W9-BWX-379
Montpelier, Vermont
WITHDRAWN

JAMES TRUSLOW ADAMS

JAMES TRUSLOW ADAMS

Historian of the American Dream

by

ALLAN NEVINS

UNIVERSITY OF ILLINOIS PRESS
Urbana Chicago London
1968

Manufactured in the United States of America
Library of Congress Catalog Card No. 68-16627

252 72452 6

Contents

I

The Busy Career of James Truslow Adams: A Personal Memoir

Ancestry and Family 1
Education and Early Reading 7
Bridgehampton, Local History, and War Service 17
The New England Trilogy 32
Marriage and English Residence 43
The Adams Family Theme and *The Epic* 58
The Scribner Contract and New Tasks 72
The Return to America: the War 83
The Fire Burns Low 96

II

Selected Correspondence of James Truslow Adams

The War and the Paris Conference 103
The New England Histories: Miss Seely 113
"Someone to Share Things With" 128
Marriage, Life Abroad, and New Aims 144
London, the Adams Family, and the Year of the Crash 170
The Epic of America: the Great Depression 200
A Change of Direction 207
America's Tragedy: Return to Connecticut 242
Factual History: Europe at War 266
Last Labors to Make History Accessible 290

Bibliography of Works by James Truslow Adams 305

Index 309

I

The Busy Career of James Truslow Adams: A Personal Memoir

By Allan Nevins

Ancestry and Family

In and after the year 1922, when I was writing editorials first for the New York *Herald* and then briefly for the *Evening Sun,* newspapers which occupied the spacious marble building erected long before by A. T. Stewart at Broadway and Chambers Street, a man in whom I took a growing interest frequently came to my office. Erect, with regular features set off by a trim brown mustache and dressed in London-cut garments, he looked rather a businessman or broker than a writer. In garb, manners, and familiarity with city life, this bachelor member of the Yale Club seemed to fit that undefinable phrase, a man about town. He walked briskly. His talk reflected not only a nimble, precise mind, but a stubborn set of opinions, some liberal, some conservative. He was clearly a gentleman, possessing high standards of conduct and a genial courtesy. His family had for three generations moved in the better circles of New York life; he knew a few leaders of finance, and he had just come through interesting wartime experiences. Essentially, however, he was a scholar.

It did not require much penetration to discern that James Truslow Adams was really a lonely man. He was reserved and meditative, with intellectual standards even more rigorous than his social and moral standards. It was partly to obtain commissions for book reviews and articles that he sought the Frank A. Munsey dailies, but partly for companionship. When he arrived late in the afternoon, we would sometimes swing into City Hall Park and down to the Battery, or uptown to Washington and Union Squares. Though shy and addicted to long silences, he could be hearty in speech when aroused, quick to chuckle over ironies of the day, scornful of the seamy side of those Harding-Coolidge years. I would have suspected a Latin vein in his ancestry even had he not mentioned it. Better read than most university men, he obviously knew literature and history more than any other subject except finance. His observations upon Matthew Arnold and Emerson were crisp, critical, and illuminating.

In his reticence, he seldom spoke about himself, a fact that made misapprehension of his position easy. Because he talked familiarly about Wall Street and clearly possessed independent income, it was natural to exaggerate his affluence, just as references to his banker grandfather William Newton Adams, and to well-placed uncles and cousins scattered over America and England made it natural to overestimate his social connections. The facts were that he had only modest means, that postwar inflation threatened him with financial difficulties, and that relatives played little part in his life. The Yale Club was generally barren of any but nodding acquaintances, for he was not really a Yale man; the village of Bridgehampton where he had his small Long Island cottage afforded hardly more society in winter than Nova Zemlya. Writing on scholarly subjects is a lonely occupation even in universities and when pursued in public libraries can be frigidly monastic. A shy worker passing into middle age, Adams made friends with difficulty.

Having been reared in an austere, gloomy home, his father a morose failure in Wall Street and his mother an invalid, Adams (as I learned later) had missed a normal boyhood and youth. One result was his studious, reflective temper. Another was a strong interest in people younger than himself. This interest doubtless accounted for his ready acceptance of me, a dozen years younger and not long out of college, as companion. Little by little he made revealing remarks about his past. From these, from letters, the memories of a few intimates, and a manuscript dictated in his last years under the title *An American Family,* it is possible to compose an account of his life.

"In American history I believe in a completely unsectional attitude," wrote Adams in mid-career.[1] "We are today all Americans, and to

[1] James T. Adams, "My Methods as a Historian," *Saturday Review of Literature,* June 30, 1934, p. 778.

adopt a provincial point of view or a sectional defense-mechanism is to invalidate the value of one's work. In this my family background has been useful to me. Settled in America since 1658, we have lived in both the North and South, and for four generations in foreign countries — South America, the West Indies, and various countries of Europe — for considerable intervals at a time. I am thoroughly American, but my father was born in South America; and though myself born in New York, my memory begins in France, although I have lived over nine-tenths of my life at home."

This statement suggests the cosmopolitan background of Adam's life. He sprang from a family mainly British, but he had one grandmother of Spanish blood; his forebears had lived chiefly in the United States, but for short periods in Venezuela and Cuba; he had been born in Brooklyn but taken immediately to Paris, where his first memories were of a wealthy American aunt on the Parc Monceau; and he had grown up in a rather large world, where some of his elders knew money, leisure, and travel. His outlook, however, was neither complicated nor cosmopolitan. He was reared simply, with no direct knowledge of Latin America, and little real acquaintance with Europe. Although his grandfathers once possessed wealth, they both lost it. Sent not to one of the great universities or ivy league colleges, but to Brooklyn Polytechnic Institute, he had been reared for a life of hard work.

People who supposed that as he was an Adams he must be of New England family or connections were in error. His first English ancestor had arrived in Maryland as an indentured servant in 1638. In time the Adamses had moved across the Potomac to Virginia, and later the center of family life had been in or near New York City. He would have called himself just a plain American of Anglo-Saxon stock, with a tincture of Spanish blood but few foreign tastes or ideas, and of no particular family. Yet his ancestral history did have much interest.[2]

The indentured servant, whose name was Francis Adams, had soon risen in the world. Only sixteen or seventeen when he arrived, at the beginning he got a poor living by hard labor. But land was cheap and could be obtained on credit. Three years after he came he was recorded in possession of 185 acres called "Troop's Rendezvous," and he added other parcels. His son, a second Francis Adams who was born the year of Bacon's rebellion, 1676, acquired more land, married well, and reared a large family. In the fourth American generation an

[2] His father searched many of the colonial records and supplied most of the data on the family line.

Abednego Adams (1721-1809) made the bold stroke of moving out of Maryland into Fairfax County, Virginia, taking a plantation between the branches of Little Hunting Creek. One creek branch divided his estate from Mount Vernon, which Abednego and his wife, Mary Peake, came to know well.

"The Adamses and the Peakes," wrote James Truslow Adams in his family record, "were close friends of the Washingtons, and I have always thought that George had his eye on the plantations of these two members of my family. In Washington's library, just to the right of the the door as you go into it from the back entrance, is a map in Washington's own handwriting of his Mount Vernon estate, and the map extends over Little Hunting Creek, indicating two houses in the first President's handwriting as A. Adams and M. Peake. I think the old boy certainly coveted those neighboring lands, although he never got them. I have, however, some china still in my house which Martha Washington gave to my great-great-grandmother, and Washington frequently spoke of his neighbors in his diary." Although not a line in this diary suggests any covetous inclinations, it does show that Washington enjoyed fox hunting and card playing with Abednego Adams.[3]

After Abednego came still another Francis Adams, who lived in Alexandria on the Potomac and had inclinations to rove. This great-grandfather of James Truslow Adams served as a private in the War of 1812, married an Alexandria girl named Mary R. Newton, and went into shipping ventures in West Indian and European waters. He unquestionably had enterprise; in 1819 he got himself appointed American consul to Trieste, and a few years later helped establish the firm of Latting, Adams, & Stewart to trade in coffee and sugar with Cuba. While still young he settled upon a sugar estate near Matanzas. James Truslow Adams owned a portrait of him painted in Vienna on burnished copper by an unknown Austrian artist, and a number of his letters, one of which told of being chased by pirates on the coast between Matanzas and Havana until he took refuge under Morro Castle.[4]

But how did the Spanish grandmother enter the family? The story, which has romantic touches, involved the son of this shipping merchant, consul, and coffee planter, a young man named William Newton Adams, the most forceful and talented of all the historian's ancestors. When his father died at an untimely age, this lad was brought

[3] See this great document as edited in four volumes by John Fitzpatrick.

[4] These papers passed into the possession of Francis Adams Truslow, who died in 1951, and his descendants.

to Connecticut to be educated. The family had means. They had also a connection with the Howland family of Howland & Aspinwall, merchants who had originally lived in Norwich, Connecticut, and it was in Norwich that William Newton Adams got his schooling. Naturally, he entered the Howland & Aspinwall offices to begin his business career. At nineteen he was sent to Venezuela to represent the firm. Here he fell in love with a Spanish girl, Carmen de Michelena de Salias, whom he married in Caracas on September 29, 1844.

The Michelenas of Venezuela were at least as distinguished a family as the Adamses of Virginia. They traced themselves back to the province of Guipuzcoa in northern Spain, a Basque area with the seaport San Sebastián its capital. In the eighteenth century two of the Michelena line migrated to Venezuela, where Jose Ignacio de Michelena married into a family from Seville. From this union sprang Carmen de Michelena, the bride of William Newton Adams. The couple, grandfather and grandmother of the historian, doubtless expected to remain long in Venezuela. Their child, William Newton Adams, Jr., was born in Caracas on November 25, 1846. But in 1848 a revolution overthrew the government, some leading citizens were slain, and the Adams family was driven into exile. In fact, family records state that they were given just forty-eight hours to leave. They made their way to Havana happy to escape alive.

The alert William Newton Adams of course remembered that his father Francis had lived for a time in the Matanzas area. Perhaps he retained his position with Howland & Aspinwall, perhaps not. At any rate, he chose temporary Cuban residence, settling in Santiago on the south coast. His talents soon made him partner in the English banking firm of Brooks & Company, which had offices in the West Indies and New York. In Santiago one of his daughters, James Truslow Adams's aunt, married into the wealthy Brooks family.

"My grandfather," writes James Truslow Adams, "very quickly took a part in all the life, business and social, of the island. Always fond of music, and an excellent businessman, he became president of the Philharmonic Society, and also of the Cuba Gas Company. In addition, he was commissioned by President Fillmore on September 24, 1850, as United States consul. He afterwards resigned that office when Congress passed a law that a consul could not occupy the position if he had a private income from business of over fifteen hundred dollars a year." While thus active, William Newton Adams helped his wife bring up thirteen children; saw that all of them were decently educated; paid frequent visits to the United States; and wrote occasionally for the American press. He remained a staunch Protestant, and a patriot of New England views. A pamphlet of his on American financial policy during the Civil War attracted some attention.

In 1865, the war over and his native Virginia back in the Union, William Newton Adams returned to the United States to become an officer in the banking firm of Moses Taylor. This was a logical choice. Taylor, the last and possibly greatest of the old school of New York merchants, had made his start in the West India trading firm of G. G. and S. Howland,[5] had gone into business independently, and had become the principal dealer in raw sugar. He was made president in 1855 of the powerful City Bank. William Newton Adams had known him for years and had joined other Cuban planters in entrusting surplus funds to his care.

But where should the repatriated merchant live? William Newton Adams considered buying a house on Washington Square, then a center of social life, but decided instead on a development on West Twenty-third Street called London Terrace. The Terrace houses had long front gardens that he thought his large family would like. Doña Carmen, however, had never learned much English and cared nothing for the social amenities of Manhattan. They therefore shortly removed to a two-and-a-half-story house with large grounds at 186 Brooklyn Avenue in a section known as Bedford Village. This place was later bought by the City of Brooklyn to house its Children's Museum.

Family reminiscences and other sources indicate that in his prime William Newton Adams was an indomitable businessman and banker of many-sided interests. He planted shade trees all along Brooklyn Avenue from Fulton Street to his house. He helped beautify St. Marks Avenue hard by, and with other prominent Brooklyn citizens, including the Seth Low family, laid out Eastern Parkway running from Prospect Park past Brooklyn Museum. While his fortune was still large, according to James Truslow Adams, he used to hire instrumentalists every Saturday night to play classical selections for the family and friends. "He spoke four or five languages with perfect ease, and would debate in Greek with the tutors whom he had for my father's younger brothers. At one time, when a number of distinguished clergy from Rome met some citizens who may have been good Catholics but were not good Latinists, grandfather was perfectly at ease acting as interpreter, talking English to the Brooklyn citizens and Latin to the Roman hierarchy."

[5] John Moody, *The Masters of Capital* (New York, 1919), pp. 59 ff.

As William Newton Adams died in 1877, more than a decade before J. T. Adams was born, these reminiscences may have passed through a dilating haze.[6]

The Spanish grandmother, Doña Carmen, has a less important place in the family annals. Evidently she was too busy rearing the thirteen children born between 1845 and 1863 to take part in community life. Then cancer overtook her soon after the removal to the United States. She was stoic enough to pay a last visit to Cuba, and died there in 1871. Her devoted husband, who had visited her assiduously while she was under treatment at Clifton Springs in upper New York, was almost prostrated by her loss.

The last years of Grandfather Adams, alas, were dark. A trusted employee absconded with $80,000 of his funds. The panic of 1873 swept away much of the remainder of his fortune. As he aged, his health declined. He spent some time on a farm he owned near Culpeper in Virginia, to get outdoor life and horseback riding. Meanwhile, he carried on real estate ventures in Brooklyn, and we hear of a trip to Havana to look after business interests. Finally, he made a sea voyage to California, and died on June 26, 1877, the day before his returning steamer reached New York. He had lived a stirring, energetic life, and if he had concentrated his energies within the United States might have left a name.

Education and Early Reading

It is somewhat astonishing that the Spanish grandmother and the Venezuelan and Cuban chapters in family history made little direct impression on James Truslow Adams. He could not read or speak Spanish, which his father and grandfather knew well, he never visited Havana or Caracas, and he took little interest in Spanish-American history. He knew some striking family stories — that was all. The most thrilling was an account of the exit of the Matanzas family from Cuba just after the death of Francis Adams, the adventurous former counsul in Trieste who had established his own coffee plantation.

This story was told with bated breath. Francis Adams, amid grief and lamentation, had been buried under the palms just when his protection was most needed by wife and children. Signs of discontent among the slaves of the island had become increasingly manifest. Half-

[6] But Miss Leonie Adams, another descendant, confirms some of them in a letter to me January 12, 1967, adding that in his wealthiest years William Newton Adams sometimes took his family to other cities in a private car.

suppressed mutterings were caught as white folk passed the Negroes. One dark night the family listened in terror as they heard machetes being sharpened, and excited fieldhands whispering about an uprising. Fortunately Mrs. Adams had been kind to the blacks, and one family servant with a sick wife was especially grateful for assistance. He gave the household secret warning, and, when the time came, carried the children in his arms to a sailing vessel to take them to the mainland. Weeks afterward, ran the melodramatic tale, the escaped family heard that a terrible insurrection had broken out, that many had been massacred, and that this particular Negro had distinguished himself by brutal murders accompanied with torture. However doubtful the details, this story laid its imprint on the imagination of James Truslow Adams.

The boy's imagination was quickened, also, by ancient family papers. Most of them were English, but some concerned the rights or *fueros* granted by Spanish monarchs to prominent Basques; exemptions from taxation, and other privileges. Nor did he forget the fact that on the Spanish side he was entitled to what Samuel Johnson called that most worthless of coats, a coat of arms. Various records showed that when William Newton Adams began rearing his great household of children, his wife Carmen had regarded slaves as essential.[7]

A family so large, and with such varied connections in banking and shipping, was certain to have interesting members. James Truslow Adams's Uncle Theodore Brooks, of the British banking family in Cuba, was long remembered. After the Spanish War, when J. T. A. was eleven or twelve, the family heard of the warm friendship of Uncle Theodore with Leonard Wood, who as military governor of Cuba sometimes stayed at the Brooks house in Santiago. A drink of General Wood's concoction is recorded. "Take a tall whisky-and-soda glass," we are told, "and pour into the bottom of it about an inch of cold tea, a great blender of flavors for a mixed drink. Squeeze in the juice of two fresh limes; and one or two teaspoons of powdered sugar; put some cracked ice in the glass; then fill with champagne, and stir well." The Brooks cousins included a young man named Richard who paid occasional visits to New York. He had been graduated from an English engineering school, married a stunningly beautiful English girl, and built canals and other public works in the Punjab. Leaving India, he

[7] J. T. Adams bequeathed the main body of family papers he held to Francis Adams Truslow, along with Truslow relics, and (after his wife's life-use) portraits of William Newton Adams, Sr., and Francis Peake Adams.

returned to Cuba, where he became head of the street railway system in Havana. Once when he brought his family, J. T. A. found that one small child spoke nothing but Hindustani.

Another cousin named Theodore Brooks had a tragic history. He chose America, went through Yale, saw naval service in World War I, and with the rank of ensign came to California to be discharged. One dark night when ship lights were dimmed he fell through open hatches to his death. On his father's side J. T. A. had a great-uncle named Charles Frederick Adams, who began his legal career in the office of William M. Evarts, and then distinguished himself in that of Charles R. Coudert. He was so prominent as a single-taxer and reformer that some of the first citizens of New York attended his funeral in 1918. It was his daughter, Leonie Adams, who became well known as a teacher in Columbia University and as a poet, being elected to the National Institute of Arts and Letters in 1951. Still another cousin, Josephine Truslow Adams, became professor of art in Swarthmore.

The most picturesquely eccentric of the family was Henry Augustus Adams, who changed his middle name to Austin. Born in Santiago, he was sent to the United States to become a clergyman. After taking degrees in Trinity College at Hartford and the General Theological Seminary in New York,[8] he became an assistant rector of Trinity Church in lower Manhattan, then pastor of a church in Buffalo, and finally rector of the Church of the Redeemer in New York. A brilliant man, he could deliver addresses that held his audience spellbound. Adams remembered attending a lecture upon the career of Napoleon, in which, to his astonishment, Uncle Henry declaimed: "To understand Napoleon, you must stand as I have stood upon the summit of the mountains of Corsica, and look out over the blue waters of the beckoning Mediterranean." As Adams knew that his uncle had never set foot on Corsica, he swallowed hard, but the statement added an impressive touch.

This Uncle Henry, if we may believe family recollections, had a commanding and luxuriant personality that carried him through rich adventures. Early in his career a wealthy widow endowed him with $100,000 to devote himself to writing religious works,[9] and he built a

[8] The alumni records of Trinity College list Henricus Augustus Adams, S.T.B. Sem. Theol. General, 1886, as a graduate of Trinity in the class of 1887.

[9] His published works under the of name Henry Austin Adams include *Larger Life* (1893); *Napoleon, a Play in Four Acts* (1894); *Westchester: Tale of Revolution* (1899); and *Orations of Henry Austin Adams, with an Introduction by His Eminence, Cardinal Gibbons* (1902). He also wrote *The Man John*

house at Great River, Long Island, as a studious retreat. Moving toward Roman Catholicism, he baptized one of his sons John Henry Newman. Then, becoming restless, he suddenly left his family and eloped to New Zealand with a girl of musical talent from Baltimore. According to the story told to Adams, the couple presently returned to British Columbia, where Uncle Henry brought a suit for divorce from his first wife on grounds of desertion! The Adams family sometimes said that when all Gaul was divided into three parts, Henry had seized the largest share. Ultimately it was the discarded wife who got the divorce. Besides his religious writings, Uncle Henry brought out plays, one of which, " 'Ception Shoals," ran for thirty-seven nights in New York early in 1917, with Alla Nazimova as star.[10]

When Adams became acquainted with the colonial historian Charles M. Andrews, he found that he had roomed with Uncle Henry in Trinity College; and Andrews told Adams that after a long life he still regarded Henry as the most fascinating man he had ever known.

The Truslows, a family that Adams ascertained to be of Yorkshire origin, produced no such salient personalities. Their most distinguished scion was the artist Edwin Austin Abbey (1852-1911), best remembered for his murals in the Boston Public Library depicting the legend of the Holy Grail. He was the great-grandson of a John Truslow born in Reading, England. When Abbey left his native Philadelphia to work in New York with Harper Brothers, he sometimes came to the house of William Newton Adams, Jr., for Sunday dinner, a shy young man who blushed when addressed. This was just before the birth of James Truslow Adams. Later he lived for some years in the Cotswold village of Broadway, where Adams once visited him. He died in London.

In the Truslow line as in the Adams line it was the historian's grandfather who was the most successful and impressive figure; James Linklater Truslow became a successful manufacturer of corks and by the end of the century was rated a millionaire. His business was eventually absorbed by the Armstrong Cork Company. For years he lived at 783 St. Marks Avenue in Brooklyn, a house that Adams remembered vividly. It had a spacious central hall paved in black and white marble

---

Spreckels (1924), an interesting character study, for the sugar magnate Spreckels, who did much to develop San Diego into a great city, was a close friend. Adams, who finished the biography on Spreckels's yacht, declared that he had watched the magnate in moments of exultation, hilarity, and crushing sorrow.

[10] See the reviews in *The Theatre,* XXV (January-June, 1917), and Burns Mantle and Garrison P. Sherwood, *The Best Plays of 1909-1919* (New York, 1933), p. 592.

running from front to rear, a large first-floor library, and parlors of Victorian dignity. J. T. A. always recalled it in association with the opening of Brooklyn Bridge in 1883, the cork factory being only a short distance from the eastern end. The day the great suspension bridge was opened members of the family attended the ceremonies, and in the evening gazed in wonder at the brilliant illumination of piers, cables, and gracefully arching roadway.

"Grandfather," writes J. T. A., "gave a party for the family and some of his friends on the roof of the factory, where we could see the fireworks. It was the first time, at the age of four and a half, that I had ever stayed up till ten o'clock to eat ice-cream and cake, and watch the world burst into flame. The sight made a tremendous impression."

In all this period we obtain no clear view of J. T. A.'s father, William Newton Adams, Jr., and the glimpses we have are not happy. We know that he studied finance in Germany, reading and working in Bremen; that he had scholarly tastes, evinced by his life membership in the Virginia and Long Island Historical Societies and in the Brooklyn Library; and that late in life he joined the brokerage firm of Henderson, Linley & Company at Two Wall Street. In the risky brokerage business lack of financial acumen kept him unsuccessful. He was handicapped also by the fact that his wife was a lifelong invalid. One acquaintance recalls the elder Adams as a sour, disappointed man, who never forgave fate for the loss of the family fortune; ill-tempered, and complaining. Other associates found him pleasanter but inclined to excessive worry about money. It may be significant that the historian wrote nothing about him.

The principal boyhood reminiscence that J. T. A. has left us deals with the great blizzard of 1888, which he witnessed at nearly ten. "That storm," he writes,

the only really great one which New York has had to fight, started in the morning in ordinary fashion. My father went to business. The storm steadily increased in intensity. About two o'clock the stock exchange decided to close and let the people go home. By that time not a wheel was turning in the whole city. My father had to walk the three-quarters of a mile or so from the corner of Wall Street and Broadway to the Brooklyn Bridge, across the mile-long bridge in the face of blinding snow and biting wind, and then begin to walk the three miles out to where we lived on St. Marks Avenue. When he got to within two blocks of our house he fell completely exhausted. The snow was over his knees at every step, and he was not a strong man. Fortunately, he fell in front of the house of a Mr. Carpenter, a friend of ours. . . . Mr. Carpenter and his two boys went out and gathered my father into the house, and revived him. After three or four hours he finally made the last two blocks to his own house. We had no idea where he had been or what had happened to him, for in those days hardly anybody had telephones.

Father got home, but the snow kept up all night and next morning, so that in Brooklyn and New York the drifts were up to the second-story windows. Front stoops had disappeared entirely, and in order to clear some of the snow away from the area-way, we had to take it from the inside, carry it through the house, and dump it into the back yard, where the wind had not drifted it. The next morning, my grandfather sent his coachman from his house to ours to see if we had enough food. From the bay window in the front of our house I watched Daniel work his way along. To walk was impossible, for the snow must have been fifteen or twenty feet deep. He lay on his stomach and practically swam on top of the snow, and it took him a half hour to make the six hundred feet from grandfather's house.

Early in 1888 Adams's father removed from Brooklyn Avenue to St. Marks Avenue, where the family were just getting settled when the blizzard struck. In 1901 Grandfather Truslow died. His once large fortune had dwindled, for he had placed much of his savings in real estate, which for years proved practically unsaleable. At his death his estate was estimated at about $600,000. He had two sons, to whom he bequeathed his stock in Armstrong Cork, and two daughters (one of them J. T. A.'s mother), to whom he left the realty. The stock declared handsome dividends, and rose rapidly in value; the land brought little, and this little by the terms of the will had to be invested in bonds legal for trust funds, which yielded only about 3½ per cent. Thus losing for the second time his great expectations, Adams's father showed greater moroseness than ever. If only Grandfather Truslow had given the cork stock to the daughters!

In a general view, James Truslow Adams's American ancestors were interesting but not significant figures. Not one of them made any name in the United States; not one appears in any biographical dictionary or state or city history. The only touch of distinction discernible is that in William Newton Adams, Sr. Yet, although J. T. A. always spoke scornfully of genealogical studies, he took much interest in his own family history. Its color and adventure appealed to his imagination and widened his vision. Confined mainly to his book-lined study, he found refreshment in thinking of the indentured servant seizing upon Maryland land, the Virginia planter riding to hounds with George Washington, the Alexandria shipmaster and merchant coming back from Trieste to buy sugarcane holdings near Matanzas, the Caracas don bestowing the hand of his lovely daughter Carmen upon a Yankee adventurer while revolution rumbled in the background, and this adventurer, grown older, becoming a respected figure in New York banking.

Of James Truslow Adams's early education we have scanty records. In 1889, when he was eleven, he entered the private school of a Miss Parsons in an old-fashioned Brooklyn residence at Pacific Street and New York Avenue. After a year or two he was transferred to a boy's school across the street kept by a man named Maury; a military school that put him into a gray uniform with silver buttons. He disliked Maury, the strict discipline, and the necessity of running five or six blocks around the drill hall with a heavy gun on his shoulder. By emphatic complaints he got himself removed at the end of a year.

Meanwhile, he began to enjoy some country life. His mother's brother, James Truslow, rented a place in South Woodstock, Connecticut, an old farmhouse on a lake, and during summers in the middle 1880's Adams's parents boarded nearby. He played with other children of the family, mostly Truslows, in a group who called themselves, after Louisa M. Alcott's book, the Eight Cousins. They got acquainted here with the household of Hamilton Wright Mabie, whose essays and lectures were then in high repute. They rowed, swam, climbed on haywagons, petted the farm animals, kept rabbits of their own, and had a thoroughly satisfactory time.

In the autumn of 1890 J. T. A. began attending the Polytechnic School on Livingston Street. It was reached by horsecar on the Bergen Street line, the Kings County Elevated Railroad not being built until a few years later. He thought the ride delightful, especially when open cars were used in spring and summer — the horses jogging along, the bells around their necks ringing, at three miles an hour.

Meanwhile, by a stroke of fortune, a genial attendant in the Brooklyn Library gave the boy access to the stacks, where he often spent his Saturdays. He came upon books which not only assisted him to good marks at school, but delighted him by their variety. He was an avid consumer of Jules Verne's *Twenty Thousand Leagues Under the Sea,* the *Journey to the Moon,* and other romances; he devoured the inevitable G. A. Henty; and in time he progressed to Walter Scott. Before long he discovered some secondhand bookshops. Thereupon he dropped the horsecars, for he found he could save money by walking the three miles and use it in buying books.

One bookstore on Court Street, managed by an old gentleman named Farnell and his son, became a favorite. "After fifty years," Adams writes, "I still recall them both well, for they seemed to take an interest in me. A high spot in my purchases at Farnell's was when I bought a copy of Brydon's *Tour of Sicily* for ten cents. I called Farnell's attention to the fact that there were two volumes bound in one, and I still remember that he said: 'My God, I thought it was only the first volume. If I had known there were both, you would not have got it!' I began to feel like a real book collector." The remarkable fact was that the boy should want such a book.

Adams spent four years in the lower grades of the Polytechnic School before emerging into the Polytechnic Institute, where he was a pupil in the preparatory department 1890-94. When he thus completed his high school studies he should have gone to one of the older Eastern colleges. Columbia even in pre-subway days was within easy reach. But his brother Herbert had recently died of scarlet fever; his mother, still a semi-invalid, felt in her bereavement that she must keep him near her; and his father always practiced economy. The Polytechnic was now giving college courses, and they decided to keep him there. He would have done better at Columbia, Yale, or Harvard. Significantly, he mentions no teacher by name. However, he found some unusual fellow students. One was Paul Dougherty, who became a distinguished marine painter; another was Dougherty's younger brother, who, going on the stage, shortened his name to Walter Hampden; and a third was Clayton Hamilton, later a distinguished dramatic critic, playwright, and author of several books, including a life of Robert Louis Stevenson.

Throughout four years of work in the Brooklyn Polytechnic for an arts degree, Adams felt concerned over his future occupation. He considered becoming a lawyer, and always believed that he might have made a good one, for he loved legal and constitutional problems. But since the weekly declamations that the Institute required were tortures to his shy spirit, and he supposed lawyers had to do constant public speaking, he gave up the idea. He thought of engineering. That dream vanished, however, when a friendly mechanical engineer sent him a copy of Ganot's *Physics* as a book to begin. Toward the end of his four years he suspected that he had some literary talent. In 1897 he became editor of the monthly school publication, which he converted into a weekly. That same year he wrote the libretto of a fairy opera, which with music by a neighborhood violin teacher, was performed by forty girls of the Packer Institute; and throwing enthusiasm into helping stage "The Culprit's Quest," as he called it, he had the satisfaction at nineteen of seeing it achieve a local success.

He was clearly a brilliant young man, for he was graduated in June, 1898, as president of his class, valedictorian, and class poet. Thinking he might become a teacher of philosophy, he made the mistake of going to Yale for the year 1898-99. A competent adviser would have sent him to Harvard, where William James, George Santayana, and Josiah Royce might have instilled a lasting interest in the subject, but Yale offered little inspiration. Adams perhaps never really knew, and certainly never spoke of, the principal figure in philosophy at Yale, George Trumbull Ladd, better remembered for his books on Indian and Japanese life than for his *Theory of Reality*. In disappointment, he returned to his father's office in New York as unpaid messenger. The firm paid for his carfare and lunches, but by paternal edict offered not a cent more, until, at Christmas in 1898, the senior partner gave him an envelope out of which, to his astonishment, he shook a $500 bill.

Another unexpected gift followed. A Japanese student he had known in New Haven dropped into his office and asked if he were going back to Yale. Adams returned an emphatic "No!" But, expostulated the Japanese, if you simply write them they will give you an M.A. virtually as a matter of routine. This information proved correct. Adams wrote the authorities, went to commencement, paid a $10 fee, and became Master of Arts, "upon examination" — the "examination" meaning nothing.[11]

About the same time he made a favorable impression on a railroad executive, a Scot named Ewen, in his building. This man, a former officer of the Southern Railroad who had left it to help reorganize the Central of Georgia, not only proposed that Adams enter his employ, but gave him more business instruction that he had gotten from his father. The first day, Adams later recalled, Ewen looked at a typewriter on his desk, and remarked meaningly: "You know, when I went on the railroad the first thing they did was to make me run a locomotive." Catching the hint, Adams learned typewriting. He also kept account books, handled routine correspondence, and held a power-of-attorney enabling him to sign his employer's name to checks on the First National Bank not exceeding $500,000; he worked long hours at an initial $3.50 a week. Presently Ewen began reorganizing a little railroad in western New York called the Jamestown & Chautauqua.

"In order that I should be an officer and do some of the work, he had the directors make me secretary. For this I once more got $3.50 a week, but I was not a little proud of being secretary of a railroad cor-

[11] See the *Catalogue of the Officers of Graduates of Yale University 1701-1924* (1924), p. 422. Not until two years later was control of the M.A. degree transferred to the new Graduate Faculty, and the standard raised to demand two years of postgraduate instruction. See George W. Pierson, *Yale College and University 1871-1937,* I (1952), 227.

poration. It was a nice little thing twenty-nine miles long, but just as wide as any other, and connected with five trunk lines. I being an executive officer, it gave me in those happy days free passes on all the railroads of the country, and just to see what it felt like I once went to Chicago for dinner."

For his $7 a week Adams learned so much about transportation, analysis of railway accounts and general investment business that he could well have made larger sacrifices for his tuition. He inspected the Jamestown & Chautauqua from time to time, using his own private locomotive. Eating at cheap Italian and Spanish restaurants in downtown Manhattan, he made the $7 do. Finally, aware that he had learned all he could, he asked Ewen to audit his books, certify that his accounts were correct, and accept his resignation.

Then came the crowning touch of his education, a trip to Europe. He had saved a little money, and Grandfather Truslow, who approved him as a cleancut young businessman, gave him $500. After three weeks in London, where he celebrated his twenty-second birthday, he went to Paris to view the Exposition of 1900, later recalled as "one of the ugliest things I have ever seen." In a long run on the Continent he saw the Emperor Franz Josef face to face in a Vienna hotel, made friends with a Scottish publisher named Isbister and an old Irish lady named Mrs. D'Oyley Carte, who both took a fancy to him, and finally spent three weeks in a Florentine *pension* where he got lodging, three meals, and afternoon tea for ninety-five cents a day. In 1901 he was home again, refreshed and instructed, but still uncertain what he wanted to do.

The family situation was changing. His Uncle James Truslow had died in 1899, and Grandfather Truslow followed in 1901. His mother, to whom he was devoted, did not wish to remain in the Brooklyn neighborhood where she had lived almost a lifetime with all of her family about her, and the four of them — father, mother, sister Amy, and Adams — decided to go to Summit, New Jersey, a place full of acquaintances. Here, after several moves, they took a house built by Uncle James for Hamilton Wright Mabie, in which Mabie had written a popular volume of essays called *My Study Fire*. Mabie's study fire became J. T. A.'s. In time, also, his father served two terms as unpaid mayor of Summit, while he himself was elected a councilman. They made friends, for Summit was full of interesting people. One was Rollo Ogden, editor of the New York *Evening Post;* another was Constance Adams (not related), who married Cecil De Mille.

From Summit, Adams could commute to a new business post that he soon found in Wall Street. A smouldering coal of literary ambition, a suppressed passion for writing, however, burned in his bosom, and neither business nor Summit was to hold him long.

Bridgehampton, Local History, and War Service

Adams, who had a way of avoiding disagreeable topics, never told me why, after his experience with a railroad and his European trip, he turned to the kind of brokerage business in which his father had fared badly. He repeatedly made it plain, however, that he thought Wall Street a dangerous wilderness, its atmosphere hectic, and its routines deadening. Supposing that it was a place where men made money, I once spoke with compassion of an elderly Staten Island friend who had come to grief there, his family suffering. "That doesn't astonish me," said Adams emphatically. "Men are always coming croppers in Wall Street. A lot of them end by ruining themselves and their families." He never said that he thought his father's life there was unhappy, for he seldom spoke to me of his father at all, but I later concluded that he felt it was. When he did turn toward the street it was temporarily and unwillingly.

He went to Columbia for six weeks, thinking that history might prove more attractive than philosophy, but found sitting in a classroom with undergraduates intolerable. He then attempted entrance into book publishing, not realizing how many neophytes in letters besieged the offices for jobs and how low the salary levels then were.

Armed with a letter from Hamilton W. Mabie, he called upon Frank Dodd, head of Dodd, Mead & Company. The firm was then one of the most conservative and compactly organized in the city. As one publisher said, "it made money by never spending any," and Frank Dodd politely told him that it had no opening. He met a different rebuff when he went to Frederick A. Stokes & Company. Stokes thought he might be given a job, took him to dinner at the Yale Club with champagne, and offered him a two-year contract — at $15 a week. "We believe in the apprentice system," he said. "I do not," replied Adams. A call on Frank N. Doubleday of Doubleday, Page completed his exploration. They had a pleasant talk. As Adams explained his recent connection with the Jamestown & Chautauqua, "Effendi" was delighted. "My secret ambition has always been to run a railroad," he exclaimed. Adams responded happily. "You are a publisher who has always wanted to get into the railroad business," he pointed out; "I am a railroad man who wants to get into publishing. Let us trade jobs!" But Doubleday declined.

At this point an old friend, Allen L. Lindley, intervened with an attractive business offer. Holding a seat in the New York Stock Exchange, Lindley and several associates established the firm of Henderson, Lindley & Company, and invited Adams to take an interest, contributing experience and talents but no capital.[12] Adams set to work. Although the profits proved fairly good, he chafed under the uncertainties of the market. When the panic of 1907 fell upon the country, he suggested to his partners that as business was slack, one of them might travel over the country to investigate the economic situation and look for opportunities. The result was that, setting out with introductions to manufacturers, bankers, and railroad executives, he inspected enterprises ranging from the Cudahy meat-packing plant in Chicago to a large shirt factory in Kansas City. Finally, in Idaho he found an opportunity he could recommend to the firm.

The capitalist Charles R. Flint, who arranged so many mergers that he became known as "the father of trusts," had run up heavy obligations with the United States Rubber Company, and wished to use the Pacific & Idaho Northern Railroad in Idaho as part payment. Adams's firm volunteered to examine it. By personal inspection J. T. A. found that after winding up the valley of the Snake River the railroad stopped at a dead end in a canyon so narrow that it did not give room for a turntable. Some thirty miles beyond, however, in the Meadows Valley, the bed of a prehistoric lake filled by soil eroded from the mountains, lay about 100,000 acres of remarkably rich land. As long as this area remained sealed, land could be bought for $10 an acre, but a good rail connection would lift it to $100. Adams suggested that the company buy large holdings, extend the railroad, sell its land to apple growers at reasonable prices, and thus establish a thriving community with trainloads of fruit going out and trainloads of supplies coming in.[13]

[12] Adams spoke to me of four men initially in the firm, but notices in the *Commercial and Financial Chronicle* show that it consisted of Francis Henderson, D. A. Lindley, J. A. Janney, A. W. Howe, and Allen L. Lindley. It appears from the brief statement about William Newton Adams, Jr., in *Who's Who in New York, 1909,* that he also had a brief connection with it, and that its offices were at Two Wall Street. James Truslow Adams at first held an interest without being a full partner; surviving letterheads list neither him nor his father. However, he was admitted to partnership December 1, 1908, the offices then being at 100 Broadway.

[13] The Pacific and Idaho Northern reached the town of New Meadows, and

Ultimately Adams had the satisfaction of seeing this terminal stretch of the Pacific & Idaho Northern constructed, the district about Meadows become a rich horticultural district, and his firm turn a neat profit. He had enlisted Governor James H. Brady in Boise, and others helped. When he completed his business tour with a swing from the Far West through the South, he found the country rapidly recovering from the panic. "As a result of what I had seen," he wrote later, "I think my firm was the first one to turn bullish and advise people to buy stocks." Taking a vacation trip up the Saguenay, he sent an account of an old French-Canadian newspaper vendor he met there to the New York *Times,* which paid him $20. On June 7, 1907, he wrote the poet Robert Underwood Johnson: "I enclose my check for $5 drawn to the order of the Keats-Shelley Memorial Fund. This is part of the first payment I ever received for literary work, and I take great pleasure in applying it for this purpose."[14]

During the next few years Adams was irritated and rebellious under the daily routine of his firm. Much as he enjoyed adventures like the promotion of Meadows, Idaho, he detested his eternal preoccupation with bonds, shares, and syndicates, the sickening risks of the daily rise and fall, and the necessity of mastering business trends. He felt that like everybody else, he thought and talked too much about money. Moreover, he worked in an anxious round chained to a clock. In Summit he gobbled a hasty breakfast facing the dining-room clock, left the house at 7:45 precisely, strode a mile to the station, and caught the 8:06 train. He was on his office telephone at 9:00; the stock exchange opened at 10:00; loans were called at 10:30; stock deliveries ceased at 2:15; and the exchange closed at 3:00. A Western Union clock stood in each room of the firm's offices. With the evening schedule of trains back to Summit fixed in memory, he watched the hands, ready at the last moment to spring from Wall Street to the Hoboken Ferry. It was much too mechanical a round for a young man of literary tastes.

He bought books — all kinds of them, including poetry, but more and more history. His father grumbled over the cost. "We can't afford them," he complained, so Adams smuggled expensive titles into the

---

people in Idaho for a time dreamed of a ninety-mile connection with Fenn in Idaho County, thus giving Idaho the north-and-south railroad it needed; but this connection was never built. Sister M. Alfreda Eisensohn treats the subject in *Pioneer Days in Idaho County* (Caldwell, Idaho, 1947), II, 547, 548, and has written me additional information.

[14] Robert Underwood Johnson Papers, American Academy of Arts and Letters, 633 West 155th Street, New York, New York.

house under his coat; but the old gentleman, like the sister Amy, read them.

Adams often said to himself, "I shall get out of Wall Street as soon as I reach thirty-five or save a hundred thousand dollars, whichever comes first; and then I shall try writing." On his thirty-fifth birthday, in 1912, he cast up his accounts. He had his hundred thousand. "This is Kismet!" he exclaimed. "I shall defy fortune no longer!" Next day he told his associates he was quitting. They expostulated, but he was adamant.

"I remember that day walking to the Hoboken Ferry for the last time," he later recalled. "On Broadway I passed the show-window of the Waltham Watch Company. When I saw all the watches it suddenly struck me that, as I had retired at a very early age, my time was all my own, and I ought to keep track of it. I went in and bought a watch — the watch I carried in my pocket for the next thirty-five years."[15]

He knew that, for a writer, he was getting a tardy start. He had not drilled himself in historical method or rules of scholarship; his Wall Street cell had taught him little about life; he had never played the assiduous ape, like Stevenson, to some great stylist like Hazlitt. He could say that he had done an immense amount of careful reading in the better English and American authors, and that few men knew the novelists, essayists, and historians from Clarendon to Parkman better. He had written a good deal of doggerel verse, realizing that it was not worth sending to any magazine, but pleased when he hit out a felicitous word or phrase. Shy, reserved, with only one really close friend he had made in Brooklyn, Ed Schermerhorn, spending much time with his mother and his sister Amy, but without other feminine companionship, and giving his complex emotions expression mainly in his fondness for children, he knew that he had not yet found himself. But he had two eminent virtues: he was thoughtful and he was independent-minded, reaching and following his own conclusions.[16]

For a time, uncertain of his course, he looked into another corner of

[15] His mother's sad end in 1911 had disturbed him greatly, for he was a devoted son, and helped persuade him that he ought to make a new start, if possible, away from his father and sister. She had become paralyzed in 1910. After that Summit was distasteful.

[16] Once in these years, he told me later, he fell in love with an attractive girl, but she was of a very rich family, he was poor, and he seized upon this absurd reason for withdrawing. Various letters indicated that in youth he had the romantic impulses common to adolescents and had his share of flirtation, hampered by shyness.

business. He took a part-time position as treasurer of a rock plaster concern, thinking he might unite this job with writing. He soon found it excessively time consuming, and he was troubled by its ethical problems. The fierce competition in the plaster business, so that a price variance of a fraction of a cent might mean the difference between decent profit and ruin, tempted executives of major companies to reach agreements on their charges. The Sherman Anti-Trust Act had steel teeth. If Adams attended a meeting where price collusion could be proved, he might pay a $5,000 fine or spend a year in jail. Meanwhile, the firm was using a lad to carry a valise with the cash payroll from the bank every Saturday. Although the route he followed had seen some dangerous holdups, it was unlawful to carry a revolver without a license, and to get one he had to pay a police captain $15. Adams had the choice of risking the life of the boy by sending him out unarmed, or bribing the police. Such dilemmas helped him make up his mind to quit business forever.

For a time, he occupied himself in studying Persian. Like George Nathaniel Curzon and Anthony Eden, he learned to read the language and speak it a little, familiarized himself with Firdousi, Omar Khayyam, and Hafiz, and explored the Bagdad and Ispahan schools of art. This, he remarked later, was "just for something to get my teeth into." He never taught Persian or tried translating.[17] Meanwhile, he gave more attention to Summit affairs, becoming head of the finance committee and street committee of the city council. He had to meet curious problems when a horse fell dead in the middle of a boundary street, so that Summit and a neighboring town quarreled obstinately over disposal of the carcass, and when a spring suddenly gushed up in front of the Episcopal Church, defying the engineers.

The autumn after leaving business in 1912 Adams bought a little land and began building a cottage at Bridgehampton, far down the south coast of Long Island; a seemingly casual decision on which his whole future hung. His original plan was to erect a cabin where he, Ed Schermerhorn, and other companions could go camping, and where he could write alone, a first step in his plan for striking out independently. But Amy vigorously demurred. Why not make the house large enough for herself and their father as well? So, on his two-acre site he reluctantly finished a cottage big enough for all, at first without a furnace because he meant it only for summer use. The Summit house

[17] When I first knew him long after this, he had a Persian dictionary, the two volumes of Lord Curzon's *Persia,* and related books, and still read Persian.

was sold. Then, as the family failed to get a suitable substitute in that town, he installed a furnace in the Bridgehampton place. His plan to gain solitude had failed. But in this new house he at last sat down to write.

"The three requirements of life which I have always made," Adams later wrote, "are quiet, space, and service, three of the most unobtainable and expensive things of our present life." The two acres gave him space. He ensured quiet by buying his land opposite one of the oldest graveyards in New York State, long since disused. The cemetery stones not only fascinated him, but suggested the theme of his first printed book. Working hard, he produced a little volume thorough in scholarship and charming in style, called *Memorials of Old Bridgehampton.* This he published at his own expense in 1916, through the local newspaper office. It was not quite his first venture into authorship, for he had previously issued two pamphlets on financial affairs, distributed free.[18] He regarded it as apprentice work, however, and thought that at $1.50 a copy the *Memorials* would sell very slowly among residents of Bridgehampton, Southampton, and East Hampton, three towns lining the coast from Patchogue to Montauk. He was astonished to see the edition rapidly sold out, and still more astonished — "my eyes popped" — when a year or two later he saw a copy advertised by Goodspeed's in Boston at $75.

Actually Adams was unjust when he wrote later, "I think it was a very rotten book." Treating Bridgehampton primarily as a whaling village much like its north-shore neighbor Sag Harbor, he brought out the picturesqueness of its economic and social past. Even he admitted in time that "it had a lot of interesting information." He was fortunate in his subject, for in colonial days the town had sheltered not only whalers and various other adventurous mariners, but a considerable number of slaves who gradually achieved freedom. The reason the price shot to $75, however, was that he had printed in an appendix the complete inscriptions on all gravestones in five old cemeteries of the vicinity, beginning with the one just across the way. While the quaintness in the epitaphs was pleasing, they attracted eager students of genealogy. Professor Albert S. Cook of Yale, influential in English studies,

[18] *Some Notes on Currency Problems,* New York, 1908, 38 pp. and *Speculation and the Reform of the New York Stock Exchange,* Summit, New Jersey, 1913, 27 pp., both privately printed. The former dealt with the complicated circumstances leading up to the Aldrich-Vreeland Act of 1908; the latter argued for a closer oversight by the New York Stock Exchange of the books and practises of members.

found so much in his copy that he hunted up Adams, with the result that they became warm friends.

The logical ensuing step was to expand this little volume to cover the whole coastal township of Southampton, thirty miles long and holding a number of villages settled in the early seventeenth century from Old England and New England. This offered larger opportunities for a treatment of whaling, piracy, and merchant voyages European and Asiatic. Adams seized them with enthusiasm. His book, *History of the Town of Southampton, East of Canoe Place,* appeared in 1918 from the Hampton Press in Bridgehampton, in handsome format. It met a reception worthy of its thoroughness, scholarly accuracy, and literary merit. Professor Dixon Ryan Fox of Columbia, later president of Union College, a specialist in New York history, called it almost a model piece of local history. Professor Marcus W. Jernegan of the University of Chicago gave the same verdict in the *American Historical Review.*

This time the sale was gratifyingly large. The United States was being drawn into the First World War as he finished the book, and his ardor made him so eager to be free for enlistment that he had worked day and night. Although his last chapters were hurried, they were not in the least scamped.

The book began with a careful physiographic study of the area, and a description of Indian life. He proceeded to a realistic account of town government and included spirited narratives of the Revolutionary period and the War of 1812. As he covered whaling and the growth of commerce, he paused to offer honest studies of the social groups and town life. Numerous photographs of mills, houses, ships, churches, and landscapes helped give the story life and color. Maps were interspersed, and an appendix provided valuable documents, including inventories of estates. Readers could see that the research had been laborious, that the author had unusual literary ability, and that he scorned a filiopietistic approach. Only through scholarly studies of this character, wrote Jernegan, could the country gain an understanding of the spirit of local history, and of "the development of a most important characteristic of the native American, the notion of self-government." People who paid $2.65 for the 424-page volume got one of the best bargains of the time.[19]

[19] Both the *Memorials of Old Bridgehampton* and the *History of the Town of Southampton* were reprinted by Empire State Historical Publications in 1962.

At last Adams had found his proper occupation, only to encounter the interruption of war.

A late start in life — there was no doubt of that, for he was thirty-nine in the autumn of 1917. Most people would have thought it unfortunate that he had gone to a technological college, third-rate in the humanities; that neither there nor in his brief attendance at Yale had any teacher inspired him; and that he had spent his best early years in a deadening Wall Street routine. Such a statement would have been unjust. His incessant reading in literature and history more than atoned for any deficiences of his colleges; given his literary tastes and ability, he had been fortunate in escaping the graduate school pedantry of the time; and he had learned a good deal of economics from Wall Street. Nobody who crossed the barrier of his shyness could talk to him for five minutes without seeing that he was informed, thoughtful, and tolerant.

The Southampton book completed, he received a telegram from Isaiah Bowman, president of the American Geographical Society, asking if he could come in to help meet an emergency. Bowman was facing a tough problem. President Wilson had asked Colonel House to assemble a commission to gather facts, ideas, and documents in preparation for an eventual peace conference, and House had made his wife's brother-in-law, Sidney E. Mezes, a Californian once head of the University of Texas and now president of City College in New York, director of the enterprise. Mezes had then chosen Bowman as executive officer. They had gathered about ninety specialists from all over the country, begun a survey of the history, geography, ethnology, economics, and religions of fifty lands, and wound themselves up in such a ball of detail that they needed a few systematic men to unwind them. When Bowman asked Cook of Yale to suggest somebody, Cook named Adams. Within a few days Adams was living at the Yale Club, working in the Geographical Society offices, and looking after a variety of assignments.

At once he began meeting new men, new adventures, and new ideas. Bowman got him elected a member of the Explorers' Club on the ground that he had explored the "Upper Reaches of the Bronx River." He talked there with such scientists as Stefansson, William Beebe, and Peary's associate Robert Bartlett, while his work on the Mezes commission brought him in touch with Robert Lansing and Walter Lippmann. One of his main jobs was to prepare accurate maps, using newly invented photostatic apparatus. Once he worked until two in the morning to produce a large-scale map of a debatable area from more than twenty small maps on different scales. He was pleased next morning to hear Bowman tell a high government officer: "I went home, and left Adams to do the job, and of course he did it."

His superiors, including Lippmann, praised his zeal and competence. After some months, however, as the war situation grew more critical, he felt he would be happier in uniform. Bowman protested that he was useful just where he was and that plenty of others could go into the trenches. Adams nevertheless insisted and shortly got a commission in Washington as captain in the Military Intelligence Service, doing more map work. He never forgot some of his experiences in the summer of 1918. The capital that season had equatorial temperatures. For a whole week, declares Adams, the official thermometer several hundred feet above the street never went below 100° day or night.

"I used to see it one hundred and twelve degrees in the drugstores. There were no cold drinks, as the ice gave out. It was rather ghastly, because at that time we had the flu epidemic. Not only was there no ice, but after a while there were no caskets. My secretary, a nice girl and a very competent one, got the flu and was dead in three days. I had to look after that, as she came from Minnesota. The girls were often living four and five in a room owing to the crowded housing conditions, and to add to our difficulties, many of them had come to Washington to do war work as a sort of lark, and had come under assumed names and with false addresses, so that when they died it was a mess."

Besides making maps, he compiled guide books for field officers. One that he wrote on the Murmansk Peninsula in Russia, where American, British, and French troops were to stage an expedition against Communist forces, and where the Germans had a coastal submarine base, gave him endless trouble. He had to assemble the data, write his text, and see the brochure through the press within six weeks. The otherwise impossible task was made feasible by the help of Secret Service men. These sleuths found a Russian woman, for example, who before the war had lived part of the time in a Murmansk village, and part of the time in California. She gave the Secret Service all kinds of information, with photographs showing the very harbor in which the German submarines were concealed. A year or two after the war Adams was told that his booklet was so good that the British and French had gladly made use of it; but he gave the credit to the Secret Service, which had covered even details like the availablity of standing timber to repair damaged railway bridges, and the facilities in various villages for quartering troops.

Adams spent most of October, 1918, in New York, doing little but putter about in his old offices in the Geographical Society. Bowman wanted him to go overseas on the *George Washington* with Wilson and the Commission, taking charge of numerous cases of books and papers, but some eager soul in the State Department seized that assignment. He lingered on through the false armistice and real armistice, still doing nothing but draw a captain's pay for living at the Yale Club, until his sharp protest brought him back to Washington. Again he did little but look after some secret files in his 1330 F Street office until one evening he went down in the elevator with a colonel named Dunn. The colonel asked if he had on his seven-league boots. Startled, Adams demanded an explanation and got the reply: "Oh, you are going to Paris tomorrow." Sure enough, he received immediate orders, and hurried to Hoboken to board the *Leviathan* — only to sit in his cabin for ten days while the vessel stayed tied up at the dock. She finally pulled out on January 23, 1919, with a contingent of about 900 homegoing Polish troops aboard.

The voyage to Europe was enlivened by an ebullient, self-assured Major Colby, who had been a lawyer in Boston before the war, and since a recent transfer from the Belgian artillery to the American army was now going to Servia as military attaché. William S. Sharp, the Ohioan then ambassador to France, was also abroad. The crossing took ten days, during which Adams mounted guard over a heavy case containing additional books and documents for the Peace Conference. The one bit of drama occurred when they reached Brest to find that a single train ran to Paris every twenty-four hours, and that the one then puffing in the station was already full. The despairing Adams saw himself perched for a night and day on the precious box! Major Colby, however, was equal to any occassion. "Leave it to me," he said — and Adams records the sequel:

There was a whole car for the ambassador, his son, and suite, but that was sacred ground. Colby went in and talked to the *chef de gare,* and came dashing out. He said, "Come along, we're going." I asked where, and he said, "In the ambassador's car."

A little French official was making an awful fuss about weighing my box of documents when we heard the whistle begin to blow. Just then a big Negro, as black as the ace of spades, who looked as if he had come out of the rice plantations of Georgia, a private in our army, saw my captain's bars and said: "Boss, you want something?" I told him that I had to have that box weighed and put on the platform of the train before we left, and there was no time. He grabbed the French official by the back of the neck, threw him aside, weighed my box, called two or three other men, and put it on the platform. We followed and sat down in one of the sleeping compartments of the ambassador's sacred car.

I said to Colby, "This is fine, but what are we going to do with the ambassador?" He said, "That is all right; I told the *chef de gare* that I was attaché to Servia." And here is where his Belgian uniform came in. In the few minutes that Colby possessed he had not only arranged with the *chef de gare* that we were to have part of the ambassador's private car, but had somehow picked up two bottles of Burgundy, which he pulled out of his large Belgian-uniform pockets. He rang the bell for the attendant in the car, gave him the two bottles, and told him to give them to the ambassador with the compliments of Major Colby, Colonel Van Atta, and Captain Adams, who unfortunately had found it necessary to occupy one of the compartments of his special car. We sat and waited, and then came a rap on the door of the compartment. It was the ambassador's seventeen-year-old son, who said: "The ambassador wishes to thank you gentlemen very much and to ask if any of you has a corkscrew?" We spent the rest of the eighteen-hour journey in peace.

The Crillon was jammed by the restless American officials, staff workers, and journalists attending the Peace Conference, but Bowman had reserved for Adams a steam-heated bedroom where he was comfortable. When he went down to dinner the first night he had the pleasant surprise of espying an old friend, the anthropologist Farrabee, who had been a member of his special circle in Washington. Adams specially liked Farabee for his endless string of stories about life in the Amazon Valley, where he had lived among the Indians for two years, his philosophical temperament, and his unfailing courtesy. One story especially pleased Adams. In getting out of his Amazon home Farrabee had arranged with an Indian chief for a caravan, which he hustled forward at top speed. The second morning he found the chief and all the savages sitting on their haunches in a meditative circle. "What is the matter?" he inquired. "Only one thing," replied the chief. "We have hurried so much that we have to sit down for a while to let our souls catch up with our bodies." Farrabee displayed his courtesy by hunting up two relatives of Adams, a half-sister of his mother and her husband, whom he knew to be resident in Paris, and inviting them to dinner.

On inquiry, Adams learned that he had been designated archivist of the American delegation to the Peace Conference. In reality, he never had anything to do with the archives, but instead found himself saddled with many-sided duties respecting the maps.

One duty was to act as liaison officer in map work for the American delegation, British delegation, and geographical service of the French Army. Another duty was to assist in the purchase of maps and atlases in Europe to be distributed to the War College, American Geographical Society, and Library of Congress. His most important job, however, was to take care of the confidential maps. He had five rooms full of them, with sentries night and day at the door, and he alone could give visitors access. In spare hours he prepared a variety of useful new maps, and had some of them reproduced in poster relief, as the exigencies of the Peace Conference required, by a corps of workers housed in the Invalides above the tomb of Napoleon. In one day this staff could finish a surprisingly complete relief map, with hills, plains, and rivers delineated and place-names accurately lettered. Eminent European statesmen sometimes pored over these maps.

"I remember one interesting day when the boundary between Greece and Albania was under consideration," he writes. "Venizelos, the prime minister of Greece, came in with some of the other Peace Conference people to look at the boundary suggested." The map that Adams had ready for him, laid out in blocks about eighteen inches square, covered almost one side of the room on a slanting wooden frame. A red line indicated the suggested boundary. Venizelos, a mild-mannered little man of soft speech but infinite persistence, looked it up and down, minutely scrutinizing the red line. Then, putting his hands in a meek, semi-prayerful position in front of his chest, he exploded: "This will never do." Colonel House had a way of meeting such statements with an equally disconcerting "Why?" Somebody else asked the question this time, and Venizelos replied: "The line is halfway up the slopes of all those mountains. The Greeks live in the valleys, and all their wealth is in the cattle they keep there in winter and drive to the mountain tops in summer. With this boundary as drawn, twice a year the Greeks will have to carry their movable wealth across an international line. That will mean incidents, and incidents in the Balkans mean war, and Balkan wars always lead to war in Europe." Venizelos got his alteration.

Another prominent figure at the Conference was King Albert of Belgium, well over six feet tall, blond, and athletic. Then or later, for Adams in his London years spent some time with him writing a specially commissioned magazine story, he related the particulars of his marriage. He had gone to Vienna, he said, to visit the Emperor Franz Joseph. There he met a daughter of Duke Charles Theodore of Bavaria, with whom he fell in love. The girl's father belonged to one of the best families of Germany; she had received an excellent education, and was in every way eligible. But King Leopold of the Belgians, who still had a full decade to reign, made objections. He bade Albert wait, go away for a time, and then see how he felt about marriage. "If I must go away," said Albert, "I would like to go to America. It must be an attractive country, for so many Belgians go over and never return." In 1898, therefore, he spent a good deal of time traveling in the United States. On his return he renewed his courtship, the King yielded, and in 1900 he married Elizabeth.

Adams made one short excursion to Chateau-Thierry to see the battlefield, continued to Soissons, where he found the cathedral a mere shell, and got as far as Rheims, which was full of ruined buildings.

Later he wrote of the miles and miles of barbed wire and the sad sights. "We slept in an old ruined house at Chateau-Thierry, and found a spring cot with a mattress. The fellow I was with and I drew to see who would get the spring and who the mattress. I drew the spring. The walls were full of holes from shells, and it was very airy. The roads were awful, full of shell-holes. The landscape looked like the moon, all dead and full of trenches and shell-holes, the fields around Soissons still uncleared from the battle. We would pass a woman in black hauling a cart with a few little belongings, two or three children trudging along, going back to some little farm. It all seems like a nightmare now from another life."[20]

He took a longer trip as companion to Professor Douglas Johnson of Columbia, a geologist who had been busy on topographical work, and who asked Adams to accompany him to army headquarters on the Loire to get his discharge. Although a journey so far from Paris seemed almost impossible, for the maps had to be guarded and absences were restricted, Adams went to see the officer in charge of personnel. This dignitary was out of his office, but a soldier doing secretarial work inquired into the circumstances and found out what orders Adams needed. His face lighted up.

"Well, captain," he said, "that officer is hardly ever in. He is always out at teas in the afternoon, and when he comes in before dinner he is in a tearing hurry, and signs all the orders that I put on his desk without reading them. If you want to make out your orders, I'll take them to him."

The plan worked like a charm. The soldier typed out orders that Adams dictated. He was to leave Paris at 8:00, proceed to Blois for the night, visit headquarters, and return within three days. The personnel officer duly rushed in, signed the orders, and Adams was off next day with Douglas Johnson.

[20] From a letter to Kay Seely, August 20, 1924.

In general, however, Adams found the Conference dull. The American experts at the Crillon lived like monks in a dark, crowded, and chilly monastery. The hotel remained so jammed that the lounge had to be added to the dining room. This left no place to sit at night, and when the downstairs lights were put out at 9 P.M. and all city restaurants and cafés were shut at 9:30, most men repaired to their gloomy rooms, for the streets were shabby and dreary.[21] "It was the blackest, coldest, wettest winter in that city in ninety-six years," writes Adams, recording a statistic that seemed accurate. "Perhaps that had something to do with the failure of the Conference. Along in midwinter I felt quite unwell, and had pains in all my joints." A doctor told him he had rheumatism, and he began taking long walks in the gray drizzle to limber himself up. "Finally, one night I could not sleep at all. It seemed to me that I had what we used to call a charley-horse all over. The army doctor, a major, came up to my room. He looked me over, examined my chest, and asked if I had ever had measles. I told him I never had. His answer was: 'You are a damned liar — you have them now.' "

As Adams had been riding in the elevator that President Wilson occasionally used, this disconcerted him. Although it turned out that he had only German measles, the major ordered him into a hospital for infectious ailments on the Marne. As he was driven out by a soldier in a Ford, he asked the name of the destination. "It's Jonesville on the Pond," was the reply — doughboy French for *Joinville-sur-le-Pont*. Here, in what had been a dilapidated boys' school, nervously aware that he was surrounded by diphtheria, spinal meningitis, and typhus, Adams ate poor cold food, avoided a black cat that wandered from room to room, and shuddered at plates and cutlery that were distressingly unclean. Fortunately, he found some congenial companionship in a Salvation Army man until, his measles disappearing, he abruptly left, telling his doctor: "I am going A.W.O.L. Call up the Peace Conference and order a car to take me back to the Crillon, and keep your eyes shut while I am leaving."

As the Peace Conference wore on early in 1918, Adams felt the deep-

[21] But, wrote Adams in an article, "How Our Peace Agents Live," in the New York *Times,* July 27, 1919, men knew that they were taking a part, however, minor, in one of the great events of history. The atmosphere was that of a board of directors meeting, but they had glimpses of Lloyd George and Clemenceau. And such Americans as Haskins of Harvard, Day of Yale, and Douglas Johnson of Columbia "would humanize even a peace conference, if that were possible."

ening chilliness of the French people toward Wilson. Late in January the President was toiling sixteen or eighteen hours a day. Irked by the criticism of the press, he had Dr. Cary Grayson hint that if Gallic harassment continued, he might have the Conference removed to another country.[22] Soon afterward, he let it be known that he must sail February 15 for a short stay in Washington, to sign bills and perform other official duties, and would leave Brest on the *George Washington.* Thereupon, men attached to the Conference were astonished by the sudden receipt of an ornate invitation to a gala performance at the opera in Wilson's honor. Adams, assigned a seat in the box just above the President, made some inquiries.

"Oh, don't you know?" an American lady told him. "When Wilson came here the excitement was tremendous, and he was hailed like Christ entering Jerusalem. Now that his stock has gone down, the prefect of police has become worried over his departure. Not only would he go to the station in insulting silence; somebody might hurl a missile at him. The prefect had the brilliant idea of a farewell performance, ending when all the streets are dark and empty anyway." The lady further explained why the opera chosen for the night was not the familiar *Faust* of Gounod; by special decree of Clemenceau, she said, it was Berlioz's *Damnation of Faust.*

Adams made a lasting friend at the Conference in the English-speaking Baron Korff, a Menshevik Russian leader of ability whom Kerensky had appointed governor-general of Finland. When Kerensky fell he and his wife had abruptly walked out of their house in Finland, leaving everything, even their hats, behind them. He had accompanied Prince Lvoff, once prominent in the Russian Zemstvo organization, to Paris where Lvoff settled permanently. J. T. A. took a liking to this impoverished expert in international law, who later lectured at Johns Hopkins and Columbia, and literally worked himself into the grave, dropping dead at his lecture desk. Meanwhile, Adams continued seeing a good deal of Bowman, the leading territorial specialist in the American group, and later got from him an elaborate theory that the break between Wilson and House was attributable to indiscreet promises that House made during Wilson's absence respecting the Trieste situation.

By the middle of March, 1918, Wilson was back in Paris, facing a multiplicity of new problems, and resuming the overwork that early in April prostrated him for three days and left him physically weakened.

[22] Arthur Walworth, *Woodrow Wilson, World Prophet* (New York, 1958), p. 253.

Question after question was somehow settled. Of these decisions Adams, an unimportant figure on the periphery, knew nothing. He had no understanding of the European snake pit, and no comprehension of the political and economic currents weaving such fantastic patterns under the surface of events. But by the end of April he perceived that the work of the Conference was practically finished and that he had nothing more to do. The peace treaty was finally submitted to the Germans on May 7. Fidgeting to get home, Adams did not witness its presentation.

"My father had had pneumonia and he was getting old," he writes. "My sister was running the furnace and the car at our house on the end of Long Island." Time to return!

He reached America only by packing himself into a battered ship, the *Potsdam,* with 2,500 returning soldiers, and enduring army rations, a diphtheria epidemic, and a fire on the way. The greatest diversion came the final day. An order was issued that all the troops had to take a bath before landing; and Adams saw the 2,500 men pop up one hatchway in the cold dawn, stark naked, run under heavy jets of sea water played on them by hoses, and disappear down another hatchway. Never did the Statute of Liberty hold a more welcoming mien.

The New England Trilogy

The return from France ended a disheartening but instructive episode in Adams's life. Although still uncertain of his future, he was deeply relieved to be home again. He had been laying plans while abroad for following his successful history of Southampton by a more ambitious book on the colonial period. But he did not get down to it at once. A bachelor with a modest but adequate income, he could use his time as he liked. For some months in the spring and summer of 1918, while the country returned to peacetime pursuits, he devoted himself to family and village affairs in his Bridgehampton cottage, where he was to remain until 1927.

"I loved Bridgehampton," he wrote later. Although the place had a number of "summer people," it was essentially a simple farming community, quite different from the smart social centers of Southampton on the west and Easthampton on the east. His war experience had given him a new outlook, and although forty in 1918, he found in his leisure there a stronger appreciation of youth. He had never cared much for outdoor sports. But now he made friends with a number of lads of fifteen to eighteen, who used to go camping, swimming, fishing, and shooting with him.

More and more devoted to the village, he left two substantial memorials of his residence. A bathing beach with dilapidated bathhouses had been managed for years by a Coast Guard veteran who leased the cubicles from the Methodist Book Concern at a dollar a year. Suddenly the villagers received word that two Pittsburgh millionaires were buying the property to turn it into walled estates. Adams intervened, got E. J. Berwind, head of a large coal company, to subscribe money on condition that the community raise a little, and finally arranged for creation of a six-acre bathing beach lined with bathhouses that the village rented for only $25 apiece, as compared with $150 at Southampton. At the same time, he helped others devise a plan for an American Legion center that grew until he found himself raising money for a large Community House that would shelter the local fire department, the grange, various fraternal organizations, a large auditorium for lectures and motion pictures, a dance hall, bowling alleys, and other amenities, as well as the Legion. Some shabby structures that had grown up piecemeal for club purposes were scrapped in favor of the new $75,000 hall.

At the height of this effort a scornful summer resident told Adams that he could not raise $5,000 for his undertaking. Adams responded: "Come with me tomorrow morning and see!" He was at the point where pledged payments were due, and in less than an hour had $25,000 in hand.

His boldest postwar adventure, however, was embarcation upon his first large-scale book, *The Founding of New England.* He had thought of this when writing his Southampton volume, and talks with some of the Peace Conference specialists had heightened his ambition. One day at the Crillon he discussed with Clive Day of Yale the deficiencies of John Gorham Palfrey's five-volume *History of New England.* Begun in 1858, it was hopelessly outdated in many particulars. A strong Puritan bias in the first volumes and a violent Anglophobia in the Revolutionary period robbed it of objectivity. Adams also perceived that Palfrey's Massachusetts residence and Congregational inheritance (though later he became Unitarian) had made him peevishly unfair to New Hampshire and Rhode Island. "When I get back," he told Day, "I shall try to get out a really modern history of New England."

At the beginning, as he later protested, he had not the slightest intention of being iconoclastic. He then held the old traditional view of

New England history. His intention was simply to rewrite it. He meant to do this first by considering not only the original sources but the latest results of scholarship, and second by trying to understand New England's record in relation to the whole empire rather than as a detached provincial espisode. But when he came to study the sources, he formed an impression very different from the picture given by all the traditional historians. "My reaction was sharp," he later admitted. In trying at the same time to put Massachusetts into her imperial setting, he felt sure he was moving in just the right direction, and most later historians have agreed that his attitude was correct. The effect of his work, therefore, *was* iconoclastic. It upset old concepts.

In the *Founding,* as the first of three books, Adams laid a careful groundwork of physical geography and Indian history before he dealt with English explorations prior to the *Mayflower's* immortal voyage. He brought his story to a climax with the witchcraft frenzy near the end of the seventeenth century, and the fanatical insanity of men like Cotton Mather. His narrative struck refreshingly new notes. It did justice to British rule in New England, condemning various instances of the crown's neglect, confusion, and oppression, but praising the statesmanlike policies of Lord Clarendon, pointing out how essential British protection against France really was, and explaining how intemperately the stubborn Yankee colonists disputed British claims to any authority whatever. He was severe upon the Puritans in more ways than one. He showed how sharply the contributions of Connecticut and Rhode Island to political freedom and civil liberty differed from those of the Bay Colony, and how superior they were. His descriptions of Puritan land greed and Puritan cruelty to the Indians were fierce enough to wring the hearts of descendants of the early settlers. Nobody could read his account of the inhuman Puritan torture of Quakers, men and women alike, without horror and indignation.

Palfrey had devoted thirty-five pages to excuses for the Massachusetts persecution of the Quakers. Adams was too honest to extenuate the whippings, brandings, mutilations, imprisonments, and executions of those who incurred the wrath of the Puritan divines. After describing the heroic death of Mary Dyer, the sale of two Quaker children into bondage to pay the fines assessed upon them, and the flogging of some half-naked women through eleven successive towns, he penned an unrelenting verdict upon the clergy of harsh John Endicott's time. "The theocracy had now reached such a height of intellectual pride, of intolerable belief in themselves as the sole possessors of the knowledge of

God, and as the only legitimate interpreters of His will to the world, that either all freedom of thought in Massachusetts must die, or their power must be destroyed." Fortunately, the King declared that the bloodshed must stop, royal commissioners interfered, and no less a person than Cromwell demanded in Parliament: "Is it ingenuous to ask liberty and not to give it?" Such a revulsion of opinion took place in the Bay Colony itself that at two of the most outrageous executions heavy guards had to be posted to prevent a popular outbreak.

Touches of cutting sarcasm enlivened Adams's history of the rebellion led by the Wampanoag sachem "King Philip." He noted the colonists' failure to understand the Indian theory of property, or indeed any theory of property not the white man's. He described the contempt the settlers developed for the heathen and the savages, "who incidentally were in possession of lands coveted by the Saints of God." It was the fatal error of the chieftain Miantonomo, a consistent friend of the English, that he trusted in the white men's justice, knowing they had no real charge to bring against him. "He had not, however, reckoned on the church." It always had charges up its sleeve. Again, the men of Massachusetts could never be pinned down to precise boundary lines. Protesting their unshakable integrity, they got some "skilful artists" to draw their southern lines, combining guesswork with an old map, a pen, and a ruler, and meanwhile they were laying claim to New Hampshire and Maine on the north. Thus "the colony slowly expanded, like a balloon filling with gas."

Happily, the bigotry of the Puritan church-state could not last, and Adams traced its inevitable transformation even more vigorously and decisively than Brooks Adams had done in *The Emancipation of Massachusetts* (1887). Such a transformation was necessary to the whole future of America. Before men could legitimately proclaim the motto, "No taxation without representation," it was essential that the "people" should be identified as the whole community and not just a religious sect. Before Massachusetts could join Virginia in asserting that "All men are born equal," she had, as Adams put it, to abandon her politico-religious distinction between a minority born to everlasting sainthood, and a majority doomed to eternal damnation. The way in which the transformation was effected Adams described briskly and graphically in his last three chapters, one of which did larger justice to Sir Edmund Andros than he had previously received.

Adams also emphasized the economic foundations of the growing colonial self-assertiveness. The real struggle among Britain, France,

Spain, and other nations in the colonial era, he argued, was not for geographical empire but for raw materials, commerce, and markets on a worldwide scale.

As his book neared completion, Adams was at a loss to bring it before the public, for he knew nothing of publishing. He even feared that he might have to make his own arrangements for printing it. Happily, some officers he had known during the war had spent a weekend with him in Bridgehampton, and one of them, Charles Johnson, was a literary Irishman who had married a daughter of the distinguished Russian veteran of the Russo-Turkish War and First World War, General Alexei Brusilov. While teaching at Rutgers, Johnson wrote for the *Atlantic Monthly* and other magazines. He looked at Adams's unfinished manuscript, and advised him to send sample chapters to Ellery Sedgwick, editor of the *Atlantic.*

Sedgwick, a perceptive man with a liking for new authors, fancied the manuscript so much that he at once offered a contract for book publication by the Atlantic Monthly Press. "Incidentally," wrote Adams later, "it was an extremely rotten contract. The editor of *Harper's Monthly* later told me that he thought it was the damndest contract he had ever seen, and he wouldn't mind telling Ellery Sedgwick so to his face." This was a bit unjust; Sedgwick had merely taken account of the risks of publishing a scholarly book by an unknown writer, and though his contract was poor by standards of 1950, it was not too indecent for 1920.

The volume was an immediate success. Reviewers were enthusiastic, although some Massachusetts men, including Samuel Eliot Morison, protested that it was unfair to the Puritans. Its flyleaf later recorded: First Impression, May, 1921; Second Impression, November, 1922; Third Impression, May, 1926; Fourth Impression, April, 1927. And the title-page soon bore evidence of academic recognition, placing after Adams's name the letters LL.D., Litt.D. It gratified him that the doctorate of laws came from Rhode Island State College, for he had taken pains to emphasize the debt of New England to little Rhode Island's sturdy independence of thought. The prompt award of the Pulitzer Prize for history gave him pleasure, and so did his election to the National Institute of Arts and Letters, with Worthington C. Ford, M. A. De Wolfe Howe, and Ellery Sedgwick as sponsors. It pleased him also that early visitors at his door included the tall and courtly Dixon Ryan Fox of Columbia, who came to urge Adams to write one of the first volumes in the *History of American Life* series just launched by himself and Arthur M. Schlesinger.

The sharpest criticism of the *Founding* was shortly presented in Samuel Eliot Morison's *Builders of the Bay Colony* (1930), and Adams briefly replied to it in the *New England Quarterly* of October, 1930. The issues presented were not susceptible of decisive settlement. The two men differed upon the question whether the great mass of migrants to Massachusetts were motivated most heavily by religious impulses or by economic considerations. Each historian seemed to the other indulging in unjustified inferences from hazy data, and consequent half-truths. In demonstrating that "church members" meant communicants rather than church attendants, Morison unquestionably demolished one bit of statistical evidence that Adams had put forward. Both agreed, however, that no firm statistics upon religious fealty were available, and that explorations into motive never achieve clear and dependable conclusions. That Adams may have been too drastic in his minimization of religious impulses was plain; that Morison may have been too sweeping in his rejection of economic impulses was equally clear. And Adams was able to score a moral point against Morison when he argued that the latter's defense of Puritan intolerance and persecution as "necessary" was a very disagreeable if not a flimsy kind of defense. As H. L. Mencken published the later volumes of his *Prejudices,* it became evident how much ammunition Adams had furnished him and other anti-Puritan writers.

The impression made by *The Founding* had not faded when two years later he brought out its successor, *Revolutionary New England, 1691-1776.* In a well-illustrated volume of 480 pages, even better in style than the first, he again seized a large opportunity. Monographic studies, compilations of documents, and histories bearing upon the crowded years beginning in 1763 were almost innumerable, and every year added to their number. That period was momentous, dramatic, and full of patriotic appeal. Little sound recent work, however, had been expended upon the period between the so-called revolution of 1688, strongly felt in America as in England, and the victorious close of the Seven Years' War in 1763.[23] In this three-quarters of a century, as Adams said, lay the origins of radical thought in the colonies, the growth of grievances, and the development of parties; yet writers had neglected these subjects. So long as people thought of the American Revolution only in political and military terms, the neglect did not greatly matter. But they were beginning to think of it as a great socio-

[23] Adams pointed out this gap in a paper read to the American Historical Association at New Haven, December 27, 1922, and published in the *American Historical Review,* XXVIII, No. 4 (July, 1923).

economic movement, the roots of which ran far back into colonial history.

Adams therefore set himself to deal in scholarly but readable fashion with a variety of subjects either ignored or poorly treated. What was the administration of the British Empire when the Stuarts were thrown aside by William and Mary, the ideas of John Locke triumphed, and Massachusetts received her new charter? Why was crown administration so inefficient? Just what was the effect of the constant strife between crown governor and popular assembly upon public feeling? In the wars with the French the colonies and their militia made a bad showing; could they have done better, and how? The importance of land policy, the navigation acts, the paper money question, and the appearance of nascent industrialism, had never been fully brought out in New England history, and Adams treated all these subjects compactly but trenchantly. He had something cogent to say on frontier commercial ethics, colonial Indian policy, and the land question.

His discussion of Jonathan Edwards and the Great Awakening threw fresh light upon New England theology (Edwards, he writes, preached "a gorilla God of fiendish deviltry"). With freshness and independence, he carried his narrative through the defeat of the French, the conquest of Canada, and the appearance of "the insoluble problem," imperial taxation.

Once more he made his dislike of Puritanism, which in spite of the spread of Episcopalianism and Deism remained a dominant influence, emphatically plain. He emphasized its harshness, its belief in its own infallibility, and its bigotry as more than counterbalancing its finer qualities. Once more, also, he did justice to the best British leaders in colonial administration; especially to William Shirley, the doughty, far-sighted royal governor of Massachusetts who showed more grasp of the imperial problem than anybody else. Once more, too, Adams brought out the striking evidences of a steady broadening and secularizing of the colonial mind, and the rising importance of business in all its aspects from land speculation and smuggling to honest trade and manufactures.

Like the *Founding of New England,* the second volume rested almost wholly upon printed sources, but they were so numerous and his study was so thorough that exploration of manuscript collections could have added little. His footnotes showed how voluminous had been his researches. The book had greater appeal to the general public than the *Founding* for several reasons; the period was closer, the mind of New England had become more modern, and the author wrote with greater eloquence. To the tune of laudatory reviews the book sold briskly. The most critical notice came from Evarts B. Greene in the *American Historical Review,* offering strictures upon Adams's "emotional" disparagement of Puritans and the landed aristocracy, but conceding that the treatment was very able and showed a distinct advance in workmanship. It would long be indispensable to serious students of New England and the Revolution, wrote Greene. He might have said more about its literary distinction, exemplified in the final paragraph — a paragraph in which Adams characteristically pointed to the need for additional investigations:

> In telling the story of New England (wrote Adams) from the first scattered settlements founded in cold December upon the little strip of land between the stormy wintry sea and illimitable forests, down to the time when four populous colonies, strong and proud in their strength, united with the rest of their younger and older sisters to form a new nation, we have been able to indicate but a few of the sources from whence, both for good and for ill, that new nation drew its own peculiar character and life. Much of the ground, indeed, remains wholly unmapped, and many an historical explorer must study the records of obscure villages and whole districts before we can understand all the causes that led to the double revolution of 1776. Much we can learn from English records, much from those of Boston and the larger towns, much from the contemporary literature of the day, but behind it all we must still learn more than we yet know of the daily life and problems, the discontents and ambitions, of the many thousands who never saw a town and who never expressed themselves in the printed page. Until then, we cannot be sure that we understand aright that great movement which spread through the throngs of common men who sailed the ships and tilled the fields and felled the forests of New England, and wrought a new hope in the heart of the world.

To complete his trilogy Adams published in April, 1926, *New England in the Republic, 1776-1850,* a provocative volume that found its central theme in "the continual struggle of the common man to realize the doctrines of the Revolution in the life of the community." It also dilated upon the growth of a sectional spirit among New Englanders, defiantly expressed in Yankee protests against the Embargo, in angry opposition to the War of 1812, and in the Hartford Convention. A sharp critical edge was clear in his treatment of Shays's Rebellion, the widening gulf between rich and poor in the industrialized states, the excesses of the anti-Catholic movement, and the general backwardness of New England in educational and humanitarian affairs.

This, however, was the least effective volume of the trilogy. Critics again charged him with unfairness, and a biased desire to emphasize shadows rather than sunshine. Covering so large a field, the book suffered at points from excessive compression. That it was a stimulating and interesting addition to history nobody could doubt, and it struck an original note of importance in showing how healthfully the New England democracy of 1850 differed from the democracy of 1776; for the later polity insisted on "the rights of man as man, and not as member of a class." But he would have done better to close this survey in 1830, thus giving himself more room for description and analysis.

In producing so broad, scholarly, and influential a group of volumes in rapid succession, 1921, 1923, and 1926, Adams had performed a notable feat. As the third went to press he was already deep in his contribution to the series that Drs. Schlesinger and Fox had planned under the title *A History of American Life,* the most comprehensive treatment of the nation's social development yet undertaken. In this he was paired with Thomas J. Wertenbaker of Princeton in covering almost the whole colonial period, getting the richer half of it in the years 1690-1763. Like Wertenbaker, he enjoyed a marked advantage over a majority of the twelve original authors in the series by having three-quarters of a century at his disposal, for he could trace economic and social changes from their origins through a long development. Later contributors, confined to twelve or fifteen years, had to take short views and write cramped narratives.

Partly for this reason, partly because he possessed complete leisure, and partly because of his scholarly acumen and literary skill, Adams wrote one of the best — probably the very best — of the books in the series. He called his 400-page volume *Provincial Society, 1690-1763.* All the critics accorded it high praise, a fact in which he took pride because the other authors, with two exceptions, were academic men.[24] He used to say he felt like a white blackbird in a flock, or a fly in amber.

He liked also to insist that he wrote the book mainly from original sources, and although he used few manuscript collections, this was a valid claim. At that time secondary accounts of life in the colonies were rare and scattered. A few monographs as good as L. V. Lockwood's *Colonial Furniture* or Elizabeth McClellan's *Historic Dress;* a few works on manners and customs as vigorous as Esther Singleton's *Social New York Under the Georges;* one remarkable diary, that of Samuel Sewall; two good economic treatises, those of W. B. Weeden

[24] The exceptions were two journalists, Ida M. Tarbell, *The Nationalizing of Business,* and myself, *The Emergence of Modern America.* Both of us were hampered by confinement to a dozen years.

on New England and P. A. Bruce on Virginia; the captivating travels of William Byrd; and, of course, the writings of John Woolman, Crêvecoeur, and Benjamin Franklin — these came near exhausting the list of valuable books. Adams properly characterized the volumes of Alice Morse Earle on home life, child life, and other social topics as "delightful." His wide reading, however, had familiarized him with many of the best articles upon colonial history, and with old travels and memoirs. He knew the great official compilations like the printed *Archives* of Pennsylvania, New Jersey, and Maryland, and the *Records* or *Provincial Papers* of Connecticut, New Hampshire, and North Carolina. He also knew where letters of warm human interest might be found in scattered places.

His method was to buy as many books as he could for use in Bridgehampton, borrow others from libraries within reach, and make up lists of newspapers, collections of manuscripts, and rare monographs to be searched during three or four winter months in Washington. Microfilming was in its infancy. He never then or later employed a research assistant, for he alone could identify what was important to him. But, following a full outline that he gradually perfected, he got through huge masses of material rapidly and efficiently.

While in the midst of his researches, working in the Library of Congress, he got word that his father had suffered a stroke. Ten days later the elder Adams was dead.[25] "My sister and I," writes Adams, "came back to New York for my father's funeral, and then on our way back to Washington stopped for two weeks at Annapolis, where I wanted to go through two thousand issues of the *Maryland Gazette* for my book. The library was in the State House, and the old librarian fortunately, like myself at the time, smoked a pipe. I spent two weeks all alone with him, as nobody else came in, going through the papers." It will be seen that he relied heavily upon colonial newspapers. Various digests and abstracts existed. "The student, however," he writes in the bibliographical essay in *Provincial Society,* "can substitute nothing for a study of the original papers themselves."

The most impressive characteristics of *Provincial Society,* nevertheless, were neither thoroughness of research nor novelty of facts. They were the acuteness of its generalizations and the finish of its style.

[25] "I had taken my father and sister to Washington for the winter," Adams wrote Isaiah Bowman. "About four weeks ago my father had a stroke which left him paralyzed and unable to speak. . . . Happily for him my father lived only nine days, for a recovery was out of the question and he had always dreaded a long illness." (February 18, 1923).

Plainly, Adams had thought more deeply upon his subject than other historians, and he brought more valuable conclusions to light. He was not a narrative and descriptive historian alone, but a philosophical historian; in his limited field he had some of the qualities not only of Macaulay and Parkman, but of Lecky. As for style, his touch was almost as graphic as that of the elder Trevelyan.

He distinguished three periods of cultural growth in the English colonies between 1690 and the end of the Seven Years' War. The first showed a civilization of transplanted character. Most of its features were copied directly from England, and lost something in crossing the Atlantic. Medicine, for example, was much below the condition of that science in Europe; education and literature were far feebler. This period came to an end with the Peace of Utrecht, which made possible the expansion of both land and the maritime frontiers. When this imported culture lost vitality, a period ensued that was marked by decline and disintegration. The settlers lost touch with Europe, society grew rougher, and the easy profits of commerce, fur trading, and land exploitation generated a materialistic temper. Fortunately, however, some substantial towns developed; contacts between colonies became easier as roads and ports were built; and the English stock was enriched by the immigration of Scots, Irish, Germans, French, and other elements. With the growth of a variegated population came a quickening of thought evinced by newspapers, colleges, travel, the Great Awakening, and science.

Adams illuminated his exposition of these successive phases of growth by special generalizations. He drew original deductions, for example, concerning the way in which the concern for physical well-being on the frontier impaired the integrity of folk art. He laid down clear deductions upon the social and economic foundations of the growing sectional animosities among the Northern, Middle, and Southern colonies. He explained how a rising tide of radicalism, economic in origin, gave birth to special types of politicians and political machinery. Yet an increasing colonial solidarity in defiance of England was also emerging, and upon this—"the fateful foreshadowing of the eventual rupture of the empire"—he made other philosophical observations.

When the book brought a shower of favorable reviews, with new honorary degrees and some suggestions of teaching positions that he did not feel equipped to accept, Adams could have no doubt as to its success. Although it did not sell widely, it confirmed among scholars and the more intelligent readers his reputation as an exceptionally able historian.

However, he always felt unfairly treated in that he received only $1,000 for so distinguished a volume. This barely met his out-of-pocket costs. The Macmillan Co. published it. He wrote the able George P. Brett, head of the American branch of that house, pointing out that Harper Brothers had paid contributors to the American Nation Series much better. Brett replied that one reason he could not pay more was that Fox and Schlesinger had demanded such large editorial fees. This did not satisfy Adams, who had been told by Fox that the reason they paid so little was that Macmillan asked such large guarantees against loss! "Somebody fumbled the truth," Adams later commented. The American Life Series seemed more risky at the outset than it was, and both editors and publisher had some reason for their initial prudence. Later, as the university world expanded, it had a wide circulation as a basic library set. Whether the compensation to authors should have been increased when the set sold well year after year is an unanswered question.

Marriage and English Residence

His war experiences, his New England trilogy, and his *Provincial Society* had left Adams feeling tired. The doctor advised a rest. I remember that about this time he looked as if he needed it and that he told me he had agreed to take his sister Amy abroad as soon as he finished his book. At that point fate intervened. Seized one day with an acute pain in his right side, he went to the Southampton hospital for examination. The sequel he has related in his manuscript upon family history:

About five o'clock, after the X-rays had all been developed, the surgeon told me that I had to have the darned appendix out. I said that I had promised to take my sister to Europe, and could I go? His answer was that I might get caught half-way across the ocean, and I had better have it done before I left; to which I replied that if I had anything to do, I wanted to do it right away, and could he take it out in the morning? He said that his operating day was filled, but that if I would come right in and get ready he would take me over at 7:30 in the morning. So I drove my car back to Bridgehampton, packed my bag, and settled in. He got me a room and a day nurse, but was having trouble in getting a night nurse. He said that the best nurse in the hospital was a young Miss Seely, and he would see what he could do. Miss Seely said she was tired, did not want any more night duty, and did not want a man for a patient, but that as a matter of professional duty she would take the case if he could not get anyone else. He wanted Miss Seely for me, and so called back to her that he could not get anybody else, and Miss Seely was my nurse that first night after the operation.

This was the night of November 22-23, 1923 — a date that Adams never forgot, for it opened a new chapter in his life.

It was a successful operation. Recovering rapidly, Adams and his sister went to England, France, and Italy as they had planned. But he came back to a world that had changed for him. For the first time in his life he had fallen deeply in love! — and he hoped that Miss Seely might reciprocate his feeling.

The next two years, 1924-25, were the most disturbed in Adams's life. A confirmed bachelor, he found himself, well into his forties, ardently attached to a girl of limited literary background half his age. He concluded that he could never be happy without her; yet he was not certain he could be satisfied in a married state, or make her happy.

A restless perplexity mastered him. His father's death, his increasing immersion in scholarly writing that required use of large libraries, a sense that he ought to be near magazine offices and publishing houses, and the winter loneliness of eastern Long Island, led him soon after his return from Europe to sell his Bridgehampton cottage. He went to live at the Yale Club, engaging Room 1313; his sister went to live in a hotel. He hated club life, and missed his sister's companionship. For several months he sank into such dejection and melancholia that he consulted a psychiatrist in New York. The advice of this expert to enter a sanatorium in Washington, Connecticut, and sort out colored yarns, almost reduced Adams to despair. When during a single week a man occupying the fourteenth-floor room above him jumped out of the window, a man in the Hotel Commodore across the street did the same thing, and the occupant of a room in the Biltmore close by chose the same exit from life, Adams felt shaken. "My own mind was in such a condition that I thought I might follow," he writes.

Fortunately, he took a grip upon himself. In this process Miss Seely was invaluable. A young woman of poise, character, and brains, she assisted him to find himself. They debated the question of marriage coolly, sensibly, earnestly — and with increasing attachment. They went to the theatre, made country excursions, and visited museums, sharing each other's discoveries — for neither had ever taken much time for such recreation. They attended church together. When they were apart Adams wrote her long letters — letters narrative, descriptive, philosophical, such as he had never written to anyone before except his old Brooklyn schoolmate and crony, Ed Schermerhorn.[26] Gradually he recovered much of his poise.

[26] Many of Schermerhorn's letters that friend, in grief after Adams's death,

Meanwhile, three of Adams's close friends gave him what aid and comfort they could. One was Mark Antony De Wolfe Howe, a scholar with wide interest in letters, history, and life, an entertaining companion whose witty talk was given flavor, like Charles Lamb's, by an engaging stutter, and the most genially lovable of men. Another was Worthington C. Ford, an authority on American and especially New England history, and a man of the world, whose travel, reading, and associations made him highly stimulating. Both were much his seniors. I was the third friend, now one of the editors of that great but ill-fated journal, the New York *World,* and some twelve years his junior. To the three of us Adams, in deep emotion, for he was a man of sensitive and candid feeling, repeatedly explained his nervous prostration.

Such advice and sympathy as we could give helped him clamber out of his psychological slough and find a firm path. A letter from Mark Howe, written at the right moment in just the right spirit, was particularly efficacious. All three of us urged him to end his ridiculous dependence upon his sister, a jealously possessive woman, and at once follow his own impulse — which was to marry Miss Seely. He and she could make a new life completely their own. Though she had her own uncertainties, her poise and common sense helped immeasurably. And the fact that Adams was now finding many acquaintances in the literary and academic worlds encouraged him to strike forward boldly.

A minor occurrence helped turn the scale. Always fond of children, he had taken pleasure in watching the growth of the teen-age daughter of a Wall Street associate and his cultivated wife, who lived in a gloomy apartment on 125th Street, then an increasingly undesirable part of town. Adams suggested that they seek a brighter home in Brooklyn. He helped them look about, until at Two Grace Street, overlooking the harbor, they found a five-room apartment with ample sunshine and fresh air, less expensive than the uptown flat and closer to Wall Street.

In this search Adams had become fascinated by a small apartment that seemed just what *he* himself needed. It had five compact rooms, with views of the East River and harbor and beyond them the fine New Jersey sunsets. He had promptly gotten his furniture and books out of storage, and settled down to makeshift housekeeping, tidying his own quarters and cooking most of his own meals. He could boil or scramble

---

unfortunately destroyed. But by this time Schermerhorn had ceased to be close to J. T. A. As he wrote Mrs. Adams later, the period of their greatest intimacy had been from 1896 to 1920.

eggs, broil a filet mignon, and bake sweet potatoes Southern style. On this limited fare he subsisted for some months.

Adams had joined Arthur Schlesinger, Sr., and me at the *World* offices, high in the Pulitzer Building dome over Park Row, on Friday, October 12, 1925, when we three talked about the general requirements of the *History of American Life.* As four of the men who were assigned volumes, including Adams and myself, finished them at about the same time, these four books appeared almost simultaneously. Late in May, 1926, he had startled me by a letter announcing that he had given up his beloved Bridgehampton cottage. "I have sold my place," he wrote, "at a very low figure, and expect to move my belongings, all too many, to town next week. I shall be at the Yale Club from June 5th onward." This was just when most people were thinking of moving *to* rustic shades, not away from them. Not until he arrived in town did I learn, in a talk with him at the Century Club, that the parting from his sister and sale of his house were connected with the queer emotional upheaval that had seized him. The Yale Club address had shortly given way to the little flat at Two Grace Street in Brooklyn.

Already the shadow of Kathryn Seely, if anything so bright can be called a shadow, was then falling across his relations with his friends. We had felt it coming. As his letter writing was diverted more and more largely to her, and to the general correspondence growing out of his books and magazine articles, he would write Mark Howe and me less frequently. We could only guess that he was pouring out his feelings to her fully and freely. Sometimes he would begin a letter to Kay on Monday, and continue it by daily installments until he mailed it on Friday. Even in the beginnings of his courtship he had given her the best of his heart and mind.

"We have tried to be serious and real friends," he wrote her, "and we both want always what is best for the other, and we will both try to help the other the best we can." He had advised her upon her small investments. He had given her injunctions upon reading, and been delighted when she appreciated books he liked, such as *The Cloister and the Hearth.* He sent her an article upon Joseph Conrad in the English *Bookman* because it contained a photograph of the novelist, his wife, and their small son at tea, writing: "There is something about the picture of the three in the peace of that room that appeals to something deep in me."

And he threw out bits of philosophy. "The more I think of the marriage relation," he observed apropos of the wedding of two Long Island friends, "the more it seems to me to come back to the fundamental mistake of regarding it as two lives running parallel, each trying to get what they can, instead of looking at it as one life made up of both, each sacrificing something and contributing something. But then, I am an old bachelor."

Later, his wife used to assert, with a twinkle in her merry blue eyes, that it was his atrocious cooking that threw him across the line into matrimony. This accusation he denied, declaring that the night they were married *he* cooked the dinner. At any rate, as he came back to a normal and happy view of life, everything was settled. He and Kay were serenely married on January 18, 1927, by a Presbyterian clergyman whom both knew, Ed Schermerhorn serving as best man; and when he brought his bride to Grace Street, they made plans for the future full of confident hopes. Here he began working with renewed energy, and preparing once more to go abroad.

His marriage of course swept him into another world. Two weeks after the ceremony he took his wife abroad, crossing to England on the White Star liner *Olympic*. It was a cold, stormy voyage, half the passengers were seasick, and some bad lobster gave Kay a touch of ptomaine poisoning that kept her in her birth. She had hung up all her frocks. "As we got near to Southampton," writes Adams, "I was wondering about two things. One was how I would get her ashore, and the other was how I would attend to the packing of all her clothes, for I had never seen so much feminine garb. We finally made it, and got into the Southwestern Hotel. It was a rainy day; I think it always is there." He worried a little about her response to English life, for he now intended a division of time between Britain and America.

England initially depressed her. The provincial hotels, first in Southampton and then Hindhead, were a shock with the single hall-and-stair carpet in red and blue, the little coal fire in a grate in their room instead of central heating, the boiled potatoes and soggy brussels sprouts, and the eternal rain. It was a shock to see navvies and other laborers who were obviously Britons; like many another American, Kay had thought of Englishmen as always wearing finely tailored suits with watch chains and always being deep in professional talk — it was only "foreigners" who did rough work. But once arrived in London, she took heart. The rain let up; the Burlington Hotel was bright as ever; and they soon found a comfortable furnished apartment — a "service flat" — at 11 Palace Court, just off Kensington Gardens. At first they contented themselves with one floor, but when the one just below fell vacant they took it also, thus gaining what New Yorkers called a duplex apartment. Possessing a dining room of their own where meals were served, they did not have to bother with servants. "I was beginning to make more money from my hard work," Adams explains, "for the public liked my stuff."

Before long Kay began to think London more attractive than New York, a view with which Adams quite agreed. In time, she came to regard England as home, and to feel nostalgia whenever they went away. Any alien staying in London for sixty consecutive days had to report to the police in Bow Street, and Adams, paying taxes to the United States and the State of New York, feared that if he seemed too clearly domiciled in Britain he might have to pay income tax there also. He therefore took his wife to Paris for a few days every two months. As they settled down, he found that he could work as advantageously in London as in America. They contentedly kept the two pleasant floors at 11 Palace Court for five or six years, making occasional trips back to the United States. This part of London was especially congenial, and when they moved it was to 61 Holland Park not far away, where they remained until the final return to the United States in 1936. The last two years in London they had also a summer place at Goring Heath in Oxfordshire.

These English years were a period of grim, stern application to work. Adams, without any editorial position or university professorship, had to wring all his income out of literary work. Seeking no foundation grant, he met all his research costs himself. One book after another was rapped out on the little Corona typewriter with which he toiled endlessly, each title requiring intense application over long months. To anticipate our story, his volume *The Adams Family,* suggested to him by Ellery Sedgwick,[27] emerged from the press in June, 1930. His still more successful book *The Epic of America* appeared in September, 1931, and was followed by two volumes of factual history, *The March of Democracy,* in 1932-33. The brief, sketchy, but at points penetrating *Henry Adams* appeared in 1933. Then came a piece of interpretative history on slavery, the abolitionist and free-soil movements, and the Civil War, *America's Tragedy* (1934). Writing these half-dozen volumes in six years would have been a remarkable feat, but at the same time Adams was sending a stream of articles to the *Atlantic, Harper's Monthly, Scribner's,* the *Forum,* and other leading magazines, and gathering the best pieces together in two volumes, *Our Business*

[27] So Edwin Weeks, close to Sedgwick on the *Atlantic Monthly,* informs me.

Civilization: Some Aspects of America (1929), and *The Tempo of Modern Life* (1931).

All this work did not prevent him from making important English friendships. Those with Francis W. Hirst, lately editor of the *Econimist*, G. P. Gooch, the historian, and James Findlay Muirhead, connected first with Baedeker's and then the Blue Guides, were the most important. Meanwhile, he not only maintained his old American friendships, but lengthened the list. In London he saw something of the American embassy staff, and particularly of David Finley, a man of taste and ability whom Ambassador Mellon had brought over from the Treasury Department. Characteristically, he pulled no strings to get into any London club. He was *not* a clubbable man. He did buy a membership in the London Library, however, which was convenient in St. James's Square, and offered invaluable lending facilities from its wealth of old books.

These were years of systematic travel, which Adams had always enjoyed, and now found more stimulating because he regarded it important in the education of his young wife. Her fascination in British and Continental life, in old towns and natural scenery, and in museums, art galleries, and concert halls, never ceased to delight him. Vienna with its concerts and opera, and Rome with its ruins, palaces, and ecclesiastical pomp, they found especially interesting. These were years, too, of certain large projects; of literary plans and expectations, some of them commercially profitable while others vanished like pricked soap bubbles. The projects of course had to be evolved or abandoned in company with publishers. His original connection with Little, Brown and its associate the Atlantic Monthly Press was fortunate, not primarily in its business results, though they were satisfactory, but in the distinction that the firm and the monthly, so important in literary history, lent to his name. He was fortunate also in his shortlived association with the ebullient young publisher Charles Boni.

Not a few American writers, from Benjamin Franklin to Henry James and Stephen Crane, have done some of their best work in England. Adams always valued his residence in London for its quiet, its freedom from social and journalistic harassments, and above all, as he often told me, for a detached perspective in viewing America that was as valuable in writing history as in his magazine commentaries. He had soon brought to London all his furniture and books. His library contained about 1,500 volumes for which he had no further use, and it pleased him that two friends, J. F. Muirhead, then past eighty, and

Sir Frederick Pollock, at ninety, immediately placed them with London University.

Both he and Kay delighted in Cockney humor. One day he heard a Communist haranguing an audience in Hyde Park, with a policeman standing beside him to preserve order. When the man got through, the bobby said to the crowd, "Now all of you who want to march on Buckingham Palace and break the windows, fall in line!" The crowd guffawed. Another time, staying in a hotel and realizing just before dinner that he had no way of opening his bottle of Scotch, he dashed out and demanded of the policeman on the corner: "Officer, can you tell me where I can get a corkscrew?" The policeman, busy directing traffic, replied without a glance, "That sounds inviting; try the chemist's across the street"—and went on guiding traffic.

Several times when I visited him I found him perfectly contented, fond of the city, the decent, courteous people, and the quaint curiosities about him. Once, combating the notion that the British were unpoetic, he took me to a large trunk of beechwood standing in Kensington Gardens carved with various Peter Pan creations: elves, gnomes, birds, wee animals, and other objects that delighted children. What other city, he asked, could offer such a medley of grace and fantasy?

Adams set down his reasons for liking London life in an article in the *Atlantic* for October, 1927, called "Home Thoughts from Abroad." After a couple of months spent in rambling about Italy and France, he found the "perennial and inexhaustible charm" of the great metropolis as fresh as ever. He deplored the fact that Devonshire House had been torn down, that beautiful Dorchester House had been sold, and that the Adelphi, with its dignified mansions above and gloomily mysterious arches below, faced an uncertain future. But then London had been incessantly changing since the Romans founded it 2,000 years before, and the modern life of the town remained singularly stable. "London still seems to me in most ways the most civilized, as it is unquestionably the greatest, of the cities of men." Here, more than in New York or Paris, the dweller might feel that he stood at the crossroads of all the world's chief highways. He was in the capital of a land whose interests were still imperial, whose business in merchandise or banking was international, and which had hardly a family without some member in a faroff corner of the commonwealth or outside world. Then, too, London was the most homelike of great cities. Its wealth of small houses, its numerous wide parks with trees, lawns, and cricket, its many squares and gardens, and general quiet, all appealed to him. At times he seemed cribbed, cabined, and confined, but in general he felt he was in what Henry James called the right place.

"One recalls the picture in *Punch* of an American motorist driving his car at seventy miles an hour while a man at the roadside calls out, 'Remember this is an island!' "

A still more charming essay upon the same theme Adams sent to the *Yale Review* under the title "Kensington Gardens and Lafayette Square." He spoke with special appreciation of the leisure and lack of friction he found in London. He had discovered the time and inclination to do all sorts of study and cogitation that he could not do in New York. "It has not been without surprise that I find myself re-reading Goethe's *Faust,* Marcus Aurelius, Epictetus, Sophocles, Aeschylus, Shakespeare, and other books that seemed never likely to leave their shelves again at home." He had come insensibly to feel himself a part of the whole stream of western European civilization from the Greeks onward. It was as though a turbulent flood, carrying the flotsam and jetsam of useless struggles, had subsided and left uncovered again the landscape of the human heart. On his table lay Robert Bridges' new volume *The Testament of Beauty.* "And so, I step out on my balcony and wonder, as I look over the lawns and trees of Kensington Gardens, how it will seem when in a few weeks I am again only one of the million scurrying ants in Times Square, a transitory spark in the blast furnace of American prosperity. . . . What, after all, is the best use to make of this dream we call life? The dusk has fallen. The curtains are drawn. The fire glows, and I turn to *The Testament of Beauty.*"

That some Britons shrank from Americans in the mass Adams acknowledged. Their distrust, he explained, did not rest on the noisiness of vulgar Yankee tourists, on resentment of American demands for repayment of war debts, or on memories of old wars. As in other European countries, it was based mainly upon a fear of the Americanization of Europe. And Adams indicated that as he watched the standardization of taste in America by mass production, mass advertising, and the mass media, he shared this uneasiness. "Of what use to travel three thousand miles from New York to San Francisco if for the most part one sees only the same kind of people, reads the same comic strips and syndicated news columns, talks the same shop, and sees the same city architecture?" This cry Adams was to repeat in other articles. He balanced his essay, however, by writing that he would not stay to live in England, and that as he looked at the tailored Warwickshire landscape he felt a nostalgia for some rough Vermont hillside or homely Carolina fishing village. Above all, he missed the contact with a great, erratic, fast-growing people carrying out one of the greatest experiments in history.

On first arriving in England he was uneasy about expenses. He and his sister no longer shared their incomes, and marriage had doubled his expenses. He did too much of the hack work just mentioned — sketches for the *Dictionary of American Biography,* reviews for the New York *Sun,* whose literary pages were now briefly conducted by Henry Hazlitt, and a professional scrutiny of the historical material in a weekly radio program that was being presented by the DuPont Corporation. These jobs dulled his palm, but brought in money that he quite unnecessarily feared he *might* need.

For business and family reasons he and Kay had to visit America regularly. Near the end of his life he computed that he had crossed the Atlantic thirty-six times, sixteen of them on the *Aquitania,* his favorite ship, and ten of them on the *Berengaria.* After retiring from business he never went beyond the Alleghenies. Britain he of course knew thoroughly, traversing it from Cornwall and Devon to Edinburgh until he could describe almost any part of it. At one time he traced his own genealogy back to Northamptonshire, the county from which the Adamses of Massachusetts had come. He momentarily considered buying a house there. "It would have been interesting to carry the family line full circle," he told me, but he saw objections, and drew back.

In France he became especially fond of Chartres, visiting it in all kinds of weather, and concluding that the stained glass of the cathedral was best on dark days. He and Kay repeatedly wandered up and down Italy, from Milan to Naples. He always recalled one amusing incident of a drive they took around Sorrento and Amalfi to Paestum to see the beautiful Greek temples. The cliffs, the blue bay, the sunny sky, and the ruins enchanted them, so that Kay exclaimed: "It is so beautiful it almost hurts!" Next moment the pain was relieved. They rounded a corner to a little inn kept by an Italian who had obviously lived in New York, and who had posted a sign: "Americans, Stop Here. Hot Dogs!"

He also recalled with amusement the speech he heard one evening in Paris from a chief functionary of their hotel. They had just arrived from Rome by the Blue Train and had seen no newspaper. The manager was sitting utterly crushed, with his head in his hands. When Adams asked what was the matter, he exploded: "This is a terrible day for France — a terrible day. The king of Jugoslavia landed at

Marseilles and was assassinated! They will say nobody is safe in France for five minutes. But worse still! The Fiat Automobile Company was giving a banquet at my hotel tonight, and has cancelled it. Sixteen thousand francs! A terrible day for France!"

Eight times the Adamses visited Holland for short holidays. Once they went to Czechoslovakia, once to Scandinavia, and repeatedly to Switzerland. As he had to economize time, much of the travel was by car, using a chauffeur who knew the roads and language. Adams had a sense of humor that brightened all his trips. He liked to sit in bars listening to the talk; he liked to inspect old houses, churches, and tombstones. "I remember in one little graveyard of a village," he writes of Devon, "reading a long inscription to some local celebrity, who had apparently occupied almost all the favored positions in the village, and the inscription ended with a cryptic note that the gentleman was 'conservative in his morals.' I have often wondered what sort of old boy he was."

In their English wanderings they had only two unpleasant experiences. Once a galloping herd of wild ponies almost forced him and Kay over the edge of a cliff in Cornwall. Another time, in Torquay, he had what he honestly thought an encounter with the supernatural. He several times told the story with earnestness to me and other close friends, and finally set it down in "An American Family." He, Kay, and his sister were staying at one of the large hotels, where he and his wife occupied a corner room, with his sister next door. "As dawn was just breaking I happened to wake, and I saw a figure of a young woman in the air about two feet above my bed. She was dressed in pale gray with a scarf around her head and neck very much like the portrait of Beatrice Cenci. She was very pretty and looked down at me, and I looked at her without any fear, but as I was looking at her, she just floated out through the closed window."

At breakfast he remarked that the most extraordinary experience had befallen him during the night. His sister at once interrupted him, saying she had been frightened by the same weird occurrence. She had awakened suddenly with a vision of someone in the room; she was paralyzed with fear, but finally mustered enough courage to turn on the bed light, and kept it on. Adams later wrote his English cousin in Devon about the incident, and the story reached the niece of Lord Lloyd, who had been governor-general of Egypt. She exclaimed that she and her uncle had been staying at this very hotel some years earlier, and she wrote Adams what had happened. Late one morning she had walked down the staircase, in broad daylight, to join her uncle for a walk. "As I went down I saw the woman in a gray dress, as you describe, coming up the stairs, and stepped aside to let her pass, but looked at her because her costume was so unusual. When she got directly opposite me she completely vanished, and I told my uncle I would not stay in that house another minute."

Among important persons whom Adams met in England was the Prince of Wales, who came to a farewell reception given by Lady Astor in 1933 for the retiring ambassador, Andrew Mellon. When Adams remarked that he had sent the Prince a copy of the *Epic,* the Prince replied: "My God, are you the man who wrote that book? I have read it all through!" Later Adams thought that the Prince had been flushed with drink, while Kay declared he had been extremely pale, a conflict of evidence that interested him as a historian.[28] Once he met Prime Minister Baldwin, who remarked that his recipe for an English leader was "to abhor logic and grow the hide of a rhinoceros." After lunching with Sir John Simon at the Athenaeum, just as Mussolini was about to send his troops into Abyssinia, he came away with a most unpleasant impression of the man. Simon had predicted flatly that Mussolini would content himself with seizing a mere border strip of Abyssinia, and had stated his emphatic opinion that the United States did not need a larger navy than Japan's. "From our conversation I thought that Sir John was perhaps the worst Foreign Minister whom England has ever had."

Adams several times met Harold Laski, "whom I intensely disliked," he writes, without quite explaining why. But when Austen Chamberlain asked him to lunch to talk about Anglo-American affairs and the war debts, Adams was pleased to find they were in complete agreement on both subjects. Philip Snowden struck him as equally sensible, and a man of extraordinary courage. John Buchan pleased Adams by his unassuming manners, tremendous energy, and warm feeling for the United States. Sir Philip Gibbs was another friend; "a very sweet and kindly man, although in my opinion rather too much a pacifist." Worthington C. Ford, supervising from Paris the reproduction of a large body of European manuscripts concerned with American history, under a program financed by the Rockefeller Foundation and conducted by the American Historical Association, repeatedly came over

[28] This was the brief version Adams gave me, but see the Correspondence for a fuller account.

from the Continent to stay with the Adamses. He and Kay liked to entertain Britons and Americans together.[29]

Altogether, they did not lack good company. Yet his best friends were still those in the United States, a lengthening list. Among the new names were Cordell Hull, his "one really good and more or less intimate friend" in the Roosevelt Cabinet, and Mrs. Hull. Shortly before Hull sailed for the London Economic Conference in 1934 Adams spent an evening with him in Washington. "I asked him just what they were going to try to do. He said they were not going to talk tariffs because the Americans were not yet ready for that, and were not going to talk war debts because Europe was not ready for that, but the one thing they were going to try to do was to stabilize the franc, the pound, and the dollar, so that international trade could come alive again." Returning soon afterward to England, Adams was in London when President Roosevelt, supposedly at the instigation of Raymond Moley, took action on gold that turned the conference into a nullity. Hull had been shown all the messages by Moley that had passed through the Embassy. One evening the Secretary and his wife called on the Adamses. "At the moment I have my foot on the Persian silk rug around which we sat," Adams later wrote, "and I have often looked to see if there were any holes burned in it from what Hull said about Moley."

Some of Adams's European friends were furious over Roosevelt's destruction of all the hopes centered in the Conference. However, one Briton told him: "At least you Americans can be proud of one thing. You sent us a very great gentleman at the head of your delegation."

Later on, somebody in the Interior Department wrote Adams that Secretary Ickes would like to talk to him. The next time he was in Washington, Adams made an appointment, called, and after an awk-

[29] "We were always having passers-by from America and elsewhere," he writes in "An American Family," "and our life with them and our London friends and the foreign correspondents of newspapers in many countries kept us very much alive. Among others who turned up from America I may mention Allan Nevins, an old friend, who was with us on a number of different occasions when he came over to lecture. He was at our house one day and among the other guests were G. P. Gooch, editor of the *Contemporary Review,* Harold Callender, European correspondent of the New York *Times,* and Francis W. Hirst, former editor of the *Economist.* My wife was the only woman. It was a man's dinner, and an extremely interesting one. Finally Gooch pulled out his watch and apologized, but said he had an appointment at three and must keep track of the time. He found it was then four!" Adams, Gooch, and Hirst had done most of the talking. Another American frequently visiting the Adamses was Stephen Bonsal, who had been a war correspondent of the New York *Herald* in the Spanish-American War, Boxer rebellion, and other conflicts.

ward silence remarked: "Mr. Secretary, I came here only because I was told you wished to see me." Ickes screwed his head on one side, scratched his chin, and blurted out: "God damned if I know what it was about!" When Adams showed him the summoning letter he picked up an interdepartmental telephone, called a subordinate, and said: "Dr. James Truslow Adams is here. What do I want to see him about?" A long explanation apparently followed, which Adams could not hear. Finally Ickes exclaimed: "Oh, there's nothing to that," slammed down the receiver, and screwing his head to one side again, courteously explained: "That bright young fellow had an idea, but there's nothing to it!" The interview was over.

All the magazine people for whom Adams wrote in these years were Americans, and some of them became warm comrades. Thomas Wells, for example, whom the House of Morgan in a financial reorganization had helped gain his place as editor of *Harper's Monthly,* was highly congenial. "He was a very able man, and as it happened, his mind and mine clicked exactly." Henry Goddard Leach, a Philadelphian of about Adams's age who became editor of the *Forum* in 1923, and wanted just the kind of essays on public affairs Adams liked to write, was another friend. With the brilliant Ellery Sedgwick as editor of the *Atlantic* he got on famously, but not always with Ellery Sedgwick as head of the Atlantic Monthly Press. Brightest of all were his relations with "dear old Arthur Scribner," as he called the publisher who died in 1932, with Charles Scribner, the equally lovable founder of *Scribner's Magazine,* and with Alfred Dashiell, who edited the magazine 1930-36. Once when he visited New York Mrs. Arthur Scribner gave a dinner for Adams and his wife. The sequel can be told in his own words:

> On another visit to America two years later we were called up at the hotel by someone who asked us to come to dinner to meet certain people. We went, and the apartment was a beautiful one with a large living room with an open log fire. I stood with my back to it talking to the guests. Suddenly a very tall, distinguished, and beautifully gowned woman came in, and spoke to my wife without an introduction. Then she came to me and said it was so nice to see me again. I thought, "Who the heck is she?" but realized that she was a New York society woman. However, I managed to meet the situation until at dinner I found myself sitting next to her, and she returned to the attack, saying again, "It is so nice to see you once more." I gulped, and the only thing I could think of was that we had met at the Scribner's dinner, so I took a bold chance, and said: "Oh, yes! I remember so pleasantly meeting you at Mrs. Arthur Scribner's." She drew herself up, and said: "I *am* Mrs. Arthur Scribner."[30]

[30] Slightly condensed from "An American Family."

With one editor and publisher, however, Adams had a special alliance over a full decade: Wilbur L. Cross, who controlled the *Yale Review* from 1911 until 1939.[31] During most of this period Cross was a member of the English Department of Yale and for eight years was governor of Connecticut. Along with Walter Lippmann and Alvin Johnson, Adams was a member of the advisory board of the *Review.* He was supposed to go to New Haven for its meetings four times a year, but as his English residence made this impossible he sent a letter on the European situation instead, to be published in the magazine. Just as after ten years he had thought it fitting to resign from the Pulitzer Prize Jury, so after a decade he quit the advisory board.

He was in no hurry to return to America, for from his flat at 11 Palace Court he could keep in fair touch with editors and publishers by correspondence. He particularly disliked the idea of going back to New York, which he decided was about the worst place in the United States for residence, though partially redeemed by its position as the metropolis of letters, drama, music, and art. When he did go back, he thought Washington would probably be the best residence; but ascendency of the New Deal, down until 1939, changed his views, for he formed a deep distrust of Franklin D. Roosevelt. A smaller place would suit him better. Yet efforts to get him to settle in Worcester, Massachusetts, and Middletown, Connecticut, he swiftly rebuffed. He also rejected suggestions that he might teach in Yale or some other university, disclaiming either taste or talent for lecturing. When Charles P. Taft suggested that he discuss with the family the possibility of executing a biography of William Howard Taft, his response was frigid. He valued his freedom to travel, write, and otherwise occupy himself as he pleased. On a visit to America he wrote V. V. McNitt how much he resented "the past weeks fairly nightmarish in enforced activities of all sorts."[32]

[31] Adams owed much also to Helen McAfee, who by 1932 had become managing editor of the *Yale Review* and was contributing a regular signed article on "Outstanding Novels." Cross, after retiring from Yale in 1930, was an able reform governor of Connecticut 1931-39.

[32] McNitt, an enterprising and liberal-minded journalist with newspaper syndicate experience, founded and edited a shortlived magazine called *McNaught's* to which J. T. A. contributed. Adams had shown disillusionment with Washington in 1931, writing his wife on April 12 that the only theatrical performance in the capital of the U.S.A. was "A Magician and his Daughter Jane." "Can you imagine the capital of any European country, even Czechoslovakia, where that would constitute the entire artistic life of the theatre? There is going to be a concert in a couple of weeks, and people are talking of it as a great event. Although this is a city of 500,000 inhabitants and the capital of what

After the trilogy and *Provincial Society* his outlook changed, as the summary list of his volumes just given shows. He sought broader themes, and took less interest in precise scholarship. The aftermath of the crash of 1930 also made him more anxious to speak out on the issues of the day, and he published an increasing number of articles not only in the major monthlies, but the financial press, *Current History,* and the *New York Times Magazine.* These essays showed a deepening conservatism, both political and economic. Inflation, the fast-rising national debt, efforts to redistribute wealth, and social welfare legislation all worried him greatly. At the same time he put into his papers a good deal of moralizing upon the values of simple living, leisure, quiet, and a happy family life, for he feared that the American people were abandoning too many of their traditional social standards.

England was actually in most respects a more radical country than the United States, but under Stanley Baldwin it did not seem so. British sedateness of temper helped nourish Adams's increasing conservatism; so did British criticism of some New Deal vagaries; so did the troubled scene on the Continent as Hitler consolidated his power in the Reich, and his partnership with Mussolini; and so did the talk of old Wall Street friends whom Adams saw on his return visits. His marriage had enhanced his sense of the importance of prudence in an uncertain world. It was a changed Adams who celebrated his forty-eighth birthday in 1936. But meanwhile he had published some books of sterling quality and had gained an international renown.

The Adams Family Theme and *The Epic*

Out of his volumes on New England, his friendship with Worthington C. Ford, and talks he had with his publisher-friend Albert Boni, who hoped that they might eventually bring out a collected edition of the writings of Henry Adams, J. T. A. developed a keen interest in the Adams family. As a preliminary undertaking, he and Boni concocted a plan for a volume of selections from the massive journal of John Quincy Adams, an invaluable record that Charles Francis Adams, Sr., had edited in a dozen large volumes (1877). It was strange this had not been done before, for the diary is fascinating. The full set was too large for a private library, and when obtainable it cost more than

Americans like to consider the richest nation in the world, the bookshops cannot compare with those in say, the little city of The Hague. As compared with Stockholm, they are a joke."

James Truslow Adams relaxing. Part of his extensive library, which he kept with him while he worked, is shown here.

Adams in uniform August, 1918.

Adams during the 1920's.

Kay Seely in training, 1919.

Formal portrait of Kay made in London.

Jay and his sister Amy L. Adams at Lewes, England.

Jay takes a nap in front of their hotel at Eastbourne, England.

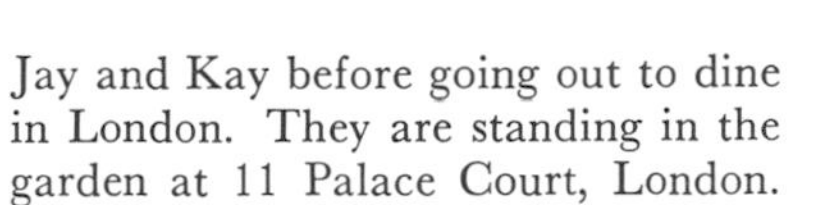

Jay and Kay before going out to dine in London. They are standing in the garden at 11 Palace Court, London.

Jay with their cat on the lawn at Chaplain's House, Goring Heath, England.

Adams at work.

James T. Adams and Charles Scribner signing a contract in the Scribner offices.

The Adams' home in Bridgehampton, Long Island.

11 Palace Court, London.

Adams' library at 11 Palace Court, London.

Jay and Kay's home in Southport, Connecticut.

Family portraits hang on the dining room walls of their Southport home.

a hundred dollars. Moreover, as it contained much dull, outdated material, a judicious reduction would vastly improve its appeal. Adams, working partly in England and partly in New York on his condensation, had marked the passages he wished to use when he suddenly found that another man had earlier glimpsed the same opportunity and anticipated him. This mischance, involving one of his best friends, he accepted good naturedly.[33]

He then went ahead trying to make arrangements for a collected edition of Henry Adams only to find, through much talk and correspondence, how difficult it was to bring into harmony the Adamses of Massachusetts and Washington, the Massachusetts Historical Society, which had originally published *The Education of Henry Adams,* in an edition of 250 copies for its members (after a tiny early printing in 1906 by Adams himself), the Institute of Architects, which had published *Mont-Saint-Michel and Chartres,* the Houghton Mifflin Company, and young Mr. Boni.

To J. T. A., as to most historians, the greatest of the Adamses was John Quincy Adams. The most challenging and interesting, however, was Henry Adams, while other members of the line were fascinating and impressive. He and Ellery Sedgwick saw what a rich literary opportunity they offered, and his lively book, *The Adams Family,* appeared in June, 1930.[34] Its success with scholars and the lay public alike was immediate. Of all his books this had the strongest human appeal and most enduring literary distinction. It also taught the largest public lessons, for as J. Franklin Jameson wrote in the *American Historical Review:* "He has produced a book which every intelligent young man may profitably read for the splendid examples it presents of manly independence, enlightened patriotism, and unselfish devotion to the pub-

[33] I was the unwitting anticipator. Adams writes in a reminiscent bit: "I had marked all the passages I wanted to use when my friend Allan Nevins came over to see me. I told him that I was condensing J. Q. A.'s Diary, whereupon he said: 'Great Scott! I have just done that for Longmans, Green & Co., and it is already in page proof.' Monday morning I called up Boni and told him the situation." Boni, who had promised an advance of $1,000, with characterstic generosity insisted on paying Adams the whole sum. My edition of the J. Q. A. Diary went through several printings with Longmans and then another when Scribner's took it over. At this time Adams and I were helping each other in various ways. For example, I did the proofreading of his volume *The Adams Family* for him, he being in London and Little, Brown feeling pressed for time. We narrowly escaped an unfortunate duplication of effort. Worthington C. Ford, for twenty years editorial head of the Massachusetts Historical Society, was close to some of the Adamses.

[34] Alfred R. McIntyre of Little, Brown also claimed credit for suggesting the Adams family theme to J. T. A.

lic service; and older persons may read it with pride that our history has contained lives so rich in the fruits of intelligence and public spirit."

Dividing his book into four parts, J. T. A. devoted the first to the Revolutionary hero John Adams — not neglecting his spirited wife Abigail; the second to John Quincy Adams, Secretary of State, President, and in his greatest years a Representative in Congress; the third to Charles Francis Adams, Sr., with emphasis on his wartime service as Minister to Great Britain; and the fourth to Henry Adams and his brothers John Quincy, Charles Francis, Jr., and Brooks. In a volume of 350 large pages, John Adams received nearly a hundred, and John Quincy Adams a bit more.

The chronicle was full of war, diplomacy, politics, and family drama, and J. T. A. made quietly effective use of the most striking episodes. They included John Adams and the XYZ Affair; John Quincy Adams's battle for the right of petition; the confrontation of Palmerston by Charles Francis Adams, Sr., protesting against the supposedly imminent escape of the British rams to reinforce the Confederacy; and the intellectual adventures of Henry Adams in the South Seas, England, and France. The most spirited historical sections were those dominated by John Quincy; the best portraiture was given to Henry. Showing wide reading though little original research, the book had consistent freshness in its grasp of men and situations, its salty narrative, and its mixture of sympathy and criticism.

For of course he did not spare the Adamses some sharp criticism. The fact that John and John Quincy Adams refused to welcome their successors, Jefferson and Jackson, into the White House seemed to him the gross breach of courtesy it unquestionably was. J. T. A. did not fail to speak of their tartness of temper, their overweening vanity, their readiness to believe that all the world was sometimes in an unfair conspiracy against their views, their frigidity of demeanor, and the *brusquerie* that Charles Francis Adams, Sr., confessed. They were unbendingly self-conscious until at the end Henry Adams wrote the *Education* in the ironic temper of a *poseur,* an aristocratic success posing as a humble failure. Yet in certain great national crises, like the approach to war with France precipitated by Alexander Hamilton in 1798-1800, the crises initiated by Southern fire-eaters in the late 1830's and 1850's, the Civil War clashes with the British Foreign Office, and the hysteric quarrels of Charles Sumner with Grant and Hamilton Fish, the Adamses played roles of principle, prejudice, and wisdom.

"A brilliant book," wrote Mark Howe. "A permanent contribution to historical literature," declared another friend, Claude M. Fuess. The Cleveland *Plain Dealer* spoke for other commentators when it asserted that the volume could be "recommended without reserve to all lovers of biography, of history, of American ideals and traditions." "It may well be that it shall long remain unique in its class," asserted Jameson, "for hardly could be found another American family to which the mode of treatment would be appropriate in anything like the same degree." Sedgwick of the *Atlantic,* and Alfred R. McIntyre, president of Little, Brown, were as pleased as Adams himself by the large sales and warm public applause.[35] Approbatory letters from members of the Adams family increased his satisfaction.

Unfortunately, the plan for a set of Henry Adam's collected writings did not gain family support and came to shipwreck in a way that bitterly disappointed him. He and Boni thought of perhaps ten volumes, and he did much hard work in searching out a complete body of contents. Worthington C. Ford, just closing his long editorial service with the Massachusetts Historical Society, not only encouraged him and lent advice, but used his influence with surviving members of the Adams family. Nobody knew more about Henry Adam's work than Ford, who had helped bring out the commercial edition of the *Education* in 1918, and would soon edit a collection of *Letters of Henry Adams 1858-1891* that he had painstakingly gathered.

"I see no objection to the plan, and much in its favor," Ford wrote the later Charles Francis Adams who, practising law in State Street, was soon to become Hoover's Secretary of the Navy. He recommended J. T. A. as "above criticism in his methods," adding: "I should strongly advise that he be favored by you and the Adams family." Apart from the *Education,* he argued, no books of Henry Adams were likely to earn much in royalties, and publication of a complete set was one hallmark of a classic — an honor accorded to very few authors.

But somewhere among the Adams family, Ferris Greenslet of Houghton, Mifflin, and others, the idea of a properly edited set met a veto. On February 6, 1929, Greenslet wrote Albert Boni that he had found it impossible to gain authorization from the family for the inclusion of five titles published by Houghton, Mifflin. Boni replied that after all the work that J. T. A. had done toward a complete edition, he was unwilling to surrender the project unless an agreement was totally impossible; was it a question of the division of royalties? It was not

[35] The Atlantic Monthly Press books were published by Little, Brown & Co. in association with the Atlantic Monthly Press Company.

mainly such a question, replied Greenslet. Some of the interested parties had taken a decidedly stiff tone, he explained, adding that their stiffness increased the reluctance of Houghton, Mifflin "to grant to an outside publisher a group of distinguished and successful titles which represented . . . an unusually prolonged campaign of editorial work." The enterprise, Greenslet slyly went on, might be turned over to Houghton, Mifflin, which would assume Boni's agreements with J. T. A. and the various publishers involved, and would then make Boni a reasonable compensation for his spade work. Adams and Boni were sorely disappointed, and Worthington C. Ford penned some cutting remarks about Greenslet. The project had to be dropped, and the world never got a useful set in which Adams and Ford would have pooled their editorial talents.[36]

Adams had confidently expected this project to succeed. He had gone so far as to write a careful introduction for the collected set; and partly to save this from oblivion and partly to furnish Boni with a small compensation for his time and planning, he allowed the firm of Albert and Charles Boni to bring it out in a handsome illustrated volume, with a careful bibliography of Henry Adams's writings. This book, dedicated to Worthington C. Ford (1933), he published as the only biography of Henry Adams thus far written. It was very far from being a satisfactory biography, as he acknowledged, but as a biographical essay, appreciative rather than critical, it had large virtues. Carl Becker, giving it a review later reprinted in *Everyman His Own Historian,* commended it highly but at the same time pointed out one obvious shortcoming, the failure to appraise Henry Adams's efforts to devise a scientific approach to history. Becker added: "One would like, above all, a less fragmentary and casual, a more resolute attempt to formulate a closely integrated psychological interpretation of the life and personality of Henry Adams." This was asking a great deal from a short study of a most complicated and enigmatic man.

In another effort to compensate Albert Boni for his losses in time and

[36] For example, Ford pointed out to J. T. A. the importance of including the "Report on Cuba" written by Henry Adams just before the Spanish-American War. "It is notorious that the report was his, although it was submitted to the Senate by Don Cameron." Ford to Adams, November 21, 1928. Ford possessed other interesting bits of information not then generally known, such as the fact that Henry Adams had written both of the printed prefaces to the *Education,* though the first was signed by Henry Cabot Lodge. It is barely possible that Ford had suggested the collected edition to J. T. A. Boni brought out a neat reprint of Henry Adam's *History,* putting the original nine volumes into four with an introduction by Henry Steele Commager.

money, Adams had earlier given his firm a sheaf of magazine essays to publish under the title *Our Business Civilization: Some Aspects of American Culture* (1929). This volume, of whose wretched physical appearance he complained — it looked like a dirty red brick — contained some of his best essays, such as "Jefferson and Hamilton Today," "The Mucker Pose," and "Home Thoughts from Abroad." Its assessments of American civilization were astringently critical. Such clinical observations upon business, mass culture, national lawlessness at the end of the prohibition era, and the luxury-spending at the height of the Coolidge-Hoover bull market, were needed and had a healthful effect. When the boom broke these ideas seemed outdated. Adams had insisted, however, that they gave but a partial view. The essays dealt only with certain aspects of the contemporaneous scene, he protested, and those the more sinister, and if he wished he could say as much or more about healthy phases of life. Some harsh statements nevertheless stuck in men's memories, such as his untenable assertion: "I cannot see that, as a general rule, American universities or colleges leave the slightest cultural impress upon those who attend them."

The collection that followed a little later, *The Tempo of Modern Life* (Boni, 1931), was not quite so good. However, it contained one attack upon the refusal of Americans to face unpleasant truths, "Pollyanna, Our Patron Goddess," which ought to be reprinted now and then, and a comment of enduring historical significance on "Presidential Prosperity" that was seen to be quite sound after prosperity vanished.[37] When some of his essays were republished in Britain under the title *A Searchlight on America,* several reviewers remarked that however severely he castigated certain tendencies in his country, his love for her showed in every paragraph; a comment that immensely pleased Adams.

The second spring after he removed abroad, as he prepared to begin work on another ambitious book, he suffered a swift crippling illness. "My wife and I went to luncheon in New York," he writes,

> and when I got back I suddenly became the sickest dog in the world. Something inside of me was coming out everywhere, at both ends and at every pore. What had happened was that it was a hot day, and I had on a new pair of blue socks which had not been washed. There was a little fold over my big toe which started a blister, and the dye got in and gave me a streptococcus infection. I was practically unconscious for about three days, when

[37] Adams had predicted the financial crash of 1930, and the ensuing depression, in an article in the *Outlook* in December, 1928, and had made his own preparations for the collapse.

the doctor told my wife that I should go to the hospital. I was there about five weeks, and at one stage they gave me only forty-eight hours to live. My wife suggested taking my leg off, but the surgeon said it would do no good, as the poison had gone through me too much and did not seem to settle. Suddenly one day he looked at me and told the floor nurse to bring the operating table at once.

Fortunately, the emergency operation that Adams underwent was successful, and so were two others that followed it. Adams soon began to recover, and after two months was hard at work again.

Hard at work in the free lancer's grinding routine, for only his little Corona stood between him and the wolf. At the end of August, 1928, when he was still too weak to get from Brooklyn to the library to compile a bibliography for his new subject, he confided to Mark Howe how much mere journalism took up his time.

I have written an article specially requested by *Harpers* and also one of a thousand words for a new eight-volume universal history being brought out in England and in which the best English scholars are cooperating. It is being brought out by the Amalgamated Press of London, one of the subsidiaries of the fifty-million dollar publishing corporation formed to take over the enterprises of the late Lord Northcliffe. They publish books, magazines, and so on, and there seems some chance of my getting work from them in England. They offered me $300 for the article, which is better pay than you get for similar work in America. I expect next to do an article for the *Atlantic.* I wish much that I could think up some editorial job like the *Hamilton* and *Jefferson* of last year. . . . That extra $1,000 comes in very handily!

If Mark Howe had been frank, he would have protested as strongly against $300 hack jobs for the Northcliffe estate as I did; Adams was not *that* poor. *The Adams Family* was adopted by the Literary Guild for mass distribution at a cut rate, with a fair payment to him, and in 1933 was republished by Blue Ribbon Books at a dollar a copy, again with fair compensation. For *Our Business Civilization* he received an advance of $2,000 from Boni, although as Edward Weeks of the Atlantic Monthly Press pointed out to him, this could be repaid only by a sale of 7,000 copies or more. (It approached that figure even before its paperback publication in Bonibooks in 1933; and it had an English edition under the title *Searchlight on America,* with an introduction by Douglas Woodruff, in 1930). The two little volumes of selections called *Hamiltonian Principles* and *Jeffersonian Principles* stood on a different basis. Little, Brown, who issued both in 1928, had initiated them, and according to Weeks they "cost us considerable." Full of well-chosen extracts illustrating their titles, with prefatory essays by Adams, they were much above the potboiler level. Little, Brown thought that Albert

Boni was adopting tactics that gave other publishers a niggardly look, but he had every right to do so, and Adams every right to profit by his generosity.

Adams was now meeting recognition in other ways. In the autumn of 1929 he was nominated to the American Academy of Arts and Letters by Nicholas Murray Butler, Wilbur Cross, Robert Grant, Henry Van Dyke, and Charles Downer Hazen. Election followed a year later. This was an honor he prized. A little later he was elected a Fellow of the Royal Society of Literature, a somewhat old-fashioned body that went back to Coleridge and Regency days. He was the third American to be chosen, and had Owen Wister for companion. Lord Lee of Fareham sent him the unanimous request of the trustees of the Sir George Watson Chair of American History, Literature, and Institutions that he lecture on this foundation at five or six British universities, an offer he declined. In the summer of 1930 the Harvard Overseers appointed him a member of the committee to inspect the Harvard department of history. Nicholas Murray Butler made him sundry tentative proposals, the most important a suggestion that he take some undefined position in Columbia, while other universities put out feelers which he rejected. Meanwhile, he kept on reviewing books, acknowledging a package of twelve volumes in one lot from Henry Hazlitt, who had transferred his talents to the *Nation*.

He reviewed partly because he wished to keep abreast of new volumes of importance in the American field and partly because he liked to have his say upon them. He was read with attention. For example, Ford on September 3, 1930, quoted to him a letter from a historian in the colonial field saying that the latest number of the *New England Quarterly* was a circus. "Truslow Adams reviews Morison's *Builders of the Bay Colony* — and how! It pleased me. Morison reviews Banks's *Winthrop Fleet* — and how!"[38] It was notorious that Adams believed the primary motivation of the great Puritan migration to be economic, and that Samuel Eliot Morison scoffed at this idea, holding that piety and

[38] The *New England Quarterly* had begun publication in January, 1928. Samuel Eliot Morison's review of Charles Edward Banks's *Winthrop Fleet of 1630* was severe, but perhaps its most important passage was the statement that "the settlement of Massachusetts Bay was due to a series of dissatisfactions with England, which centered about religion." Writing Kay from Washington in an undated letter of 1931, Adams told her: "In a speech in Boston the other night old [C. K.] Bolton said, speaking of how childen should be taught about the Puritans, 'Shall we use the pruning knife of Samuel Eliot Morison or the hatchet of James Truslow Adams?' " Mark Howe had gleefully reported this episode. J. T. A. and Morison kept on highly amicable personal terms.

idealism held the major place. Ford thought that Adams was right; others that he was wrong.

When Adams came to review Ford's first volume of Henry Adams's letters, he took especial pains with a 1,200-word paper in the *Nation* because of his affection for his old friend. "There are few men of whom I have been so fond or whose company I enjoy more," he wrote Hazlitt of Ford on September 20, 1930, "and I do hope he will eventually settle in London, as he says he will."

It was a thoroughly tired man who returned from America to 11 Palace Court that autumn, fagged and nervous after the "New York maelstrom." He found a mountain of correspondence. "This is my twentieth letter today, and the pile is scarcely diminished," he wrote me. Almost at once, however, he had to plunge into one of his greatest tasks, the composition of *The Epic of America,* a tour de force that he accomplished with astonishing speed. As October began he laid down a timetable. He informed Hazlitt that he had only five months before the British income tax law drove him to resume his temporary residence in America; he wrote Mark Howe that if he could finish the book for Little, Brown by March, 1931, he and Kay would cross for two months, returning to England in May before the summer rush; and he soon sent me exultant word that he was finishing the easier sections of the first draft at 10,000 words a week. After he completed a careful outline, he found that he had read and thought so much upon the American story that composition was easy.[39] His interpretations of national life in recent *Yale Review* papers stood him in good stead; so did his familiarity with Tocqueville, Bryce, and other commentators, including his friend Muirhead's *America, the Land of Contrasts.* By Christmas he was far along with the book and still writing rapidly.

As the *Epic* neared completion, Adams received from the well-intentioned Ellery Sedgwick about the worst piece of advice an editor ever gave his author. Sedgwick had not read a page of the manuscript. He knew nothing of it beyond a brief statement of progress that Adams had sent to Edward Weeks, and that had elicited Sedgwick's friendly comment: "Your letter to Weeks gives a good picture of what is undoubtedly an excellent volume." However, in a hasty impulse he now asked the picture redrawn.

[39] It must be remembered that Adams had read widely and thoughtfully for years. In writing a paper on Emerson for the *Atlantic* he came upon an old edition of the *Essays* that he had copiously annotated at the age of seventeen. He had also thought for half a dozen years of such a book as the *Epic,* and had assembled some of his ideas. Many of his magazine essays bore in some fashion upon the subject.

"I know well," he wrote Adams on January 13, 1931, "that what the intelligent public over here really needs is a book which, however romantic in tone, will yet tell the complete story of the American people within the contents of a single volume." He suggested that by alterations, enlargements, and a skeletonized table of contents, Adams might produce "a sort of Ploetz *Epitome* of American history." The well-known Ploetz handbook of European history is a tabulation of facts and dates drier than the Sahara. Sedgwick was suggesting that Adams forget style, interpretation, and philosophy, to furnish a marketable reference work. Such a change of goal, he wrote, would "give definiteness to the enterprise." The definiteness of the abyss!

Adams was amazed and angered. The plan of a single-volume *history* of the American people made no appeal to him; the plan of a single-volume *interpretation* of that history attracted him strongly. His book would stand or fall not by its facts, but its ideas and style. Heartened by the continued success of *The Adams Family,* he had no intention of giving way. Just before Christmas in 1930 Weeks reported that the *Family* had sold 1,900 copies in the first fifteen days of December, that fresh printings and advertising would be required, and that a full-page advertisement in the New York Sunday *Times* book section had given it the place of honor. Adams later told me he sent Sedgwick some letters so hot that when the Yale librarian saw them he suggested that they be wrapped in asbestos, but this seems to have been an illusion.

Notifying V. V. McNitt in the autumn of 1930 that he had signed the lease of a London service flat for two and a half years, Adams explained that his heart was still in his native land. "As a matter of fact, I am more patriotic in the popular sense than I used to be. I see the whole sweep of our history more and more clearly."

By March, 1931, the 420-page volume was completed. After breaking his work for a brief Italian holiday, Adams and his wife were back in the United States that month to oversee the passage of the *Epic* through the press. Even before Sedgwick read the manuscript he had abandoned his cavilling.[40] Adams found the country gripped by depression, the Hoover Administration in sunken esteem, and book sales along with other departments of business falling abysmally. Late in

[40] He abandoned it as soon as several associates examined the manuscript. "This last book of yours," he wrote Adams in an undated letter, "seems to the three people who have read it the very top of your performance. As I am shortly to go abroad I shall have no time even to run over it, but here is a book on which both hard-boiled and underdone opinion absolutely agree. It is going to be a conspicuous success. . . ."

August, however, he was cheered by word that the Book-of-the-Month Club had adopted his volume for October distribution. Its success was certain. The first commercial edition, priced at $3, was soon prominent in all bookstore windows from the Kennebec to the Sacramento, and discriminating friends who received early copies gave Adams a fore-taste of the praise just ahead.

"The work is as impressive as it is inspiring," wrote Worthington C. Ford after a careful second perusal. "You have written a book that should be recommended — nay, imposed — by every teacher as necessary reading for his students."

The central idea of the book was that American development had been dominated by a dream, the dream of a better, richer, happier existence for every citizen of whatever rank or condition.[41] That dream or hope had been a vital force from the moment the first colonists came to Jamestown and Plymouth. It had contributed to the struggle for independence, and from the hour when independence was won, every generation had witnessed some kind of uprising of the common folk to protect the dream from forces that seemed likely to overwhelm and dissipate it. "Possibly the greatest of these struggles lies just ahead of us at the present time," wrote Adams, who perceived that the hour was striking for drastic politico-economic changes. Ironically, he was to be one of their most stubborn opponents when they came.

By a happy inspiration, Adams began his book with a prologue in which, after some geographical generalizations, he described "the return of Quetzalcoatl," the conquest of the Aztec kingdom in Mexico by Hernan Cortes, his eleven ships, and his 550 Spanish warriors. Hispanic civilization was transplanted to Mexico and the Caribbean Islands. It flourished, so that 200 Spanish cities and towns soon dotted America, the University of Mexico was founded in 1551, and before the end of that century vigorous schools of art and literature had sprung up. Farther north, however, Indian life was untouched. "Meanwhile, unknown to the savages, the English and the Spaniards whom they had so often repulsed from their shores had met in fierce fight in more ships than the Indians had ever dreamed of, on a narrow strait three thousand miles away. By the night of the twentieth of July, 1588, the Spanish Armada was in full flight to the English Channel. The fate of the unwitting North American savages had been sealed." Thus felicitously did Adams set his stage.

[41] He had fought to have his book called *The American Dream,* but his publisher had rejected the title on the ground that book buyers would never pay $3 for a "dream."

Ensuing pages were marked by the same breadth of view. Comparing Spanish, French, and British cultures, for example, Adams pointed out that the French put their best efforts into religious labors and attempts at converting the savages — efforts that failed because of poverty, paucity of numbers, and dispersal of the work of a few heroic men over thousands of rugged leagues; that the Spaniards created a ruling caste possessing wealth, leisure, and power, cultivating the arts, but exploiting the sorrowful Indians; and that the English pursued a middle road, which gave them a cultural place between the failure of the French and success of the Spaniards, but a material achievement greater than either rival. In his analysis of English colonial life Adams passed with dexterous tread from generalization to generalization. At every point he laid emphasis upon the power of environment. In colonial New England, for example, two tendencies were constantly at war: the demand of the common man to share in the good things of life, and the down drag of the wilderness. Hence it was that the ideal of at least an elementary education for everybody arose at the same time that the education of the higher class declined. Everywhere the first frontier set its stamp on America, making hard work a virtue, leisure an evil, and wealth won by toil an object of exaggerated importance.

"There was probably not a gentleman of leisure on the continent north of Mexico," ran one of Adams's pungent sentences, "unless he were a jailbird or a redskin."

In the eighty pages given to pre-Revolutionary America, Adams again struck out one apt conclusion after another, many of them environmental. Americans became lawless, for example, because while they conceded the right of Parliament to make laws, they got into the habit of deciding for themselves which laws they would obey. An indigenous American culture, with increasing richness of life, sprang out of the increasing differentiation between various groups of colonists, the Yankee farmers, the New York merchants, the Virginia planters. "The New England conscience was not found among the first settlers in the South. It would probably not have survived the climate even if it had been there." Benjamin Franklin typified American culture in the middle range, without the depth of the keener New Englanders or the humane breadth of the best Southern gentleman. Able, versatile, a self-made man in every way, and as completely devoid of intellectual disinterestedness as of religious exaltation, he was "ever ready to make the best of every situation and, if there were two, of both worlds." The country in 1770 was as yet without standardization. It was marked by adventurous and colorful variations of life in far-scattered regions. But the America of the future was not to spring from its many differentiations. "A bit of all of them was to be mingled in the melody of the twentieth-century, but sternly dominant over all we hear the *stroke, stroke, stroke* of the ax on trees, the crash of the falling giant — advancing woodsmen making their clearings; Democracy; 'business.' "

The inevitability of the Revolution Adams fully recognized. In 1776 the die was cast in imperial relations and in American political philosophy. Yet the Revolution was not born of any class movement, or invincible patriot resolution, or unity of sentiment. "In plain truth we see now that the Revolution was only saved from being an abortive rebellion by two factors neither of which could be counted upon in 1776 — one the character of Washington, and the other the marshalling against England of European powers." Once the secession of the colonies succeeded, a national sentiment had to be developed and a glorious past improvised. These needs caused a nation born in war to keep re-stirring the embers of the conflict. "It had been fought against England, with France our ally. From these simple factors were born our simple hostility toward England and our sentimental friendship for France." Our historical writing, oratory, and literature all had to conform to this necessity for creating an anti-British tradition to bind the nation together.

Actually, however, the most important result of the Revolution transcended mere political change. It lay in "the breaking down of all spiritual barriers to the complete development of whatever might prove to be fertile, true, and lasting in the American dream." The nation was now to find itself increasingly divorced from the Old World, and hewing its own path.

The salient merit of Adams's book, as he pursued his interpretation down through the Hamiltonian and Jeffersonian years, the rise of the West, the battle over slavery, and on to world war, was to prove its ultimate weakness. He had a fresh way of looking at the old facts. He possessed a new realism, a clear understanding of environment and the laws of material growth, and a crisp way of showing how old truisms — "mediocrity is one of the prices paid for complete equality," for example — applied to the American record. The *Epic* was arresting and stimulating in 1931. But as his point of view and ideology were rapidly absorbed by the reading public, and as historians arose who offered yet fresher and more penetrating interpretations, the brilliant gleam of his exposition lost some of its lustre. Part of what was new in 1931 seemed familiar in 1941, and conventional by 1951. As in Charles A. Beard's history, some provocative observations had a marvelous saltiness at first, but such salt gradually loses its savor.

The book was to be read with fascination and delight, but not often re-read; to be mastered as full of stimulating insights, but not to be long pondered. Then, too, some passages inevitably lost validity with the mere passage of time and could not be rescued by eloquence.

He pointed out, for example, that the American passion for growth and size, the quantitative measurement of value, had a natural origin. A single family settling in the wilderness faced poverty and danger; a dozen families settling in a group enjoyed comparative safety. Had the first settlements in Williamsburg or Boston never increased, the value of the property would also have stood still. Moreover, newcomers brought new interests and wider social opportunities. Altogether, "all motives, safety, profit, social intercourse, educational opportunities, everything led Americans to watch mounting figures of population growth with an eye to all that made life richer and pleasanter. This was an experience repeated on every successive frontier." Some men reading this might say, "How true! I never thought of that before." But when Adams in depression days went on to write, "We are beginning today, under wholly altered conditions, to realize that size and quality are not necessarily commensurate," his statement hardly fitted the booming 1950's. He wrote, again, that the frontier, compelling men often to leave wife and children, laid down rigid rules of sexual morality. "It is possible that in respect to commercialized vice the American has been no more moral than men of other nations," he went on; but in other respects he has been. And when he added that the general rule of a strict morality had persisted "until very recent years," and promised long endurance, he once more made a statement that has been vitiated by time.

Yet the spectacular success of the book was founded upon solid virtues, and upon insights that sometimes possessed a lasting vibrancy and clarity. It was the most thoughtful treatment of the American record that the mass of readers, young and old, ill educated and highly educated, had ever seen; the kind of treatment that, as it was translated into every important language, best appealed to thoughtful foreigners. As in similar books the story quickened its pace after 1865, and he gave the later record cursory treatment. But he brought it down to the year

1930, gave an incisive brief account of the First World War, and closed with a salute to Henry Ford and quotations from Vachel Lindsay. It had not a dull page, its portraits of the greater American leaders were vigorous and convincing, and the renditions of select episodes like the crimes of the Tweed Ring and the fervors of the McKinley-Bryan contest of 1896 had kindling zest. Many a man would rise with an image he would not forget, such as Adams's remark that the Oregon Trail and Santa Fé Trail prefigured the course of empire, for as with "a huge lobster's claws we were beginning to nip the Pacific Coast at north and south." In 1967 the book was still selling.

The *Epic* might be a temporary triumph, but it was a triumph, and along with the work just preceding it, Charles A. and Mary Beard's *The Rise of American Civilization,* accomplished an important task in the awakening of the American people to the values of their past. As many readers saw, it fitted into the growing national mood of chastening introspection and critical reevaluation of forces and institutions that became evident as the Great Depression of the 1930's came on. It helped men think about the direction in which the nation was moving and think independently and critically. It was provocative in the best sense of the word. Was America a failure in its effort to play a great and noble part in human evolution? Was the national character growing on the best possible lines? Where could citizens correct wrong tendencies? These were queries that men put to themselves with more feeling after they had read the book by Adams.[42]

The success of the *Epic* raised Adams to a prominence and influence which he could use in various public ways, and with undiminished vigor he pressed on to make his convictions felt.

The Scribner Contract and New Tasks

The final years of Adams's residence in England were marked by two notable new studies upon American themes, *America's Tragedy* (1934) and *The Living Jefferson* (1936); by a growing preoccupation with political issues in the United States and the world which led him into increased magazine work; and by a new publishing arrangement with Scribner's that placed editorial burdens upon him and helped draw him

[42] By the end of 1931, according to a letter that Adams wrote me on December 11, it was reaching a total distribution of 75,000 copies, of which 45,000 were sent out by the Book-of-the-Month Club. Its total earnings, however, were then only about $20,000, not a colossal sum. The Book-of-the-Month Club had paid $10,000 for the volume, of which Adams received half.

back to the United States. He was sometimes heavily overworked. Becoming more a public instructor and less a dedicated scholar, he found himself on a course quite different from the one he had marked out in the New England trilogy and *Adams Family.* It by no means suited me, for I kept urging him to return to more scholarly studies, and it displeased most university men. It was nevertheless a useful course, which satisfied his now large public.

Like Turner and others, Adams believed two influences had been of cardinal importance in the conquest of the continent: the frontier and sectionalism. In the *Epic* he had said a great deal about the frontier; his *America's Tragedy,* a treatment of forces and events culminating in the Civil War, was primarily an examination of sectionalism. Except incidentally, he did not wish to write about the Negro, or slavery, or economic conflicts. He did not intend to produce another book of battles and campaigns. What interested him was the development of completely divergent attitudes and allegiances in North and South, giving birth in the end to two irreconcilable types of civilization and thought. Though he began with a physiographic analysis, he insisted that neither the North nor the South had geographical unity, and that their schism was traceable to historical, not natural, conditions. He was more anxious to demonstrate the complexities of sectionalism than to support the various simplifications of the problem in which extremists on both sides indulged. He took pains to point out, for example, that "except by inconceivable economic sacrifice, the slaves could never have been emancipated as a whole," and dwelt upon the tangled perplexities of the race problem.

His book thus showed a larger sympathy with the South than most Northern productions. Not only did he argue that at its best Southern life was the "most charming" that America had known, and that the Southern "sense of values" was finer than the Northern. He asserted that the Southern idea of the Constitution was as tenable as the Northern idea. The essential difference was that the Southerners took a more rigid view of the fundamental law than Northerners did; and the Civil War proved that the Constitution must be altered, even on very sensitive issues, when the opinion of a sufficiently large part of the people decided a certain form of property to be immoral or outworn.

The Southerner could argue that under the Constitution he had a right to take his perfectly legal form of human property into new territory just as the Northerner could take his forms. But this had become impossible. "Two types of civilization, two social forms, could not both occupy the same territory at the same time. Not only would free labor not go where it had to compete with the slave, but opinion as to the right to hold a certain *kind* of property had become bitter. . . . History is dynamic not static, and there is always a point beyond which no written document can save what has become obsolete or unjust in public opinion."

The book again revealed Adams's wide reading, not only in the major historical works, but in a variety of travel books, diaries, reminiscences, biographies, collections of letters, and special monographs. He had taken time to scan files of Southern newspapers. He used George Ticknor's *Journals,* and Lowell, Longfellow, Thoreau, and Whittier. The materials thus gained he knit into a rapid narrative that never flagged in interest, and that not only showed a mastery of proportion, for he covered two and a half centuries with only a few such conspicuous gaps as his failure to mention the quarrel between Douglas and Buchanan, but displayed his frequent interpretive insight. The book could be criticized in detail. In the treatment of the feverish 1850's especially it placed a reliance upon some outdated secondary treatments that betrayed him into errors. Charles W. Ramsdell of Texas, for example, protested against his overstatement of the Southern desire for a revival of the African slave trade, a movement that was defeated in the South itself.

Nevertheless, Ramsdell's appraisal of the volume in the *American Historical Review* was favorable. "The book deserves a wide circle of readers," he wrote, "for its merits far outweight its defects." He particularly commended its "fecundity of suggestion and interpretation." Avery Craven was equally complimentary. "His interpretations are fresh and vital," he wrote in the New York *Herald-Tribune Books.* From opposite sectional poles came much the same commendation. The book, wrote William C. Binkley in the *Journal of Southern History,* is "intensely interesting because of the author's remarkable ability to compress into a single paragraph or sentence a deft word picture of a broad development, or an apt and arresting characterization of a whole people." And in the *New England Quarterly* Elizabeth Foster declared the work admirable "for its combination of dignity with vigor, movement, and picturesqueness, and for its clarity."

His *Living Jefferson* encountered a much more mixed reception, for it showed Adams in the double role of historian and political pamphleteer. Published during the struggle of Franklin D. Roosevelt for his first reelection, it was far more Hamiltonian than Jeffersonian in temper. Its two final chapters, a caustic attack upon Rooseveltian ideas and policies, provoked regret in many quarters that he had sunk the historian in the political partisan.

The most balanced judgment was that of Henry Steele Commager in *Books*. "Mr. Adams's evaluation of Jefferson is shrewd and understanding," he wrote; "his appreciation is reasoned and just. He has traced, in a few swift paragraphs, the background of Jeffersonian idealism, and has understood the circumstances which developed it." But, added the reviewer, his last section simply echoed many of the objections that honest conservatism had made to Jefferson in his own lifetime, and to Jeffersonian ideals after his death. "It is remarkable because it shows how passion can becloud understanding and how fear can paralyze tolerance. It is remarkable because it shows how a liberal can be led to betray his own cause." The fiery Texas Congressman and proponent of New Deal legislation, Maury Maverick, declared in the *New Republic* that it showed an able historian at his worst, with a partisanship founded upon an outworn part of Jefferson's teachings. "There is no interpretation of the *living* Jefferson at all."

Many another able man this year, from Alfred E. Smith to Walter Lippmann, supported Landon against Roosevelt, and advocated a repudiation of the New Deal. Political feeling has seldom run higher. It is not strange that Adams, who had voted for Roosevelt in 1932 but had a special feeling for financial stability, should have shared the apprehensions that led the New York *Times* to take Landon's side, but he would have done well to confine his political expositions to his magazine papers.

For his contributions to periodicals were now a more important part of his output than ever. He kept up a large correspondence with Wilbur Cross and Helen McAfee of the *Yale Review*, and the editors of *Harper's*, *Barron's Weekly*, and other magazines. Many of his articles generated controversy and thus made more demands on his time. Banking legislation (he had published an article on "The Responsibility of Bankers" in the *Forum* of August, 1931, and continued writing on the subject); public utilities legislation (he shared Lippmann's view that Roosevelt had an excessive prejudice against utilities); the war debts, and a hundred other American topics invited his exploration. In *Scribner's* for March, 1936, he published "The Roosevelt Record—Has the President Thought It Through?," which the New York *Sun* praised, contrasting "the wild and whirling words used by Henry L. Mencken in his attack upon the Roosevelt Administration" in the

American Mercury that same month with the measured phrases in which Adams concluded that Roosevelt had not really thought his intentions through, and that although we were "on our way" nobody knew whither. In the April *Scribner's* Adams wrote on "The American Future," declaring that elaborate planning of the economic life of a people by the state, oncc initiated, was bound to extend dangerously.

Although he commented but little on European affairs, so long as he continued to live in England he took the closest interest in them. He assured Wilbur Cross at the end of 1933 that the German-Austrian situation was the critical point in Europe, that he had discussed it with Lewis Einstein, recent Minister to Czechoslovakia, Harold Callender of the New York *Times,* and others, and that the question was "whether the Hitler Government will try not only to swallow Austria but also to build up a new Mittle-Europe." Francis Hirst, then writing a little book on liberty in Europe, asked him, "who would ever have dreamed thirty years ago that in this I would have to have a chapter on the re-introduction of torture?" And he told Miss McAfee that he hesitated to plan an Italian excursion because the Continent was like Vesuvius. "You cannot predict Germany from day to day. France is seething with unrest. Austria rumbles and rumbles." His uneasiness was to grow. In short, while he was perplexed by developments in America, he was both perplexed and depressed by Europe.

"What worries me most about my own country," he wrote in May, 1935, "is the character of our people, and the Secretary of State told me that was also what worried him most. The Bonus grab, for example, is indecent to an extent that no one at home seems to realize." He added, however, that "I am too good an American to change nations."

Adams had meanwhile, with considerable agony of spirit, shifted his American publishers. He felt some obligations to Little, Brown, and some to Albert Boni, but few to the Atlantic Monthly Press. The depression had plunged half the publishing field into chaos, and he looked about for firm support. His *America's Tragedy* he planned to give to Charles Scribner's Sons, and although its sale was disappointing, he felt an increasing attachment to that house. It was impossible not to admire its position in the publishing field. He formed a liking for Charles Scribner, who had succeeded Arthur H. Scribner as head in 1932; for Maxwell E. Perkins, a modest vice-president with a reputation for helping develop such writers as Scott Fitzgerald, Thomas Wolfe, and Ring Lardner; for Whitney Darrow heading the trade department; and for Carroll B. Merritt, who oversaw the sale of subscription sets of authors. The house, founded in 1846, had published many of the important Victorian and Edwardian authors like George Meredith, R. L. Stevenson, J. M. Barrie, and John Galsworthy, had issued eminent Americans from Thomas Nelson Page and Edith Wharton onward, and had given due attention to historians, including Douglas Freeman. It had begun publishing the *Dictionary of American Biography,* under the auspices of the American Council of Learned Societies, in 1928. Adams came to know well its old-fashioned, unpretentious offices above its bookstore on Fifth Avenue. He had attended firm dinners where Charles Scribner was received with affection, and was familiar with such distinguished employees as William Crary Brownell, the critic, and John Hall Wheelock, the poet.

His negotiations for a connection on a basis that would give him fuller security in writing were conducted partly through his friend Will D. Howe. They involved the trade, subscription, and textbook departments. Howe was a shrewd, softspoken, transparently honest Hoosier with a Harvard doctorate who had left a chair in English literature in Indiana University to help establish the firm of Harcourt, Brace & Howe, and had then joined Scribner's in 1921. Adams trusted him as completely as other Scribner executives. The arrangement made assured Adams a basic income of $5,000 a year, in return for which he would give Scribner's all his books beginning with *America's Tragedy* and a factual survey of American history which he duly published in two volumes in 1932-33 under the general title *The March of Democracy.* As the plan developed, he was expected to keep this subscription history up to date by the addition of a new record each year.[43] The initial five-year contract gave Adams a greater sense of security, and he often said that he worked better when freed from financial strain and uneasiness. Its disadvantage was that it made him an indentured servant in the regular production of copy and the planning of books and sets that had a hack-work character. From this point onward his writing lost much of its spontaneity and originality.

Much as he was pleased by his contract, Adams approached the factual subscription-edition history with repugnance. He wrote me that he was slaving over it with no enthusiasm. "I am too tired to feel that emotion, and also feel that this is no job for me. It is neither original research nor interpretation. But it means so much to me and to my

[43] The first volume in the subscription edition was called *The Rise of the Union;* the second, *A Half Century of Expansion;* the third, *Civil War and Aftermath;* the fourth, *America — a World Power;* the fifth, as the set grew, *New Deal and Global War;* and the sixth, *Age of Responsibility.*

wife if I pass out, and also the chance for the rest of my life to write what does warm me, that I must do it." This was a lame excuse, for he was by no means under such financial pressure as he imagined. But, drudging away, he had produced more than 200,000 words when 1932 began, a big block of typescript in five months. "It will add nothing to my reputation and I only pray will not hurt it. As a five-volume illustrated history for Main Street on subscription I think it will do good. As a two-volume trade book I fear it. I am considering cutting my subscription to clipping bureaus for a year!"

It must be remembered that this book was written as the country was slipping into the trough of the Great Depression, as business after business was foundering (I received it just after the *World* went under), as unemployment grew, and as half the country writhed under rising personal anxieties. It was written shortly after he had rejected the suggestion that he undertake a life of Dwight Morrow, which did not appeal to him, and which he left to Harold Nicolson. Like others, Adams had to give some assistance to various relatives. He told me he could not keep up the grueling pace of his work the previous five years, and that he and his wife ought to have $15,000 a year for rising taxes, old age, and possible illness, with the costs of an American domicile.

"I had expected to take things easier," he wrote me, "but as I see no end to the extravagance of Congress and the 'soak-the-rich' policy of the 95 percent of the population which pays no taxes, at least directly, this aspect of the future worries me."

His forebodings about the subscription set were justified. The central verdict upon his book was that offered by Henry Steele Commager in *Herald-Tribune Books:* "It is well proportioned, reasonably accurate, not uncritical, and particularly full on some of the social and cultural phases of our history. But when we examine it in more detail, and by the standards which Mr. Adams himself has set, its inadequacies are more striking than its virtues." This was perfectly just, but unfortunately Adams felt that he ought not to be judged by the standards he had previously set. His intention discarded them. This was not the interpretive, scholarly type of book he had written for informed and discriminating readers, but a general narrative meant to instruct a mass audience. He was almost pathetically grateful to me when I gave the New York *Times* a review emphasizing this distinction. Stating that the book "lacks the inspiration which so often touched Mr. Adams's earlier volumes," I treated it as a venture in popular education. The *New Republic* did the same, pointing to its "real merit as a readable and useful popular summary"; and so did the Catholic *Commonweal,* balancing against its defects the fact that Adams "has the power of assimilation and selection," writes "from a well-stored background," and "has a philosophy of history which offers a coherent thread." But he could not escape the expectations he had earlier raised, or the regret that they were not met.

The fact is that to the end Adams was sensitive to reviews of his books. He had greatly resented Carl Becker's captious criticism of the *Epic* on the ground that its story did not fit Becker's peculiar definition of the epical. He was much disturbed when Henry Hazlitt as literary editor of the *Nation* got H. L. Mencken to review *The Adams Family* in order to see what the Baltimore termagant would say about these exalted exponents of the New England mind and spirit. "In other words," Adams wrote me, "he was not trying to get a critical review, but to stage a dogfight between a prejudiced mind and a topic which he knew would be anathema to it." He was disturbed again when Hazlitt turned the *Epic* over to Carl Van Doren, who as belletristic critic and former professor of English literature seemed unversed in the full stream of American history. Van Doren, who had praised *The Adams Family* highly when his *Literary Guild* adopted it, asserted that Adams had no literary gift. While others were commending what the *Saturday Review* called the "marked vigor and directness of style" in the *Epic*, Van Doren declared that such men as Adams "ought either to learn how to write better, or else to submit themselves to the warning, pruning hand of somebody who can take the trouble." Was this quite fair?

Adams was now particularly hurt by Arthur M. Schlesinger's comment on *The March of Democracy* in the *Atlantic*. "One cannot help being disturbed," wrote the elder Schlesinger, "by the thought that the commercialization of artistic and scientific effort which Mr. Adams has condemned in his criticism of American civilization is only too patent in the product of his own pen." This seemed to Adams to come with poor grace from a man who had paid Adams a cent a word for *Provincial Society*, who wrote half of a two-volume textbook with commercial ends plainly in view, and who looked down on toiling free-lance writers from the altitude of a well-paid university chair. Yet Adams had the taste never to reply to a review but once, and regretted doing that.[44]

[44] He wrote a curt letter to Becker, on reading Becker's notice in the *American Historial Review*, pointing out to him that when he complained that the book was not epical because it did not show "the tragic conflict between men's aspirations and the implacable decrees of fate," and did not cause his soul to be "purged by fear and pity," he was plainly thinking of tragedy. Aristotle had said that the qualities of an epic were "a dignified theme, organic unity, and an orderly progression of the action." "It made me rather angry," Adams wrote me, "to be hammered in that way because of Becker's own slip."

When 1934 opened Adams was installing himself in new quarters at 61-A Holland Park in the Kensington Gardens end of London. He had undergone a distressing domestic upheaval. For years he had particularly liked his Palace Court establishment for its manageress, who was an excellent cook, its maid, who was devoted to Kay and himself, and others of the staff. Suddenly, a new landlord took charge. He "proved a rotter, with a string of women." Just after Adams had signed a fresh lease he fired the entire staff and brought in disreputable people. "I was so mad," Adams said, "I could not write my book." He canceled the lease, and after much searching found the new maisonette on which he took an eighteen-months lease, bringing the old staff with him. "It is steam-heated throughout and much better than my other place," he wrote me jubilantly. "I have a large bedroom, large library, large drawing-room, good typing room opening off the library, a big dining-room, and below a huge billiard room which we use for storage, an equally large housekeeper's room, good maid's room, kitchens, wine cellar, heaps of closet space, and a garden fifty by seventy-five."

Here he set to work with new energy. "I have written 60,000 words on my book and two hundred letters in the five weeks I have been here." He planned to finish the second volume of the *March of Democracy* in time to sail on the *Berengaria* in mid-March for New York, and this he did, he and Kay making a very short stay. They were back for "a heavenly six weeks" that summer in a rented house in the Chiltern hills, and were in London by September.

It had become plain to him that they would soon have to get back to the United States for good. The requirements of the new contract with Scribner's, his intense interest in American politics, Kay's desire to be near her family, and the turmoil in Europe counseled a return. But where should they settle?

They might go to Wesleyan, where President McConaughy would reopen the door, but that place had seemed to him stuffy. Visiting it and talking with the faculty, he had found them keen, well-read, and pleasant, but of limited horizons.[45] He might take a suburban place

[45] "I met some of the men there," he wrote me. "They were excellent fellows, and I liked them, but I had an odd feeling as though I was shut up in an eighteenth-century 'powdering room.' The free air of the world at large did not seem to blow through at all. It was not that they were not up to date in their subjects, or not in touch with affairs through print. It was a curious sort of aloofness that was hard to analyze. Their knowledge was at once real and unreal. . . . I am more and more convinced that contact with the world of everyday men and of many lands is of enormous benefit to the historian,

near New York. Going to London in the autumn of 1934 to deliver the Sir George Watson Lectures, I urged him to do this, renewing my pleas that he select some broad research theme — at one time he actually thought of an interpretive exploration of the history of the Middle West — and urging him to consider giving a seminar in Columbia. He wrote me an explicit refusal. "I question whether I have the accurate, extensive, and detailed knowledge requisite. I am unfitted in every way for ordinary teaching or lecturing." Washington since the New Deal occupation had lost half its attractions for him, while its summer climate repelled him. He had no feeling for Yale, "which since I took my M.A. there in 1900 has completely ignored my existence except to ask me annually to contribute to the alumni fund." A quiet and spacious environment was as important to him as ever, and this meant the country.

Just before sailing back to England in 1934 he decided he must make a quick decision. "I had only a week before sailing," he wrote later, "and started out. I had thought that I would like to live in Connecticut, which had always seemed to me a very homelike State. I got my publishers to find me a real estate agent up near Mt. Kisco and we zigzagged down toward the coast. I told him I wanted to be near the center of a village."

Then this sober, quiet, elderly literary man, who had put so much careful planning into his life, suddenly showed how impetuous he could be. Various frustrations led him to employ a second agent. They drove along the coast east of Stamford. "I had no idea where we were going until we stopped in front of a house." He fell in love with it as suddenly and completely as he had fallen in love with Kay years before. It was the Sheffield house in Southport, a large two-story frame structure with a dormer-windowed attic, once the home of the railroad executive whose gifts had made possible the establishment of the Scientific School at Yale, Joseph E. Sheffield. He looked at its fine shade trees, its adequate flower beds and grass, its pleasant lines and the comfortable neighboring houses. He walked through its rooms, noting its wide hall and an especially spacious and sunny living room, with windows west and south commanding bright glimpses of the Sound. The porches were ample. By this cursory view he made sure it would do and bought it, leaving the tenant in possession. He did not count the bathrooms. He

who deals with man." After this letter (February 14, 1931) Wesleyan changed rapidly under able presidents and faculty members, and with greatly enlarged revenues.

failed to inspect the basement, and was glad later that he had not, for a look at that dirty cellar might have swayed him against the choice. Like many another impetuous man, he did not even consult his wife, taking her acceptance for granted.

The spring of 1935 found Adams more inclined than ever to contrast life in New Deal America unfavorably with the more placid and entertaining existence he was leading in his London flat as England celebrated the silver jubilee of King George V. He wrote Governor Cross on May 26 of a disappointing dinner party he had attended in Washington. John W. Davis, the Democratic nominee for President in 1924, was there, and Charles Warren, the eminent historian of the Supreme Court, the author J. M. Beck, and others of note. "In the smoking room after dinner all of us were placed in a circle like a farmers' Grange meeting in Bohunk, a pitcher of ice water on the table, and talked about 45 minutes before rejoining the ladies. The entire conversation was made up of personal anecdotes of very mild interest, and funny stories. That is no exaggeration. Not an idea was started, or anything important touched on. That is what I mean by going back to prep school." But in England he heard of a man in Whitechapel who asked his neighbor if he were going to decorate his house for the Jubilee. When told he was, the inquirer said, "Fine, I wish I could, but you see I am a Communist." Adams added that many stories of the festal English spirit were veraciously related to him by eyewitnesses. "At Sunderland House, where a ball was being given, the crowd outside began dancing to the music from the open windows. They then called 'Louder,' and the guests came out on the balcony to see. Orders were given the band to play louder, and eventually the guests came down to the street, and danced with the crowd on the pavement. This was not what we would call a drunken party, but this is really becoming, for a while at least, 'Merrie England' again. There has been any amount of community singing with all classes in the crowds. In Piccadilly, a crowd last Saturday night called for the band to come out and play. The mounted police — all the police have been marvelous in their tact and good nature with unprecedented crowds of people — edged in with their horses, but were rather nonplused when, instead of moving on, they stopped to pat the horses! Never have I seen such crowds or such happy and good-natured ones. One of my maids sat on the curbstone all night from ten in the evening until twelve next day to see the Jubilee procession. She said the street was filled by four A.M., all laughing and joking and dancing to while away the time. England has not been so confident and happy in twenty years or more. The contrast is not pleasant when I look at my own country. Except for a European war, England is I believe the safest, sanest, most contented land in the world today, unless we add Sweden and Norway, and I go home in the spring from a sense of duty as an American only."

Alas, the European war lay just around the corner! Adams added in his letter to Governor Cross, "the dark shadow comes from the Continent, and especially that old home of the barbarians, Germany." Within a few years he would look back on his picture of the peaceful, "merrie" England of May, 1935, with mingled wonder and regret. The days of comfort and security in Britain, as in much of the remainder of Europe, were utterly and hopelessly gone.

He was not yet free in England. His lease of the Holland Park maisonette endured until the middle of 1935, and he and Kay enjoyed their summer stay in 1934 in a fine rectory in the Chilterns, not far from Oxford, so much that they wished to go back next season.[46] It was therefore not until late in 1935 that he made his final trip across the Atlantic, and not until winter that they settled into the Southport house, which required many alterations. The moving was itself an onerous undertaking. He had two large steel vans full of furniture, silver, family portraits, and oddments to ship over, and fifty-five large packing cases of books. His sister Amy, who after his marriage had continued to spend a great part of her time with them — too much for her own good or Kay's comfort — had put many of her possessions into his London quarters, and these had to be sent over, too.

The Return to America: the War

The shift was such a sore wrench that it was fortunate they were too busy for a time to feel it. Meanwhile they found that Southport had

[46] What he rented was not properly a rectory but a chaplaincy, and the usual tenant was chaplain of the Alms House, a very English institution. This particular Alms House at Goring Heath, Oxfordshire, had been founded in 1740 with an endowment of several hundred acres of land. It had a chapel and several acres of gardens. The first year the Adamses were ignored; the second year they were accepted. Lady Rose, the local magnate, called on them repeatedly, and once told them quite casually how the previous night she had walked back from Buxton seventeen miles away in the darkness. Her husband had been killed in World War I, and her son was later slain in World War II. This second year Adams was put on a committee to judge the lively school games. Standing beside an army major and a clergyman, he was astounded to hear the cleric remark: "Mr. Adams, you know the old people in the Alms House feel you are not quite doing your duty." He learned that as occupant of the chaplain's house, he was expected to go in and chat with the dozen old couples there; and he at once entered upon a series of local friendships that he found intensely interesting.

an atmosphere all its own. It was not at all a commuter's town, only a few traveling daily the fifty-odd miles into the city. They were nearly as far from urban crowds and clamor as if they lived in Vermont. The village had a golf club and yacht club, to neither of which Adams paid the least attention. Instead, he and Kay began exploring the country roads about, diving into lanes that sometimes ended in a wooded ravine without room to turn around. Social life was not as entertaining as in London, Adams used to admit, but then as old Jonathan Trumbull had told his artist son, "Connecticut is not Athens." They made some good friends. The town library, which Adams at once began to build up, was unusually good, and as trustee he eventually made it a model collection. The Yale Library was but a little over an hour's drive east on the old Boston post-road. In another hour by train westward he could be at the Century Club on Forty-third Street. Adams found that his political conservatism precisely harmonized with the sentiments of most Republican residents about him, though not with those of his old friend Wilbur Cross. The townsmen agreed with him, that while Franklin D. Roosevelt was doubtless an honest man, he had not kept the promises of his platform.

The campaign of 1936 soon gave him some outlet for his energies. "You say Roosevelt has kept the country moving," he wrote me that summer. "I think he has given it diarrhea." He was then corresponding with Landon and Raskob, and trying to help their battle.

As he settled down he at first greatly missed England. How often he spoke of the thousand enchantments of London! — of the Chelsea river breezes, the bustle of Piccadilly, the literary memories stamped upon Bloomsbury and the precincts of the British Museum, the great houses on Berkeley and Grosvenor Squares, the Inns of Court under the elms that Lord Bacon was said to have planted, and the shops of Regent Street and Holborn. He had learned the city from squalid Bethnal Green to fashionable Belgravia, but he knew it best where he had lived and worked, about the university rooms in Gower Street, the London Library near Pall Mall, and in old Kensington. The shades of great men had walked some of the streets closest to him. Near his Palace Court apartments in Kensington William Makepeace Thackeray had died at Two Palace Green, and in his Holland Park home he had often recalled how Lord Macaulay breathed his last in his chair in Holly Court hard by. Now all this was ended; he would never go back; and in his newer, brighter land he was sometimes homesick for the familiar scenes and the well-loved people. His heart was wrung as England approached the abyss of war.

Although he kept away from New York as much as possible, for he disliked its congestion, he found a stimulating new interest in the affairs of the American Academy of Arts and Letters. The long presidency of William Dean Howells had been followed by the still longer presidency of Nicholas Murray Butler. When Butler left office in 1941 Walter Damrosch took his place, and when Wilbur Cross dropped the joint offices of Treasurer and Chancellor that same year Adams was chosen in his stead. He had already done more than anyone else for the finances of the Academy, giving unstinted effort and advice from the moment of his return to the United States. It received fairly large endowments from Archer M. Huntington and his sculptress wife Anna Hyatt Huntington which had to be protected and if possible augmented. He enjoyed reviving the studies of his Wall Street days in finance, and did it thoroughly. Before long he had more than $3,000,000 worth of property to look after, and the tasks of investment interested him deeply.

Only that part of the Academy resources called the Open Fund, he found, could be used to buy common stocks, but as the country recovered from the depression they obviously offered tempting opportunities. On November 9, 1946, he reported that from a recent rise in values he had given the Academy "a cash profit in all of about $160,000." It had made about $19,500 on International Business Machines, and $12,000 on Sears Roebuck. Much of these gains had been added to the permanent funds of the Academy in government bonds. The general income of the organization that year was close to $85,000, out of which it appropriated $2,500 for gifts to needy artists abroad, and large sums for grants, prizes, publications, and exhibits at home. Meanwhile he found the personal relationships of the Academy delightful. Once a month the directors met at the house of Dr. and Mrs. Damrosch (she was a daughter of James G. Blaine) where he talked with Stephen Vincent Benét, Charles Dana Gibson, the architect William Adams Delano, William Lyon Phelps, and others.

He disliked the rather pretentious building erected for the Academy on West 155th Street overlooking Audubon Park and the Hudson, with its large concert hall and expensive organ. Believing that a pernicious tendency in American life was the increasing emphasis on ostentation and spending, he condemned all its forms. "I was almost nauseated," he wrote Dr. Damrosch in the spring of 1940, "when I was taken through the Graduate School at Yale and found the way the Harkness money was used. The common-room there is like a lounge in a golf club for multimillionaires, and the effect on the boys is that they cannot talk intelligently unless they sit in upholstered chairs costing perhaps two or three hundred dollars apiece." At Oxford and Cambridge, he recalled, the fellows sat in straight or Windsor chairs. It seemed to him more important to get the right leaders into the Academy than to house them grandly. He was anxious to see Willa Cather and Henry Osborn Taylor elected; he thought that an actor of the stature of Edwin Booth should be chosen. For the reference library, full of manuscript treasures, he felt a special concern. When the historian C. M. Andrews died he was glad to deliver a memorial address, "a sort of Hail and Farewell to one of our members."

As the 1930's wore on his distaste for American political tendencies increased in almost every respect but one: he warmly approved of the gradual extrication of the country from its isolationist bog. He found but one able man in Roosevelt's Cabinet, his friend Cordell Hull. He deplored the Administration's insistence upon continued spending. "There can be but one end to that," he wrote Worthington C. Ford, on New Year's Day in 1939. "We are certainly in for ten years of deficits and a debt of how much over forty billions nobody knows, or in Washington seems to care." He was then paying about $6,000 a year in taxes, and was acting as historical consultant for a radio program, the "Calvalcade of America" put on the air by the DuPont Corporation, to help meet them. It was a useful educational feature, which received wide praise and took a number of prizes, and for a very limited expenditure of time (he thought about three week's work in scruntinizing twenty-six scripts) he received $4,500. He deplored such jobs, but quite improperly thought them a necessity.

His verdict as Roosevelt ended his second term was emphatic. "I think F. D. R. had one of the greatest chances any President ever had, and he took hold well at the start, but he certainly muffed the ball later, and has taken many steps it will be hard for anyone to retrace. I agree with his social outlook and humanitarianism, but to distribute a national income fairly there must be a large and sound income to distribute, and ultimate inflation can bring no good to anybody. That leads to cruelty to all and not amelioration for some."

He was pleased, however, when Roosevelt and Hull developed the principle of hemispheric solidarity both in Latin America and Canada; he approved of Roosevelt's Chicago speech in 1937 asking for a quarantine against aggressor nations; and he was heartened by the steady awakening of Americans to the Nazi menace. Francis Hirst and Worthington C. Ford sent him observations upon the progress of European events. "I feel that the old empire is growing weak and shaky at heart," Harold Callender sadly wrote him after Munich. "Britain slowly prepared, without exerting herself much, for a war in 1941 while the Germans prepared for one in 1939; hence Chamberlain's diplomacy of last month." He added that nobody could maintain an empire by these methods. "London was almost defenceless against aircraft, the R.A.F. was not much more than half as strong as the German air force, the army had only a few modern guns, when it looked like war ten days ago. Yet four years ago Churchill had warned of German armament."

Hoping to the last for peace, Adams was almost prostrated when the blow finally fell. At the moment Kay was in Southampton with her family. "Your notes about swims and picnics," he wrote on August 25, 1939, "seem to come from a different world; for we wait here moment by moment, for the possible knell of civilization and all our personal hopes and lives." He had made up his mind at last that war was inevitable. In New York nobody talked of anything but the European situation. London and Paris were blacked out — and then he broke off.

"I have just been down to listen in to Paris. They expect war except for the miracle of Hitler's giving in. The population of the eastern front of France is being evacuated as fast as possible and taken to the west. People are leaving Paris by thousands as fast as they can get away. The French general has been placed in command of all French and British forces. The British navy is holding the Baltic and North seas. Paris believes the zero hour will be tonight at twelve. I shall never forget this August. The August of 1914 was bad enough, but I was twenty-five years younger then, and we did not then know how terrible modern war could be."

These years brought the uninterrupted publication of more books — but to be honest, not important books. After the two volumes of *The March of Democracy,* he turned at the suggestion of his Scribner associates to a survey of British imperial history. The theme seemed at first to offer happy possibilities, but proved instead an elephantine burden. It was so huge in scope that it not merely involved endless drudgery, but demanded a compression fatal to Adams's best gift, incisive and original interpretation. "This morning," he confided to Kay ("Dearest Monk") on a January Sunday in 1938 when he suffered from her temporary absence, "I finished the second Elizabeth chapter, and am now down to the Stuarts in 1603, and have seven more chapters to write, about 50,000 words after doing 85,000. . . . I had hoped not to work today, but did not finish yesterday although I wrote 3,000 words, the most yet in one day on this book. I am all right, but feel the pressure and steady grind of turning my mind into cash." This suggests his treadmill gait. And Charles Scribner, always considerate, wrote him sympathetically:

"I had no idea what a laborious task the *Story of the Empire* would prove to be, and the suggestion that you should turn your hand to it was undoubtedly a mistake when you could so easily have taken some subject in American history, but I still hope that it may turn out better in the end than either of us realize at present. I do not know if you still have it in mind but it seems to me that a history of American political parties might make a very good book — better perhaps than a life of Lincoln."

His volume *Building the British Empire* (1938), thus written by a tired man toiling in a largely unfamiliar field under pressure, of course met an adverse verdict. Mary Colum stated its character fairly in the *Forum*. "The book is not really a history — there is no research; there are no memorable characterizations; there is no sense of the tragic strain and tension that historical processes are bound to have; but very pleasantly the story is told of British achievement, not only political but economic and intellectual." The London *Spectator* expressed gratitude for so lucid and sympathetic a survey. Various writers noted that the author was especially competent in dealing with the seventeenth and eighteenth centuries, where his colonial studies had given him some knowledge of the sources. His academic critics, however, were severe. Conyers Read published a sour review in the *Nation,* pronouncing the book not only superficial but dull, and J. R. Strayer delivered a still harsher verdict in the *Saturday Review of Literature,* declaring that it was little more than a textbook, and not a particularly good textbook at that. It was slightly superior in style to most textbooks, and had enough general appeal to contribute to popular knowledge of history. On the whole, however, it added nothing either to the literature of the subject or the author's reputation.

The second volume, *Empire on the Seven Seas,* which two years later carried the story from 1784 to the outbreak of the Second World War, was more spirited and appealing. Again Adams dealt with the empire as the product of British racial character and traits, and emphasized the value to the world of the expansion of English ideas and institutions. The British preference for discussion over disputation, and for compromise over partisan intolerance, especially appealed to him. No less a historian than Geoffrey Bruun praised the "charm and buoyance" and the narrative and the alertness to ideas. "The style is always readable and persuasive," remarked Reginald G. Trotter in the *American Historical Review,* adding that the author succeeded in imparting a sense of continuity to his long and variegated story. Here also, however, it was plain that excessive condensation had robbed Adams of much of his opportunity for presenting novel insights and striking new interpretations.

Being so largely dependent upon his pen for a living, Adams was worried by the disparity between the hard work he had given his factual books on American and British history, and the low royalties he received. In August, 1939, he and Charles Scribner exchanged letters on the subject. Although Will D. Howe had told him that he would probably get $5,000 a year for a long period from the *March of Democracy,* Adams complained that even after his toil gave the work an additional chapter each year, he would be lucky to receive $1,200 or so. His royalties for the first year's sales of *Building the British Empire* had been only about $3,750. Since he had to deduct from this $120 paid the indexer, $300 paid a reader who looked for possible errors, and $300 for materials, his total return was only $3,000. He still had a large public following. The stream of newspaper clippings, of letters from strangers, and of requests for articles, speeches, and lectures was undiminished, but his revenues were ominously slackening. He could not complain that the Scribner contract lacked generosity, but he probably felt that the firm might have offered him better guidance.

Recognizing that students of letters have a legitimate interest in learning about the returns from authorship, Adams later set down in his family chronicle a statement on the earnings of his principal books. It made no pretensions to exactness, and was too early for completeness. Down to about 1945, his first important title, *The Founding of New England,* which won a Pulitzer Prize, had brought him only about $10,000. From *The Adams Family* he believed he had derived about $30,000. His greatest success, *The Epic of America,* had paid him something over $80,000, or so he calculated, for precise figures were hard to find, that book having gone through so many editions, domestic and foreign. Translations had been made into at least a dozen languages, the total sales had run well above half a million, and after the German occupation of Norway ended he had been astonished by a check for $2,000 from the Norwegian publisher. His two volumes of

The March of Democracy, in various forms, including a textbook edition, had paid him something over $80,000. "One or two of my other books, which I think have been quite good," he writes, "brought in only $6,000 or $7,000." These, it must be remembered, were the revenues of a lifetime of expert labor. He had not been overpaid.

Meanwhile, he continued to contribute steadily to the magazines, and to express his views on a wide variety of current questions. In his political opinions Adams was about as consistent as an alert responsiveness to the fast-changing times permitted. He held principles that during the first twenty years of the century made him applaud what he called in *The Epic of America* "the battles cries of Roosevelt and Wilson in the struggle to realize the American dream." He supported progressive social legislation at home and internationalism abroad. He was convinced that the abandonment of laissez faire was an inevitable and wholesome process. At the same time, he believed in what Franklin D. Roosevelt on first entering the White House praised as "the normal balance of executive and legislative authority, of public procedure"; he believed in financial stability, avoidance of excessive public debt, caution in the creation of a national bureaucracy, and constructive measures for the betterment of the economy rather than radical measures for the forcible redistribution of wealth. That is, he carried the principles of T. R.'s New Nationalism and Wilson's New Freedom into the years of Franklin D. Roosevelt's New Deal.

Some dominant ideas recurred again and again in Adams's magazine essays. He seemed to most of his readers, especially after the advent of Roosevelt's New Deal, a conservative. But he would have protested that he was actually a liberal, as John Stuart Mill or Walter Begahot in England, or William James in America, would have defined that term. He certainly did not adhere to the laissez-faire doctrines of Herbert Spencer, or E. L. Godkin, or William Graham Sumner. He would have endorsed most of the positions taken by that staunch liberal, Herbert Croly, in *The Promise of American Life,* a book Theodore Roosevelt admired.

He thought that Franklin D. Roosevelt was recklessly improvident in his management of national finances, increasing government expenditures and the burden of national debt all too cavalierly; he believed that some of the new social-welfare legislation was carelessly drawn and unfortunate in its tendency to discourage the stubborn self-reliance of the American people as individuals.

Basically, however, he was governed in his thought by loyalty to principles which he held had been vindicated as sound and fruitful by three centuries of American history. In this he gave more weight to Jeffersonian than Hamiltonian principles. Vastly as he admired Hamilton's brain, he liked Jefferson's heart and attitude better, and took pleasure in the final reconciliation of John Adams and Jefferson.

Like most Americans, he was essentially an optimist, not a pessimist, and a man of libertarian, not authoritarian views. He never yielded his conviction that the republic had been triumphantly successful in achieving most of the goals set before it by its founders, and that its record illustrated the validity of its ideals. He felt that it had approached disaster only once, when sectional division had destroyed the spirit of moderation and compromise inherited from England and strengthened by the fathers of the nation.

He was conservative only in his fealty to this spirit; in his reverence for the Constitution; in his loyalty to time-tested economic and financial tenets, stemming mainly from Adam Smith; and in his hostility to restrictions upon individual liberty.

Even in these areas his so-called conservatism seemed to many contemporaries to lean to the liberal or leftist side. He criticized F. D. R. and his New Deal associates. But his strictures upon them were mild compared with his harsh castigations of Coolidge, Hoover, and Mellon. He declared that Coolidge "carried to the White House the ideals and outlook of a hardscrabble Vermont farm." Later, he remarked in his essay on Presidential Prosperity that the antiquated economic views of Coolidge interested Herbert Hoover about as much as an old blacksmith shop would interest the president of United States Steel. His opinion of Coolidge was contemptuous: "His autobiography has given us the stature of his mind." He was more respectful of Hoover, an able man and less ignorant, but equally wrong-headed. His sharp comment upon Mellon was that he measured national welfare "in stock prices, hidden assets, and dividends." "The trouble with Mellon has been that he was a market-minded financier and not a statesman." In Adams's judgment, the manner in which Coolidge and Hoover delivered optimistic predictions concerning the happy outlook for the economy, and roseate appraisals of the future of business, was absolutely detestable. They were encouraging speculation and promoting an upward whirl of the markets that was likely to end in a catastrophic crash.

On economic and social issues, however, he was always a severe critic of the old order. He pointed out in the *Epic* that despite the so-called prosperity of the country 1900-1920, "the new wealth was very unevenly distributed"; that although luxury was rampant, wage earners and salaried people felt they were not getting their share; and that flagrant injustices were evident. The strike against United States Steel in 1919, for example, showed that while the earnings of the corporation were "colossal," furnace men sometimes worked a twenty-four-hour shift. "The methods used by the managers to crush the strike were injust and un-American, including instructions by agents to provoke all the racial hatred possible between different groups of workmen." In a magazine essay on "The Cost of Prosperity" he deplored the fact that although the New York *Times* had reported the Mellon family making $300,000,000 in a single year, he did not know a single ordinary citizen who had accumulated more than the merest competency except from gift, inheritance, or stock-market speculation. His article on "A Business Man's Civilization" in another magazine attacked the increasing dominance of business in the once-independent professions of the law, architecture, and even medicine.

Adams gave his principal critical attention, indeed, not to national leaders or political parties, but to the American people. It was about the people and the quality of their life that he worried; it was upon their backs that he laid his lash.

Yet he never seriously thought of living anywhere but among them. He constantly censured their bad manners, their spotty morals (too much lawlessness, too much divorce; too much get-rich-quick spirit); their low standards in education, culture, and the arts; and their false values. He admired Americans in the main; it was only certain aspects of their life that he condemned, but these aspects he assailed fiercely. What were they?

First, he declared, Americans were deplorably reluctant to *think* — to analyze their problems realistically, and measure their aims honestly. They were incurably lazy-minded and hard-minded. They refused to look at their history realistically, accepting a hodge-podge of fables and illusions respecting it. They refused to examine their place in the world and world-affairs honestly; instead, misled by ignorance, old passions and prejudices, and their incurable cheerfulness, they took attitudes "founded in a mere mush of false historical knowledge, baseless emotions, and sentimentalism."

They would not take the facts of modern economic life seriously, Adams lamented. Men were now subject to irresistible economic forces and industrial changes, over which they had not the slightest control as individuals. They paid no attention to them; they moved on with a mere frontier restlessness compounded of optimism, illiteracy, and indifference. One of his best papers, "Polyanna, Our Patron Goddess," described the folly of wallowing in this uncritical disregard of truth, the mentality of the frontier booster. The primary needs of Americans, he said again and again, were more thoughtfulness and more discipline.

What distressed him most of all, however, was the indifference of the masses to individual freedom, once so highly prized in the United States. The story of freedom of speech and of the press, he wrote, was one of the acceptance of continually increasing restrictions. War always brought new limitations. In World War I Congress had practically abolished part of the Constitution by providing punishment up to a $10,000 fine and twenty years in jail for anyone convicted of using language intended to bring the government of the United States "into contempt, scorn, contumely, or disrepute." Attacks on any dominant form of capitalism were punishable with the same savagery. The obscenity statutes were being stretched in various States and cities to stop the circulation of printed matter in the most pernicious way. Adams wrote that Boston had little intellectual freedom left when it became illegal to circulate there certain works by Sherwood Anderson, Conrad Aiken, Upton Sinclair, H. G. Wells, Theodore Dreiser, John Dos Passos, Bertrand Russell, and Sinclair Lewis. He was as bitter in his comments on the methods used to enforce the eighteenth Amendment as Walter Lippmann was in the New York *World*. "Such a condition as exists in our country today," he wrote in "Liberty or Prosperity?" "might be understandable if our liberties had been overthrown by a tyrant with an army at his back, but we claim to be governing ourselves and to be the freest people in the world. . . . Scarcely anyone seems to care." He thought that Americans were becoming moral cowards. What was considered liberal in Europe in 1925 or 1930 was apt to be branded in America as radical or anarchistic. To rise to the heights of thought reached by the founders of the republic in 1787 was to run the risk of being sent to a social Coventry, or being deported, or being jailed for a long term.

Adams thus became, in the 1920's and still more in the 1930's, a preacher of social, economic, and political doctrines who, far from being conservative, impressed many propertied Republicans and Liberty-League Democrats, along with Volstead Act zealots, as a very firebrand of leftist thought. He seemed the more dangerous because his influence was pervasive. Such essays as "The Cost of Prosperity," denouncing current greeds, or "Hoover and Law Observance," attacking the mania for more and more laws more and more roughly enforced, and "Our Dissolving Ethics," were widely quoted when they first appeared, frequently reprinted, and potent in influencing pulpit utterances, newspaper editorials, and political speeches.

Adams was often accused of drawing comparisons between American and European life in his magazine contributions that were unfair to the United States. He certainly found more charm, more variety, and more of the artistic in France, Italy, and Britain than in the United States; and he made this impression almost unpleasantly clear in such essays as "Home Thoughts From Abroad," which he also included in *Our Business Civilization,* and "The Tempo of Modern Life," later republished in the volume of that name. Yet he never uprooted himself to live abroad, as a multitude of Americans, young and old, did; and if he found too much sick hurry, noise, and pursuit of material gains and the pleasures of sensation in America, he more and more perceived that the vitality of American life, the resourcefulness of Americans, and the social values bound up in our practical, endlessly experimental democracy, were invaluable. He saw, too, that the political frictions and international hatreds rife in Europe made life there altogether too perilous for a permanent residence. He remained an American, increasingly contented at home, and more deeply loyal.

Throughout the 1920's and 1930's he varied his essays on politics and economics, morals and manners, with disquisitions on literature that represented one of his most important contributions to adult education. They were not profoundly original and represented no large fund of scholarly knowledge, but they were thoughtful, and written with epigrammatic vigor and occasional sparkle of phrase. He wrote on history and the failure of all attempts to apply a series of laws to it, with an especially vigorous condemnation of Henry Adams's effort to define scientific laws. He wrote on "The New Biography," admitting that much of Lytton Strachey's work was admirable, but declaring that his influence upon less talented writers had been "disastrous." Rereading Emerson, he found many of his essays shallow, and like Paul Elmer More, thought that he took too brightly cheerful a view of life and ought to have wrestled more earnestly with the problem of evil. Emerson was very much the product of his land in its sunny youth, and when his country passed through crueller fires of suffering and tragedy, it might produce a thinker of darker outlook, from whose pessimism would come a deeper and more authentic note. Writing upon Matthew Arnold, he decided that he, too, had failed to produce a philosophy or even a body of thought satisfactory to the newer generations. He had overstressed the Hellenic element as a guide to right thinking and action, and underemphasized the Hebraic elements.

Such papers, if not impressive, could at least be called provocative. They gave Adams a place among not the best essayists, but the most interesting magazine writers. The "Polyanna" paper and the attack on the Mucker pose would find a lasting place among the social documents of the time.

As the United States approached the brink of war he received more and more agitated letters from friends at home and abroad. Through Charles Moore he heard how the son of Lord Charnwood, the biographer of Lincoln, had brought his wounded men out of France in the great escape from Dunkirk, and how Lady Charnwood, bedridden in an upper chamber of the house, had been nearly thrown to the floor by a bomb. His heart was wrung by his last letters from Worthington C. Ford in France, an octogenarian but still indomitable. The Germans forced Ford from his place near Paris to a beach village near the Pyrenees, crowded with refugees. "We have only the official bulletins," wrote Ford, "and no comment is permitted that is not favorable to the Germans"— but he boldly added his comment anyway. "The English are putting up a magnificent fight against tremendous odds and are fighting like gentlemen. The Germans are conducting the contest on the lowest plane, for they are liars, brigands, murderers, and of unlimited greed. London — can you picture it at present? To do so you must see how the Hun has treated the French villages, leaving nothing but the chimneys." Getting to Marseilles, Ford received government orders to sail for America — but died en route.

Adams published a moving tribute to this old friend in the *Saturday Review*. He joined William Allen White's Committee to Defend America by Aiding the Allies. He responded to the appeal of Lion Feuchtwanger for a gift to the Exiled Writers' Committee to help rescue some one hundred anti-Nazi writers who were in French concentration camps, or crowding into Lisbon to await passage money to America. He lent his talents to the promotion of war savings bonds, and was shortly gratified by a letter from Undersecretary D. W. Bell of the Treasury Department telling him (July 9, 1942) that 14,000,000 persons owned these bonds. He wrote for the New York *Times Magazine* a telling article upon national unity in wartime. He had supported Wendell Willkie for President in the 1940 election, but Willkie had come out for support of the Allies. The energy with which he spoke out for Lend-Lease early in 1941 brought from Burton K. Wheeler a violent protest. In every feasible way, in short, he supported the Allied cause.

From Cordell Hull that spring came a delighted telegram. "I have been very pleased to note your support of the President on the question of aid to Britain," stated Hull. "I have taken careful note of your suggestion regarding the possibility of this government making a 'dramatic move' at the present time, and I can assure you that your suggestion will receive our most careful consideration." Within three months came the promulgation of the Atlantic Charter.

The Fire Burns Low

During the crowded war years, when so many of us were sent far and wide, losing old associations and occupations, the friends of James Truslow Adams could take satisfaction in his serene absorption in a variety of home tasks. "As usual I am tied up with all sorts of work," he wrote me from Southport at Thanksgiving in 1940, as I was leaving for battered London; and he continued busy. He was then giving a month's work to the revision of J. M. Beck's book on the Constitution, pushing forward the six-volume *Dictionary of American History* that he had initiated, collecting material for the chapter he added each year to *The March of Democracy,* and writing occasional magazine articles. The declining health of his sister Amy cost him time and anxiety. Long hours had to be given every week to a correspondence that now embraced political figures from Willkie to La Guardia, as well as journalists and scholars. He was too busy for much recreation or any exercise whatever, though not for attention to the Academy, or for enjoyment of the house that he and Kay had made comfortable, its big sun-drenched library on the ground floor, with a long solid wall of favorite books surmounted by white plaster busts, being especially attractive.

By this time he had nearly as many friends as he wanted in the village or the towns about, and could always meet others by prearrangement at the Century Club in the city. "I have never been a 'groupy' person," he wrote Felicia Geffen of the Academy staff apropos of some gathering she was arranging. "My social circle has always been made up of people who for one reason or another I like regardless of whether they were bankers or brokers or sculptors or lawyers or what-not." Shy and reserved elsewhere, in such circles he was a cheery conversationalist, ever ready with an incisive remark, witty sally, or quiet laugh, always genial, but never taking the center of the stage.[47]

He was thinking now of another large task, the book that he eventually called *The American: The Making of a New Man.* This was to be a study of the American temperament as shaped by the political system of the republic, its religions, its land and maritime frontiers, its relations with other lands, and its economic development. Charles Scribner wrote him that the theme precisely suited his gifts and was certain to appeal to the public. He plunged into it with enthusiasm, finishing chapter after chapter with his old verve and sparkle until a series of misfortunes befell him. His sister became so ill that be brought her to Southport, where after nine months in bed she died late in 1942. Early next spring Kay broke her ankle, and was on crutches for two months. The ensuing summer he himself was prostrated. Taken ill in June, he went to the hospital, and although he emerged late in August, was not himself again until autumn, for in succession he had a streptococcus throat, virus pneumonia, and a bad case of sulfa poisoning. "I nearly moved from the hospital to my lovely plot in Greenwood Cemetery," he wrote me. Altogether, for two years *The American* was constantly interrupted.

"I had to pick it up so often and drop it and start afresh," he told Solicitor General Orrin Judd of New York, "that I myself thought it rotten." But he kept on, because he really wanted to find out what gave the 135,000,000 Americans of his day their character.

When this 400-page book finally came out in 1943 it was far from rotten, its best sections almost representing the Adams of the earlier successes. "A book worthy of its subject," declared the *Atlantic;* "refreshing in the best sense of the word," said *Commonweal;* "a comprehensive, readable job with here and there a new insight," remarked the *New Yorker.* One seasoned historical writer, Gerald W. Johnson, not merely declared that Adams wrote "luminously, learnedly, charmingly, and for the most part plausibly," but set down a sweeping commendation: "I am acquainted with no other work that within as small a compass presents so lucid an account of the major forces that have molded and shaped the lives of the dwellers upon this continent." It

[47] His closest friends were now far away. The ocean and battle lines sundered him from Francis W. Hirst; M. A. De Wolfe Howe, his spirit unquenchable, was eighty in 1944 and kept to Boston; Henry Osborn Taylor died in 1941; Henry Hazlitt was busy from 1946 with *Newsweek.* I spent the blitz winter of 1940-41 in England, returned in 1942 on war work, was in Australia and New Zealand in 1943-44, and went to the London Embassy in 1946-47.

was selected by the government for an Armed Services edition of from 50,000 to 80,000 copies. Even its critics, who found too much praise of rugged individualism, acknowledged that it welded together fact, quotation, and anecdote in an illuminating way.

But it did not escape the charge that it rehashed a great deal of old material in a way that André Siegfried could make valuable to Europeans, but that Americans found familiar, or the charge that some of its generalizations on democracy, opinion, classes, and constitutional principles were too loose for working definitions.

It was at this point, after the exhaustions of illness and the last sustained book, that an inner spring in Adams's mental and physical constitution seemed to lose resilience. He began to speak and write with a new lassitude and resignation.

Occasionally he showed all the old sparkle, humor, and zest. For example, in the spring of 1947 he wrote Leonard Bacon of an evening at the Century Club.

> I was quite late and sat at the long table entirely alone. After a little while, another man came in and sat opposite to me on the other side of the table. I recognized him but could not think for a moment or two who he was. As a matter of fact, I had met him personally only once before at a meeting of the Royal Society of Literature to which I was elected. He turned out to be H. G. Wells, as sore as a wet hen. He had been down to LaGuardia Field three times with his hand luggage to get a plane for London which would get him home for Christmas, but the fog was so thick that he was told to go back and spend the night in New York. Incidentally, he told me that he usually got his meals in New York at Foyot's on the Park Avenue corner by the Ambassador Hotel.

Adams, knowing Foyot's in Paris, thought he would try the New York branch, but was taken aback when a modest meal cost him and Kay $14.

The Adams of this anecdote was the oldtime Adams, alert for new faces and new experiences, but we met him less frequently. As the war ended, as others turned to their peacetime tasks with fresh hope and zest, he showed a detachment we had not before seen in him.

"You ask me why I have stopped writing," he wrote me on January 14, 1947. "It is partly because I am getting old and will be sixty-nine this year and am tired and have watched other men like Charles A. Beard write too long, and I think it well to stop while I still have some reputation." He would maintain his editorial labors and magazine articles. "But I cannot see myself facing the beginning of a whole new book. I am willing to build a chicken-coop but not plan a large building." He recalled that his forebears had shown neither marked physical vigor in their later years, nor unusual longevity. The biographies of historians reveal as many instances of early cessation of work as of protracted composition; as many men like Gibbon (who completed his *Decline* at fifty-one) and Macaulay (who flagged at fifty-seven) as veterans like Bancroft and Von Ranke. Having worked with unremitting intensity for a quarter-century, he might well feel that mental and physical health demanded more leisure.

Moreover, his editorial labors, though on a lower level of achievement, were heavy and important. With the support of Scribner's, and the collaboration of one of the firm's staff members, R. V. Coleman, he carried through three notable undertakings: the six-volume *Dictionary of American History,* the large, one-volume *Atlas of American History,* and the five-volume *Album of American History.*[48] The first, his own conception, deserved the adjective "monumental" that the *American Historical Review* applied to it, and the second the term "impressive" given it by the same authority. Coleman, a man so quiet that he was little known even by his colleagues, had three valuable qualifications. His knowledge of American history was truly encyclopedic; he was familiar with the hundreds of writers and scores of institutions that had to be enlisted in preparing great reference works; and his industry was prodigious. Adams and he developed organizational plans for the enterprises; he then collected the materials, which Adams edited and gave his own inimitable touch.

The *Dictionary* filled a large need so effectively that it became an indispensable reference work in every library. American history had been completely rewritten during the previous generation. Thousands of new facts had been discovered, thousands of verdicts on figures and events had been revised, and a thousand new interests had been revealed. How could the ordinary man get quickly and accurately the essential facts on every occurrence, controversy, or public policy? Harper's had once published a cumbrous historical dictionary that was as dead as the dodo. Adams and Coleman induced more than 1,100 historical scholars to pledge their cooperation; prepared a careful plan; assigned nearly 7,000 articles to the proper authorities; and then whipped the whole work into shape. It was at once revealed as a work that every student, teacher, journalist, and wide-awake citizen would have to know and use. As Dean Harry Carman of Columbia said in

[48] The sixth volume of the *Dictionary* and fifth of the *Album* were devoted to indexes.

raising a scholar's cry of joy: "It will save countless hours of searching through stacks of books!"[49]

The object of the *Atlas* was of course to present geographical history. In scholarship, graphic workmanship, and general utility it set a new standard in the field. There were critics who thought that with fewer war maps, and more maps of railroads, industrics, and population, the volume might serve a larger purpose; but on such matters readers would always disagree. As for the *Album,* it made an earnest effort to provide authentic contemporaneous pictures illustrating every aspect of the multifaceted life of the American people. These pictures had to cover art, music, household utensils, the implements of farms and workshops, ships, churches, dwellings, restaurants — everything that touched the experience of the people. Literally hundreds of museums, historical societies, libraries, and other respositories were persuaded to contribute their treasures. Maps, paintings, silverware, costumes, schoolbooks, were all brought into the volumes, for they were documents of history. The text was kept to a minimum — most critics thought within too strict limits. Emphasis was placed upon authenticity and comprehensiveness. Although complete success was impossible, it was plain that Adams, Coleman, the art director Atkinson Dymock, and their aides had put a prodigious amount of pains and toil into the undertaking, and had achieved a result of real usefulness to students of social history. "Valuable and stimulating," wrote Esther Forbes in the New York *Times,* though she added that the commentary should have received more thought.

These labors alone would have kept Adams well occupied. He took time, however, for other tasks. One was a book on adult education written for the Carnegie Corporation, and entitled *Frontiers of American Culture.* Another was a study of the workings of the General Motors Corporation, written quite independently of that business but with its cooperation, *Big Business in a Democracy.* Both were well done. In fact, Carl Bridenbaugh thought the adult education volume one of the best of Adams's many books, "a rare example of the application of history to the understanding and solution of current problems." Both, however, were the kind of books that other men could have written, and both were transitory, becoming outdated after a few years.

[49] An additional volume in 1961 brought the *Dictionary* up to date, since when it remained unrivaled in its position. In 1962 a reduced one-volume edition was published by Scribner's with Wayne Andrews as editor and Thomas C. Cochran as advisory editor, under the title *Concise Dictionary of American History.*

At the same time Adams was giving attention to some new ventures in public service. He became a member of the board of the Bridgeport Savings Bank, which soon had deposits exceeding $100,000,000, taking his duties very seriously; while he also gave time and money to a South Dakota organization called Friends of the Middle Border, which had for its main object the creation of a cultural center in Dakota Wesleyan University at Mitchell, South Dakota.

This Dakota movement was near to his heart. Three of the ten incorporators of the Friends were members of the American Academy, Adams, Hamlin Garland, and Stewart Edward White, while its advisory board included other academicians: John Erskine, Carl Sandburg, and William Allen White. The museum which they founded included books and manuscripts of these men, an original Albrecht Dürer given by Adams, examples of the work of Audubon, Catlin, Grant Wood, and other painters, and historical objects of importance. This, wrote Adams proudly in 1943, "is the only museum in the whole vast area covered by the two Dakotas, and perhaps we might include Montana and Idaho. It is the only place where young and old Americans of that section can see original works of art. You never know when from such contact a spark of inspiration may fire some youngster, but it is an experience also for the old. Recently a retired farmer became so rapt in contemplation of Harvey Dunn's fine painting "Dakota Woman" that he had almost to be pulled away by his relatives!"

Working hard at his many avocations, Adams could feel that his central vocation, the writing of history, had produced works that would outlive him. He took no excessive pride in the valuable reference works that he created in these last years, or even in sound contributions to contemporary thinking like *Frontiers of Culture.* He did take pride in the vitality of his best books; in the fact that *The Epic of America* sold steadily on an international market, that a continuous demand existed for *The Adams Family,* and that every serious student of the American past knew *The Founding of New England, Revolutionary New England, Provincial America,* and *America's Tragedy.* From any point of view, he was one of the most successful American historians of his time. He had played his part, too, in public affairs, contributing to the public debate upon political questions, defending the more sober values of social and intellectual life, and championing a responsible internationalism.

His strength gradually ebbed. In 1948 he went into New York only four times; he ceased to write magazine articles, and conserved his energies as far as his duties and his social temper permitted. But it was no surprise to his friends when in mid-May, 1949, he was felled by a stroke. On the 18th he died.

The train that carried friends to Southport two days later did not usually stop at that small town. For May it was a gloomy day, cloudy and chill. I asked the conductor to make a special halt, saying that a number of writers and artists wished to alight for the funeral; and a little knot of mourners wended their way from the station up the hill and through the streets to his "Sheffield House," where the ceremony was to be held. There was the familiar library, before whose fire we had often sat, the wall of English and American classics with the white busts above them, the grandfather clock, the Viennese painting of the consular ancestor, the view southward to the Sound under leaden skies.

It was an hour not for sadness but for recalling the bright aspects of the fruitful career just ended; the career of a largely self-taught scholar who had written his name among the most effective historical teachers of his generation. Everyone present possessed special memories. One friend, the youngest there, possessed especially dear recollections. They ran far back to the early 1920's, until they brought before him a vivid picture. It was a vision of the massive old marble building at Broadway and Chambers Street; the trees of City Hall Park shimmering in the background; the big clamorous city room of a metropolitan newspaper, and the quieter editorial rooms adjoining; the erect figure of a youngish man of impeccable dress, regular features, brown mustache, and shy look entering from the wide stairway; and of his face breaking into a pleasant smile at the words, "Shall we walk up to Washington Square together?" How much had happened in his life since then, and how much upon which we could think with happiness!

II

Selected Correspondence of James Truslow Adams

The War and the Paris Conference

Dr. Isaiah Bowman, as World War I approached its end, brought Adams into the curious organization for supplying information to Woodrow Wilson and his aides called The Inquiry.

If the State Department had been adequately equipped, this inquiry into the conditions of peacemaking would not have been needed. But in facing the questions of boundaries, reparations, security, trade arrangements, and reconstruction that would soon demand answers, the government realized that expert facts must be assembled. It was announced in September, 1918, that Wilson had asked Colonel E. M. House to gather the data, the "who's who and what's what" that a peace conference would need. Money would come from the President's special fund. The best available historians, economists, geographers, and jurists would be enlisted. As we have noted, House deputed the management of the Inquiry to Sidney E. Mezes of New York, and Mezes turned the executive direction over to Bowman, who asked Adams to help him.

This was a stroke of fortune. Bringing Adams into association with such scholars as J. T. Shotwell of Columbia and C. H. Haskins of Harvard, it offered him an acquaintance with ambassadors, army officers, and journalists like Walter Lippmann. Best of all, it gave him an opportunity to go to Paris early in 1919 and to see a little of the disorderly process of peacemaking. He never pretended that his services were important, but they did offer some training to a future historian.

To His Family

New York, April 19, 1918

Dr. Bowman wants me here until this work is over, which probably means for the war, including perhaps some months more for the purpose I told you of.[1] But beyond that he has today definitely offered me the position of curator or head of the map department, of the [Geographical] Society, beginning at the end of the Enquiry work. The trustees have approved my name. The pay is not very big, he says, $2,000 or possibly $2,500 a year, but the position is of some importance from a scientific standpoint, and can be made as big as I can make it. When I spoke of not wanting to live in the city, he suggested that I might be willing to take the work with three months' leave in the summer each year, being on hand only for meetings of learned societies, and so on. The Society is the most important one of its kind in either North or South America, and the position would be a dignified and interesting one. As to the Enquiry work, it has been decided the time has come to make it public.[2]

To His Family

Tuesday

I had hoped to get out for dinner but my "easy week" has turned out a heavy one. Miss Hines (photostat) is in the hospital for an operation, and will not be back for six weeks, and tonight my secretary left for Canada her father being ill. I hope, however, that she will be back

[1] The genial Isaiah Bowman (1878-1950), whom Adams found endlessly helpful, was a Canadian by birth who had taken degrees at Michigan State, Harvard, and Yale. He became director of the American Geographical Society in 1915, holding that place for twenty years, and then became president of Johns Hopkins. The earliest of his books, chiefly on South American exploration, included *South America* (1915) and *The Andes of Southern Peru* (1916). A member of learned societies, the holder of half-a-dozen gold medals, and a leader of important exploring expeditions, he was a practical man of affairs. He now became chief territorial specialist with the Commission to Negotiate Peace.

[2] Sidney Edward Mezes (1863-1931), a Californian by birth with a doctorate from Harvard, had taught philosophy in the University of Texas before becoming its president. In 1914 he was chosen president of City College in New York. Connected by marriage with Colonel E. M. House, he was made director in 1917-18 of the Inquiry or Enquiry. Later he became director of the territorial section of the Commission to Negotiate Peace. He was part author of the not very enlightened or enlightening book, *What Really Happened in Paris* (1921).

Monday. Meanwhile the work has piled up on me. All kinds of "extras"— for example, last night there was a robbery in the Hispania, and I have had to find a night watchman. Late this afternoon General Altaschul, of Honduras, came in and took up about two hours. Friday I am to meet Bonilla, ex-President of that country.[1]

To His Family

New York, July 26, 1918

It has been a pretty tiring week with its hustling and uncertainty— mainly the latter. I shall be glad when the next three are over. Last night I got all my papers off to Washington, questionnaire, letters of recommendation and release, affidavit, certificate of army surgeon, etc., and this morning heard that they were all in order. I am to report for probation Aug. 1st and so will go to Washington Wednesday. They tell me that after a few days probation to comply with the law I will be recommended for a captain's commission and they promise— unofficially— that I will get it. That takes 10 days more of red tape. So that is the situation. If it goes thro'— and I don't see why it shouldn't, I am in luck.

As to next winter there is no use planning yet. I shall be in the army and subject to orders. I might be in New York again or Washington or France or Siberia. My work for a while will be in the General Staff in Washington, but I can't count on being settled anywhere.

To His Family

Washington, August 1, 1918

Although this is Willard paper I am now at the Harrington, having spent last night at the Willard and having paid $6.00 for a room and innumerable tips. To room and eat there both would cost about $10-11 a day, I think. Here I have a room for $3.50 and meals are much cheaper, but this also is only temporary. Capt. Furlong is trying to find a room in a private house for me and I am to hear about it tomorrow — $24 a month if I get it. I shall take it for a week or two, I think, which will give me time to look about. . . .

Yesterday I saw Bowman and had a very interesting talk with him. He agrees with me that I ought to remain here six months if I get a commission even if called back to the E. later, which he wants to do if he is in it before they go to the P.C.

[1] General Manuel Bonilla was President of Honduras 1912-16.

Night Letter to W. N. Adams

Washington, August 16, 1918

Have received my commission as captain. . . .

To His Family

Washington, August 18, 1918

I am now in uniform and have been learning saluting with a vengeance. The city is full of army and navy men, and downtown I suppose one easily salutes a half a dozen times on each block. As all enlisted men in army and navy and officers below Captain in army and senior lieutenant in navy have to salute me first, while those two salute with me simultaneously, and I have to salute from major and lieutenant-commander up — you see I have to keep a sharp lookout for shoulder straps! It is an awful nuisance. I really had quite a jolt this morning. I have been used to passing the guard at the door with a nod and smile, but today as I came in all four jumped to their feet, saluted and stood at attention as I passed in. I have bought two summer uniforms ready made — a "palm beach" and a light serge. My winter one, I may have made. So far I have got off rather easier than I had feared, about $150, including a very good rain coat which I can use after the war. My boots and leggins are of dark purplish Cordovan leather, which look very well and cost only $27. Pigskin leggins are now $90!

To His Father

Cosmos Club, Washington, August 22, 1918

You ask what I am in. I do not suppose I will get my actual printed commission for two weeks or more yet, so do not know just how it will be worded. I understand I am commissioned as Captain in the "Military Intelligence Branch" of the Executive Division of the General Staff, U.S. Army. At any rate that is where I am assigned to duty. My telegram from the Adjutant General notified me that I was appointed Captain, and ordered me to report at once for duty to the Chief of the Military Intelligence Branch.

To His Family

Hotel Harrington, Washington, August 25, 1918

I felt so stale I thought I would try to get outside the city and see what I could find, so I took a Chevy Chase car to the end of the route.

Then I took a chance on a road which led off into some woods and walked for a mile or two, where it opened into meadows again and at a bridge over a stream met a small boy, whom I questioned as to the possibility of there being a swimming hole. He told me there was a fair one about a mile down stream. So I followed down and found three kids about 14 years old in swimming there. They invited me to come in, so I stripped and joined them and spent the rest of the morning with them, and came back to town much refreshed every way!

To His Father

Office, Monday night, September 23, 1918

They say the government is going to bring 12,000 more people here, but I do not know where they are going to put them. As I went out to supper tonight, about six, there was a line at Child's running through the restaurant, out the door and 30 or 40 feet down the street, waiting for chairs. All facilities are overtaxed. . . .

Rock Creek Park is the prettiest park, by all odds, I have seen anywhere. Amy would love it, for there are real woods with pretty paths everywhere and a sense of untouched nature, with no crowd anywhere. Yesterday I walked about 15 miles, going out to the Brooke Tea House, near Chevy Chase, for an early luncheon and then tramping out through Maryland, and back into Washington along Rock Creek. . . .

There is nothing much to report from here. I usually get home by 8 or half past now (after dinner) and have made a beginning of studying Russian. Not that I expect to really learn it, but even a little of it is useful to me. It is a perfectly rotten thing to learn. I have certainly been fortunate in what the war has done for me so far. I have had a chance to widen my perspective very much and have a far better grasp of things in general. If, as I hope to do, I should write when I get back to civil life, my work ought to show the results of my present training, I think.

To His Father

Washington, October 13, 1918

Yesterday was a holiday. As luck has it I was on duty in the afternoon, but as I had been on also on the previous holiday Furlong got Capt. Johnston to take it for me. There were showers all day, but the Cushings had invited me to motor so we went in spite of the weather, and finally got as far as Frederick, Md. about 110 miles round trip.

The change in physiography from the coastal plain to the "Piedmont" is very marked, and the latter far more rugged and hilly than we had thought. It is beautiful country in western Maryland, and from Frederick one gets a fine view of the Blue Ridge. I saw the site of Barbara Fritchie's house, which I had never dreamed of visiting. Two weeks ago I ran out in another direction to Blue Mount in Virginia about 20 miles west of Bull Run so have now seen quite a bit of country. Yesterday's trip to western Maryland has increased my desire to go down the Shenandoah valley some day. The country is ever so much finer than the coastal plain, and more prosperous. A few evenings ago Capt. Rich, of the War College, motored me around the country east of Washington to show me the physiographic features of that part, so I am getting quite a scientific view of the lay of the land around this part of the world. Today I have been for a walk with Capt. Johnston through Rock Creek, and this evening am to have tea home with the Cushings.

To His Father

Washington, October 16, 1918

This morning there was a little incident which will be rather pleasant to remember. As we were hurrying along Connecticut Avenue, I saw the President's car come bowling along, with the usual motorcycle guard on each side. As it went by I suddenly realized the President himself was in it and looking at me. I clicked my heels and saluted in a hurry, just in time to get a smile and bow before he whirled on. Cushing didn't wake up until too late. It is rather pleasant to have had the chance to look the most powerful man in the world in the eye and to have had my personal greeting from him. Lansing,[1] I met in New York. If I could only meet Col. House I would have pretty good memory pictures of the three main figures in American history for this period.

From Major Charles W. Furlong[2]

November 18, 1918

1. As you have been transferred to other duties, I take this opportunity of expressing to you my appreciation of your efficient service

[1] In a letter written from New York, May 3, 1918, Adams states: "According to our last news the S. of S. [Secretary of State, Robert Lansing] will be here tomorrow and I am tied up therefore."

[2] Charles Wellington Furlong, a man of many-sided talent, educated in Cornell, Harvard, and the École des Beaux Arts in Paris, had a spectacular roving

while on duty under me in the Military Monograph Sub-Section, M.I.D., M.I.2.

2. Since reporting to this office, August 1st, 1918, you have acted as executive officer and have also been in charge of some of the very important work of this Sub-Section. This has envolved executive ability, the collecting, assembling, writing and revising of certain data to be incorporated in field handbooks for officers. This has also envolved careful weighing of values, systematic and prompt handling of difficult material, and putting it into final shape. Besides this, you had charge of certain other work requiring tact and business ability. All this work you have done with exceptional efficiency and interest, carrying it out promptly. Your appreciation and adaptation of a military attitude toward whatever work you have undertaken has made you a most valuable officer.

To His Family

Washington, December 12, 1918

Huntington wants me to stay in until July but I am not very keen about that. However, so much may happen first that I am not giving it any thought. I do not think that the troubles are through on the other side by any means yet.

To His Family

On board U.S.S. *Leviathan,* January 22, 1919

The boat is simply colossal. It is the biggest thing of any kind I have ever seen. It is nearly twice the size of the *Mauretania* (58,000 tons against 32,000, I believe) and really seems unbelievable.

I find I am to share my room with Major Furlong,[1] but it is nearly as large as mine at home; has four beds, four arm chairs, a center table, a writing desk and two wardrobes. . . .

I wish you could see Colby's baggage![2] There is a mountain of it in

---

career behind him. Between 1900 and 1917 he had discovered the wreck of the frigate *Philadelphia* in Tripoli Harbor, headed the first scientific expedition across the heart of Tierra del Fuego, won the world's rough-riding championship at Pendleton, Oregon, and published books on the Sahara, Tripoli, and South America. He was commissioned a captain in 1917.

[1] Major Furlong, whose many-sided talents have just been noted, was on his way to Paris, as he later wrote, to take charge of Military Intelligence, and of the Conference Room and Reference Room of the American Commission. He was therefore Adams's direct superior.

[2] Bainbridge Colby (1869-1950) later became Wilson's final Secretary of State.

the corner. Apparently he is taking everything necessary for every sort of life from campaigning to diplomatic, including a couple of fencing masks unpacked. What in creation he is going to do with it all I cannot imagine.

To His Family

American Commission to Negotiate Peace
Hotel Crillon, Paris, February 2, 1919

Well, here I am at last, safely stowed away bag and baggage. I never got separated from the latter though I stayed by it with difficulty in spots. The trip from Brest to Paris took 15 hours, and was a wild scramble at both ends, the details of which will have to wait. The boys in the A.E.F., however, are ready to help at every turn, and they are really a fine lot. . . .

Paris is jammed full and as far as I can make out costs at least $10 a day to live and not well at that. I am taken care of, however, and am most comfortably fixed here at the Crillon with a delightful room and bath. The place is well heated, and the table simple but good, so I have neither comfort nor expense to worry about. The place is not large enough to house everyone, so I am very fortunate in being assigned to it, and hope I can stay. Bowman thinks I can.

To His Family

Paris, February 5, 1919

I cannot, of course, say much of my work here. It is more or less like what I did for the H. C. in N.Y. and is interesting for its setting and personal contacts rather than for itself and the sooner it is over the better I will like it. My room and office are both in the hotel, which I am glad of, as the Parisian climate is rotten in winter. I shall, however, try to get out a bit each day. Sunday I walked up the Champs Élysée as far as the Bois, have been up and down the Seine a bit, but naturally have little time for sight seeing, for which I shall use Sundays as I can. Next Tuesday I have been asked to a box party at the Opera for a gala performance of Faust with all the best singers in honor of Wilson and it ought to be good. I expect, however, to keep pretty steadily at work and do not expect to go in for much gaiety. . . .

Today I passed Gompers[1] in the hall and had a good look at him.

[1] Samuel Gompers (1850-1924), one of the founders of the American Federation of Labor in 1886, and later almost continuously its president till his death; he represented the A.F. of L. at the Peace Conference in Paris, 1918-19.

He has rather a shrewd fine face, a little heavy but rather a good type. I have also run into a number of other lesser notabilities, like George Creel, Hoover,[1] etc. Well, I am going to read *Le Temps* a bit and turn in.

To His Father

Paris, February 15, 1919

I cannot write of my work and do not do much outside of it. Yesterday, as the cables told you, I suppose, the text of the League of Nations was made public. Everything here, however, runs along much as it might in any business office and there is little sense of anything more important going on than the drafting of any ordinary contracts. The whole atmosphere is matter of fact; I would like to write my own views of the whole situation but suppose I had better not.

The weather continues simply abominable — absolutely no sunshine, and rain and fog much of the time. If . . . this is the usual thing here in winter, nothing in the world would induce me to live here. The sidewalks have not been dry once since I have been here, and everything, buildings, trees and sky are grey and black. Paris may be gay behind closed doors but is about as depressing as can be in appearance outside.

To His Father

Paris, March 31, 1919

I have just seen my superior officer here and he has agreed to arrange to have orders issued for me to sail from Brest "on or about April 15th." I have also fixed it up with Bowman. That will be 3 months from the time I was ordered here and, for various reasons, the moment seemed opportune to get away. I shall certainly be glad to get back. If I reach the States by May 1st, I may be able to get my discharge and go home for good by the middle of May. I cannot tell over here how long the process is. It is possible 6 weeks now may see me free and with you again. It certainly sounds good.

On my return this morning, I found a nice note from Elie de Fesquet saying his mother and father would be glad to have me dine there Thursday, and I shall go. I judge they are very nice people and it will be pleasant to see a real French home, and I shall be glad to see the kid again.

[1] George Creel (1876-1953), Western journalist and former editor of the *Rocky Mountain News,* had been appointed chairman of the Committee on Public Information in April, 1917, and served for more than two years. Later he wrote *The War, the World, and Wilson* (1920).

To His Father

Paris, April 3, 1919

Having just come in from the de Fesquet's and having had black coffee there and not being at all sleepy, I will get off a few lines to you about the event. It was very interesting and very pleasant, though I must confess it took a bit of courage to go to a dinner where I had never laid eyes on my host or hostess, who I knew did not speak English and to possibly encounter others in similar state. It would have taken still more had I known what was coming, although it needn't have for it all went off very nicely. They are evidently people of very considerable wealth (connected with the DuPonts before the latter family left France). The dinner was an elaborate and perfectly delicious one with ten people — the Naval Attaché of the French Embassy at Washington, a Count somebody, an old Abbé and others. I was evidently the guest of honor, took Madame de F. to dinner on my arm and sat on her right. The old butler, the wines, everything was perfect and I imagine I saw a certain type of French life at its best. One or two spoke English, and Elie was put at my left and was most attentive and helped me along.

Life is certainly a funny thing — all this from a chance street acquaintance! Having decided to take me in, they certainly did it up brown! Madame Bonfré (wife of the Naval Attaché) knows all the State Dept. people here and it is possible enquiries were made about me, though I do not know. The two older sons were both killed in the war and Elie is the only one left, and Madame's first remark, "Vous avez été très aimable à mon fils, Monsieur Capitaine," accounts for my honors of course.

To His Father

Paris, April 9, 1919

I have just come in from luncheon with Baron Korff at the Lutetia. His wife and father-in-law, Admiral Van Reyper, have taken a house at Inogne for the summer. He wants me to go to see the Baroness in Washington and give her news of him so I suppose I must. Tomorrow I lunch with Dr. Hudson of Harvard, one of the international law experts. Friday Capt. Stoika, of the Rumanian army is coming to dinner with me. Saturday I dine with Dr. Grey, a Persian scholar, and his wife. Monday I still hope to leave for Brest with Farabee. It sounds very interesting but to tell the truth I shall be very glad to get away and can hardly wait. I feel as though I would give anything to lie on the beach and watch the ocean and do nothing for a while. The prospect in Europe depresses me. . . .

I do not know whether a New England history would be profitable or not and shall probably talk the matter over with Abbott when I get home. I had a letter from Prof. Cook a few days ago. A couple of days ago I was lunching with Dean Haskins of Harvard who told me he would give me every facility for work in the Harvard Library.[1]

The New England Histories: Miss Seely

Returning from Paris in 1919, Adams soon devoted all his energies to reading, research, and writing. He also kept busy through 1923 visiting libraries of documentary sources in Worcester, Providence, Salem, and other New England towns. He immersed himself in a mass of monographic studies and special articles, not forgetting to save time for reflection. His object was to upset "the old conception of New England history, according to which that section was considered to have been settled by persecuted religious refugees, devoted to liberty of conscience." This revolt against a worshipful attitude toward the Puritans had begun when Brooks Adams published (1887) *The Emancipation of Massachusetts,* a book which showed the faultiness of the ideas and practices of the Puritan leaders. James Truslow Adams meant to complete the revolt.

He toiled upon his scholarly and realistic refutation of the old picture of a glorious company of saints and patriots as founders of the section with earnestness. Meanwhile, he had to make a living and a reputation by magazine work. *The Founding of New England* in 1921 and *Revolutionary New England* in 1923 proved instantly successful, appealing to scholars and general readers alike.

But these were not years of scholarly industry alone. Blossoming in the hard-working routine of the time was his friendship with Kathryn M. Seely, which soon became something more than a friendship. His other letters pale in comparison with those to the Long Island girl who helped him to capture a sense of the larger horizons of life.

[1] The various persons here mentioned include Manley O. Hudson (1886 ——), who was taken to Paris as an expert on international law, and who later served in the secretariat of the League of Nations; Albert S. Cook (1853-1927), professor of English in Yale, and editor of various classic texts in English literature; and Dean Charles H. Haskins of Harvard (1870-1937), author of *The Normans in European History* (1915), who was sent to Paris as an expert on Western Europe. William Curtis Farabee, the anthropologist (1865-1925), has been noted in the biographical introduction.

To Kay Seely

Bridgehampton, December 10, 1923

Dear "Youngster" —

(Miss Seely sounds so very formal, but I will be respectful and use it next time!) I am still rather shaky as you can see, but I want to thank you for your part in contributing to the picture of the smoker's reverie, which I found in my pocket and which helped to cheer an evening which had some very lonely spots in it in spite of my natural pleasure at home-coming. I knew I would miss the happy comradeship of the past two weeks, — and I *do*. It certainly is the unexpected which happens in life. How little I thought a month ago I would be in the hospital, and when that was settled, how little I thought I would find new friends there, and be really down-hearted at leaving. I shall keep the "reverie" as a souvenir of what was a very happy time — thanks to you both.

I will write to you again after a while, and meantime let me thank you again for all you did for me, — more than you know.

To me, younger friends are both a help and a happiness. Perhaps an older one would not be wholly useless to you. Count me an honest and sincere one to you if you wish, certainly one who has high hopes of you and counts on your developing into all that he has seen of the best in you. Stick to it! Do not try to live too many years all in a day, — and may courage and good fortune go with you.

Faithfully your friend,
James Truslow Adams

To Kay Seely

New York, December 31, 1923

Dear Kathryn —

If your experience in life is anything like mine, I think you will find one of the hardest questions to answer is one that is always coming up about all sorts of things, — "Where shall I stop? Where shall I draw the line?" I tell you, Kathryn, if we could only always answer that right we would have solved the art of living. The old Puritan tried to answer it by cutting almost all the joy out of life. In Massachusetts and Connecticut there could be no dancing, no songs except hymns, church all day Sunday, no one allowed even to go for a walk that day, boys and girls not even allowed to get together in the evenings, penalties for kissing, &c, &c. I have made a study of the results, and they are startling, though what might be expected, and in my writings I have attacked the Puritanic attitude toward life.

To Kay Seely

Paris, February 27, 1924

When I said I did not remember that first night [at the Southampton Hospital] it was so, but haven't you discovered yet that things that you don't remember for a while come back clearly later? . . . Things come back and settle down in the right order. And now I remember every detail of that night. Mrs. P. bustled about and got ready to leave, and then brought you in, and you stood in front of the bureau, with your stiff collar, and she said "Here's little Miss Seely (she said little), who will look after you." After a little while you offered to get me a bit of aeorozone or whatever the stuff was, and when I hesitated you said "It is all right or I wouldn't give it to you," and I said I knew that, and so on. And I shall never forget the absolute sense of well-being that your rubbing my forehead brought me. I like Mrs. P., and she is a good nurse but your rubbing is worth ten of hers, though perhaps I shouldn't tell you so, but then women are never conceited or babies with the toe ache, are they? Well, I was baby enough then to love to have you rub me but I will tell you something also. There was more than one time when I was not asleep when I pretended to be and would have loved to have you keep on but thought it was not fair, and your patient heard you tiptoe out ever so carefully, leaving him apparently asleep but really wishing you were not going. But then all men are babies!

To Kay Seely

Oxford, April 13, 1924

I feel very far off and out of touch with things. Last week I had a shock in a letter of a few lines telling me one of my best friends, Baron Korff of Washington, had died suddenly, ill only two hours. He was a very fine fellow. His career in Finland ruined by the Russian Revolution, he never uttered a complaint or a whimper but came over here and had already achieved success and was at the beginning of a brilliant career. His mind was a delight and he was so simple, frank and manly. I shall miss him very much, and his death is an absolute calamity for his wife and two children. Well, the older one gets, the more one has to meet these things.

The more one sees of it and thinks of it, the more extraordinary and utterly incomprehensible life becomes. We start out like any other animal, the fertilization of a protoplasmic egg so small you can't see it, and, well, I needn't go into all the physiology, you know it as well and probably better than I do. But then the human being is so unlike anything else in the whole universe in its capacities. In our thought, in our moral sense (however applied morals may differ from time to time), in our consciousness of ourselves and our own existence, in our control of the forces of the universe, in our search for knowledge of the nature of which we are a part, and all the rest. . . . If we think it is better to try to see and make beauty than ugliness, let's try to do so. If we condemn suffering, let's try to prevent it. If we believe in justice and loyalty and so on rather than what the universe seems to give us, let's try for that. As for faith and hope, well all we have is that we see that man has already outstripped the rest of the universe apparently and perhaps he may go further. Man seems to be headed in a different direction from the rest, a direction which would lead to a very different universe. If we don't march in that direction, what is the alternative? We can slip down to the level of the rest of things, we can prey on others, we can, well, we can do all the things that occur to us, but we will have the feeling that we are betraying all the struggles of the best types of men for tens of thousands of years and, in the long run, we won't be even as happy as if we had tried to stick to the best ideals of what we have evolved. Do you see anything else for it, Kathryn? I confess I don't. I am not preaching. I am simply thinking aloud in my present mood.

To Kay Seely

London, April 15, 1924

Well, the American mail came and no letter from a kid who wears soldier caps and, the first night she meets her patients, a high collar. . . .

We came up from Oxford yesterday, and this morning went out to Warwick Castle. It is really beautiful and although it covers some eight hundred years of English history, most of it is in good repair and is still the home of the Earls of Warwick. One has the sense everywhere here of being in close touch with all periods of English life, from the very beginning. For example I was in a Saxon water mill today which is still running and grinding! In the castle I was in the present Countess's music room, a magnificent great hall in which one goes back from the photographs of the Countess's present friends through the centuries and remembers that in that same room Piers Gaveston, the favorite of Edward II received his death sentence and was hurried out to be beheaded in 1312, and much of English history both before and since has taken place in it. Everything tells of the movement of life through all of it. In a corner there is an enormous iron bowl, which was used in the 13th century to cook meals for the Earl's retainers and is now used only to brew punch, 120 gallons, as each new earl comes of age. On a stand is a helmet which Cromwell wore, and so on through the whole enormous room, down, as I say, to the present day with photographs of friends who were in the last war. The grounds are lovely everywhere, as are the views from the castle windows up and down the river Avon as it winds between woods and meadows. We also went over to see the ruins of Kenilworth Castle but although very interesting, it *is* in ruins and one does not get the same sense of continuous historic life there as at Warwick.

To Kay Seely

Washington, May 31, 1924

I have been through 330 newspapers today from the 1770's to 1786 making notes and my eye muscles have had fast exercise running up and down columns of faded yellow print. . . .

Tuesday I go to New York, my sister staying on here. I get there late in the afternoon and have to be up at 120th Street for dinner with Murray Butler, the president of Columbia University. In fact, I am to be one of the guests of honor. Then next morning I have to be up there again before ten for the commencement at which I am to be given an honorary degree as Doctor of Letters, and a luncheon afterward — about five hours of publicity which I shall be jolly glad to get through with. It is considered quite an honor and now you know all about it. . . .

In the past two years I have had quite a few honors but do you know, they are beginning to make me feel rather old and lonely. I do not mean that I do not enjoy the recognition of my work and the consideration shown me but one has to have someone to share such things with, someone who really cares more than one does one's self, to get much zest out of them. My sister is proud of them but we are getting old, I guess, and take everything in a very matter-of-fact way. I ought to have had a wife and some kids, and, if things had been different, I might have. The only real fun I have had out of it, I had from my little friend of fifteen I spoke of the other day. I told her a couple of days ago and got back, by special delivery, the loveliest letter, bubbling over with affection and pride. It warmed my heart all the way through. . . .

It is odd that, without any connection between them, I have come into three friendships with girls, counting you, since I went to the hospital. I say it is odd because I had been so many years without any at all. Many years ago, well, I had an experience. She had some millions and I had practically nothing, and at any rate when that was all over I steered clear of girls for a long time. I had family cares, worked like a dog in business and had no girl or women friends at all beyond mere social acquaintances. I gave up all idea of ever getting married and never shall now, but I missed a great deal. . . .

I shall certainly be glad to get back to Bridgehampton in a little over two weeks. It will be seven months since I left home for the Southampton Hospital, the longest time I have been away from my shack there since I built it, except the year and a half I was in the war. If I am up to it, I have a busy summer ahead. I want to make a fair start on my new book so as to be able to finish it next summer after this; I have promised quite a number of book reviews and several magazines are going to send me work of that sort to do, which helps to pay bills; the book I wrote last summer has to be whipped into shape a bit for style and to fit into the volumes before and after, which are being written by other men, (there are to be twelve in all, each by a different man); several editors have asked me for articles, which I am not sure whether I shall try to write or not; but at least I shall be home and can do as much or as little as I seem fit for. I think I shall be all right. They wrote me the other day that they were waiting for me to help them organize the Boy Scouts but I am not going to get deep into village things this year, beyond doing my share on the Community House committees. I was chairman of both the finance and building committees of that, and the legal work of organization, the raising of the more than $60,000 we got and all the rest nearly finished me.

To Kay Seely

Washington, June 6, 1924

Tuesday evening was the dinner at President Butler's given in honor of Mellon, Tarkington, a man you know, and the other five who were getting the special degrees. There were about thirty other guests, all distinguished men and it was hard to realize that they were supposed to be there to honor *us*. Butler has a beautiful big house, the flowers were really wonderful, and the guests all interesting, so I had a good evening. I liked Tarkington, a big, rather clumsy, quiet chap. Mellon, the Secretary of the Treasury, I liked immensely, a distinguished looking man, very quiet, with rather tired looking eyes, extremely modest, almost shy, evidently a sensitive make-up and as far removed from the type of most men in high public office as could well be. He is one of the ablest financiers in America, worth some fifty or sixty millions, and it has meant nothing to him to be the head of the treasury except the performance of a public duty while all sorts of mud has been slung at him, as usual in politics. I had a long talk with H. H. Kohlsaat, who has been the friend and adviser of every Republican president since McKinley, and got a lot of interesting bits from him.[1] Brander Matthews, the veteran dramatic critic, was there, and, oh I don't know, a lot of others. It may interest you to know that in spite of Butler's speech about prohibition there was absolutely nothing to drink either at the dinner or after, although it was a man's dinner only and in a private house, so you see the Constitution is observed sometimes.

The next morning was commencement. I got up to the university about half-past-nine and got into my robes as a Doctor of Laws, the degree I had received last spring. I assure you I am quite gorgeous in them, — a black silk gown faced with purple velvet down the front, big sleeves slashed with the same purple, and a velvet cap with a gold tassel. I met a lot of people and about an hour later the procession of between three and four thousand graduates got under way to march across the campus. The students coming up for their Bachelor degrees were all in black but our part was quite gay with the colored robes and hoods, and we eight had an escort of twenty naval officers in white and gold uniforms. . . .

As I wrote you from New York, your letter touched me very much. It was a *lovely* letter, and full of the Kathryn that I am fond of. I loved that page about the kids. So it did you good when the little six-year-old kissed you and put her arms around your neck after her prayers? Of course it did. I remember when my godson was a little tike and I used to go up to Connecticut once a month to see him, — he was about eight to eleven then, — he always insisted on my going up to be with him while he got to bed. He would get undressed and into his pajamas, and then always sit on my lap for a while and talk. Then he would get down and say his prayer at my knee, give me a

[1] Herman Henry Kohlsaat (1853-1924), born in Illinois of immigrant parents, had made a fortune from a wholesale bakery and a chain of restaurants, and had invested some of his money in newspaper properties. He used the Chicago *Inter-Ocean* and *Record-Herald* to support the Republican Party, and took pride in his friendship with McKinley, Theodore Roosevelt, and Taft.

kiss, and I would sling him up on my shoulder and carry him out to his bed on the sleeping porch and tuck him up with another kiss. Do you good morally?

To Kay Seely

July 10, 1924

This may not be mailed to you for some time but I am enthusiastic at the moment and might as well pass it on. What about? Well, the last thing I ever thought I would be, a New England minister of a hundred years ago.[1]

I was rather dreading having to go through his diary in four big volumes but the introduction has made me wish that both you and I had known this old chap. He was extremely learned and read and spoke twenty languages. That I give you just as a background for the rest. What first struck me was a passage from one of his sermons. He said "When a man is found, who does not profess much, nor despise all, who is pure from guile, peaceable in his life, gentle in his manners, easily dissuaded from revenge, with a heart to pity and relieve the miserable, impartial in his judgment and without dissimulation, — this is a man of religion. This is an apostolic description of a good man; and whatever opinions he may have, and he has a right to choose for himself, this man is after God's own heart." Now that is good talk!

One day during service in the War of 1812 (he lived in the seaport of Salem), he saw a man look through the window and speak to one of the ship-owners. He stopped his sermon and said "Mr. Brown, is there any news?" He was told two British cruisers were chasing a Salem vessel into the harbor and likely to catch her. Dr. Bentley at once said to the congregation "this is a time for action not for words. Let us do what we can to save the *Constitution* [the vessel]. God be with us, Amen," and put on his hat and rushed out with the rest, and they saved the boat.

The list of things he did for the poor and sick, and the way he did everything is really wonderful. Nobody in those days thought much or did much for children. All summer he used to take a dozen children or so, different parties, off for long walks in the woods or on the shore, tell them about the things in nature, and then end up with a supper for them. Apparently the boys of the village adored him. Once the schoolmaster suddenly died and the selectmen announced that the

[1] The Diary of William Bentley (1759-1819) was published by the Essex Institute, 1905-14.

school would be closed as they could not get another teacher. Dr. Bentley at once said he would teach until they did. Next morning after the news had got about *every* boy in the place turned up to go to school! And it tells how this man, who was perhaps the most learned man in all Massachusetts at the time, taught the kids. . . .

Friday afternoon, Hello, Kitty-kat! No letter from Southampton in the mail. And I have no time to write one. I have been delayed with one thing and another all day and must get down to work. Just had a letter from the *Atlantic* asking me to review a book and have it reach them by the 23d, — and the kid here most of next week! I shall take it to New York with me and sit up and read it Thursday night.

I was looking over one or two of your letters last night. I want to say seriously, Kathryn, that I appreciate very very deeply the affection and trust you feel for me. You need never fear I will misunderstand, and I will try to deserve them both as though I were really your big brother. You say you could not misunderstand me now, and I don't think I could you. I know perfectly well that there is "no harm" as you say in your feeling for me, and as for me, I think your trust is safe. I have talked absolutely openly to you, on purpose, and you know me pretty well.

To M. A. De Wolfe Howe

Long Island, July 27, 1924

I was very glad to hear from you and will answer from my new quarters. For I have become very luxurious and have built me a study back of the garden where I can retire to perfect privacy. It is only 12 x 16 but it is fitted up as a literary workshop and will be a delight. I have rigged up shelves for all the books I am using constantly, more shelves for photostats and maps, a broad shelf about ten feet long, just high enough to stand at comfortably for spreading out notes and so on when I want to get a birdseye view of a mass of material, a few comfortable chairs, a smoking table, and my typewriter. There is a window on each side to catch the breeze from any direction, and to the south I look over the level meadows to the dunes with an occasional glimpse of ocean. From the front door, as I write, I look down the garden path, which just now is a riot of hollyhocks and phlox. It is far from the telephone and other intrusions. Aren't you envious? I am so exceedingly pleased with myself that I hope that I can do some work, tho' I doubt it. Possibly the necessity of paying for it will spur me on!

I sent an article to Sedgwick[1] which he seemed to like and is going to use on "Historic Determinism and the Individual," tho' I do not know what issue it may come out in. I should hear from him this week again about it. He had the rough draft and I sent him the finished one a few days ago. They also seem satisfied with a book review which I got off to them *on time* last week. I got the book from them Thursday afternoon just as I was leaving for New York and had to mail the review Monday morning. The book was a little disappointing on examination but they promise to send me something better next time. Last night (Saturday) I had a two-column review in the *Sun* of Osgood's life and work which occupied the leading place on the book page.[2] As I shall not have a book out for two years I suppose signed articles and reviews will help a bit to keep my name going. I noted the *Transcript* but remained tranquil. It was unfair in that I had not claimed that the Revolution was all due to class conflict and a few radicals at all, but was merely trying to trace all the contributory causes. But I am not worried. The review in the *London Times* (two columns) was very good and spoke of *Revolutionary New England* as "a brilliant book." I do not know who is gratuitously acting as press agent, but various items are going about the press about me, such as my getting the Litt.D. from Columbia; and one item stating that I am busy disinterring the best Boston family skeletons comes from Alabama, Wisconsin, and elsewhere. This publicity is an odd business!

To Kay Seely

Bridgehampton, August 4, 1924, at least I think it is the 4th. It is Sunday.

I am writing this in my new study which I do not think was finished when I wrote to you last. I am as pleased as a kid with a toy over it, and I really think I am going to get lots of work done in it. I have shelves for books and photostats, a high shelf table which I can work at standing up, a few green wicker chairs, my typewriter table, and a

[1] Ellery Sedgwick (1872-1960), had become editor of the *Atlantic Monthly* a decade before this date. This article was the first of Adams's contributions to the magazine.

[2] Herbert Levi Osgood (1855-1918), long professor of history in Columbia University, who was best known for his history of the American colonies in the seventeenth century, had just been given a careful biography by his son-in-law, Dixon Ryan Fox (1887-1945), who later left a chair of history in Columbia to become president of Union College. Adams admired the painstaking if stylistically dry work of Osgood.

little wicker table, on which are tobacco, pipes, magazines, and a picture of my "daughter." From the front door I have a very pretty view down the garden path, which, just now is a riot of hollyhocks and phlox. The little shack was quite honored this morning by a visit from Charles Andrews of Yale, who is the greatest scholar in America in colonial history, and, incidentally, a very charming chap. . . .

I have cleared up all my outside writing but one review now for a time and am working only on my book.[1] Next month I expect quite a few reviews to do again with the autumn books so want to make hay on my main work now. I hope before so very long to drop in at the hospital again if it is all right and won't bother you.

Last week I felt rather rottenly, a sort of "all-gone" feeling nervously but am much better again. The week before I had been very much worried about something and I guess I was having a bit of reaction after too much happiness with the youngster down here. . . . It is a perfectly heavenly day today, as you probably know yourself! and I wish you were here in the "study" where we could have a good chat. How does it feel to be only a month off twenty-six? . . . Just think, I will be forty-six in October. I would like to drop twenty of them and start again with what I know now!

To Kay Seely

Bridgehampton, August 12, 1924

Heigh-ho, I have finished chapter I. I don't like it and it will have to have a good deal of revising later on, but such as it is there it is on the shelf. I think I am getting into the swing a little more.

You see I had not done any book writing since last November and one does strike a stride. The first chapter always bothers me, and this book does not interest me as much as the other two did anyway. I have got worked up a little painting the miseries of the private soldier in the Revolution and one of these days, when I am in the mood for it, I am going to end chapter I with a good slam at the comfortable people who wouldn't either go into the army or pay their share of the taxes. The U.S.A. was not chock full of patriots in those days! It was the same old story of greed and selfishness on the part of large classes while some poor beggars and some real patriots did the work and took the knocks. Well, it will always be so, I suppose. At any rate, it always

[1] Having published *The Founding of New England* and *Revolutionary New England, 1691-1776,* Adams was now engaged upon *New England in the Republic, 1776-1850,* which he published in 1926.

has been. Perhaps some day human beings will learn to order all things better and there will be a happier world.

I often think that even with all the physical suffering which there is in disease, old age, and so on, nevertheless what a wonderful world it would be to be happy in if we only knew how to handle things and ourselves. In the first place the world itself is wonderfully beautiful with its oceans, its shores, rivers, and lakes, the woods and clouds, the sunsets and stars and all the rest, except where man spoils it. We have learned to produce all we need for the comfort of everyone if we could only distribute things rightly. Then there is our love of making things. We all love to make something ourselves, and the vast stores of lovely things that have been made by the people of different ages and nations, shows what we can do, the pictures, furniture, poems and books, statues, buildings, if we could only make things for their beauty instead of to sell quickly in mass for profit for a few. Then there is all the wealth of human love and affection, if we only knew how to use it without getting into trouble. Think of all those who want to give love and affection and those who want to get them, and yet how many do neither but just stay lonely and dry up because of all the possible troubles that may come, things being as they are.

It is really an extraordinary world for possible happiness and yet we ourselves make such a mess of it, and then blame the universe. It is not the fault of any one of us. We are all caught in the great machinery but perhaps some day a better ordering of everything may come, and if it does what a wonderful chance for happiness there would be. The four things a man needs are simple enough, play, work, love and worship. (Did you ever read Cabot's *What Man Lives By?* It is worth your looking at it if the library has it. The B.H. one has it.) But we have largely spoiled work by modern conditions, we don't know how to play, a large proportion have to go without love, and the churches with their dogmas and cold intellectuality and our own self-consciousness have largely taken away our worship, in its wide sense.

I had no idea of getting on this tack when I started to write. I had just finished my chapter and thought I would chat with you a few minutes before going on to other work. . . .

My, how it rained on the roof of my shack this morning. There is nothing but the shingles over my head and it made such a racket I could hardly hear the Corona clicking. Yes, the shack is masculine, all right and is going to stay so. It is very simple and there is not much in it but it is a great success for work. I spend the whole day out here all alone and just go in the "other" house for meals and at night. I could really be quite content to bring a cot out and live here! I was figuring the other day that I could not replace my house and grounds as they are today at present costs for less than $22,000 (don't tell the tax assessors!!) and the stuff in it is insured for about $18,000 more, and here I am living quite as happily in a $400 shack on the other side of the hedge. Isn't that a commentary on modern life?! If the other house ever burns up I shall never accumulate such stuff again. . . . What I would do with all our stuff I don't know. One can't sell family portraits, family heirlooms in big mahogany furniture and all that sort of thing, and little by little one gets overwhelmed with one's belongings. Sometimes I wish almost it would all burn up! One gets tied up as life goes on. My friends think of me as being perfectly independent, a bachelor without a family and enough money at any rate to be independent as a bachelor, whereas the fact is, with my place here, which cannot be left in the summer or rented without ruining it, and my sister, I am as much tied up as if I had a wife and three children! She has it in her head now that she ought to give me a month's "vacation" next winter and is talking of going to Cuba, but I doubt it. As I shall be working about eight hours a day in the Library of Congress my vacation does not promise to be exciting in quiet Washington. It rather amuses me. As a mater of fact, it is well for everyone to get away from daily contacts once in a while and her theory is all right for neither of us has gotten away for years.

To Allan Nevins

Bridgehampton, October 31, 1924

You can tell Mr. Sherman from me that overwork does *not* pay.[1] Two years ago my doctor told me I had been using my head too much and ought to have a rest. Like most males in fair form I laughed, and signed up with Macmillan for the book for Fox. I wrote the whole thing last year and had it beautifully planned to get clear just short of a breakdown and go to Europe. Then I landed in the hospital with appendicitis, and on account of my nervous condition it has taken me a full year to get back, and I am not quite back yet. I have discovered that one needs extra vigor laid up for a rainy day quite as much as pennies.

I am sending off a review of your book this morning to Dr. Canby

[1] Stuart P. Sherman's death in the summer of 1926 was occasioned by a heart attack while swimming, but followed years of sedentary overwork.

and thinking you might care to see it I have knocked off an extra carbon. I honestly think you have done a very good piece of work. I returned the copy the *New Republic* sent me and do not know who will now do it for them. What do you think of Andrews's book?[1] I have just finished reading it for Canby. Far be it from me to criticize Andrews, who probably knew more twenty years ago than I ever shall, but it seems to me that he does not bring out the radical tendencies in the colonies and the local matters, such as you deal with, sufficiently. The English background is finely rendered and he has a remarkable grasp of the imperial relation but he does not bring out, to my mind, the complex situation on *our* side. Although he pays his respects to the influence of the frontier, I do not think he gives any hint of a conflict of interest between our frontier and tidewater. I would like to know your first impression. The book is a fine piece of work and if he had called it the "Imperial Background" instead of the "Colonial Background" there would be no question as to his having fulfilled the promise of the title.

To Kay Seely

Bridgehampton, November 1, 1924

Good morning, Kay!

(Ugh! Chilly in the shack this morning!) Well, how is everything? Did you sleep well Wednesday night, and eat, and get rested a bit? I certainly hope so, Kay, and that you are feeling better. The goblins didn't get you *last* night, did they? I have just been taking a stroll around my "estate" and nothing was disturbed, but the kids — and goblins — never do bother my place now. If the kids like you they are good to you — "trust them and they don't sting"! Ugh, Ugh, Ugh, I wish I had our beach fire here right now. You know I enjoyed that. *I* am a kid about things like that. I love to gather the wood and start the fire and watch it. Luckily *I* don't mind tending it!

Did you enjoy it, Kay? Or don't you care as much about a fire as I do? It is the greatest discovery man ever made in his rise from the brute. It has meant cooked food, and so agriculture instead of roaming after wild fruit and raw flesh, and it meant smelting of metals, and so tools and instruments and the whole of science and invention, and it meant a home life. Think of the change when our early naked or skin-clad ancestors, instead of shivering in the dark and cold could gather in front of that marvellous thing, a "blaze," giving warmth and light

[1] Charles M. Andrews had just published a short book on *The Colonial Background of the American Revolution,* on which Adams makes a just comment.

and drawing the man and his mate and the "cubs" together with a new sense of comfort and tenderness! It was man's first great step up from the brute, this making and tending of fire, and he is the only creature that has ever done it. Well, I suppose we cannot have a fire on the beach in summer but we can find something else to do.

Thursday I went gunning in the afternoon with Ralph. We had no particular luck but had a good afternoon tramping the shore of the bay. It was a beautiful day and it was lovely down in the high marsh grass, all turning red now and shot with light as one worked through it. The colors of water and sky were marvellous and when the sun dropped, the "baby moon" was there in the west, and then suddenly night fell. There is no stillness like that of a marsh at twilight. I scared up a big heron with a squawk in the quiet but did not shoot at it and let the awkward thing fly lumberingly off to safety, its heart pumping with terror, probably, at the big beast which had suddenly disturbed it. The lad had a good time, although he got only one plover. He said he didn't care so much about actually shooting anything as just to tramp about and try to stalk them, and then with an unexpected show of affection for a boy of that age, he said, "It is so good to have someone you like to do things with." Human nature! . . .

Later. Did I say I had a clear desk? I have just had a great big mail and I am no clearer now than ever. Two of the "letters from strangers" came from opposite ends of the earth. A man from San Francisco writes me of an article he has written, which he is sending, with a good deal about me. That will have to be answered. Then I got a *very* nice letter from Sir William Ashley, a well-known English writer on economics, praising my work very highly and saying he is going to do all he can to make my work better known in England.[1] I have now had complimentary letters from the universities of London and Birmingham and Oxford and am beginning to be a little bit known. It takes time and *work,* and now *to* work! Isn't this (Saturday) a marvellous day for Nov. 1st? Too good to stay in and type but it can't be helped. One can't get results unless one works.

To Kay Seely

Bridgehampton, Sunday, November 9, 1924

Oh, Kay, but it is raw and cold! My feet were beginning to get

[1] Sir William Ashley, who had been professor of economic history at Harvard, 1892-1901, and since then professor of commerce in Birmingham University, was author of the widely known *Introduction to English Economic History and Theory,* and other books.

frozen so I put out my stove and have retreated to my own room. Unless the weather cheers up, the days in the shack are numbered for *this* year. I was working up here from breakfast until a two o'clock dinner over accounts. I loathe them! But I have quite a bit of book-keeping to do and the income-tax has added a new terror to them. I don't mind paying my share of running the government but I *do* object to all the extra book-keeping involved. . . .

Oh, Kay, there is so much I want to do and so much I ought to know in order to do it! The more I get into history the more I feel that we have got to go way below the old surface, and deal not with kings and statesmen and people who wrote books, but with the lives and difficulties of the great mass of men and women. Of course that is not a new idea, but I am stressing it rather more for our Colonial period than any one else has. Sir William Ashley says I am "rewriting American history." At any rate, I am trying to write it in a way that has not been done before. I ended my second volume by saying "Much we can learn from English records, much from those of Boston and the larger towns, much from the contemporary literature of the day, but behind it all we must still learn more than we yet know of the daily life and problems, the discontents and ambitions, of the many thousands who never saw a town and who never expressed themselves in the printed page. Until then, we cannot be sure that we understand aright that great movement which spread through the throngs of common men who sailed the ships and tilled the fields and felled the forests of New England, and wrought a new hope in the heart of the world." And so I end the first chapter of my new book in which I have treated of the revolution by showing the lives of the soldiers rather than telling of battles, by saying "we must turn to yet other aspects of the lives of the silent millions who were forced by the struggle to face new hardships, new temptations, new problems, new conditions in every phase of daily life. For it is, to a great extent, the dumb tongues of the multitudes that will one day speak the living words of history." But all this is the hardest thing to get.

"Someone to Share Things With"

Encouraged by the warm reception of the first two volumes of his New England trilogy, the award of a Pulitzer Prize, and favorable reviews, Adams by 1924 was well launched on his third volume, *New England in the Republic.* His attitude toward history was changing.

He began seeking larger themes, and applying to them principles of a more analytic character. After the trilogy his next important work was to be a piece of large-scale social history. At the same time, he was turning to the contemporaneous scene in politics and economics. The postwar reaction under Harding and Coolidge disgusted him. He was beginning to write articles of dissent for the best magazines, and to gain a national influence. He protested against the crass materialism of the Harding-Coolidge Administrations; the neglect of the farmer, laborer, and clerk; the reluctance of Washington to aid other nations, or support an effective world organization for peace; and the blindness to grave social problems. He was a moderate liberal, not a radical, imbued with the ideas of Theodore Roosevelt and Woodrow Wilson.

He had found himself intellectually, and worked with a rising sense of power. But the rather shy and lonely man realized that he could not relish prizes, honorary degrees, and public applause because he had no close associate, no partner, to share his emotions, and could not accept disappointments as he should because nobody sympathized.

To Allan Nevins

Washington, February 10, 1925

As I do not know much about what I may call the business end of reviewing, I am going to ask you to let me consider you a good enough friend to ask a bit of advice. As you know, I began my reviewing in the *New Republic.* I am not very keen about that journal these days, but Littell has always been extremely courteous, they pay well, and immediately upon acceptance regardless of date of publication. I have also reviewed for the *American Historical,* the *Catholic Historical,* the pay being nominal but I consider it something of a duty and I suppose it does no harm to have my name there occasionally. The *Atlantic* will send me things but their reviews are limited to 500 words and $15. I have also reviewed for Canby but they are slow, do not pay particularly well, and I don't like dealing with an office that you never can get a letter out of. As I said, Sherman has also asked me to do something for him when the right thing comes along. Now this is the point. I would be glad to do the bulk of my work in that line for you, and for the next few years anyway would like to knock out a few hundred dollars extra by it, though this year I have a pretty full schedule if I am to finish my book by autumn. Next year I am not going to start writing my next big thing but spend the summer studying, so will be much freer. Would it not be well, however, for me to review for these other papers occasionally both to have my name appear before other sets of readers and also to keep in touch with other editors? I am asking for your frank advice. You spoke the other day, for example, of rather wanting to leave journalism and get back to university work. Suppose you should leave the *Sun* and I had concentrated solely on that paper, and a new editor came in who didn't care for my work, would it not have been better for me to have kept a certain amount going elsewhere? Forgive my trespassing upon your time and good nature for personal advice and I promise not to do it again. I hope you are still planning to try the east end of Long Island next summer.

To Allan Nevins

Washington, February 13, 1925

Thank you very much for your letter, and its kind expressions. I shall be glad to make the arrangement you suggest, and you can count upon me. I shall also take your advice as to the *New Republic*. Would it be proper to say to Littell sometime that I had made an arrangement with you by which I was to do the major part of my reviewing for you but that it was not exclusive and that I should be glad to do something for him from time to time? It merely occurs to me that by saying something of that sort in the proper way that it would simplify the thing and not make it look all the time as though I were trying to dodge individual books he might suggest. I am relieved at what you say as to the probability of your remaining with the *Sun* and that being the case I shall not pay any particular attention to Sherman or Canby, though I might do an occasional book if I were asked. I would much prefer such an arrangement as you offer with you so long as your leaving the *Sun* would not leave me standing alone after I had burned my bridges elsewhere.

As I said, this summer I have heavy work to finish my book but I think I can handle everything you will want in addition and this is the last summer I shall be so pressed. It is owing to my having got behind last year on account of my operation. With regard to English books, I may say that I have been interested in the current imperial problems as well as the colonial one of the past. I always get the minutes of the Imperial Conferences from London and for a while I subscribed regularly to South African and Australian journals. I think I am one of the few men in this country who read all the debates on the Peace Treaty in the Hansards of all five Dominions! I say that because when I tried to get those for South Africa at the Library of Congress, I found that, owing to some mistake, they had received none since 1914, and I was the first man whose enquiry had brought it to their attention. I felt that I did not want to get merely handpicked English versions or the matter as filtered through the *Round Table,* and I found a lot of interesting stuff. My interest has not been in local Dominion politics but only as relates to the empire. It is a fascinating evolution at the present time and an unholy mess!

I expect to leave here for New York about the middle of next month, and will advise you of the exact date later. After a week or so in town, possibly in Boston, I shall go to Bridgehampton and be there until December, so you will have no trouble on that score. I shall make a point to see you in town, and would be glad, after I get home, to have you run down there for a night or week-end when I could show you a little of the country and perhaps help you clarify the summer situation.

To Kay Seely

Washington, February 17, 1925

I put in rather a stiff day at the library today and came home a little early so will start a letter to you as the rest of the week is likely to be full. Oh, no, it won't be sent to you for a long long time yet!! What news have I got? Tomorrow night I am going to the theater to see Joan with my sister, and Friday dine at the Jamesons, with some other people, as yet unknown. . . .

Yesterday I lunched with Herbert Adams, one of the best sculptors in America, and liked him very much, — a simple, sincere sort of person. I was interested in looking at his hands, supple and strongly knit but not at all tapering as to fingers, rather square. (I was going to say "on the other hand," but that expression hardly fits this time for I should say on both hands!) Today at lunch there was the chap who is the best player on the flute in America, (the first flute of the New York Symphony orchestra), who is just back from Havana; an official from the State Department who is at the head of the "rum" end of the State Department, and who has been to Mexico for the radio conference of all the countries of North and South America; and the usual men from the library. The talk as usual ran over all sorts of topics and countries. That is about all my social news. Otherwise I have been digging among newspapers of 1807. I find that somewhat oddly there are almost none here for 1845 so, as I want a matter investigated in those years, I am having a girl do it for me at Worcester, Mass., where there is the best collection of newspapers in the country, and I am anxious to see what she makes of it. I am gambling $20 on her finding what I want. I have written abroad declining the suggestion made to me of which I wrote. I am too tired to undertake such heavy work of a worrying sort; would probably be a good deal more lonely there than here; and don't know enough for the job.

To Kay Seely

Washington, March 2, 1925

Dear Puss-Cat:

Yesterday you would have smiled to have seen me. The other day I happened to say to Colonel Martin that I was getting tired of going with almost nobody but men of an intellectual type and wished I could talk to a kid. He said "come and play with my baby" in fun. Anyway he asked my sister and myself to dinner yesterday and I did play with the baby, a girl one year old, just able to toddle around very unsteadily, I was quite tickled because it came to me before it would go to my sister! I really found myself quite taken up with it and thought of you as I was playing with it. This afternoon I went to the other extreme of age and had an interesting call on old man (excuse me, ANOTHER OLD MAN) of 95. He fell down stairs the other day and cut his head very badly so he told me he was not feeling quite as well as usual but he was wonderful. I wanted to see him because he is the only surviving member of the Brook Farm Community which was started in Massachusetts in 1845 and of which he was a member from then to 1848. He was born in 1830. Just think of all the things he has in his mind, which is clear and active! I asked him if he knew Emerson and he said he knew him very well, and told me more or less about his personality. . . . Time's up. Oh, Puss Cat, I would much rather talk to you than read about the constitution of the British Empire! Night, Kay!

To Kay Seely

Atlantic City, March 19, 1925

As I look down in the street there are some little school girls of about fourteen going by, all in their fur coats and sporty things. Aren't some of them adorable? I haven't the faintest idea what sort of people live in this city. One never walks anywhere but the board-walk and there one sees people from everywhere except Atlantic City! It is rather a quiet crowd at the hotel here but not an interesting one at all. There isn't a man who looks as though he had a thought beyond business or the women beyond clothes, though doubtless that is an injustice. But they all look to me like the type whose one idea of success is a little better house and a little bigger car every year or two. I wonder where we are all headed in this country. We have the most magnificent country, the greatest resources, the greatest wealth that any nation ever had. What are we going to do with it? There is much we learn only through suffering, and as a people we have had no great suffering since the civil war, and that was two generations ago. Only a very few old people recall it. I wonder if we are going to "get ours," as they say, some day. I often wonder very seriously whether we are really *happier* for all these things in "civilization"— all these motor cars and radios and plumbing and artistic and intellectual and scientific interests and all the rest, because it is not only the machinery of life that becomes more complicated but ourselves also. By introducing all sorts of needs doesn't it make the attainment of a simple human happiness harder? I have in mind sometime writing a few more essays on history and using them with the two already in the *Atlantic* for just a small volume.

To Allan Nevins

London, April 29, 1925

On arrival at Southampton I was greeted by a letter of welcome from a rather pet cousin in Devonshire telling me that the family place there, old "St. Michael's," had burned to the ground while I was on the sea, so we altered our plans and came here first until things could be straightened out. We are leaving tomorrow for Bath, and go to Devonshire Monday.

We spent a week here, a London cousin taking my sister about a good deal and thus relieving me of a certain amount of sight-seeing and feminine shopping. I was not in the mood for either and outside of a moderate amount of tailoring and the picture shops in Bond Street, I have devoted myself to tramping the Strand, Regent Street, Pall Mall, Piccadilly, etc., watching human life rather than seeing the sights tourist fashion. I have forgotten just how it goes but Browning says in "The Last Ride Together," speaking of art and of the sculptor there from his finest work:

> – – – – – – – – we turn
> to younder girl that fords the burn.

If my garbled quotation sends you back to one of my favorite poems my letter will have been of some use!

As my sister is of a sight-seeing disposition, I ran up to Edinburgh with her for the week-end as we neither of us had ever been in Scotland. I have now been and shall never be again. It is a marvellous city for architectural composition, for location, for tone, and lights and shadows, but it depressed me beyond words. The country is dour, and the people sad with none of that ennoblement that real tragedy brings. There is none of that purging of the emotions of the Greek tragedy — merely a sad-eyed soddenness. For once I find myself at one with Sam Johnson — which is unusual, for although I am a Boswellian I am not a Johnsonian.

The palace [Holyrood] stirred a new interest in Queen Mary, a motor ride to "Queen's Ferry" brought "Kidnapped" back to me, and one must be blind not to realize the beauty and appeal of the Scotch scenery, but as far as my mood was concerned, I was glad to cross the Tweed again and speed at 50 miles an hour through Yorkshire, Lincolnshire and southward on the eight hours journey to King's Cross again.

Yesterday, a London cousin arriving to take my sister off for the day, I resolved to despatch Scotland from my mind and spent the day rambling about the gayest streets of London, lunching at Prince's and having tea at the Ritz! Although I have been here many times, I find London inexhaustible in its multifold appeal and its vast extent. Beside it all other cities I know, New York, Paris, Rome, Vienna, what not, seem small and restricted. They are like a patch of woods compared with a vast stretch of primeval forest, for that is the effect London has on me, of some vast growth of nature through which the incessant streams of human life pour in every direction. In other cities I find myself looking at buildings and streets and vistas as man's handiwork — here I look only at the stream of life itself flowing as naturally down the streets as rivers between their banks. I have grown utterly conscienceless about sightseeing in Europe and come over only to see friends, relatives, and get in a new atmosphere. *If* I feel like the "Cheshire Cheese" I lunch *there, if* I feel like the Ritz, I tea *there,* and after all isn't one just as historically important as the other?

I had tea this afternoon with De Wolfe Howe, who happens to be here, at his brother-in-law's house, Muirhead,[1] who now gets up the

[1] James Fullerton Muirhead, born in Glasgow in 1853, had married Helen Quincy, great-granddaughter of President Josiah Quincy of Harvard. As editor of the English editions of Baedeker he had lived for some years in Leipzig, and as author of the Baedekers on the United States and Canada had spent much time in America. He had published a work of insight, *America, The Land of Contrasts,* in 1898, and later helped his brother Findlay organize the Blue Guides. He became a warm friend of Adams.

Blue Guides for Macmillans, which have replaced the Baedekers. They have a delightful house out Kensington way.

I have just stopped to drink your health in my last mug of ale before turning in!

To Kay Seely (then visiting in Syracuse)

New York, Sunday, May 17, 1925

I am writing on my knee in bed but it is too late to run the Corona so I will chance your being able to read my scrawl. I want to let you know I am back in the U.S.A. safely, and to thank you for your letter which came this evening. It was just six weeks since I had heard and I was a good deal worried. . . .

I wrote you last from Bath, a rather mixed letter, as I remember it, on a very rainy day. . . . From Bath we went to Torquay which is on the south Devon Coast. My cousins were at the station to meet us, and we stayed there from Monday to Friday, motoring every day. The weather was a joke, sunshine and heavy down-pours alternating every few minutes, but one gets used to it. One day we drove about 30 miles along the shore to a little picturesque village called Slapton, with perhaps forty houses and some eight hundred years of history. My family knew the vicar of the church there so we stopped in for tea with him — a real English country "sporting parson" who, I suspect, cares more about fishing for sole than souls. Another day we drove about eighty miles up in Dartmoor, in the high moor country. . . . Some of my family clan in Devon are amusing, my cousin is really a dear. . . .

And now as soon as I can get her business here settled, I must get home and buckle down to work in earnest. I have loads to do, and I hope I can do it.

To Kay Seely

Bridgehampton, June 21, 1925

Heigh-ho! I am tired and am going to have just a word with you before going in. It is a quarter to eight but I am out in my shack. I love it out here. It is sort of out of the world and suits the "lone wolf" side of me. Luckily for Mr. Rabbit I am *not* a lone wolf. There has always been a big brown one about the place, and this evening I discovered that the beggar must have stolen a march on me and set up a family, for there is the dearest and tiniest little one I ever saw out on the lawn. Honestly it isn't over about six inches long and not old enough to be frightened of man yet. He almost let me get him to play with. But not quite! And then out here near the shack there is a female red-winged blackbird who nearly goes frantic when I stroll down near a certain spot in this little stretch back here, I have left rather wild. Of course she has a nest somewhere, — the place is full of them, — and the poor thing is paralyzed with the fear that I shall harm her kiddies! . . .

I wrote a 2000 word review today of the two volumes on "Great Britain and the American Civil War" so with the one on "The Essential American Tradition" which the *Sun* hasn't used yet, I am two up and won't work next Sunday. The *Atlantic* has given me two weeks more to finish the book and made it November 15th if I send them ten chapters before long. In another couple of days I shall have my material organized for chapter X and begin writing. There is so much that I am afraid the chapter will turn out twins. The other day I ran my sister over to Quogue for her to see a friend of hers, which took the whole afternoon, and that and my two days in town put me back at bit, but I am going to be all right on time now. I am sick of the book but have time enough to do it, especially if I can find someone perhaps to do some typing for me of the clean copy for the press, which would save me a couple of days or more on each chapter. Well, I am going in now to start reading another book for review. . . .

. . . .

Just read in a letter (dated 1806) "A conscience is a plague to a man — and yet a man is worse for having none." Quite so!

. . . .

I have been glancing at Epictetus again. He is too much of a Stoic for me. We are, after all, men and women, of flesh and blood and affection and pains and sorrows and we can't make ourselves into marble statues, but this is not bad advice: "What ought not to be done, do not even think of doing."

To Kay Seely

Bridgehampton, Thursday, July 17, 1925

And you have been reading some? Good for you, but can't you find something more interesting than *Revolutionary New England?* . . . Honestly, I am afraid you will find it rather a dull book. It is a dull period, the earlier part of it, and has been neglected by historians, and is now considered a bit as mine because I have dug in it a little more than most. The valuable thing I did in the book, if anything, was to show that for many decades before the Revolution — that is the war with England — splits had come in New England society and that parties had been formed there between the rich and poor, etc., and that we must take all that class feeling into consideration when we come to the question of the struggle between the colonies and England later. When my smaller book on the social and economic life of all the colonies in that period comes out next year I will send it to you and I think you may find that more interesting.

I have been cleaning out some of the drawers in the secretary in my room and found a whole lot of duplicate clippings. They are old but I am sending you three of them. One is the Boston *Transcript's* review of the Revolutionary book, which gives a fair idea of what I was driving at. Another is an editorial from the N.Y. *Times* about my ideas, and the last is a review I wrote, at the end of which I give the same idea. This is what I have specially tried to teach. I don't want them back. I don't remember whether I ever sent you an address I made before the American Historical Association on the same topic, but anyway I won't smother your budding interest in history by too much all at once. . . .

Yesterday I finished the rough draft — *very* rough — of chapter XII but am not satisfied with it. I will do it over when I come to revise the whole thing and meanwhile am going on to make up my notes for XIII. Only five more now, but there are three books on hand to review for the *Sun,* and two of them are two volumes each. . . .

Sunday. "I'm busy and tired and all out of sorts." That was K. to J., but today we'll make it J. to K. I am. This morning I wrote a 500 word review of [Harry Elmer] Barnes's book for the *Sun,* and this afternoon have to make a call or two I don't want to. I wanted to take a good slap at Barnes but restrained myself. He is clever but he has a badly swelled head and at thirty-six seems to think he can sit in judgment on everybody. The book is on the relations of history to the social sciences.

To Kay Seely

Washington, November 14, 1925

I am a very ignorant person in many spots! Honestly I am. I have read lots of things most people haven't and haven't read lots of others that almost everyone has. No, Honey, don't think I can hold up my end in talk with anybody. I can't and I feel my culture is very slight as compared with what it ought to be. . . .

I am not particularly sympathetic with Frenchmen but you must not forget some things. In the first place, the frothy life of a part of Paris is not *France* any more than a certain type of fast rich-man-chorus-girl-Broadway, etc., is *America*. And in no country is there to be found a more beautiful family life than in France. Taken as a whole I should say that between husband and wife, children and parents, brothers and sisters, there was a more happy relation there than here. Like all nations, they have their good and bad.

To Kay Seely

Washington, Saturday, November 21, 1925

Honey-dearest: I am enclosing the article on early American women which may interest you or may make you laugh at me. I have sent a copy to McNitt for *McNaught's*[1] but as he may not like it I send you this carbon so you can have a look at it if it never gets printed. If it does you have an "advance copy." Honey, you have taught me a lot about women and I not only understand them better but I think heaps better of them than I did before. I am willing to admit now that they are much better, deeper, finer than men. There! If through you I have come to feel that way about "women" it shows that I must have been thinking about you, doesn't it? Smile, Honey! . . .

It is perfect weather, too warm to walk far, and — come, let's look out of the window. See how the sunlight seems to lie so softly over everything, as it does sometimes at Happy Hollow? And people are walking lazily about, like a summer day. Girls, lots of them. I do not believe there is another city in the country that has so many girls in the twenties, for they come here from all over to work in the Government offices. There is a big office on that corner — see it, that big white stone building? — and at 9 in the morning this street is alive with girls rushing along to get in before the bell strikes, and at lunch time, and 4:30. What do you suppose that one is thinking about? Over there. See? She has been sitting all alone on that bench for over an hour now. She has a brown cloche hat (ha ha! is that what you call them?), a tan coat with a fur collar, a blue suit with a red tie, short skirt and flesh stocking, black ties. There! She has *some*thing on her mind but I can't see that as I can her clothes. Now, I have described the outside, you describe the inside. Make up what you think *she* is thinking and tell me. I'll give you one page of your letter paper to tell me the story.

[1] V. V. McNitt was founder and editor of *McNaught's Monthly*.

Now, don't forget. And don't you love the big grey squirrels running around, heaps of them? See that one there. The beggar wants to cross the street and he is looking up and down. *He* isn't going to get run over by any auto! Zip!! There he goes. And pigeons by the hundred. The girl has shifted now and is sitting sideways with her shoulder against the back of the bench, her head down showing a long stretch of white neck. Wouldn't she be surprised if somebody leaned down and kissed it?! That would start something, wouldn't it? I could pretty nearly throw something into her lap from my window. If I had a Hershey bar I might try it and then duck. Now, she has hitched forward again, crossed her legs, and pulled her skirt down modestly over her knee. Yesterday morning while I was dressing I looked over there and a girl came along who met a young chap, gave him a kiss and then they went off together arm in arm. You see the park is quite human. Now the girl on the bench has her hands crossed in her lap and is turning her head this way and that looking up and down her path. Perhaps she is waiting for some one to do it to her and go off. Well, it is none of *my* business and I ought to be reading that book for review. Yes, I ought and must stop talking to you. Here's a chair and you can watch out the window while I get to work. If anything exciting happens you can tell me. Do you mind my smoking my pipe? I have cut down lately, really. You see, I can't smoke in the Library. Will you light it? All right — thanks. Now I'll settle down. Oh, I say, look. That's interesting. She has taken a letter out of her pocket, and is reading it. How many times do you suppose she has read it before? There's a lead for your page as to what she is thinking. I am off. Bye-bye. J.

To Kay Seely

Washington, Thanksgiving morning, November 27, 1925

Well, I have heard from my Woman article. . . . McNitt says "it is the sort of article that should be read twice and if the reader is wide awake, he will carry on his thinking from the point where you leave off and will reach conclusions of his own as to the importance of womanly qualities to the future of the country." Were you "wide awake?" That is what worries me sometimes, as it does a good many thinking people, about the feminist movement. It is not that I do not want woman to have every right and every opportunity to go into any sort of work, and to express herself in any way, and all the rest. But I honestly believe that woman, as woman, has a far greater contribution to make to the welfare of the race than man. A man's world would be a heck of a place. Without the devotion of woman and her spiritual influence I believe we would all go to the devil, and it is a question — an open one which I do not pretend to answer — whether if woman copies man in all his activities and tries to live a man's life, she may end by losing her own distinctive qualities and begin to assume his. If she does, God help us all. I mean it.

I want woman to go in for athletics, and do everything to expand her mind, and to have every opportunity of becoming economically independent, and so on, but can she do everything that man does and keep her own distinct qualities? That is the question that only time can answer. If she can, she will be the most glorious thing in all creation, far finer than any man. But if she gradually becomes a sort of second man merely with physical differences in her body, then the world will have lost its soul. For that is what woman is. If it were not for woman's capacity for self-sacrifice, her love that is so much finer than man's, her spiritual way of looking at things instead of man's physical way, and all the rest, the world would be more like a society of bees or ants or other animals than it is. What is it in you that makes me love you and makes me a better man and makes me want to be good? It is not your knowledge or mind. I can find intellect in dozens of men in a far higher degree than in the most intelligent woman ever made. It is your goodness, your self-sacrifice, your depth of love, your way of looking at our relation when you spoke of the sacredness of our memories and of the sacrament on our anniversary — qualities that a woman has in far higher degree than man. Men who can understand appreciate that and even those who do not understand somehow feel the influence of it. If women were just like men, the world would lose that, the most precious thing we have. . . . It is all mysterious and it is a very mixed up world, isn't it Honey? But do you see that the "woman question" is a good deal deeper and more complicated than merely giving her the vote or the chance to compete in business or the professions?

Friday, 5.30 . . . Three women invaded the "Round Table" as guests at luncheon.[1] We were having a good quiet talk when they suddenly came in with one of the men. They were the energetic, club-women type which I hate, and one of them started in by saying that she could hardly believe she was at the "celebrated Round Table," she had heard so much about the conversation there and was dying for us to begin, — a perfectly silly remark which of course killed all decent talk for about

[1] Luncheon table at the Library of Congress.

ten minutes. After a few more things had been said "oh Mr. Adams do tell us what you think about the Puritans!" One of the men chuckled and I could have thrown my fishball at her. I said "I am afraid I can't quote my books as they are copyrighted" and let it go. She seemed to think we were performing seals. After a while somehow rational conversation did get started and the other two women were somewhat more sensible. After they went I sat on and smoked a pipe with one of the men who is writing a history of science in colonial America, and recovered. She was simply trying to show off — such a contrast to the women yesterday, quiet, intelligent, interested in the subject and not at all in themselves. These "active" women, "intellectuals" and leaders do rub me the wrong way. I love an intelligent woman even if she has never read a book; if she has, so much the better because it widens the range of topics, but I cannot stand the woman who tries to impress you with the fact that she is intellectual or clever. As you see, Honey, my fur has been rubbed the wrong way and instead of purring I am growling!

To Kay Seely

New York, November 28, 1925

My writing has got to be my main life, and I have been looking about to see what I can do in the way of apartments or houses if we[1] decide to make this city our winter home. It certainly does cost to live now! I looked at one apartment of two small bedrooms, a living room about half the size of my library, a small dining room, and a kitchen only four feet wide, and that was $1700 a year. One downtown here, with fair sized rooms and plenty of them was $3600! There is an ideal place for me right here in the club, or rather in an adjoining building the club owns, and which has a door cut through. It is an old fashioned house and so has large rooms. There are two which are practically one and which would give me a library about 40 feet long, much larger than my present one, a small study, small bedroom and bath. I could have my meals at the club and no trouble with servants. It would have just the one thing I want, a great big room for my books, but as it would not house my sister too it is out of the question. . . . If we are going with more or less a certain group of people here, we shall have to be somewhere on this side of town, and have a place big enough to get callers into. That means, of course, a certain level of expense. I

[1] "We" still meant J. T. A. and his sister Amy.

care nothing about show and society, but I like to go with pleasant, cultivated people. . . . while you do not have to have as big houses as they do or live on their scale, you have to have a reasonably good place or it makes the interchange of social courtesies difficult. . . . I have the feeling that I do not know what is ahead in life and don't want to tie myself to a house again. Anyway, there is nothing to be done for another year, and I am just looking around in a general way. I do think, however, that whatever time we might spend in Bridgehampton in the summer it would be better to get my things and books over here for what is going to be the longest stay of each year. The winter rather than the summer ought to be my working time and I need my library to do the work well. I don't like to be cooped up in two hotel rooms with my sister all winter either.

To Kay Seely

Saturday, December 12, 1925

I was at the Library until 2.30 when I came back to take my sister to an art exhibition at the Corcoran Gallery . . . and then I came up to my room to write a review, which I have just finished and mailed. And within a few minutes another book — 400 pp. — has come to be read and written about — Mowatt's *Diplomatic Relations of Great Britain and the U.S.* I have told the *Sun* that I do not think another book that came is worth giving the space of a review to. The one I have just done is a selection of letters between John Adams and Thomas Jefferson. Adams, you know, was the second president of the United States and Jefferson the third. They had worked hard together in the days of the Revolution but later politics estranged them and they had no communication until 1812 when a mutual friend, Dr. Rush, brought them together again. They were then 68 and 76 but they began writing long letters to each other about everything in life, evidently delighted to be friends again. These letters as given here are only extracts but I compared them with the originals and they give the spirit and character of the whole. They discuss all sorts of things — the origin of Indians, eugenics, God, the future life, whether they would be willing to live life over again etc etc. They read enormously — but I needn't go on for I shall send you the review when it comes out. . . .

Phelps is all right. I do not know that he is a very profound critic of literature but he has done a lot to make people enjoy the good things and his courses at Yale were always crowded. I remember the first time I saw him — "Billy Phelps" as he was always called. I was rushing into the "Co-op" at Yale to buy something and he and his big dog were just coming out. The dog rushed out as I rushed in and we collided and I nearly took a header over Bow-wow into Phelps's arms! A professor was a more august personage to me then than he is now and I was embarrassed.

I hope you are right about woman being able to become more intelligent and interested in everything in the world and yet not lose those qualities that make her so much better than men. What you say about man having to use his mind and woman not having to in the past is true. Man's work has to be done to a great extent by the use of *reason,* not only in such things as the law and scientific work but in lesser mental work. It comes natural to him whereas it does not to most women. Take the running of a car, for example. A man will study his car and then if anything goes wrong he will try to reason out what it may be. I have noticed so often that a woman does not as a rule, and that if she knows anything it is generally what some man has told her. She will say if something happens, "so and so told me to do this or that." Of course there are some who are good mechanics but not many. The whole thing leads to a consideration of the part played by reason in life, and it is a subject that we could talk about a long time. I am coming more and more to believe that reason is just *one* tool, one way of getting at things, and that there are others. It is necessary to get at things and understand the world from the scientific point of view, but there are other points of view. It has been a tremendously useful tool for doing some things and without it we would be animals yet, but it does not do everything. Now woman has her own ways of getting at things and she does it well. There are few men who do not owe much of their success to some woman, not merely to the inspiration of her love and their love for her but to her advice. . . . Many women have an intuitive judgment that may be extraordinarily good without her being intellectual at all. I was talking with a man about it the other day and said that it would be very interesting if we could know what influence the wives of the presidents had exerted on history. The Roosevelt papers, for example, are still sealed up and will be kept secret for many years yet, but when they are opened I happen to know that it will become evident how much help the present Mrs. Roosevelt was to him and that many a time she saved him from doing foolish things although her knowledge of affairs was much less than his. She was the balance wheel of his life.

Reason is not all of mental life at all. It is, as I say, an essential tool for doing *some* things in life, but some of the finest things in life, and in our *mental* life, do not spring from reason. They come from faith and love, which have nothing to do with reason, and from love of the beautiful. Sculpture, painting, poetry for example. Take the great cathedrals. Reason played a part in the physical construction, yet, but what was it that made the people of the Middle Ages rear those wonderful buildings so much finer than anything we can do today? It was faith in their religion, not reason. Reason builds railroads and steamships and ugly farm houses. Where is reason in your worrying over your patients and being such an angel to them that we all love you? It is something deeper and higher than reason. A very great deal of the very best in the joint life of man and woman does not come from reason at all. I think that man and woman *are* different and that it is just conceit and silliness in man to think of woman as a "lesser" or undeveloped man. I think that human life should be thought of as a joint thing in which man and woman each contribute their share. It is not simply physical sex-needs that makes a man need a woman or a woman a man to live their lives most fully. Franklin used to say that man and woman were like the halves of a pair of scissors, neither was any use without the other. That is not so altogether but they do need each other to make a full life. And that joint life should not be thought of as just *two* lives lived together, but as a wholly new thing, a real joint life which each helps to make. When hydrogen and oxygen combine they make a new thing, water, H_2O. They are not just hydrogen and oxygen.

Now, the only point that I wonder about is whether if women lead men's lives, that is, are forced to use their *reason* as man has had to, will that develop their reason at the expense of their other qualities? To use a somewhat raw comparison since the Indians have become civilized, or at least ceased to lead their old lives, they have lost their keenness of smell and all their old ability of woodcraft senses. I asked one of the officers in the war who had Indians under him whether they were of any special use in scouting, etc. He said no, that they had lost their old senses for all that sort of thing and no longer had any special keenness as compared with white men. I do not say that women will, it is just an open question in my mind.

Marriage, Life Abroad, and New Aims

"I have rarely been so uncertain as to what is ahead," Adams wrote as the year 1925 ended. What lay ahead in 1926 was his last year of bachelorhood, for he and Kay decided to marry at the beginning of 1927. What lay ahead also was publication of the third volume of his trilogy, *New England in the Republic,* in the spring of 1926; a book which dealt less with politics and religion and more with the broad social and intellectual life of the people than its predecessors. As 1927 arrived he gave the final touches to a volume of purely social history, *Provincial Society,* one of the best books thus far written in America in a neglected field. The failure of the careful plans he and Albert Boni had made for a collected edition of the works of Henry Adams was discouraging, but in 1929 he found the writing of a book on the entire Adams line a fascinating task.

An equally important fact of the years just after his marriage was his embarcation upon foreign residence. Settling in London, he found the surroundings and social atmosphere highly favorable to literary pursuits. He and Kay found frequent trips to the Continent both refreshing and educational. At the same time, he kept in close touch with American affairs, pouring out a stream of articles for periodicals, and corresponding frequently with his friends. Various invitations to resume his residence in the United States, of which one to become an advisory scholar at Wesleyan College in Connecticut attracted him greatly, he resolutely repelled. Although apprehensive over some developments of the time, he led a life of almost unshaken contentment.

To Allan Nevins

Bridgehampton, May 31, 1926

I was very glad indeed to get your good letter a couple of days ago and wish your optimistic forecast of the sale of my place to some inspired millionaire had come true. I *have* sold it but at a very low price, about what the house alone is insured for, with out-buildings and two acres of beautiful grounds thrown in. The boom down here was only in acreage and waterfront and never affected houses. This is a small and very quiet village and I am about two miles even from that. My place is very attractive but I felt that it might be a year or two before I could sell it to the right man at the right price. In the meantime it would have cost me nearly a couple of thousand to own and keep it up and that was too large a proportion of my income to use up on something I was merely gambling on. I do not know just when the final break in America's prosperity may come — in two years or three — but all signs point to the fact that we are nearing the end of a cycle of good times,[1] and if one should be caught with a country place for sale when the end arrives he could not sell it for some years. So, as I had definitely decided not to live in the house any longer, I made up my mind to sell it to somebody who wanted to speculate and let him take the risks. The contract is signed and title will pass the 29th of June. Meanwhile we are moving to town this week — four vans — and putting the things into storage. My sister is going to Connecticut and to visit about for some months and I am going this week Saturday to the Yale Club, after which my plans are entirely uncertain. I am afraid the Historical Association cannot count on a very heavy contribution from me the way I am feeling at present![2] After a winter in England I was staggered when I got home at the prices for everything and the reckless way in which everyone, even the village people here, are buying anything that takes their fancy regardless of price. Apparently the way to live in America now is to pay 10% down, get everything you want, and say "I should worry." But I can unburden my mind on this score when I see you, which I hope will be soon.

I was much interested in your program of work in hand, and will be glad to talk it over with you. It is always a marvel to me how you accomplish what you do and it makes me feel a slow plodder. I have nothing ahead at the moment. My publishers are urging me to go to Boston to talk over some project they have in mind and another house wants me to write a Life of Jefferson but I am not sufficiently settled in life or mind to start in on a work of long breath. When I get this move accomplished, my sister settled somewhere and myself at the Club, I shall sit down and think things out.

I left England the week before the strike, which turned out much as I anticipated it would. I entirely agree with Lippmann as to the character of the English and his feeling about our native land.[3] I am a "good" but thoroughly disgusted American. There will be an anonymous article in the August *Atlantic* on the subject, the authorship of which you will readily guess! I sputtered in a letter to Sedgwick on my return and he asked me to write an informal article.

[1] This prophecy, which Adams made to other men at various times, he later recalled with satisfaction in his acuteness.

[2] The American Historical Association, a body with large ambitions and scanty financial resources, was striving under Albert J. Beveridge and others to raise an endowment fund.

[3] The general strike which began in Great Britain at the beginning of May, 1926, had involved about 3,000,000 workers, and brought to a practical standstill a number of important industries, such as coal mining, building construction, railroads, iron and steel, and the printing trades. Its course, however, was marked with great moderation.

To M. A. De Wolfe Howe

New York, August 2, 1926

I have just returned from a week-end with Nevins and find your note of the 29th, which accounts for my not having replied more promptly.[1] The past two or three years I have been so tied down at Bridgehampton that I have had to refuse all invitations in the summer and now that I am living alone at a club my friends are inviting me in every direction. It is very pleasant but I have been gadding so that I have decided to give up the suggested motor trip. . . . I note, however, that you will be back by the 24th, and if convenient for you I might see you on, say, the 26th. You suggest a varied line of entertainment but, although I should be glad to do anything you wished, my requirements for contentment as a guest are few. Sailing is a somewhat tender subject at the moment for about ten days ago I tried to sail from Philadelphia to New York and was mostly becalmed for two days with the thermometer 116. A pipe and a book on a cool porch offers more to my imagination.

From M. A. De Wolfe Howe

October 10, 1926

Since you have treated me with the confidence of a friend, I have come to feel that I should not be fulfilling my part in the relationship were I to withhold something that came to me as a sort of illumination as I journeyed to and from Newport yesterday. It involves some plain speaking, but I am sure our relation has grown to be such that you will not take it amiss.

What I have seen, in the new light of reflection, is that instead of laying your troubles before a mere friend of the laity, you should have consulted a wise, up-to-date doctor. I am sure he would now be telling you that you have worried yourself into a pathological condition calling for the opinion and advice of a psychologist. You happened to come to me instead of to him, but I believe the advice I have to give you is just as sound as any doctor's — provided only you will think it so.

[1] In this weekend stay Adams talked frankly of his attachment to Kay Seely and his perplexities. Could a man so much older make her happy? Did his limited inome permit the responsibilities of marriage? Would his literary career be benefited or impaired? Should he think first of his duty to his sister and aging father? The answers seemed clear to his friends, who spoke to him in the same terms as those of M. A. De Wolfe Howe in the next letter.

You must shake off the habit of deferring to another member of your family, and make a definite strike for personal happiness before it is too late. No state of mind brings greater unhappiness than the consciousness that one has not had the courage or the independence of thought to follow one's own instincts. — You may remember my saying something of this very sort [to] you in Cotuit. — Even an unhappy marriage of one's own choosing would bring less mental suffering than that of impotent regret. The illumination I have seen tells me, however, that the marriage you have been contemplating would not be unhappy. Accordingly my earnest advice — which I wish you could regard as a psycho-medical prescription — is to stop playing Hamlet at once, stop thinking, stop analyzing, stop wondering and worrying, and marry the girl you care for as soon as she will let you — this very week if possible. My firm conviction is that, acting on this advice, you will never regret the Declaration of Independence I suggested as we walked up the Embankment.

To M. A. De Wolfe Howe

New York, October 12, 1926

I certainly do not take your letter amiss and thank you most deeply for it and for the spirit of friendship which prompted it. I agree with you as to my having got into a pathological mental condition. Much has contributed to that unfortunate end. I could analyze my own case perfectly! That is just the devil of it, analysis, introspection, months of solitude with no companionship or routine work which must be done, the first affair of this sort coming at 47 years of age, many things combined to play the dickens with a mind that was always Hamlet-like, the facts of my sister and I being alone in the world, the great difference in age between the youngster and myself for her sake, the other extra gambles in the case as compared with two who have shared the same sort of life etc., etc. Your prescription is probably the right one. If I could do the thing this moment I would do it but I have learned that there is no trick my nerves and mind cannot play me in it. It is the case of Lincoln without the genius. At any rate nothing can be done this week or perhaps longer as she is on a case. Within the next fortnight, however, I shall either make the jump or clear out. There is no use trying any longer to live alone in one small room and try to do intellectual work. I might dig a trench or do bookkeeping but I cannot write books.

To M. A. De Wolfe Howe

New York, November 1, 1926

It is no use. My mind is sick. I can get nowhere — which the girl realizes — and I am simply stalled. I have got to get away from the pacing of this one small room but cannot decide as yet where to go, alone. This is the loneliest place a man can live, I think. Everyone is so rushed and centered on their own affairs and tied up with all sorts of things that simple companionship is out of the question. I have eliminated my sister from the problem but on other matters my mind goes back and forth like a shuttle and there are inhibitions that hold me as firmly as physical bonds from acting and yet I cannot break my mind away from the thought of the possibility, though even that is now probably too late. She herself is tied for the rest of this month for an operation on her sister, a serious matter.

To M. A. De Wolfe Howe

New York, November 9, 1926

Thanks for your very kind letter. I would love to see you but am so utterly fagged mentally that I am not fit for a guest. I suppose some day some spring will start or break but at present I am just stalled in every way and cannot seem to plan or work or even read. I am doing nothing but a little reviewing, and that, I fear, stupidly. I enclose a note I wrote on your Quincy for the *Sun,* taking double the trifling space they first suggested.[1] It does not amount to anything but then neither do I at the moment. I know that all things pass and that, happy or unhappy, one somehow gets through in time. Forgive the exhibition that I am making at present.

To Allan Nevins

Brooklyn, January 12, 1927

I have read your *Frémont* with a great deal of difficulty because I had to do it in your double column galley proof which I found hard to handle for purposes of review. I wrote about 1300 words on it for the *Herald-Tribune* and I have sent it to Mrs. Van Doren.[2] Harpers are

[1] M. A. De Wolfe Howe had just re-edited in scholarly fashion the volume by Josiah Quincy (1802-82), member of Congress, mayor of Boston, and president of Harvard, *Figures from the Past, from the Leaves of Old Journals.*

[2] Irita Van Doren succeeded Stuart P. Sherman, after his premature death the previous summer, as editor of *Herald-Tribune Books.* The book here mentioned was the first edition of a biography of Frémont published by Harper's, and later in successive editions by other publishers.

to tell her when it can be released. The sewed sheets came today but, of course, too late to use. If the review is not all it should be you will have to make some allowances for the conditions under which it was written. I think it is by all odds the most readable book which you have written yet and you have certainly reached your aim in that. I enclose a carbon copy of my review which you may be interested to see. I think you handle your whole subject extremely well but I confess that I do not like your hero even after you have done everything possible for him.

Thank you for your kind words about my last book. I quite agree with you as to Macmillan and nothing could ever induce me to write for them again. Fortunately, I am very happy with my regular publishers.

My address abroad after January 27th will be as usual, care of Barclay's Bank, 1 Pall Mall, London.

To M. A. De Wolfe Howe

Brooklyn, January 14, 1927

I expect you wonder what has happened to me and I have been meaning for the past ten days to thank you for your Christmas greeting but as it happens I have just been through the crisis of my affairs and have been waiting to write until I could tell you positively of what I was going to do. I can say now that I am going to be married next Tuesday, very quietly in New York.

The move over here did me a lot of good. The furnishing of the apartment, the having to do all my own cooking and housekeeping — which I did purposely — the view of the harbor, and the generally more quiet life over here, all helped to stop the whirling of my brain.[1] By a month ago I was so much better that my sister went to England and I was left free to work things out as fast or slowly as I wanted and as I wanted. The result has been that I have worked them out as I started this letter by saying.

We are going to stay right here in the apartment for two or three weeks and then go to Europe for possibly four or five months. The youngster has never had a chance to see the world and will be wild with delight over everything. After that our plans are uncertain except that I hope to get down to work somewhere and do better work than

[1] The date of Adams's marriage, as already stated, was January 18, 1927. The apartment-furnishing, housekeeping, and cooking had reference to his residence at Brooklyn up to his wedding.

I have yet. I have this apartment until October so we can use it as a base in the summer and perhaps cruise around New England in the car looking for the right place. We both prefer the country and, of course, living there will be cheaper.

Although I fully realize the responsibilities and some of the problems that I am assuming, my condition is entirely normal again and I am facing them with a good deal of interest and am assured that whatever difficulties may come my happiness lies in what I am doing. I was a very sick man, mentally, in September and I know that as the good friend you have proved yourself to be you will be glad to know I have "come back."

To Lawrence Gipson[1]

Brooklyn, January 29, 1927

I trust that you will pardon my delay in replying to your interesting letter with the enclosed outline. It is needless to say that your undertaking appeals to me very much and I would have answered more promptly had I not been busy getting married and now preparing to leave for Europe on the 11th for four or five months.

As you say, your outline will probably be modified from time to time in the course of such a huge undertaking but it seems to me that the subjects noted cover most thoroughly the whole ground. My criticism would be that you are planning a work that will take not one but several lives if carried out with the thoroughness of research throughout that you indicate. I know well from your previous work your capacity for research and for the proper marshalling of facts but I do not see how you can cover all the varied fields you have in mind by yourself. Perhaps you are a much more rapid worker than I.

To M. A. De Wolfe Howe

Brooklyn, February 9, 1927

Kay and I were both rather done up by the time that the event finally took place and we have had an unconventional and extremely busy honeymoon. We were married quite promptly after making the decision so that Kay had everything to get in the way of clothes and so on for the trip. I was also committed to certain reviews, etc., and had much to do to get my business affairs into shape to leave for five months. She very sensibly decided that as we were going to Europe

[1] Then beginning his history of the British Empire in the eighteenth century.

and as we both had so much to do that there was no use putting off the trip abroad by taking time and money for a short trip first, so we came right to my apartment here and have been busy almost every moment since. The dust and smoke of the Harbor front calls for extra care in packing everything here and it has been no small job to get even this small apartment all snug for so long an absence.

I think the decision was a wise one and that life is going to go much better now. We are going to England first because I [get] no accomodation for Italy direct until the middle of March but we shall stay only a fortnight in northern Europe and then head for Italy and perhaps Sicily, coming north again with the early spring and spending a couple of months in England again later. I have this apartment until October 1st and before then hope to have decided where and how we shall live. I do not want to undertake a book until we are settled somewhere and I can get my library out. Meanwhile I have signed on with Allen Johnson for about 40,000 words of lives for the new *Dictionary of Biography,* which is work I can readily do here and which comes in handily as a pot boiler.[1]

To M. A. De Wolfe Howe

Paris, April 25, 1927

It warmed the cockles of my heart to get your letter a couple of days ago, and I only hope we can have the suggested chat and "stock-taking" soon after my return. I have taken passage on the *Mauretania* June 25th due at New York the 30th. I shall be at 2 Grace Court, Brooklyn, thereafter for the summer, for I contracted with Johnson for about 30,000 words of biographies for the *Dictionary* and they must be turned off as soon as practicable.

I have thought of you often but you know how hard it is to settle to correspondence when travelling and living in hotels, a test that even the indefatigable Worthington Ford did not pass last winter, as he told me. Moreover Kay has been far from well and the trip, most happy otherwise, has been punctuated by anxieties on that account. Her own worries before marriage were similar to my own and to those were added three extremely trying cases in her profession so that when the decision was finally reached and action taken she was much run down

[1] The first volume of the *Dictionary of American Biography* was published in 1928. The index for the twenty volumes completed in 1936 shows that he had written ninety-eight biographical essays, including not only colonial leaders but such historians as John Fiske, John Gorham Palfrey, and Francis Parkman.

nervously and physically. The three weeks before sailing were very hectic with all sorts of things to be done and it was an exhausted couple that finally got off on the Olympic. Then as luck would have it she got a very bad attack of ptomaine poisoning from lobster on the trip so that she was laid by the heels for two weeks in Surrey on landing. The total result was that she has had to go very slowly and has had to give up several times on our travels much to her discouragement and disappointment, for she has been very keen to see and learn as much as possible. She is gradually getting stronger and I think will be better when we cross to England again on Saturday. . . .

I have my small apartment on the Heights[1] until October 1st. We are both anxious, within a reasonable time to settle in a small house somewhere. However, I have my doubts if she will be well enough by late summer to face the possibilities of American housekeeping. I cannot write a book until I do get settled and my library out of storage. The summer's work and a fair amount of money to help out is assured by the *Dictionary*. Kay would much like to come over here for another winter to settle and study before settling permanently in America, and in view of her health and of the fact that if I give up my apartment in October I would have no expenses other than hotel bills, it seems rather wise to do so if I can. Once settled, rent and other expenses will be running and I hope work will be more or less continuous and perhaps now would be a good time to see a little more of the world and give her more chance to study. That decision will have to be made during the summer.

Between you and me, I have also just been offered a post in America at $7000 a year which, as it would make me entirely comfortable financially, has its temptations.[2] It would necessitate, however, giving up writing, and I am loath to do that. Kay says she can be perfectly content on what we have and thinks I ought not to sacrifice my independence and to keep on writing, and I shall probably do so. . . .

I was glad to get away from Italy, much as I love it and can tell you some interesting episodes throwing light on the Fascist regime. The method is distinctly terroristic and something is going to blow up some day. When I was in Milan there was a Fascist celebration and 60,000 young men throughout Italy were added to the ranks of the organization. The oath they took was to obey implicitly and without question

[1] Two Grace Court on Brooklyn Heights.
[2] A publishing position which Adams rejected.

any order issued by Il Duce — never a mention of king or country. The Black Shirts are in evidence everywhere, enter all railway carriages with revolvers in their belts and scan you over, sometimes with no little insolence. As to more than that I could give you a good many instances of what has happened to people I know in Florence. As one resident of 25 years told me "never have we been so comfortable, and never so uncomfortable," meaning that the machinery of life runs more smoothly but that there is constant mental anxiety for reasons obvious enough. The tourist sees only the smooth running machinery but when you get beneath that you realize the odd Jacobin-terroristic-nervous atmosphere of the whole place. It was all very interesting.

To Allan Nevins

London, June 19, 1927

I was very glad to get your letter yesterday just as I was leaving for St. Albans altho' I cannot tell you how sorry, from a purely selfish point of view, I am to hear that you are going to abandon New York. Since I left, my oldest friend has sold his house and is going to move away also, and I begin to feel that I am being abandoned to the Armenians.[1] Except to see some of my friends I am dreading going "home" this week and exchanging the peace and quiet and sense of decency here for the conditions in my native city.

As for your plan, I can see the wisdom of it for you and think you did wisely in accepting. You ought to have an exceedingly pleasant scholar's life, with a minimum of anxiety of any sort, and agreeable surroundings, social and other, and, incidentally, I think your children will be much better off than in 112th Street. But I certainly am sorry to lose you!

I also have had lately to consider a position. I will not go into details here but the salary added to what I have would have relieved me from all financial worry and it was a scholar's job. On the other hand I would have had to give up nearly if not all writing of my own, have given much time to the executive aspect of the work and undertaken to learn and direct what would have been professional work of an entirely new sort to me, almost learning a new profession. I am ever so much better — have gained ten pounds.

[1] I had accepted a professorship in Cornell University. Edward Schermerhorn was the oldest friend who was moving away.

To Mrs. Adams[1]

Brooklyn, Sunday, 4 p.m.,
January 1, 1928

Dearest Honey-pet,

I was certainly glad that you were not here last night for there was no chance to sleep until long after twelve. At midnight I think every steam whistle on every boat in the harbor and every factory in the city blew its darndest for fifteen minutes. The din was literally terrific, and, of course banished sleep for sometime afterward. . . . The butcher shop was open so I got a chop and cooked dinner. I also got a small chicken for broiling and had that for dinner today, or at least one-quarter of it. I went out to breakfast for I thought I would rather do that and get coffee. As I have not got the material yet for my final two paragraphs, although letters tell me it is on its way, I have not been writing but just loafing and taking it easy. . . .

I had a review in Saturday's *Sun* and the *Saturday Review* and that pretty nearly cleans up that sort of work for this season, though not quite.

Get all the benefit you can from the country and don't worry about me, though I miss the wife and working-partner both more than you can know.

From Ellery Sedgwick

Boston, January 7, 1928

First, let me say that your paper on Hamilton and Jefferson is a miniature masterpiece.[2] I think it singularly effective. I have another subject which I am very anxious to have you treat. You will see, I think, its importance, and it seems to me that God and New York have given you just the experience to fit you to cope with it.

You and I have talked of the phenomenon of the Stock Market. It is evidently manipulated by persons to whom it is essential that the appearance of prosperity does not fade until the hoary old bugbear of a Democratic administration looms on the horizon. Yesterday the climax was capped by Mr. Coolidge who, over the radio, went beyond his usual length of extolling prosperity by specifically declaring that the enormous expansion of brokers' loans, which earlier in the week had

[1] Adams was working at Two Grace Court; Kay had gone to Southampton to visit her family.

[2] "Jefferson and Hamilton To-day, the Dichotomy in American Thought," *Atlantic Monthly,* April, 1928.

produced a shiver, was simply a healthy manifestation and proof of increasing prosperity. Both Mr. Mellon and Mr. Hoover have given out supporting statements, and we are evidently in for a further rise in the market which will, I suspect, drop about Election Day. . . .[1] Now this whole subject of psychological politics is most interesting.

To M. A. De Wolfe Howe

Nürnberg, March 3, 1928

We had a very rough crossing, and I have not yet been able to account for the ten days which rolled by so swiftly and happily in London. We then crossed the channel to Belgium, a "leprous" place as English slang has it, and next passed to Holland, which is wholly delightful. Why I have avoided it in ten trips to the continent, I cannot imagine. No one can know Dutch art at its best unless he has been to The Hague and Amsterdam and I was swept off my feet by the Rembrandts and Vermeers. Next, as neither my wife nor sister had ever been to Germany, I acted as courier up the Rhine along the same route I took as a youngster in 1900. We pass to Munich tomorrow, and then our plans are uncertain, although we are all moved to return to Holland for a few days about April 1st for the tulips. The first week in April will find us back at the Burlington Hotel in Cork Street, London, and it would be unthinkably jolly if you should be there also. I pray that you do not find your letters by any searching through the post and that your personal presence on the spot will prove essential. Incidentally, I commend the Burlington as very central, quiet, English and not too costly. Worthington Ford's first question when he met there by appointment was, "How did you ever discover this delightful tomb?"

One of our London days went to a motor trip down into Surrey to investigate the possible purchase of "Little Twits" but, whatever I do, I have decided not to buy in England until I have given it a trial, if we do. I find my income tax would be about $1600 and that counting that and an annual trip to America, it would cost me about as much in England as at home. Clarence Brigham has written me many details of living costs and conditions at Worcester and I shall run up there to look about after my return in May. I would very much like to have a few years in England but do not know whether I could afford it, for

[1] An error; reference to the press shows no unusual drop in price. Stocks continued rising in November despite much profit-taking, trading was suspended for a time on November 23 because of the rush of business, and seats on the Stock Exchange this month sold at the high figures of $575,000 and $580,000.

a good part of my American income would be lost there. For example, this year, although I missed the spring reviewing I made about $700 at that, about $1500 on the D.A.B. and more on other odds and ends. I would like to drop much of that and do considered articles and books but begin to question a little if I could keep sufficiently in touch with American life to write articles in sufficient quantity if my English expenses should equal my American. At any rate I am nearing a decision and this summer will settle the matter, one way or the other, as I had planned. The income tax and the annual, or even biennial trip, to America are the stumbling blocks.

My article in *Harper's* has brought me more letters than any other I have written, not excepting "Home." By the way, I have an interesting echo from my *Atlantic* article "Home Thoughts" in a long letter from an Englishman in New Zealand, who incloses three editorials from the Wellington *Evening Post* speaking of that article and my other work in highly laudatory terms. I had no idea that the *Atlantic* nor my own more modest fame travelled so far.

From Ellery Sedgwick

Boston, April 24, 1928

Your case went to the jury this morning, and I can assure you that no life was ever more carefully considered. We talked your projects over fore and aft, and it was our unanimous opinion that the next solid work for you to attempt would be a biography of Daniel Webster. There is no doubt that the public is waiting for a full-length portrait of the man who, though not as majestic as he looked, has never been described as he really was. We have taken into consideration the desirability of taking up work that does not involve at the outset excessive reading, and if you cable me a favorable word, I can ship to you a small traveling library of Websteriana, including the Works and Letters and one or two scarce biographies.

It so happens that Little, Brown and Company in their early days rather specialized in Webster, and they are as keen as we are to get out a substantial one-volume Life. Of course, Jefferson was a more interesting and a more remarkable man, but there have been many lives of Jefferson, and Webster's career leaves a blank in American letters painful for a publisher to note.

We none of us have any doubt whatsoever of the success of this enterprise. Sold at five dollars, it would be the biography of the year, and there would be money in it.

To M. A. De Wolfe Howe

London, May [?], 1928

I shall soon be in New York again — we sail May 16th — and I confess I dread it. The early part of the week we were down at Cambridge and in the warm sunshine the peace and beauty of the backs seemed more perfect than ever. We saw Ely as it should be seen, — on a grey, lowering day which makes the old tower more hoary by several centuries than does bright sunshine, — just as I have learned by repeated visits that Chartres should be seen in the rain, or, as I have never seen it, by starlight, to get the full beauty of the glass. The last suggestion, starlight, was made to me last week by an acquaintance of yours and a friend of your brother Wallace, Stewart Campbell, with whom we spent last week-end.[1] He has leased for 21 years an old 15th century house at Shere in Surrey, a gem of a place. It is the old tavern where the pilgrims stopped on their way from Winchester to Canterbury 500 years ago, and the old "pub" room, which they use as a dining room, has a splendid old fireplace and a ravishing flagged stone floor, and with their old furniture, lit by candles, it is a room to dream dreams in. He has about an acre of ground, forming a secluded garden back of the house, and, between ourselves, for all this he pays $400 (not £) a year! He is very anxious that I should take another old house there, including the old jail (!) which dates from the 13th century and which may come into the market. It is a charming village, recently voted the most beautiful in England, all owned by the Duke of Northumberland who will allow no modern buildings.

However, next week we are going up into North-Hants to visit the rector of Charwelton and have a look at the old Adams house from which my ancestor went to Virginia in 1658, and which is just now to be let. It is not certain but is rather an interesting story. We had a ring in our family which was always worn by the head male in it since long before the revolution (when arms were protected legally) with the arms of the family on it. Three generations ago, when the Spanish government wished to make my grandfather a hidalgo and grant him arms, he told them he only wished for a confirmation of the arms on the ring and which had come down in the family. The government did so and I have that grant with the signatures of the queen, prime-minister etc. I had a long session yesterday with the Windsor Herald at the Herald's College and these arms are identical with those of the

[1] Charles Stewart Campbell, C.B.E., a graduate of Cambridge and retired lieutenant-colonel.

the Adams's who held the Manor of Charwelton. He got out old manuscript pedigrees, one of 1680 and one earlier, which show that at the time my first ancestor Francis Adams appeared in Virginia there were two Francis Adams's of the Charwelton family, cousins, of whom nothing is known after boyhood. Would it not be odd if I, who am the last male in the direct line for nine generations should go back to the exact spot from which the family came 370 years ago, after the family had lived in America, Austria, Cuba, Venezuela, and America again for all the intervening time? It is also odd that, although I have never believed and do not now (our arms are different, I think) that my family had the slightest connection with the "Braintree Adams's (John, John Quincy etc) that I find their ancestors lived within ten miles of Charwelton. The places are just on the borders of Warwickshire.

The days here in London slip by with marvellous contentment and speed. It is all so sane that I can hardly believe that in three weeks I shall be headed for home where, I see, Billy Phelps has been having Gene Tunney lecture at Yale on Shakespeare! And where I shall have to get into a welter of book-reviewing, articles, etc., to pay bills. I got Sedgwick's rather surprising cable about my doing Daniel Webster but will wait to write you about that until I get the letter which doubtless is following the brief cable.

To M. A. De Wolfe Howe

Brooklyn, May 27, 1928

We had a delightful last three weeks in England and I think I wrote you of part of it. Briefly, we made a pilgrimage to Church Charwelton, the home of my ancestors, and were charmingly entertained by Sir Charles and Lady Knightley, now the owners of the property though they live in their own rather noted manor house at Fawsley. From there we motored through the Warwickshire country, through Gloucestershire to Gloucester, and back to London by rail. There we found an invitation from the Archbishop to Canterbury to go to Lambeth Palace and have tea with his wife and see the whole place, which we did. We stayed in town just long enough for that and then went to Lynton, in North Devon, and motored thence all along the coast — Clovelly, Tintagel, etc. — to Land's End, and back through southern Cornwall to Torquay to stay with my family there. I know Devon better than any countryside in America, except east Long Island, but it grows more beautiful to me every year. This time it was simply indescribable, acres and acres of the wonderful beech forests being literally carpetted solidly with blue-bells, such a blue-bell spring as comes but once in a generation even in England.

And now I am "home" and must quickly get to work. I was exceedingly sorry to learn of your giving up your connection with the *Atlantic Monthly,* though I can understand your desire to be free from bothersome detail. Nevertheless, it leaves me a little feeling at loose end. Can you tell me to whom I should write now about projects in general or details in particular. I have, of course, met McIntyre and Jenkins but have no personal relations with them as yet. I always have the feeling that Sedgwick works at such high pressure and is so busy that he should not be bothered except in the most important matters and then by as brief notes as possible. Candidly, between ourselves, I think that, like most Americans, he is so rushed that he does not always take in what his correspondent is driving at. If you will recall my letter to you, I expressly said that I would have to do some back work, editorial or other, this summer which would bring me in immediate money, to pay for my trip and also the expense of moving and settling this fall. Also that until settled I could not begin a long sustained book. To my surprise I got a cable asking me to write a life of Webster. On April 24th he wrote me enthusiastically about that project, stating that he thought it would be profitable but that he had not had time to calculate at all the possible returns.

From Alfred R. McIntyre

Boston, June 19, 1928

I talked to Mr. Sedgwick this morning about the book on the Adams family, and he thoroughly approved of your plan for it as outlined to me last Friday. He is just as enthusiastic, I think, as I am with regard to the book and we both hope you will decide soon to go ahead with it. When you are ready let me know and I will send contracts for your signature, and as Mr. Howe told you, we will then make an advance payment on account of royalties.

As a matter of record, I am setting down here that we have not the slightest objection to your editing for Boni and Liveright the diaries of John Quincy Adams.

To M. A. De Wolfe Howe

Brooklyn, June 21, 1928

After much consultation the die is cast and we are all three going to England in December for about two years, as residents not tourists for that time. I shall leave my library and things here in shape to be forwarded on receipt of cable as soon as I have found a house and hope there will not be much delay. I do not intend to remain permanently, for business and other reasons. As I work it out, the financial strain will be greater, not less, there than here, for with the income tax living costs just about the same, and there we shall want to travel and must come home every two years or so whereas if living here we do not have to go to Europe unless we wish. On the other hand, once settled I want to be settled for life and think this would be an extremely interesting experience for all of us before settling down for good and all in a small American city. I think Worcester, as such places go, unusually attractive, especially up on the new hill section. Mr. Washburn was delightful and the American Antiquarian an ideal place for me to work in. The temptation is great to go there at once and dig in. However, as you know, the cultural atmosphere of any small American place is pretty thin and not very stimulating unless one can bring to it stored memories and a mind trained and broadened elsewhere. My sister wants to go over. For my wife, two years of residence in England with trips to the continent will be a college education and much else thrown in. For myself, I shall have the chance to study England and the English as I have not yet, even with all my visits as a tourist. I shall fill out my knowledge of the continent with Spain, Norway, and other countries not yet visited, and when I come back it will be with a much better background than I have now, and, perhaps, cured of the desire to live there! Now that we have decided even on two years, I have many qualms already when I think of the nuisance of the move, the distance from all my investment affairs, from editors and publishers (who, after all, are excellent fellows!) and the rest of what is involved. So far from regarding it as a prelude to living there I look at it now as the Japanese looks at his few years in America or Europe.

To M. A. De Wolfe Howe

Brooklyn, August 5, 1928

This is just to let you know that I think I am at last on the road to real recovery. I would say it unqualifiedly but for the fact that my leg, as the surgeons said, did not go at all according to the books, and after a date had been set for my leaving the hospital I had to have two more operations. However I *am* home now, with all my leg, and the incisions all healed and no signs of more infections. (Tap wood!)

I am also getting my strength back. The fever took it pretty well out of me (as high as 105 and for many days close to 104). I sincerely hope that the episode, which has taken a lot out of my wife and myself in this hot summer, cost me over $1000, and broken all my plans of work, is now in sight of a happy end. I shall therefore suspend medical bulletins.

I am at work again on a moderate scale. Before October 1st I am supposed to condense old J. Q's Diary of twelve volumes into one, write an introduction and have it ready for the press; also to write a 10,000 word article on Colonial Life in America for an English concern and have it in London by October 15th. Those are the two most pressing things. Next come 26 lives for Johnson; an article for *Harpers;* two or more for Sedgwick; and the accumulation of all the data and printed material needful for the Adams book for you. Next comes the settlement of all my and my sister's business affairs before sailing; the finding of houses if possible in England; the transfer of all my household effects and the settling down to writing over there. Incidentally I have to put everything here into storage temporarily when I close my apartment next month. I shall be jolly glad when all is over and I can seat myself once more among all the Lares and Penates which I have not seen in two years and more.

As soon as possible I shall finish the Diary and English article — I hope by early October. (I shall also have to do a lot of reviewing to pay for my leg.) Then I think I shall run over to Boston to talk to Ford and get what I can there for the Adams book. Probably I shall also have to go to Washington on it and might as well write the lives there. Who is there of the Adams's now? I know nothing of the personal lives of Brooks and C. F. (The last is also dead, is he not?) My idea to make the book rather philosophical than biographical — to throw the four generations of John, J. Q., C. F. and the three of my day, against the background of changing America, but shall have to have somewhat more than I now have as to Brooks and the last C. F. So un-Bostonian am I that I am utterly ignorant of the activities and personality of the last C. F. (brother of Henry.) Did George, son of J. Q. ever do anything? I have the impression, perhaps from ignorance, that C. F. ult. compromised with current life rather more than Henry and Brooks but will call for much less consideration than his brothers. . . .

I think as I mean to treat the subject it will be a very entertaining book to write, tracing the line of development of family mentality and character from its start and the line of development of the national social life and outlook from *its* start, the two gradually diverging from a primary coincidence to where they become poles apart. As you see, I intend to deal with thought and tendencies much more than with biographical detail. As my literary counsellor not my publisher may I ask whether you do not think this is the way to do it? As I sit here with the thermometer at 90, the humidity Heaven knows what, praying for a thunder storm I wish I could talk these matters out with you today on your charming porch at Cotuit. (That is not a baited hook for I cannot leave town for many weeks yet.)

From M. A. De Wolfe Howe

August 23, 1928

Charles Francis Adams, the brother of Henry and Brooks, died some eight or ten years ago. He was president of the Massachusetts Historical Society and much besides both in letters and in affairs. Characteristically saying that he did not want "the awkward squad" firing over his grave, he forestalled the usual Historical Society memoir by writing the extensive *Autobiography of Charles Francis Adams.* . . . The present Charles Francis Adams, his nephew, a son of a younger John Quincy Adams, is the treasurer of Harvard College and a famous yachtsman. The living Charles Adams is a man of very uncommon capacity.

To Allan Nevins

London, January 2, 1929

I am becoming less and less inclined to consider Wesleyan, between ourselves. For a good many years now I have been used to a multiplicity of interesting international contacts, and have moved easily between New York, Washington, Paris and London, to say nothing of travel in many countries. I am afraid a small town on a branch line four hours from New York would seem very cramped, and, what with the rail fare and a hotel for the night, it would cost us about $50 every time we went to town for anything, which, having tried that sort of life at Bridgehampton, I know would mean that we would not go and would feel rather imprisoned. $3500 is welcome but as taxes for me would be about $500 more in Connecticut than New York (owing to the tax laws and the form of my property) it would really be about $3000, which is the price of six magazine articles. Light and informal as the work would seem to you, it would be so utterly new to me that, with my nervousness and conscientiousness, it would take far more of my time than of yours in a similar position, and be more of a strain. For a year or two at any rate, while it was strange to me, it would, I am sure, reduce my working time and energy considerably for my writing. . . .

I realize all you say about the permanent expatriate and know the dangers are great. I am not contemplating that but only two or three years more until my wife gets strong. I have learned there is no use planning too many years ahead. As for myself, of course, I may live to be ninety but the fact that my mother's two brothers died of heart disease without warning at 50 and 51, and four of my father's did the same at about ten years older warns me against planning for a long old age. Quite apart from that, perhaps fantastic thought, I am now 51 and I doubt if wherever I was I should settle down to a magnum opus. My New England trilogy took me six years of incessant work, doing nothing else. . . .

What you say about America as my subject is also true but to some extent I may get away from that, although in part only. That is one of the points that worries me about living over here even for a few years more. On the other hand, there are two things to be said. One is, that with annual visits home I could keep in touch more or less and one does see the scene in some ways better from here than at home, — the annual contrast enables one to gauge the changes better. The second thing is that my mind has been steadily enlarging, and, without meaning to "talk big" I now look at the world whereas I used to look at the U.S.A., just as my books show a steady progression from the history of my village, then the history of the township in which it was, then the history of a section, then the history of the whole seaboard, then a criticism of the whole country. What I am wondering is whether, living on both sides of the water I might not better be able to disentangle the purely American tendencies from world tendencies, and while still writing to some extent on the former do so with an understanding of the latter. . . .

I am relieved to hear that you have left the *World* and are really going to have a free summer. Do not let anything interfere with it! Even if we decide to come back here for a while longer we shall be in America some months. There is lots to do there in connection with starting my books through the press and I want to get thoroughly in touch with America again. We would probably stay until the 15th of August, when winter rates on the steamers go into effect again. At first I shall have to be in New York, and go to Washington and Boston.

To M. A. De Wolfe Howe

London, January 26 [1929]

Congratulations on having reached the proof stage of your *Rhodes.*[1] Would I had got that far with the Adamses! . . . Your suggested covered wagon trip across the continent appals me, even though the wagon have a motor in it. I hug my fire closer here as I think of those two thousand level miles of that vast midwest that you will have to spin your mileage over. I have done it four times and dread the thought of it even in a railroad train. Why, oh why, do you consider that when you might be sitting comfortably in London with good old ale, the wonderful exhibition of Dutch art at Burlington House and all sorts of good and pleasant and civilized things beside? But your letter sounds a hopeful note as to the eventual possibility of that also.

We have been house-hunting at Epsom and elsewhere but have come to no decision except that we shall probably decide upon a flat in town instead for a trial year if we remain. The rent of a house includes only the landlord's interest on his money — all else, taxes, insurance, upkeep, etc., are usually paid by the lessee, which adds about 50% to the rent. When I come squarely up against that, the problem of starting housekeeping in the country etc., the uncertainties, financial and otherwise until we have learned our way about a bit more, seem too great, as I want this year to be less troubled by financial matters. The rent of a furnished flat includes everything. One knows where one is as to expense, and in a service flat one has only to buy food for their cooking. On the whole that would seem wiser. One object of being here is rest and the opportunity, both for my wife and myself, to study and travel. A flat has the further advantage of being shut-up-able at any moment without bother and would much facilitate trips. We shall investigate that phase of living, therefore, this week, and I shall try to content myself with going yet another year without my Lares and Penates. My books, on account of the Adams book, I must have, and they hang on my shoulders like the old man of the sea. What to do with 4000 of them in a furnished flat? I have arranged with the Customs authorities for their entry but have no place to put them! Were it not for the Adams book I would not bother with them for the first year until we decided what we would do permanently but simply study, travel, edit the Henry Adams and write articles, but I am bound to the other and the undertaking being so wide in scope requires a whole library.

[1] Howe published his life of Rhodes in 1929.

We are not looking beyond the year as yet. We both like it here and the atmosphere is assuredly far more inducive to study and culture than is that at home. The last few evenings I have been reading Horace's odes and Goethe's Faust with the same inevitability that I do the stock market at home, and Kay, in spite of her not being particularly fit, has read three books on Dutch art, Strachey's *Elizabeth* and been three times to the Dutch exhibition with the same inevitability. Being a bit tired the other day we decided to refresh our minds with some of the Italians at the National Gallery, and, if you will forgive my saying so, it was, after the Boston Fine Arts, like a glass of fine old tawny port after dandelion home-brew. Of course, for some years now I have annually been having the very best in the world, and at home one has to starve for it.

From Albert Boni

New York, February 15, 1929

I regret having had to delay so long giving you any word on the Henry Adams matter, but shortly after I cabled you the advice from Ford regarding the Massachusetts Historical Society decision, I had a call from Mr. Greenslet of Houghton Mifflin, who, while expressing his chagrin that they had not thought of it first, stated that they had no desire to be obstructive in the matter, and asked whether we would agree to a 15% royalty on the books which they hold. This of course I assented to, whereupon he informed me that they were still awaiting the decision of the Institute of American Architects, and just so soon as they had definite word from them he would confirm the whole arrangement.

The first word I had was the letter of February 6th — copy of which I am enclosing. I also send with it copy of my reply to it, and a letter I wrote Mr. Ford which will give you my impression of their behavior.

I went up to Boston three days ago to see what could be accomplished in conference. The upshot of my talk with Greenslet and Scaife — both of Houghton Mifflin — was first: that they revealed quite conclusively that they had been lying in their presentation of the situation to me with the object of prying us loose from the idea. Among other things, they claimed that the consent of the Massachusetts Historical Society had been secured only with difficulty and "much hemming and hawing." Second: I refused absolutely to consider turning over the plan to them. Third: they agreed to reconsider the whole matter on the basis of our proceeding with our edition and then making an arrangement with them for another edition to be sold by subscription. I am under the impression that no definite decision will be made by them until after Mr. Greenslet has had the opportunity of seeing you in England. He tells me that he is sailing on February 23rd.

Worthington C. Ford was splendidly indignant and was all for bringing pressure immediately to force their hand. I thought it the better policy to endeavor to further isolate them completely; and the copies of the letters which Ford has written to Mrs. LaFarge, Mr. Cram, and Francis Adams will show you what we are attempting to accomplish.

To Allan Nevins

London, February 17, 1929

I have thought of you often since leaving home and been wondering when we should expect you over here.

Time flows gently but with immense swiftness here and it is hard to realize we have been in London five weeks. Were it not for the extraordinarily cold weather we should be in our flat by now, and, as it is, hope to get in this week. After discovering some of the complexities (for our particular and private case) of taking a house for a year only, we determined on a furnished flat and have found one in which we can camp out comfortably enough for our trial period of England. As I know you are interested in wages and cost of living here I will tell you what we have. The house is a handsome former private residence at 11 Palace Court, Bayswater, a few hundred feet from Kensington Gardens. It is run by an Irish lady whose house in Dublin was blown up and who lost £30,000 in the Revolution, and the other tenants are all agreeable people. We have the whole 3d floor (they call it 2d here); a drawing room about 22 x 22, a large bedroom and small study. For this, with full maid service, we pay $34 a week. Our meals, when desired are served in our rooms at 65c, 75c, and $1.00 for breakfast, lunch, and dinner. I have sent for my books and shall install about a third of them in the flat. We are about five minutes from the Marble Arch and fifteen from Trafalgar Square.

We had planned to go to the continent next week but shall not unless the weather moderates considerably. A letter today from a friend in Florence tells of two feet of snow there, frigid hotels, frozen plumbing, and a flight of tourists as trains permit. Tomorrow my sister and an English cousin start for Spain, the only corner of Europe untouched by the "great frost." As soon as my books come I shall get started on the Adamses and editing Henry. Houghton Mifflin have made difficulties about the latter but I hope they will soon be straightened out.

From Ellery Sedgwick

Boston, February 20, 1929

We are transfigured and transposed. From your letter to Weeks, you are consuming your restless energy rushing up and down, in and out of elevators, with a flying word or two to every friend you meet and a flashing glance at Van Eyck and Teniers, while I sit quietly and leisurely at my desk, a quaint monument to timelessness. So much by way of leisurely approach.

Now I will fall in with your humor and dash to the point. Matthew Arnold nowadays strikes me as an exceedingly good subject, but, Lord I don't have to read *Culture and Anarchy* again to remember him. Those essays were my staff of life forty years ago. As a boy, Mr. Arnold came to Stockbridge and we saw a good deal of him. Only last week there tumbled out of my bureau drawer a funny oldfashioned photograph of the Arnold family sitting in a garden in Victorian poses, but I could identify all the characters with ease. The point of the paper would be, of course, not to remind readers of what Arnold used to be, but to show how America and indeed the world has turned the way he would not have us go — how Hebraism has conquered Hellenism, and how Sweetness and Light can no longer be understood without reference to Schrafft's and Mazda. I think you could throw the old plea for sanity and soundness against the crazy quilt background of the modern world with effectiveness. At any rate, I'd rather bet on that paper than on a more generalized Victorian one.

From Worthington C. Ford

Boston, March 18, 1929

As to Mr. Boni, I am with him entirely, and think that H. M. Co. are engaged in a little trickery of which I cannot approve. In fact, it has so much disgusted me that I have made no contract for the letters of Henry Adams, and I do not intend to. . . . Mr. Boni sailed last week and says that he expects to see Mr. Greenslet in London, and if an arrangement is reached he will cable. All that I shall be glad to know, for it might decide me in my action on the letters. When I consider that I sail July 27th the things that are still to be done rather appal me, and the days are flashing by too rapidly to leave me with any sense of comfort.

To M. A. De Wolfe Howe

11 Palace Court,
London, March 18, 1929

We are back from Paris and this afternoon Kay (my wife) and I had tea with Lady Bryce (the widow of the ambassador). . . .

Yesterday I had a long talk with Ferris Greenslet who always stays at Garlands. Houghton, Mifflin & Co. have acted very meanly in trying to block the Henry Adams in order that they should publish it themselves but after two months negotiations in America I finally won out here yesterday and Boni is to have it though H. M. may have the rights to a limited subscription edition. . . .

We are comfortably settled here until next Feb. 16th according to my lease, and after that our plans are undecided. Although we both much prefer the life here to that in the States I suppose we shall go back for other reasons. Death and old age are problems for the déracinés, and there is the further one of writing for the American market on American topics from here if one stays too long. If we stay a year and a half or a couple of years we shall have had an interesting experience, have learned a lot, and be able to make our final decision with a full knowledge of both sides of the question and ocean. What do you know about Wesleyan University at Middletown, Connecticut? Confidentially, I have had a suggestion from there that rather interests me if I decide to live at home. It is intimated to me by the president that they would like to have me come there and live much on the same basis as Robert Frost the poet lives at Amherst. I would be a member of the faculty, paid, of course, but have no regular teaching to do. Certain selected honor students would come to my study in my own house and discuss their problems in American history with me. There would be no classes, lectures, examinations, papers, etc. only five or six boys talking informally around my own fireside. I would have ample time for writing all the year and three or four months completely free. . . .

Greenslet told me that just before he sailed he personally handed to Mrs. Beveridge the check for her royalties for Lincoln for six months and that it was the largest single royalty check they had ever given out — $51,000! You might know it would go to a person who did not need it!

From Worthington C. Ford

Boston, April 6, 1929

As to the position you suggest, Frost enjoyed his stay in Michigan very much so far as association and sphere of action were concerned. He took a house a little outside of the town and somewhat inaccessible so that it acted as a sort of sieve preventing his being overwhelmed by a crowd, as it involved a little cost of time to see him. Still he was quite enthusiastic about it when I met him there. A year after he resigned because he thought the field was not one that excited his poetic capabilities and he wished to return to his New England home. This he did, and has published one volume since. I do not think that in history you would meet with the same difficulty. You have not only facility in writing but also the ability to get subjects before you; and they could be accomplished just as well from a place a little remote from civilization and yet near enough to keep you in touch with your best interests, meaning by your best interests those on which your living depends. I have more than once raised the question as to your future in England. I do not think you would ever have the position there that you have already gained here, and certainly contact with English publishers would not result in encouragements such as you could have with American publishers. A man is rarely free to live where he wishes, or even to engage in the kind of work that he wishes, unless he approaches independence. I have always been controlled by the bread and butter question, and on the whole it has worked out pretty well.

London, the Adams Family, and the Year of the Crash

Adams felt happy to be in England as the so-called Coolidge-Hoover Bull Market brought stock market prices rising rapidly from the spring of 1928 until they broke catastrophically in October of 1929. With his experience of New York finance he did not like the excessive investment in industrial plants, the excessive production of goods, and the excessive profits in the favored parts of an uneven economy. Still less did he like the atmosphere of hurry, standardization, and extravagance in the United States. In his magazine articles he sounded much the same satiric note that Sinclair Lewis sounded in *Main Street* and Sherwood Anderson, H. L. Mencken, and Ellen Glasgow in their stories and essays. It pleased him to celebrate the older American virtues in his portrayal of the Adamses in their long and elevated line. In these productive years he kept in touch with his country through magazine editors, book publishers, and a select number of friends.

George P. Brett to Henry Osborn Taylor[1]

New York, April 29, 1929

I don't know personally James Truslow Adams who, I see, has just been taking a crack at us in the *Saturday Review of Literature* in the following words: "Recently one of the most eminent publishing houses in New York insisted on paying its authors a beggarly $1,000 each for an important series of 100,000-word volumes."

I confess *mea culpa* that $1,000 is very little to pay for the work that went into these volumes, but at the same time if we had to pay more we probably should not have paid anything. You understand what I mean by that because the enterprise would then have become so costly that we could not have afforded it at all. As it is each of the volumes published in the series so far shows a very heavy deficit, with little or no probability that the books will ever show a profit.

James C. McConaughy to James Truslow Adams and Henry S. Canby[2]

Middletown, Conn., May 8, 1929

I hope Mr. Canby had in mind the one feature of college teaching which absolutely differentiates it from any other profession and which I feel is one of the biggest handicaps to adequate compenstaion for superior service, namely, permanency of tenure. With the possible exception of state and federal judges, I know of no other profession where a man continues to hold his job and salary, usually until seventy, quite irrespective of whether he loafs or not. If teachers want to demand proper compensation, should they not place themselves somewhat on the plane that every other professional and working man does? — i.e., pay while one is worth it, and not if one's worth vanishes. This would destroy some smug academic security. It would be a sad blow to the quite numerous incompetents in the academic world, many of whom are now being paid more than they are worth, from the crude market standpoint. It would, however, show those who must finance better teachers' salaries that the recipients of their gifts were willing to demand higher pay only when they were worth it. Isn't this type of

[1] Brett, head of the Macmillan Company, commented upon the *History of American Life* to which Adams had contributed a volume.

[2] In this letter President McConaughy of Wesleyan comments upon a discussion between Adams and Henry Seidel Canby, editor of the *Saturday Review of Literature,* upon academic compensation and the conditions of university education.

action the most immediate thing for the American intellectualist to do, if, as Mr. Canby urges, they are "in order to avoid becoming a servant class, to risk job and even profession in the attempt?"

Mr. Arnett, past President of the American Association of Colleges, who knows about as much about college salaries as anyone, urged this in my hearing at the recent meeting of the Association, but I have grave doubts whether college teachers, except in very isolated places, are going to be willing to give up this proud academic privilege. I fear they want these higher salaries — which most of them should have — and also the smug security of permanent tenure. Certainly, the Yale professors, in their recent report, so demanded (page 87, on permanency of tenure): "to abolish permanency of tenure would be to reduce the University's faculties entirely and completely to the status of employees." I vigorously dissent: I think, as is true of every other profession, a good man will always find a real opportunity; with the American Association of University Professors so active, the chances for unjust treatment by arbitrary boards of trustees are greatly minimized; but I am willing to wager any amount that 99% of college teachers will say "Amen" to their Yale colleagues, and in the same voice demand the larger salaries, — in the Yale case amounting to $15,000 or $16,000 a year.

Mr. Adams' most interesting comparison of the results of modern industry on the teachers' situation points to the deadening result of mass consumption and group conformity. One of the results of this is that teachers seem to wish to be treated by groups, in classes, instead of allowing an unusual man to be paid an unusual salary, and a mediocre man to be paid a mediocre salary, or perhaps lose his position. The Yale professors demand, on page 86: a salary scale based on rank and length of tenure, with "the salary to be determined by the position, not by the individual." I think this a beautiful illustration of the result of mass production and conformity in the academic world. What other profession in the world, (except, barely possibly, the bench, which is really in a different category), would have the effrontery to say this? Yet, college professors, with the timidity which Mr. Canby denounces, urge that they be treated as a group, with little or no recognition of individual differences and superiorities. I doubt whether we can get men of wealth to finance $8,000 at Wesleyan, and $15,000 at Yale, on salaries, if they are dealing with the mass.

College teachers bemoan the apparent evidence of business practice in academic matters. They want to keep their jobs almost for life, (and they are very unhappy, and sometimes vituperative, if they are asked to retire before seventy, even when the college's welfare demands this action by the trustees); they want to be treated as a group instead of as individuals (when obviously some are "worth" twice as much as others ever can be); they urge salaries to put their incomes on a comparison with those of young bankers, lawyers, and other business men.

From Ellery Sedgwick

Boston, May 18, 1929

A week in London is like a day in Rome. It is physically impossible to accomplish anything. Your note reached me at the Burlington Hotel, but not until I had achieved the quiet of the steamer was I able to read your piece.[1] I agree with it profoundly. I was a sophomore, I think, when first I fell under Arnold's spell. As a boy I had known him during his summer in Stockbridge, Massachusetts, and his daughter has been a friend of my family since I can recall. But I was twenty when the full realization of what *Sweetness and Light* might mean came flooding over me. After that, the pregnant phrases with which his essays are strewn grew to be aphorisms in my daily life. And almost more than his prose, his poetry in those years seemed to express my waking thoughts. *The Dissidence of Dissent,* the Protestation of the Protestant Religion and all the rest of it became automatic press-buttons in my consciousness, and as I look back I have no doubt my native scepticism was reinforced and perhaps given its final cast by Arnold's point of view.

I say all this because it will make you understand with what vivid interest I turned your pages. So closely indeed I followed your argument that at first I was unconscious of what I believe are several extravagances of statement to which my attention is now drawn by my young associates educated in a very different school. Of course, it isn't literally fair to compare the great Daniel's thoughts born of job trot, with our own Judge Webster's lucubrations at a rhythm of forty miles an hour. One or two of these statements there are which would lay you open to reply. Would you care to have any slight alterations made?

From George P. Brett

New York, June 5, 1929

Certainly up to this time the enterprise as a whole, aside from our pride in the individual volumes, has not been one to afford us very

[1] A reconsideration of Matthew Arnold written for the *Atlantic.*

much satisfaction. The facts do not, however, I think, bear out the suggestion that the total charges which the individual books bear is either inadequate or ungenerous.

While we had long had in mind the preparation of a large American history from the social point of view, somewhat perhaps after the style of the Cambridge History Series, this enterprise came to us in the first instance as a conception of the editors who planned the whole thing and to whom we were in the first instance responsible. Our own position and our freedom to determine the return to editors and authors was, therefore, somewhat more circumscribed than would have been the case had we ourselves initiated the program. The editors were quite unwilling to go on with their plans except on a royalty arrangement, which, since there are four editors, had to be sufficient to give each of them an appreciable return.[1] Furthermore, since the main sale anticipated was a college sale, the price per volume had to be moderate. Each book, therefore, had to carry a royalty to the editors and a payment to the author.

While it is perfectly true, therefore, that a cash payment of $1000 to the author of each volume might in itself seem small, particularly in your own case, when it is combined with the royalty payment to the editors, the aggregate would compare very favorably with the amount paid by any publishing house in the country, and indeed, more than favorably with that paid on a great many books of this type. It is, in fact, quite all the books could stand with any appreciable of ultimate commercial success.

From Worthington C. Ford

Boston, June 18, 1929

There is no objection to saying that both prefaces in the *Education* were written by Henry Adams. The book was actually printed in 1906, but I find that he was distributing it in January, 1907. I should therefore take 1907 as the proper date. The distinction between "printed" and "published" is one that few would raise.

Henry Adams was assistant professor of history in Harvard University, 1870 to 1877. That is sufficient. My recollection is that he declined the LL.D.— certainly it did not come from Harvard. Looking at the Harvard Quinquennial I find that it was conferred by Western Reserve, Ohio, 1892. That means that it was through his friend

[1] The four editors were Fox, Schlesinger, Carl Becker, and Ashley Thorndike of Columbia, but the two latter held a consultant position.

Charles F. Thwing, President of the University and a member of the class in Harvard of 1876. It is possible, therefore, that he may have been a pupil of Henry Adams.

To Wilbur Cross

London, June 26, 1929

As to an article on [Henry] Adams for the [Yale] *Review,* I hardly know what to say just at the moment and would like to think it over. I had intended at first to make my Introduction rather a critical study but later decided, in view of the fact that there is no biography of Adams and not likely to be (though I have been asked to write one), to make the Introduction rather biographical in form. A careful study of the *Education* shows me that in quite a few cases Adams jumbled the sequence of events and in some cases even gives as determining motives events which did not occur until several years after the points at which he placed them. Of course twenty years are left out entirely. Allen Johnson's account in the *D.A.B.,* is of necessity brief, and in some respects inadequate as biography. As the Introduction stands now in its rough first draft, it is thus a 23,000 word biography, touching only briefly on the mind of Adams which I leave to speak for itself in the Works, although, of course, I indicate and discuss briefly the nature of each of his writings as they appear in chronological order. It may be that I shall decide to expand this part, or even, possibly append a short critical essay to the biography. I am going to read it over today with a fresh mind after having left it for a fortnight, and decide. As it stands now, it is a closely knit narrative and it would be difficult to lift any section out for a separate article for the *Review.*

In addition to this difficulty, as I may have told you, I am at work on a history of the four generations of the Adams family — John, J. Q., C. F. 1st, and Henry, Brooks, C. F. 2d and J. Q. 2d, which is neither history nor biography, but a sort of combination. In that I shall have to treat Henry again. I hope to finish this before the end of the year and think if I did anything for you, that probably an entirely new article from some aspect would be best. Henry had hold of an important idea in his trying to link up history with scientific thought. As it happened, however, he took as his basis the physical thought of about 1900, just the moment more or less at which physics was to begin to alter most radically. What he would have done with Einstein, Bohr, Whitehead, and the whole of the new physics of the past decade is a very interesting problem. I think that this new physics means that science is entering upon a wholly new stage metaphysically, and bears out most interestingly Adams's prophecy that about this time thought would enter upon a new phase. In fact many of his prophecies were rather remarkable; for instance, the one he made about Europe's being attacked in its thought and values by probable changes at the two peripheries of Russia and America, on which today, nearly twenty years after, a whole literature has sprung up in France. Perhaps, if it did not prove to overlap my other two things on him, a short article on his method, the changed basis of physics, and his prophecies, might be interesting.

From Allan Nevins

Columbia University, July 5, 1929

I have just come back from a vacation — alas, too brief — in which my mail did not follow you, and am at once taking steps to forward you the fullest Adams data possible. There are almost no Adams letters in my collection. What few I have I shall send you copies of. But I am going through the privately printed edition here at the Public Library, and by tomorrow's mail shall send you a full schedule of dates and places. I trust it will meet your needs.

We are having a very hot summer here, and for me it is a very busy one. I still have one foot in the *World,* and one at Columbia, where they have elevated me to a professorship. Indeed, I am to have charge of all graduate students in history for their first one or two years, and to oversee the preparation of all the M.A. theses. Lippmann has been very nice about the *World.* On condition that I merely come in every day, and do what is up my street if anything is up it, he will continue my full salary. Even so, the two places cannot be combined forever. Meanwhile, the White book approaches its completion.[1] It will really shed a great deal of light on recent American diplomatic history, for White was on the inside, both in Europe and in Washington, from 1895 to 1910. Then, of course, there is much of interest in his daily letters to Lodge and Root on the Peace Conference.

To M. A. De Wolfe Howe

London, July 12, 1929

We came home to work and last week took three days off, ostensibly to track the Adamses to their origin in the villages of Barton St. David's

[1] Henry White, diplomatist and member of the Peace Commission.

and Charlton Mackrell in Somerset. We put up at Somerton, a delightful village where nothing has happened since the battle of Sedgemoor, and where we stayed, for 10 shillings a day each, at an old stone inn which had last been done over in 1605, and where we were the only guests. In the register I could find only one American registered there since the record began. I got a countryman to motor us about at sixpence a mile, and we scoured all that part of Somerset, some of which I knew before. We included Glastonbury and Wells and crossed your recent trail at the Cheddar Gorge. We also visited Wookey Hole, which is far finer and more interesting than the Cheddar caves, and where there were no charabancs or tourists. We ended by a scamper across Dorset to take the train at Weymouth.

So far from objecting to your comment on the *Forum* article I appreciate it as a friendly act. I feel much as you do and have been fighting *Harper's* for some time to let me write on something besides criticizing America. I think, however, that the effect of my articles must have been cumulative for in the Hoover one I thought I did suggest some remedy on the last page, i.e. that we must begin to reform from the very bottom, the springs and motives of our lives, and that for that a leader would help who would take that line. Much as I disliked [Theodore] Roosevelt in many ways, I believe he did do much to stir the conscience of the country. The war and the huge prosperity since have swept over all the old ground gained and we need a new leader and a new regeneration. Perhaps I did not make my point clearly enough. Boni is negotiating with me at the moment for a small volume of my articles on America and if they are republished, I shall have had my say and shall fight hard to vary my new articles. Editors, however, insist on slashing attacks — the *Forum, Harper's,* and even the *Atlantic.* When I asked Sedgwick to let me write on Matthew Arnold Sixty Years After he agreed if I would twist it into an attack on current life.

To Henry Hazlitt

London, July 25, 1929

I suppose we shall go home next April though as far as the life here is concerned both Kay and I shall be very loath to do so. Not only do we like London but the having all Europe at our doorstep to play in. We are off to Denmark and Sweden next week but shall be back by the first of September. Also, for the first time, I have enjoyed society. Here, in drawing rooms, you meet all the world — social, political, literary, artistic, etc. instead of having them all segregated as we do in

America — one sort in the East 60's, another in Greenwich Village, another in Washington, and so on. We have become quite swanky and have even lunched twice this week at Lady Astor's, with the Archbishop of Canterbury, and a general collection of specimens from the titled, parliamentary and artistic worlds. Such jumbles are good for all concerned and, so far as my own experience goes, are not often to be encountered home. I have been extremely busy also lately as Boni cabled me to whip a dozen of my magazine articles into shape for a book this autumn. It is to be called, I believe, "Our Business Civilization: Some Aspects of American Culture" (Boni's title).

To M. A. De Wolfe Howe

London, July 25, 1929

We have had a lot of interesting social things lately, at the Hirst's and elsewhere, and have lunched twice at Lady Astor's. I like her and she has been wonderfully kind to Kay. The last luncheon was one of about thirty, the Archbishop of Canterbury, Lady Duveen, and a lot of other titled and parliamentary people, but she put me by her at table, and Kay by her son, and when the ladies went to the drawing room for coffee she and Lady Duveen took Kay in tow and were very kind to her. I had lunch with Philip Kerr the other day and he wanted me to go down with him to speak at Cambridge but I am no good at that sort of thing and declined. I must say that I enjoy society here much more than I ever did at home. I think it is the mixture of all sorts of people — pure society, politics, literature, art, etc. The conversation is certainly better. I was thinking today, I have not heard a person in England (I mean at social affairs) mention business or automobiles since I have been here. The conversation ranges over every conceivable topic but not those, which, like plumbing, seem to be considered necessary and useful but not interesting socially. A London season is a very curious thing. Once one is started, invitations just fall from the blue. People you do not know at all, ask you to tea. I suppose they know who you are, but the workings are mysterious. At any rate, it is very interesting and valuable experience.

We are going over to Paris on the 6th to pick up my sister and then go to Denmark and Sweden. We shall be back about September 1st. I want to finish the Adams book by December and shall cut my travels accordingly, although in September I want to go to Devon for a few days to see my cousins there and have a day or two on the moors while the heather is still in bloom. Have you read *Lone Voyagers* by Neff?

Greenslet sent it to me with the request that I give it a good word. I went through it last night and it makes me dread getting into Middletown more than ever. It does for the small western college what Lewis did for the small town. It may be overdrawn but too much of it is true, and it makes you want to scream.

We probably shall go back to live but I do dread it. One has so much freer play here. One can drink what one likes, read what one likes (I see I cannot take my English unexpurgated copy of *All Quiet* home), one has the accumulations of 2000 years and more of culture to stimulate not only one's mind but one's taste and emotions, one can find someone to talk to about anything, and there is no stock market.

From Edward Weeks

Boston, September 9, 1929

As my cable has already informed you, I was immensely pleased with my reading of the first installment of the Adams biography. I took the manuscript away with me on my vacation and annotated it at my leisure.

It is in every sense a distinguished piece of work. The characters are drawn with that freedom and naturalness which so often alludes the most determined biographers. In part I think this is due to the skill with which you have enabled them to speak for themselves, and in part as a result of your wide and vigorous understanding of the times. These two strands — the one of historical delineation, the other of authoritative quotation — are interwoven with a third. I refer, of course, to your own critical interpretation which, derived as much from your own experience as from literary sources, adds verisimilitude, pungency and discrimination to the whole, and so completes the effect. This fragment allows me a sufficient glimpse of your general design and of your particular style to make me not only confident, but expectant of the book's success. I know it is poor policy for a publisher to boast or prophesy. Let it be enough, then, for me to say that I think "An American Family" will be one of the most distinctive books that we have ever had the pleasure of publishing.

From Samuel Eliot Morison

Cambridge, Mass., October 1, 1929

Reading your most interesting and stimulating article in the current *Forum,* reminded me that you have never contributed to this magazine, possibly because you have never been asked! Now I am wondering whether you will not help us by a review of Charles K. Bolton's *Real Founders of New England.* I am sure that you will enjoy reviewing the book, which is a pretentious but a very silly one, making out that the fishermen and scattered settlers of the New England coast who didn't found anything, were the "real" founders rather than the Plymouth and Massachusetts-Bay people. One of the heroes of the book is Pastor Lyford, and the author expresses his deep regret that you should have called that noble clergyman and upholder of the Church of England "a lascivious Uriah Heep." The book deserves to be slashed thoroughly, and of course you can do it better than any of us here who have to live with Bolton and see him every few days.

Please do not say 'no' to us until you have seen the October copy of the Quarterly, which I am sending you. We are trying very hard to produce a regional historical journal in which style and humor are just as important as matter and scholarly worth. If you will cable me collect: "Professor Morison, Harvard University. Consent. Adams," I will mail you Bolton's book at once, so that we may have the review for the January number.

Your letter in the lentern was much appreciated. We are founding a new Civil Liberties Committee, in the hope of relieving the situation by legislation. The situation looks rather brighter this morning, for the Irish Mayor of Quincy not only allowed the "Strange Interlude" to be given there, but also has endorsed the performance without qualifications.

To Wilbur Cross

London, October 5, 1929

I am greatly obliged to you for your cable received yesterday morning. I have added about three pages to the essay and shifted one page from around the middle to the beginning. Personally I think the paper much improved. Your cable seemed to me to embody a rather large order for two pages, i.e. to discuss the *Chartres* and *Education,* and to tell how they affected other writers, and how their standing has been affected by the criticism of twenty years! As all that obviously could not be done in 600 words, in any detail, I hope I have complied with what you wished in a general way. I assumed that, as the essay was concerned with Adams's theory and the new physics, you would not wish a dispersion of interest, and that what you did wish was sufficient comment on Adams's more conventional achievements to afford a sort of background for the mind that went wandering into the theoretical side of his art. For that reason I now start the essay with a note on the charge so frequently made, and implied when not openly made, that he was an amateur, if not a trifler. I pass next to show briefly the body of his solid achievement along the best of conventional lines. Then on to the discussion of his theory, the effect on it of the new developments of science, and, last, a mere note on the possibilities of continuing his effort along more promising and feasible lines. This seems to me to give coherence and logical structure to the whole essay.

I did not want to linger over the *Chartres* and *Education* because even Henry himself gave up the attempt to make them fit into his theory as establishing "points," and their influence is another matter. To speak of his work, to give him, so to say, a "union card," is right and proper, but I am dealing now with Adams and physics, Adams's mind in relation to American intellectual life, the influence of his most characteristic work (*Chartres, Education, Degradation*) on American thought, the history of its reception and criticism, his growing public, and what that public makes of him, are all subjects for an essay the central theme of which would be quite different from the present one. As I think all this must have been as clear to you when you cabled as to me, I have tried to follow what seemed to me the spirit of your suggestion. I am greatly indebted to you for it, for I really do think the essay is better.

From Edward Weeks

Boston, October 5, 1929

For some time I have been troubled by the knowledge that Mr. Boni was making friendly overtures to you of a sort that tended to place your other publishers in a somewhat niggardly regard. I say so without any reflection upon Mr. Boni of whom, though I have never met him, I know nothing that is not honorable. Now comes his large advance upon your forthcoming volume of essays, an advance, which naturally attractive to you, can only be justified, candidly, when regarded in the light of a deliberate encouragement to you and a large gamble on a risky undertaking. You are close enough to the literary market on this side to realize the hazard that is attached to any collection of short pieces, whether of short stories or of essays and almost regardless of the author. This hazard has been intensified in the course of the past year. The Book Clubs by giving extravagant publicity and emphasis to their selections have practically compelled the bookseller in his turn to play up these favored volumes in preference to the less popular volumes, and it is common knowledge that today first novels and volumes of collected papers are handled only in the most modest quantities. . . .

I want to speak to you now in an entirely different capacity. In addition to my direction of the Press, Mr. Sedgwick has lately appointed me to serve as Editor of the new Atlantic Bookshelf, which is in the course of undergoing a very thorough revision. More space is to be devoted to the reviews, the type is to be enlarged, and as you will see from the enclosed announcement, every effort is to be made to combine discriminating criticisms with a broad, and to some extent, a personal survey of each season's books.

I am very anxious to have you serve on our staff as one of the experts in the field of biography and history. Your associates will be Mr. Charles Johnston, and I hope, Miss Elizabeth Shepley Sergeant. Each of you will be expected to contribute in the course of a year three or four critical essays of a thousand words in which you will be at liberty to discuss in whatever proportion you prefer the merits and defects of a selected and, to some extent, a homogeneous group of biography or history.

To M. A. De Wolfe Howe

London, October 21, 1929

Your letter has just reached me on a day you would have loved in London — an air like spring, a haze softening every distance in Hyde Park, and the brown foliage and slowly moving groups of nibbling sheep composing into a perfect Constable landscape. Kay and I have just come in from hunting up an old editorial on Henry Adams in the newspaper room of the British Museum, travelling home by bus, and now, in front of a fire and with my five-thirty mug of ale, I shall answer you.

If I were you, I would not trouble myself at all about the reviews. I have not seen Schlesinger's or Miller's (who *is* Miller?) but I have Fox's. I know Fox well, Schlesinger slightly, and consider them both the sort of men who are all too common in our universities. They are both very capable in their fields. They "know their subjects"; but outside of that they are barbarians in the Greek sense. They both, I imagine, had exceedingly meagre backgrounds, socially and culturally, unextended by travel and contacts until an age when their minds and natures had become set. They know American history as you and I will never know it, but they are not cultivated men, as at least *you* are.

They are exactly the type which I mention in my essay "May I ask?"; men who know their subject but are helpless outside of it. I consider Fox's question: "How does his [Rhodes] treatment of a given episode compare with that of Von Holst? with Schouler? with more recent writers?," when asked of the man who has been writing the life of Rhodes, as a perfect example of that soul-killing specialisation and intellectual provincialism that I am fighting in American life. You were not writing a critical essay on Rhodes' methods as historian. You were writing the life of a man; not a Ph.D. thesis on his method. I do not doubt that if you wrote a charming, and, to a cultured man, wholly satisfying life of Charles Lamb, some "teacher of English" would attack you because you had not shown Lamb's relation to other writers of essays, with a disquisition on essays as a genre in English literature, and all the rest of it. . . .

I know of no subject more narrowing than American history, when pursued as most American professors of it pursue it to the exclusion of all other intellectual and cultural interests. Beginning in 1609 it is cut off from all the currents of western European culture before. It is provincial in the extreme. From the Civil War on it is almost current politics. When, in addition, most professors start with no background or culture, the result is hopeless, for them and their students. . . .

. . . I hope to have the [Adams family] book completed in another ten days but shall hold it for any further information I can insert about J. Q. L. B. decline to publish, in any case, until the autumn of 1930. I am praying that nobody brings out such an obvious book first. You may recall that they did not wish to bring out a Jefferson on the ground that the market was over-stocked with Jeffersons. A month ago, I had a letter from Weeks, praising my Adams book very highly and suggesting that Little, Brown might now want a Jefferson, although he had not consulted them. A week later I found they were bringing out a Jefferson by Chinard. Meanwhile, I had been trying to get Chinard's book for Boni on the score that L.B. had declined a Jefferson, so would not want it, and a Jefferson by Chinard would spike one by me, so Boni ought to have it to make up for not getting one by me. Suddenly both Boni and I discover that L.B. has had Chinard's book all along. I do not like the episode at all, indicating as it does that I cannot trust L.B., and also that the *Atlantic* Monthly Press is not at all in McIntyre's counsels. I have intimated so to Weeks, adding that I have nothing but the most cordial and friendly feeling for him. Oh, for the good old days when I could deal with a Mark Howe! So far, my little

Russian Jew Boni has proved himself not only more generous but much more of a gentleman than our Puritan friends L.B. I am tied to them on a contract for the Adams book but I am much inclined to make that the last.

To M. A. De Wolfe Howe

London, November 1, 1929

I presume that today you received my book from Boni, which, to my horror is as atrocious a piece of bookmaking as I ever have seen! Had I been in America I might have prevented that terrible binding, but as it is I am ashamed to send it to my friends. . . .

I much wish that I might now get away from this sort of writing but suppose I cannot entirely. This book, in the aggregate, must represent less than a year's work and has brought me in, even although I got lower prices for some of the articles than I now get, close to $8,000, whereas all four of my histories, the New England series and the Macmillan one, took seven years to write and have brought me just the same amount as a total, exclusive of the Pulitzer Prize that will not be repeated. I get for two articles what Macmillan paid me for *Provincial Society,* $1000, which is all I have also got thus far, about, for *New England in the Republic.* Harper's publish immediately such things as "A Business Man's Civilization" and "Is America Young," whereas they have not yet published an article they paid for last February on "Science and Art." Even my article in this month's *Atlantic* Sedgwick insisted should include a "sideswipe" at America, though written on Matthew Arnold. I suppose the editors know what their readers want but I myself am getting deadly tired of articles on marriage, the cost of medical service, our colleges, etc., etc., etc., and turn to English magazines like the excellent *Realist* to try to get in touch with an occasional eternal verity. American journalism and literature is beginning to make me feel like a man in one of those amusement park places where every wall is covered with distorting mirrors and one sees one's self in distorted form every way one looks.

I have greatly enjoyed writing my biography of Henry Adams, which will be published in a small limited edition (Little, Brown would not allow Boni and myself to make a trade edition) as well as an Introduction to the Collected Works. I am going over to Paris Wednesday to see Ford and let him read it. I have also finished my Adams book for L.B. and am merely holding the MS in case you or others turn up some good bit on John Quincy for me. I think these two things and the article on Henry Adams for the *Yale Review* the best things I have done. Cross seems much pleased with the last and writes he is trying to make space to get it in the December issue and that if not it will be in the March one.

Have you seen Randall's *Our Changing Civilization?* Hartman of Harper's (associate editor) wrote me in high praise of it and told me to be sure to get it. I have spent four evenings on it and have been much disappointed, and wonder what you thought of it. Hartman seems to consider it a sort of new gospel and said it had changed his thinking. Tonight I shall read Aristotle, a cowardly "escape," as the moderns would consider, from the problems of the present!

I sincerely hope you did not get caught in the Wall Street debacle, which I selfishly welcome and would be glad to see go further. I have been wondering about Sedgwick, for the last time I saw him he was a wild bull, told me he had put practically everything into common stocks, and had accepted the belief that American finance had changed forever and we would never see low prices again. Of course, even with the smash to date the prices are not low in many cases, with many stocks still yielding only 2½ to 4%. I look now for some rally and then a long slow decline provided there are no failures of such magnitude as to bring about another crash. I think it would be a good thing if people would have to live on their legitimate incomes for a while, instead of those plus gambling profits, but of course that will play hob with consumption, and industry is geared to high consumption.

The losses must have been terrific and the steamship offices are besieged by people trying to get passage home. One man said he had just got here with his wife and three children to place them at school in Switzerland and spend the winter travelling but that the break had cleaned him out completely and he did not have a red cent left. This sort of thing must be a fairly common story, and it is silly for a chap like Stuart Chase to say the slump cannot hurt business for there have been only "paper losses." Last December I pointed out one great danger in the huge mass of money being loaned on stocks not by banks but by the big corporations, money which could be withdrawn with no sense of responsibility at a moment's notice. I see by the Federal Reserve Statement that $1,300,000,000 of that money was withdrawn last week, much of it to be used by the corporations in buying the very stocks they shook loose from their speculative holders.

Here such English friends as I have all live on what they have or what they make from their professions and although they spend much less than my American friends, their homes are much more peaceful. I am afraid I am hopelessly un-American! If I could only afford it, I should like to spend my time trying to learn the best that has been said and thought by our race and passing it on to others of like mind in an occasional book or thoughtful article. I shall try a biography next when I get settled somewhere, for I find I enjoy writing it immensely, and incidentally it is ten times as easy as history. I parted from old John Quincy Adams with really deep regret when I came to the end of his section in my book and think I am a better man for having lived a few months in his life and thought.

From Samuel Eliot Morison

Cambridge, Mass., November 7, 1929

I cabled you today "eight hundred," as I entirely forgot about sending you the copy of the *Quarterly*. It will go tomorrow, though. I have been frightfully busy giving some lectures on early Massachusetts Bay, and if they are printed, I hope you will review them for the *Quarterly*, as you are the only person I can think of who will say exactly what he thinks about the book. Colonial historians are very few and timid. The book will probably not be out until spring, so if you change your address, perhaps you will be so kind as to drop me a line. Our January number goes to press about December first, and of course we should like to have your review of Bolton for it. A strange sort of book, isn't it? "800" is only for guidance — anything you think it may be worth will go with us.

From Abraham Flexner

New York, November 8, 1929

Ellery Sedgwick has been kind enough to give me your London address. I should like to express to you the pleasure which I had in reading your paper in the current *Atlantic*. I read everything you write that comes my way and always with profound sympathy. In the present instance, I was particularly pleased to note your admiration for Matthew Arnold. I happen to be re-reading his Letters at this time. I have always regarded him as by far the most important influence under which I have ever come. It is pleasant to see you recalling him to an American generation which needs him as badly as did his own in England.

May I venture to send you with my compliments a copy of a little lecture which I gave at Oxford a year ago? If you have time to glance through it, you will see that we are not so very far apart in our way of looking at American and modern developments in general.

From Worthington C. Ford

Hotel Louvois, November 11, 1929

Your Introduction is admirable in tone and in performance. Resting heavily upon the *Education* as it should, your additions are pertinent and illuminative. You give the man a place to which no one can raise objection and you do it by a weighing of his work and authority that is neither prejudiced by personal knowledge of him nor colored by the flippant judgments that pass for criticism. I see nothing to excite my adverse comment nor am I able to suggest additions. The last paragraph does awaken a doubt. The nieces (both recent Catholics) have sought to give a twist to Henry Adams's last years which will not hold and which the rest of the family resented. It is impossible to imagine H. A. surrendering himself to any creed, sect or church. He had too much independence — and knowledge — and his mind remained clear to the end. I would like to see the last paragraph so modified as to say that in his last years he took great interest in old 12th and 13th century music, etc.; which would imply church music and not bring in a daily request for a hymn to the Virgin. . . .

The essay on the Phase is also extremely well done and carries on his trial to an application that would have astonished him, even though it meant disaster. The fourth generation of Adams was explained mentally by Darwin and Lyell — both not to be understood by the father. They were eager adopters of the Darwinian theories and applied them much as Spencer did. The father never understood them, but he left them alone and that allowed them to develop unruled by him. He must have had moments of surprise — and doubt; but he acted wisely, and four decidedly individual sons resulted. I am delighted to have your high estimate of Henry, for he was the most difficult to appreciate.

To M. A. De Wolfe Howe

London, November 16, 1929

You are at present in close contact with one of the things that is not only the very best in America, but in the world, the marvellous instrument called, with no sense of its full significance, the Library of Congress, and which, in my opinion owes its present significance solely to

Herbert Putnam, one of the greatest of contemporary Americans, though his bust may never be in the Hall of Fame and Mediocrity. Your letter raises the question that I put to you some time ago, of whether I was concerning myself too much with the shadows on American life. It is one of the greatest blessings that a man can have to possess a friend who is willing to comment and criticize freely, and I hope you always will. . . .

It has seemed to me that certain things needed saying, certain tendencies pointed out. On the other hand, I realize that a voice of which people tire, has no effectiveness. The question, therefore is, does the fact that I have dealt only with the seamy side interfere with my being listened to at all, and should I throw in some praise to widen my audience and strengthen my position? That is what I wonder.

I get a constant stream of letters from strangers and newspaper clippings about myself from every state in the Union, or at least from New York to San Francisco. Some praise, some criticize me. But so far, I find the quality of those who praise better than those who blame. For example, take my last mail. There was an atrocious letter from a man in Chicago called Murphy, ill-spelled and the sort of thing you want to put in the fire. On the other hand, here is one from a man in Puyallup (lovely name!) Washington, who says he has been a clergyman forty-five years, and who says my articles in *Harper's* help him greatly in his work, stimulate him to thinking and make him hopeful of the future. A few days ago, a woman in a small town wrote that I had no right to talk about the American colleges and American mental life as I did and that I did not know what I was talking about. Yesterday I got a newspaper clipping on the conferring of honorary degrees on Lowell of Harvard and Butler of Columbia, as the two leading educators of America, at the 65th Convention of the University of New York at Albany. Murray Butler in his speech spoke of me by name as "one of the foremost of contemporary Americans in the fields of letters and history" and proceeded to quote verbatim a long passage from one of my articles on the very point on which the woman had told me I knew nothing, about American colleges and intellectual life. I could go on, but I quote these things from my mail because I am myself genuinely concerned as to what is best for me to write about. I am not muck-raking or scandal mongering, nor am I trying to be sensational. I am trying all the time to stand for certain values I believe in. My articles appear to impress different people very differently. Most men, like generals, are better at either defence or attack. I think I am better at the attack. . . .

There are always two opposed types — there are the Platonists and the Aristotelians, the conservatives and the radicals, the attackers and defenders, and I believe the world needs both all the time, as a cart needs at least two wheels. I have no wish, however, to become a common scold. But it is curious that, for example, in the article that you say first made you think I was assuming too much of that role without any suggestion for construction — Hoover and Law Observance — was the one in which I had tried to be constructive, and to point out that Hoover's panacea, to obey laws or get them repealed, could not possibly work out in present-day America, and that what we needed was a man who would preach a doctrine far deeper reaching, a doctrine that would go to the root of the *moral,* not the legal, life of the nation. I tried to point out that lack of law observance was a disease deep seated and that merely to make new laws or repeal old ones did not strike at the heart of the evil, and that we should have to do that to get anywhere.

It seems to me, to go back to other matters, that while there are some very fine things in American life, the major tendencies are working for evil. For example the increasing dominance of business ethics and ideals, the democratization of higher education, and other things, and that the main attack, for a man who sees them, should be made on them. Murray Butler says, and I think him right, that the American school system has gone far backward in the last twenty-five years. Lowell says the American college cannot continue as it is going on at present. I am trying to get at the controlling principles of the evils in our life. To my mind a good deal of the best in American life at present is due to the hang over of principles that are steadily losing in power and influence as contrasted with the new ones now becoming more and more effective. The question is, should I desist from studying and analyzing these new, and to me baneful, influences in order to praise the by-products of the other principles that I think are losing power? . . .

I am delighted that you are finding Washington so much to your taste. I do not wonder that you enjoy the Round Table. I am inclined to consider it the best university in America, and a man who lunched there for four years would be better entitled to an A.B. than most college graduates. It is, in my mind, one of the chief foci of civilization in America, and there again you have Herbert Putnam at work. You ought to have a very delightful winter and I hope you do with all my heart.

I shall sail for home on the *Aquitania* March 12 and hope to see you in your Washington quarters. If I can find a house somewhere within my means and my wife can find a cook, we shall probably stay, somewhere over there.

From Samuel E. Morison

Cambridge, Mass., November 25, 1929

Thanks very much for the review of Bolton. It is just what we wanted, and what only you could do. Bolton is an excellent Librarian who has the misfortune to fancy himself an historian; and the public naturally thinks that the person who runs the Boston Athenaeum with all those books around, must know something.

It is no wonder that the public takes you seriously as an historian, and properly so, because you write unusually well, and your works on New England are the results of considerable study and research. In doing my Lowell Institute Lectures, I had frequent reason to consult your *Founding of New England,* and find no reason to change the opinion I expressed when it came out: that it is a notable and on the whole sound piece of work. There is, of course, one fundamental fault with it from my point of view: that, starting from an inherent dislike of puritans, you did not take the trouble to know them, much less to understand them. Consequently you have made a good many off-hand statements about them which are not correct, including the one about preoccupation with the devil and hell. Old Dr. Fenn remarked the other night, that when he was a young man, the Calvinists were accusing the Unitarians of continually throwing stones at the Trinity, while the Unitarians could never speak of a Calvinist without accusing him of preaching a hell paved with infant skulls. Dr. Fenn said he had gone to sermons now for about fifty years, and had never heard either doing what the other accused him of. Our ideas of puritanism in this generation are apt to be derived either from some prim old great-aunt, or from an anti-saloon league person, both of whom represent a degenerate and negative type of puritanism. I feel when reading your books & articles that you are continually putting up this latter type as a sort of straw man in place of the veritable positive puritan of the seventeenth century. Of course, to people who know their New England background, your books are provocative, stimulating and informing.

I hope that this will prepare you to write a slashing review of my printed lectures, when they appear. Do let me have an address when you get here. Certainly America is not a favorable place for a person with a limited income to set up housekeeping. At the same time, the servant problem is much easier in the cities than it was ten years ago. According to my experience, one can live better on about $10,000 a year in England than here — i.e. what I call better, more service and less plumbing —; but that the heavier taxation over there more than balances. Middletown would be an easier place to get a cook than Dartmouth. I have a house at Peterborough, New Hampshire, and when we go up there to spend the weekend, we have to import a cook from Manchester at a cost of twelve dollars, including train fares, for the weekend.

From Nicholas Murray Butler

New York, November 25, 1929

It is a great pleasure to have your letter of November 15, and to know where you are placed at the moment. I have inquired several times as to your whereabouts but no one has seemed to know just where you were. If you are planning to come back to America why not consider settling down in Morningside Heights and becoming, informally at least, one of our academic family?

Some time ago we had here for several years Mrs. Gertrude Atherton, who moved in and about with us on terms of familiarity and friendship, and who was kind enough to say that until she had these associations she had never known or suspected what it meant to live in a university company.

We need to draw to us productive, creative and critical minds of our time, whether men or women, to have them use our libraries and collections, and to come to know our scholars and to be known by these. Various forms of academic association, formal and informal, are possible for such if any given individual should wish to avail himself of them. A number of suggestions occur to me, but I forbear to go extensively into them until I learn whether even in a general way such an academic companionship and contact would be agreeable to you.

From Ellery Sedgwick

Boston, November 26, 1929

Dear Adams:

I hear that the Adamses are finished and done for! Well done, indeed, good and faithful clerk! I regard this as a milestone in your career, and I trust it may so prove in ours. My comment to you on *Sweetness and Light* was personal, but it might have stood for a hundred congratulations which have reached me from all sorts of people to whom I supposed that Arnold was a tradition long since forgotten — exploded perhaps. I should welcome an "Emerson" to follow it. Before me as I write is your letter of a few days ago to Weeks. I quite agree with you that the angle of reflection is very different, and that the piece might be quite as fresh as the Arnold. I think it might be worth your while in case you can find a file of *Atlantics* in the library to glance over a couple of papers which John Jay Chapman wrote on Emerson quite thirty years ago. My guess is that it is more than that, but if I am not mistaken, I talked them over either with Walter Page or possibly with Horace Scudder (who was also another old friend of mine) when I was a senior at College in the days of Martin Van Buren, or thereabouts. That would put it in '94 or '95. Chapman is, of course, a native moralist, but his papers represented very truly what Emerson meant to the high souls of his generation, and I think that his estimate would form an interesting half way point in your review.

From Claude G. Bowers

New York, November 27, 1929

Since your letter came I have been literally swamped or it would have been answered long ago. I was very much delighted with the review in the *Sun* and would have written you had I known your address. I am surprised and yet not surprised either that it should have been somewhat expurgated in the interest of traditional partisan falsehood, but the book editor is not to blame. I had expected a great deal of that sort of thing and have been delightfully disappointed. Even the Philadelphia *Public Ledger,* the Chicago *Tribune,* the New York *Tribune* and *Evening Post* have been most generous and only the Boston *Transcript* reviewed it in the spirit of a partisan tirade. Perhaps it was too much to expect any other attitude from that quarter. In the nature of things the story is not a pretty one for those in power in the period treated, but the suppression or distortion of the facts would have been dishonest. I was amazed myself at the depth of the depravity when I get into it.

The thing that has pleased me most perhaps is the attitude of the southern press, all the leading papers down there devoting from two to four columns of editorials to it in addition to good review. I had feared that these papers might give the rebel yell. They all wrote with fine restraint and toleration, expressing complete satisfaction with the result of the war, but saying that the one remaining bitterness had been their inability to wipe out the misunderstandings of the North due to propaganda after the war, and that now that a Northerner had written the truth, and a Boston publishing house had printed it, "the South has no further grievance." It has led the "best sellers" nationally for two months — which is good in that it may enable me to go to England again next summer.

How I envy you your present habitation. I was in London just long enough to fall in love with it. By the way, have you been out to Holland House? It fascinated me enormously with its associations, its long walks, its enormous statue of Fox. Politics here? It has not, to my mind, been so low in generations. We got tired of the gods and decided we would have nothing to do with anyone but the most mediocre. This is the day of the little fish. The last three Presidents have been utterly without any capacity for leadership. One was the associate of scamps. One was the office boy of Big Business. The present one wants to be one of the board of directors. His administration thus far has been a wretched failure. There is a perfect analogy between the first year of Hoover and the first of Taft. Both elected overwhelmingly, they both summoned Congress to deal with the tariff. Taft wanted a downward revision and Hoover a limited revision. Taft lost out on his downward revision and Hoover lost out on his limited, and both got upward revision of the most intolerable sort. Both encouraged by their lack of courage an insurgent movement, and that of today is more serious than that of 1909. Neither had enough guts to lead, and just as Taft lost the House in 1910, Hoover will probably lose the House in 1930.

I have it on excellent Washington authority that at the Capitol there is a feeling of contempt for the President. Among the people he seems without popularity. They tell me that at moving picture houses his picture on the screen never brings forth one handclap. His conduct during the market crisis has been contemptible in its weakness. When everything was crashing he held his hands until the *Post* here editorially scourged him, and then acted with his reduced income tax. I find that business men hate him for not having acted in time. "Reduced taxes?," snorted one of them to me. "Great good that will do when there will be nothing on which I can pay taxes."

The conditions here are bad. The press generally is lying outrageously, heroically trying to prevent depression. The cancellation of

Xmas orders has been unprecedented. In every nook and corner are victims of the market — ruined. The General Motors had arranged a very expensive advertising campaign in the Wall Street Journal, and it has postponed it "indefinitely." Merchants all over who have been wrecked on the market will be unable to meet their bills and commercial crashes are probable within four months.

The press — Democrats leading — are trying to make a hero out of Hoover as a "leader" because he summons groups to consider means of continuing prosperity, and the railroads announce a billion dollar expansion program this year. Sounds fine, but they will not spend it unless they can sell bonds and they won't sell bonds so low as to make a heavy loss certain.

The Republicans are utterly demoralized and if there were a militant, constructive, united Democratic Party it could sweep the country in three years. Unhappily it is not at all certain that solidarity is possible with it, and it is certain that an adequate leader does not now appear in view. Unless the Democrats unite, and upon a definite and sane programme, and with a militant leader with a constructive mind, we shall have two bankrupt parties, and the Democrats may win merely because of the protest against those in power. And that would be a futile victory. So you see I am a pessimist just now.

Am going over to England again next summer. If you are to be there then shall look you up. What are you up to? What writing? I have just got your book and shall read it within a few days. Nevins is working hard — too hard, I think.

To M. A. De Wolfe Howe

London, Thanksgiving Day, 1929

I want much to see the Sherman Letters[1] and agree with you as to the possibilities of producing such a mind in America, but are you sure you have taken all "the implications" as you say into account? . . . Here is the point I would make. America can produce minds of a fine type, such as Sherman, Osborn Taylor, Brownell, More, and so on, but in the newer America rapidly arising as a result of mass production and other economic changes can they survive without a heavy foundation of cash? Henry Adams and Taylor both married money. Taylor told me recently in Stockholm that he never had to think of money.

[1] Stuart P. Sherman's *Life of Letters,* by Jacob Zeitlin and Homer E. Woodbridge, was published in 1929.

He has a town and country house, servants, room in both houses for a library, and the rest of a scholar's equipment. So did Adams. I do not know about J. J. Chapman.

But look at Sherman. He did not marry money, had a wife, and a son ill with tuberculosis in Colorado. Like me, Sherman could not bear the thought of giving up his library and living in a small flat. He bought a house in Jane Street in a veritable slum, full of push-carts and yelling dirty tenement brats, for which he paid $20,000 and about $5000 more to fix it up. There he slaved for the *Tribune,* giving lectures, summer courses, and so on simply to keep going. No one can say that he tried to live like a prosperous business man. He was merely trying to have a home that a business man would despise. . . .

I lunched with Sherman the spring of the summer he was drowned, drowned because he had so weakened his heart. The man looked utterly worn, and I told him he could not keep up the pace. "The bills have to be paid," was his answer. Yet I suppose he was making at least $18,000 a year. But what with $2500 or so for the equivalent of rent, a considerable expense I presume for life insurance, the cost of living, and the cost of illness, I doubt if he was getting ahead much. America did produce the mind of Sherman but killed it in the forties, just as it killed Korff at 47.

To Allan Nevins

London, December 1, 1929

I am myself very tired. I have done, for me, a big lot of work this year and also have travelled thousands of miles and some months, never knowing just how much my wife will be able to do or whether a plan made one day can be carried out the next. Unfortunately she gains nervous strength but very slowly. . . . Except for her health, the experiment of marriage has been a great success and at the end of three years we care more deeply than in the beginning. *That* problem was well solved, but now we are faced with the one of where to live. We are going to Italy in January and then back here to sail for America March 12. I told you that Wesleyan wants me to go there to live much as Robert Frost does at Amherst, and talk to some of the boys, ostensibly on American history but really about Shakespeare and the musical glasses *et al* in my own study. I have never taught. I cannot lecture, from a constitutional shyness I cannot overcome, and I dread being tied to an institution, but they offer me $3500 a year and, except for the full time job at the Library of Congress a few years ago, nobody in America has seen fit to offer me a nickel a week! I am told I *may* be able to get a maid there at $90 a month. That is the crux of life in America for me. My wife is simply not strong enough to do the housework even if I wished her to, which I do not. She cannot, that is all, and if she could just do it would have no energy for anything else in life. I did not marry her to make her a cook and chambermaid, and if those are the terms on which American life are possible only, I shall come back here. I can get a good house even in London for $1500-1700 a year and maids at $250 a year. . . .

I have written any number of magazine articles this year, *Forum, Harpers, Atlantic, Current History, Saturday Review,* etc., book reviews, prepared my essays for the press in a terrific hurry on cabled orders when ready to drop from work, have written a 135,000 word book on the Adams family which Little, Brown will bring out next autumn, a 25,000 word life of Henry Adams for an Introduction for the ten volumes of the Collected Works, which I have also got ready for Boni, and all of which will be published the fall of 1930 with the Life as a separate also in a limited edition, have written an article for the Dec. or March *Yale Review* which Ford and Cross think rather good on Henry Adams and the New Physics, and so on. This is little as compared with what you do but I cannot keep up even this pace, and must cut down a bit next year. What with $600 for storage of my things, $500 for bringing my library across the sea, $1200 for furniture, building bookcases, etc., $600 insurance, and all our travelling it has cost us about $14-15,000 but even so I shall save about $3000, but I cannot keep on at this rate. We have done a good bit of travelling and in a rather expensive way. Incidentally we have had the unenviable record of crossing the Channel ten times so far this year! Apart from shorter trips, I think I wrote you of the long one to Germany, Czecho-Slovakia, Austria (heavenly opera in Vienna!) and so on. We have been many times to Paris, and I have now been there so often in my life that there is no more thrill in arriving at the Gare du Nord than at Forty-second Street and even my wife finds it an old story though she loves to go there. We have been to Holland four times, and, with my sister, had an extremely interesting six weeks trip through Denmark and Sweden, dropping down to Berlin and coming back from there. Sweden and Holland, of course, are the countries in which to see the new architecture . . . but I will not write a travelogue. Here in England we have been off occasional week-ends and had a fine trip up to Shropshire where we were entertained by Lady Gaskell, the widow of Henry

Adams' English friend, at Wenlock Abbey. It was very interesting to sit in front of his fire at the Priory (the habitable part of the Abbey) and chat with the same woman he used to. I also hung over Wenlock Edge and looked off to the blue hills of Wales, all of which you find in the *Education.* It is one of the loveliest counties in England and we enjoyed the trip immensely. A fortnight ago we ran over to Paris for a week to let Ford read my Henry Adams, and made our fifth visit to Chartres cathedral, which is more marvellous each time and always different.

Soon, however, is arising the question what next? Unfortunately for American life today I have too much of the old tradition back of me. Both my grandfathers were millionaires, and for generations we have been used to comely living. I do not mean that at all snobbishly. I merely mean that space, privacy and such horribly expensive matters are in my blood. I have been used to large rooms, and my old mahogany some of which is very fine and much of it heirlooms, is too large for a flat. There are my family portraits, that of my great-grandfather being a lovely thing. There is my library. What in creation am I to do with such things in an America where it is ten to one you cannot get service and if you do you pay a cook $1000 a year and get that yourself for a volume like *Provincial Society?* Incidentally I got under Brett's skin by a reference to the atrocious pay they gave us. You know Harpers averaged $1500 a volume for the American Nation Series when living costs were half what they are now. Brett[1] got Henry Osborn Taylor to say a good word for him, and Taylor and I had a fine time together in Stockholm. . . .

I am far more at home in London than I am in New York, for it is psychologically much more like the New York of my childhood than is the sky-scraper hustling New York of today. My sister is living a few blocks off. She has the whole second floor of a good house in a good neighborhood. She orders her own meals and they are cooked, and served in her own drawing room. For her rooms, meals, and good maid service, she pays about $1600 a year, and has a comfort and a privacy that she simply could not get at all in New York without enormous expense for her. . . .

[1] George P. Brett, American head of the publishing firm of Macmillan, was a figure of wide influence until his death in 1936. Henry Osborn Taylor (1856-1941), who devoted himself to the study of ancient and medieval culture, had published his *Ancient Ideals* in 1896, and his more important work, *The Medieval Mind,* in 1911. His work on *Thought and Expression in the Sixteenth Century* was to appear in the year after this letter.

That is merely the working of democracy the world over, and I am rapidly becoming an anti-Democrat. Recently here in England they revised the Statutes of the Realm and the men who set the type got more per hour than the lawyers who made the revision! France is extremely worried over her intellectual life because wages have gone up so much faster than the numbers of the Intelligent public, that have not gone up at all, that it is now impossible to publish many books that would unquestionably have been published in an edition of 1000 copies before the war. I suggest you read *Isis, or the Future of Oxford* in the excellent Today and Tomorrow series. . . .

From Worthington C. Ford

Paris, December 14, 1929

With everyone — from Hoover down — preaching on the dollar; with a man like Grundy to represent a great State in the Senate, and with one like Edge to represent us here, where is the point in which a needle could be inserted carrying the virus of true living? It is depressing and the more so because it is becoming more fixed daily. Even in the University of Paris they complain of the decreasing study of the humanities and the decreasing influence of the old university spirit — with some 22,000 Students, as against more than 33,000 Students at Columbia (God save the mark!)

But your series of studies are an admirable record of things as they are and contain not a little suggestive autobiography that interested me. I doubt if the book will sell, for the U.S. are too busy to read outside of what is forced upon them by the absurd book-clubs; but you will find every penny-a-liner borrowing from it for years to come, and without credit. That is greatness! . . .

I also read yours on modern biography. Excellent. With all good feelings for my friend Gam Bradford he has introduced a pose which he now states as a gospel, and it is mischievous, because it proffers a somewhat commonplace sketch of outer conditions as a study of a "soul." Bosh. A good writer of fiction can do better, but he would not be read as a writer of a gospel. You have held the mirror up to a lot of fakirs — and the number will increase. I have seen the birth of the Am. historian at the Am. Hist. Ass'n's inception and he has never existed to this day. He remains a worker, a producer and a teacher. It is like an ant hill — all alike to the causal observer.

From M. A. De Wolfe Howe

Washington, December 15, 1929

With all my limitations, I must try to oblige for a statement about the contribution of America to world civilization. Your list of its defections from the highest that might have been hoped for it is indeed impressive, and of course so true in many particulars that there is no rejoinder. Is not this, however, to be considered as weighing heavily in our favor? — that here for the first time in the history of the world, the lot of the average man, the equalization of opportunity, the possibilities of turning leisure from incessant toil to worthy account, are realizing the very demands upon society for which the philosophers of Europe have been clamoring for several centuries? You will point at once to the unworthy uses to which hordes of our countrymen are putting their opportunities — but is it not to be considered that the country as a whole is still in the active process of lifting a level, and that the peaks of distinction cannot be expected to emerge from it in any considerable numbers until the level is somewhat stabilized? This, I know, is all very general, and exposed to exceptions at many points, but with such an agency as the Library of Congress under my immediate observation, and that a national, no merely local, phenomenon — and with many other instrumentalities busy throughout the country with lifting the level with widely various effect, I feel no small confidence that we can afford to wait for the better things that are reasonably sure to come.

From Allan Nevins

New York, December 16, 1929

Your letter was a great pleasure for me, and cleared up a good many questions I have been asking myself about you. As you surmise, this has been a busy year for me; chiefly, as I shall explain later, because I have been unable to get away from full-time work at the *World* while supposedly doing full-time work at Columbia. I am sorry to hear that Mrs. Adams continues to be somewhat unwell, for I had hoped a good rest, with change of scene, would bring her back to full health. And you stagger me by the list of all you have done since you have left these shores. I feel like a sluggard when I contemplate it, though to tell you the truth I have been working under some grave handicaps. I don't wonder that you feel rather tired.

The important news in your letter, to me, is that you are coming back in March. I hope you will give the place at Wesleyan a try.

Evidently the duties will not be heavy, the salary will help meet your bills, and I am told it is both a pleasant and an inexpensive place to live. Of the probable intellectual companionship I know nothing, but in almost every college of that size there are a few good men — often the best are quite obscure so far as the world goes — and Yale is not far distant. I shall ask Canby about it. It seems to me that you are a bit inclined to exaggerate the difficulties of living in America. You ought not really to have any trouble getting a good maid at $90; we have a very good one at $70, an Irish girl who is conscientious, neat, a fair cook, and reasonably intelligent. Rentals in Middletown should be low, though after my experience in Ithaca I should say that you might have to do a bit of house-hunting.

At any rate — if you will let me speak as a friend, who has a much greater admiration and affection for you than you suppose — I don't think you ought to give up being an American. Spending an occasional year or two in England will do you good; spending the rest of your life there, I fear, would not. Even the ablest men run the risk of becoming déracinés. Moreover, this country needs you. All your equipment, both as historian and as social critic, is for work in and about America, and you will lose time, momentum, and perhaps expertness if you either transfer your activities to an English scene, or try to work in England — indefinitely — upon American materials. What I especially covet for you just now, and for Mrs. Adams, is a happier experience of American life than you have had in the past five years. I also covet for you the chance to take up some larger piece of work again, like your New England trilogy. These scattered books on diverse subjects are all very well, but they do not count in the long run (as I have decided for myself) like some large enterprise. Come back to the United States, give Middletown a good try, and let the country have the benefit of your presence.

The Epic of America: the Great Depression

The years 1930 and 1931 were those in which the United States descended into the trough of the Great Depression. They were also the years in which Adams's untiring labors achieved two of his greatest successes, first in *The Adams Family* and then in *The Epic of America.* And during this busy, distressed time his articles in the principal American periodicals were as widely read and commented upon as those of any writer.

Living for the most part in London, Adams witnessed the successive blows that struck Western Europe: the failure of the largest Austrian bank in the spring of 1931, the collapse of German finance, the departure of England and most other nations from the gold standard, and the general devaluation of currencies. He heartily approved of the moratorium that President Hoover induced European nations to declare on reparations, but thought Hoover too tardy in other policies. As the American economy sank further and further, the Reconstruction Finance Corporation seemed to him a step forward, but he thought other steps needed.

It depressed him to hear such bad news from home, to see England in such straits, with processions of the unemployed filling the streets, and to find that much of the Continent was worse off. Yet these were among his happier years. "I have very heavy work to do," he wrote one friend, "and can do it with less strain here than at home." Amid his toil it gratified him to get appreciative praise from all kinds of people. "You are undoubtedly writing American history today better than any other man," wrote David S. Muzzey of Columbia.

To M. A. De Wolfe Howe

London, January 4, 1930

We have just heard one of the most beautiful things we ever did. The carillon of bells made for New Zealand for its War Memorial is supposed to be the finest in the world, and has been set up in Hyde Park for a few days before being shipped out so that "we Londoners" could hear it. The best carilloneur has been brought down from Birmingham to play them, and it was lovely beyond words this afternoon. I shall never forget "Sweet and Low" as it came to us across the meadow from what is really a marvellous carillon. We had also Shubert's "Serenade" and a half dozen other things, ending with "Just a song at twilight" when twilight was really falling; and the vast crowd melted away without a sound. I do wish you might have been there.

I did not begin this letter to tell you that, however, but merely to enclose the obituary in this morning's *Times* of George Woodberry, which I thought might interest you. I believe you knew him. I never met him but have always been fond of his "North Shore Watch," and once had some correspondence with him.

Much to the frosting of our spirits we are beginning to clear out the flat and leave on the 18th, although we do not start from Paris for Rome until the 26th. From now on it would be best to address me care of Barclay's Bank, 1 Pall Mall, London, until we sail on March 12th.

Have you read Bridges's *Testament of Beauty,* and if so what does your poetship say to it? Also have you seen a rather good small volume on Keats by Takeshi Saito of Tokio? I dread seeing the coffin lids go down on my library again and the months of hotels ahead. Rome and Naples are some compensation, and a good look at the U.S.A. again for purpose of study, but I must get settled. The waste of energy is too great. However it will be good to hang over my balcony again on the Via Vittorio Emmanuele on the San Martino hill, and watch the Bay of Naples take every shade of mother of pearl in the sunrise. I have been there twice, once for several weeks, but not for twenty years, and the hills and bay both are haunted with memories of young friends, every one of them killed in the war. I once said that I would never go back unless I were married, little dreaming I ever would be, and now we are going.

To Alfred McIntyre[1]

[London,] January 11, 1930

As I come more and more to study the production of books, I see the author as contributing his research, time, and literary skill to the writing, and the publisher as contributing the capital and work for manufacturing it, and his selling organization and expense of distributing it. The author can produce only one book at a time on which to make a profit whereas the publisher produces many. I presume that a fair division of profits would be represented by the terms of contracts which publishers in general make.

With regard, however, to sales effected through book clubs, the author, as I see it, contributes considerably more than the publisher. It is the special quality of *his* work rather than the trade name or the capital or work of the publisher that secures its acceptance by a Club. In addition the publisher, in this case, does not take any risk whatever or increase his advertising cost to secure sales through the Club, or make use of his own selling organization. He merely submits a copy to the managers of the Club. That being the case, I do not see why the publisher should receive 60% and the author only 40%. I may not understand the matter clearly but would like to investigate further. . . . Again, as the author receives a royalty on the retail price and not on that less discounts in cases where sales depend entirely upon the publishers' selling organization, I do not see why the author should be penalized in the case you mention in your second clause, and receive

[1] Of Little, Brown.

a royalty on the amount *less* all discounts when the publishers' part of the work is much curtailed. That *some* allowance should be made for the extra discount to Clubs is reasonable, but that the author should not only make such an allowance but lose his royalty on *any* discount does not, frankly, seem just to me. . . .

I shall certainly see you, or Mr. Sedgwick or Mr. Weeks,[1] when in America, and shall be glad to discuss new books. It is possible that my next work may be a Jefferson for Boni. I harbor no grudge against you, assuredly, but these are the facts. On my first volume, which your reader, Worthington Ford, pronounced the best history of New England yet written and sure of a sale, 3000 copies were exempt from royalty. That book has sold between 8 and 9000 copies. The second and third had each 1000 copies exempt. You accepted by suggestion of the Jefferson and Hamilton volumes, for which I was offered $350 each, and on my request was paid $500 each; but to my enquiries as to whether you had any editorial work which I could do, I never received any ready, altho' repeated several times. Also, when I wanted to publish some of my essays, you would not take the risk on any terms. On the other hand, when I asked Boni for editorial work he gave me $3000 worth, and he requested permission to publish the essays, which have brought me much good publicity and already $2000 in royalties, and as the sales are mounting prospects of more. I therefore feel that I owe Boni a certain obligation. Harpers also offered to bring out the essays if I would promise them another volume. You, as my regular publishers, were the only ones who declined utterly. I do not mean that I am intending or contemplating any permanent change in publishers, and I think it a mistake to do as some writers do and hawk each work about for the highest bidder.

To Allan Nevins

London, January 16, 1930

I write amidst bales and packing boxes for my move tomorrow, at least all our Lares and Penates do and we clear out the following morning. Jove, how time flies as one get older! A year flashes by like a day. We have been in England over a year and now as we are leaving it seems as though we were just arriving. It has been a comfortable, happy, interesting and successful one, but this next one must see us settled somewhere if possible. . . .

Confidentially, I was offered the post as head of the Library at Cor-

[1] Ellery Sedgwick and Theodore Weeks, both of the Atlantic Monthly Press.

nell. Nothing was said as to the amount of the salary but I could not see anything in it in any case. To do the job well would mean losing myself in administrative work and having no time or energy for writing, at what I think would undoubtedly be a sacrifice of income, although perhaps a less wearing and hazardous occupation. I question whether I am fitted for the academic shades now. My life has been one of a good deal of movement and freedom. . . .

I made a rather interesting excursion a few days ago into a hitherto unknown part of London to me, along the docks and the poorest part of the East End. I now understand Dickens far better than ever. The day had begun fine but turned into a foggy drizzle and then a downpour, and I got the full flavor of the dismalness of Wapping Old Stairs and the Ratcliff Highway. In that district and on toward Whitechapel I saw what I never expected to see in England, the bobbies patrolling in couples, which, if you know England, tells a rather startling story. One expects that sort of thing in Italy, where the picturesque police always stroll in twos even on boulevards and railway stations but I never dreamed of seeing it here.

Did you notice Stephenson's review of Bowers' book in the *Saturday Review?* I thought it very sneering and did not like it at all. What is the matter with Stephenson the last few years anyway? I haven't found him reviewing anything he does not sneer at, and certainly his own work lately has been nothing to brag about. I thought his publishing a lot of rather badly edited extracts from Lincoln's writings and calling it an Autobiography to mislead the public was about as cheap a thing as any scholar had done for some time. By no stretch of the word could it be called Autobiography. I have been rather disappointed in our American historians this past year. Abbott's book on New York in the Revolution, Van Tyne's Revolution and practically all the books I have seen seem to be pretty skimmed milk of wisdom for our scholars. Is nobody doing anything at all great or at least really thoughtful? The two best biographies of American statesmen this year are both by Frenchmen, Fay and Chinard. Of course, it is pretty slack water everywhere these days. Murray Butler wrote me that he thought my historical scheme "intensely interesting" and I want to talk to Shotwell about it if he is in America when I get home. I have always liked him and I think him much your biggest gun at Columbia, head and shoulders above the Ph.D. type.[1]

[1] The books here mentioned are Claude G. Bowers, *The Tragic Era* (1929); Nathaniel W. Stephenson, *Autobiography of Abraham Lincoln* (1926); Wilbur Cortez Abbott, *New York in the Revolution;* L. H. Van Tyne, *The War of In-*

I have been quite surprised at the commotion caused by my reprinted articles in the Business Civilization. They have had a great deal more press notice than anything else I have done and have called forth puffs from different sources as Harry Barnes, the Hearst papers, and the Mass. Inst. of Technology Review, as well as praise from such other men as Butler, Canby, Dr. Flexner, etc. Incidentally as articles and book it has brought me in more than I got from all three New England volumes, Provincial Society and the Hamilton and Jefferson volumes, combined.

To M. A. De Wolfe Howe

Rome, February 8, 1930

Your most welcome letter found me where the Tiber, not the Wairora, rolls, examining the only Eternal City I shall probably ever reach. It is my third visit but my wife's first, and she is completely under the spell of its infinitely varied interest. A few days ago we were in the Forum looking at the new excavations that have revealed the Etruscan remains below the lowest level of the earliest Roman Forum, and a few hours later were standing in a huge crowd of about a million modern Romans in the Via Nazionale to watch Mussolini march in the funeral parade of the great Fascist general, Bianchi. In a few hours we had passed from the dim dawn of history to the great movement of the present moment. The incessant calls on one's knowledge here are appalling and one realizes one's abysmal ignorance as nowhere else. Egypt and Babylonia, although older, would have no such effect for they do not link up at every point with things one ought to know and does not. We are not far from the Street of Humility but all Rome is that for the scholar!

A few days ago we motored out to Tivoli to spend a morning among the terraces and high cypresses of the Villa d'Este, and sitting there in the shade of the old Cardinal's trees, the sound of plashing waters from fountains coming to one from every direction, looking out over the olive and vine-clad slope of the Sabine Hills down to the wide expanse of the campagna rolling like a sea to where the dome of St. Peter's rose against the sky twenty miles away, one strove in vain to find a common denominator for that and America. On Monday we

---

dependence; Gilbert Chinard, *Thomas Jefferson, Apostle of Americanism;* and Bernard Fay, *Benjamin Franklin.* Adams's praise of James T. Shotwell, professor of history in Columbia University 1908-42, was founded upon his labors as historian and planner of efforts to promote international peace.

are going to motor to Orvieto for the night, about eighty miles away, as I have never been there and want to see the cathedral which is said to have the finest polychrome facade in the world. A week later we go on to Naples, Pompei, Castellamare, Amalfi, Sorrento and Paestum. Then a twenty-eight hour run to Paris, a fortnight in London, and the Custom House at Pier 54 North River.

I am glad you liked the article in the *Yale Review*. It is the sort of thing I would like to do more of and which I honestly think there is much more likelihood of my doing here than at home. . . .

. . . My Adams book bids fair to be my greatest popular success. The Literary Guild has accepted it for June publication, so Little, Brown cable me, which means they take 70,000 copies in a lump. Of course, the Book Clubs leave the author little but his skin, and they pay only a lump sum of $13,500 in royalties on the whole 70,000, but it is good advertising in Little, Brown's opinion, and after some negotiating I have agreed with Little, Brown to accept $5900 for myself, they to get $5400 and put $2200 into extra advertising for the trade edition. The book thus ought to bring me in $10,000 in royalties altogether if there is a halfway decent trade sale. I do not think there is anything confidential about the Club's having taken the book but perhaps it would be well for you not to mention it yet. Altogether the actual writing I did in my London flat last year promises to bring me in about $18,000, although I was travelling for about five months of the year. Of course I do not expect to keep up that rate of work and luck, but even at a heavy falling off I am inclined to think I would make more money as well as do better work in this atmosphere here than in America.

I cannot quite make out wherein the greater sense of leisure, that "wide unhaste" you quote from one of my boyhood idols, Bliss Carman, lies here as compared with any part of my home land. Your lack of it even in Washington with a post that as I understand it does not levy too greatly upon your time, makes me wonder even more. I did not reach England until well into January last year. I did not get into my flat until about the first of March; my library did not arrive until April. We have spent nearly five months rambling over France, England, Belgium, Holland, Austria, Germany, Denmark and Sweden. I wrote sixteen major magazine articles, edited Henry Adams, wrote a 25,000 word biography of him and the 135,000 word Adams book, and had a good bit of social life, yet never felt as pressed and hurried as I used to at home. I managed *The Testament of Beauty* easily and since I read that have, for the first time in my life, read through the whole of *Paradise Lost* as well, in the course of the year all Marcus Aurelius, and much else classical as well as many current books outside of the twenty or more I reviewed. I take no credit to myself. There is something in the atmosphere over here, "an ampler ether, a diviner air" perhaps, that makes such things easy.

To M. A. De Wolfe Howe

London, February 22, 1930

Your dictated *Ave* has been unanswered far too long but, yes, I will admit it, I was very busy even in England as you surmised. Last year I took on, as you know, a large part of the literary washing of the U.S.A., and have been trying to get it laundered and delivered. I had to reach America around March 15th as chairman of the Pulitzer Jury in history. I had to finish the Little, Brown book, for various reasons, before I went. I had to have some change and rest after that was accomplished. Hence I worked like a dog up to January 15th, when I could cry "done", and fled on the *rapids* to the Italian Riviera, where I picked up my sister en route back from Corsica, and the three of us settled for a week of perfect peace at Rapallo. Kay and I had a huge room and bath, both opening on a private terrace thirty feet long where we lounged and looked over the blue of the Mediterranean, splashed with the orange of the trees in our garden. We breakfasted out doors and for the rest of the day, my chief excitement was to stroll down to the water side, buy French, German, and English papers, and read them at a cafe table in the sunshine. The little town, nestled in a cleft of the mountains on the edge of the sea, was charming and quiet, never a sound at night save a cockcrow now and then far up the mountain side.

A Change of Direction

With his greatest literary successes completed, for *The Adams Family* and *The Epic of America* will be remembered as long as his New England trilogy and had broader appeal, Adams entered in 1932-33 upon a period of temporary uncertainty. Not only had his proposed edition of Henry Adams's writings fallen through, but this had left his biographical study of Adams unsatisfactory. He did not have time or means to make it either a full-length biography or a thorough critical treatment of the man and his works. For various reasons he rejected a proposal that he write the life of Dwight W. Morrow. Meanwhile, he continued contributing to American magazines, with essays now more and more upon politics and business. He continued to draw comfort and perspective from his residence in London, which was well, for in 1931-32 he felt that he had to "work like mad" (as he wrote M. A. De Wolfe Howe) to maintain his family future.

It was at this point that he signed a long-term contract with Scribner's, and embarked upon his first long piece of factual writing, *The March of Democracy* (1932-33). This was a change of direction about which he himself was doubtful. His age must be remembered, however, and his utter dependence on his little Corona typewriter. Keenly interested as ever in American and world affairs, Adams witnessed the election of Franklin D. Roosevelt in the fall of 1932 with satisfaction.

From Henry Hazlitt[1]

New York, January 4, 1932

I don't see how it is possible to know when revival is coming unless one is able to guess pretty shrewdly what certain key figures are going to do. One has to know the psychology of M. Laval, Herbert Hoover, the railway union labor leaders, a few key members of Congress, and in addition a more widespread opinion that helps to dictate the opinion of these persons at the top. If the January 18 Debt Conference both postpones and materially reduces the reparations payments, irrespective of what America does for the debts, then a slow revival might be possible. If the miracle were to happen here of a sharp reduction of the tariff, a more rapid revival would be possible. If Germany is allowed to sink, then things will get far worse in the next couple of years.

I wish I could have more faith in British policy. Whether England should have returned to the old sterling parity after the war is a difficult question to answer even now. In view of developments (the failure of British wage levels, costs of production, and prices to adjust themselves to competitive world levels) I think it would have been better to have devaluated then, but it seems to me that it was mainly stupidity and incompetence that put it off the gold basis last Fall. The British were building up a situation against themselves for several years by their artificial cheap money policy; and their bankers, of course, made things worse by borrowing at low interest from Paris and New York to lend at high interest in Germany.

[1] Now of the editorial staff of the New York *Nation*.

From Herbert Putnam[1]

Washington, January 20, 1932

Deferring my own curiosities to those of our privileged readers, it was only a fortnight ago that I began *The Epic;* and only last evening that I encountered the references to the Library of Congress in its concluding pages.

You will realize how they must have moved and stimulated me, and will move and stimulate all of those associated with this recent development — convinced of the soundness of it, eager to promote it, and grateful for every recognition of it. Your recognition of it as an expression of the valid Democracy which may be the substance of the "Dream," carries an authority that should be far reaching. And we appreciate it the more in that the illustration wasn't necessary to your exposition, but important, in the determination to emphasize to the American public the rôle with which we should be credited among the agencies for culture.

But how generously you have done it! and as regards my self personally, how lavishly! We are proud to think that the characterizations will reach the many thousands of readers who will follow with absorption your extraordinarily dramatic review and analysis.

From Worthington C. Ford

Paris, February 2, 1932

My congratulations on the practical completion of the work — to my mind a colossal undertaking and performed in record time. It bespeaks the orderliness of your mind and the almost perfection of your methods of work. Do you fully realize the position you occupy in letters? Your *Epic* is selling in a year when nothing else is, when the world is complaining of economic ills unmatched in two centuries. You have two publishers at your call, bearing not the head of a Baptist on a golden salver, but a signed blank check. You command entrance to any American magazine at will. Scribner's has always been regarded as the aristocrat among publishers, selective, leaning toward good literature, generous and sympathetic. As a permanent connection it is the best to be had. I do not see that you are tied to Little, Brown however much our good friend Howe might wish it. He now has no connection with the house, so you are free to act as you wish. . . .

[1] Head (1899-1938) of the Library of Congress.

To Henry Hazlitt

London, February 3, 1932

I am pretty near down and out with all the work under pressure of the past six months — can't sleep and all that — and have a lot to do of all sorts of things to clear up before sailing three weeks from to-day. Would you mind if I did not do Denison's book or anything at the moment? There are over 100 unanswered letters on my table as my semi-secretary is ill and I cannot seem to get anyone in for just a couple of days. I really am up against it, but when I finish this big job in Washington I am not going to take on anything big again for a long time, and could do what you want for *The Nation.* Excuse this brief note but I am just plowing through this pile of mail — all kinds of stuff from all kinds of people. The letter just before this was to a teacher who is working for his Ph.D. degree and who asked me where I got certain statements I made about the panic of 1837 (his subject) in *Harper's.* I got them all from McGrane's book *The Panic of 1837* published by the University of Chicago. How in Hades could a man doing a doctoral thesis on the panic have never heard of this book with its bibliography, its citations of authorities on every page, etc.?

From Allan Nevins

New York, February 6, 1932

Indeed I shall be delighted to read your latest book, all the 235,000 words of it, in manuscript, and to give you my most conscientious criticism. I do not think so slightingly of it in advance as you seem to do, for I know you are incapable of writing anything that does not have distinction. Do you recall that I had to hold your hand, so to speak, over the *Epic?* — that same *Epic* which has been the outstanding success of the year in the field of history. If Scribners make the request, I shall assent to it. We are glad to hear that the date is set for your return to these shores, and I am impatient for your arrival. . . .

We are all well. The *Cleveland* marches forward steadily, and while I promise nothing to anybody, least of all to myself, it is possible it will be finished by July 1. Even if it is, I shall perhaps simply lock it up in a drawer for some months, and then rewrite it. I am also, with some hired help, getting on with a collection of Cleveland's letters authorized by Mrs. Preston, and at Lippmann's request, I have promised to scramble together a volume of his journalistic essays for fall publication. This will be the labor of only a few days, but he wants some hand other than his own to appear. But my teaching burden being light, I am giving three-fourths of my time to the *Cleveland,* and in the ability to do so feel myself in an enviable position. Much as I mourn the *World* sometimes, I am glad to be out of journalism.

To Miss McAfee

London, February 9, 1932

A few weeks ago I spent an evening with Hermann Kantorowicz who is professor of law at Kiel, and who wrote the recent book *The Spirit of British Policy.* (Allan & Unwin). He struck me as something of an extremist but he was exceedingly interesting on Germany. He claims that the German people want the *form* of democracy and to be told they can do everything, and then immediately want to turn everything over to someone to do for them, i.e., that they crave a dictatorship with control over the selection of the dictator. I can elucidate this in conversation, but there might be a good article on the attitude of the Germans toward the democratic idea and the military dictator. He had some very good anecdotes. . . .

What I had thought perhaps of doing myself was an article on the increasing difficulty of being a good and intellectually honest citizen, given on the one hand the abandonment of the *representative* for a rubber stamp in Congress, and, on the other, the extraordinary complexity of the problems to be solved by modern governments. I am myself getting sick of it. I have to earn a living. I want to use my mind for all sorts of things outside of working hours that have nothing to do with the problems of the day. If I work all day, and read, say, Dante or Aeschylus in the evening, how the devil am I to know what I ought to know, if I am to vote intelligently, about the Sino-Japanese situation, legislation for the unemployed, old age insurance, farm relief, and scores of other things? I can't. I have tried to. I have tried to be a "good citizen" and to have intelligent opinions. But I have only a few years to live. Why should I devote all my waking hours to making a living and trying to have an opinion on subjects which only specialists, if they, can have a worthwhile one on? Life is too short to make a living, to go tramping, to be a companion for one's family, to know something of the best in art and letters and to know also whether Hoover and Congress have made asses of themselves or not as mirrored in a highly partisan press. What is the answer? Compare what a citizen is supposed to know to-day with 1776. Where shall we draw the line between living the good life as a citizen or as a human being? Is there an article here?

To M. A. De Wolfe Howe

London, February 21, 1932

Confidential

This last year, as you know, I have devoted almost solely to "getting ahead," having wanted ever since getting married to add to my capital as rapidly as might be so as to work up an income from capital on which we could live comfortably without my writing, in case of my own illness or death. For that reason, having done the *Epic* for Little, Brown first. . . . I have worked like mad this year to get the 275,000 words down on paper at least for Scribner so that that "property" would be established. That is now all accomplished except the last chapter, which I am going to do in Washington, as a result of my having written 10,000 words a week every single week since July 20th, besides some magazine articles.

The success of *The Adams Family* and the extraordinary success of *The Epic* (which comes out in London next week and is being translated into French for publication by Payot), swung me a good stride forward on my capital run. The Scribner contract, besides the $20,000 advance, which I shall save entire, promises a comfortable addition to income for 25-30 years, but that will not start beyond the advance, I suppose, for two or three years.

All these past six months I have known I was driving myself to the limit literally and must get a rest as soon as the Scribner work was finished. I made up my mind as soon as I could do that in America to come back to Europe, go off somewhere in the Tyrol, Sweden, or wherever we decided, and lie completely fallow for a while. . . . When Howe[1] came, he brought a message from Arthur Scribner to the effect that they thought I needed above all first a complete rest without thought of another book. Next they felt that for the next few years while writing I should not have any financial anxiety, and that I would do my best work that way. They offered me a contract for five years to act on their staff in a (nominal) advisory capacity at $5000 a year, payable monthly, and for that they wanted a first call on any books I might write in that period, the contracts for the books to be based on a 15% straight royalty and $5000 advance or whatever per volume I thought fair or needful, the $5000 a year having nothing to do with the book contracts but being a sort of retainer. This meant that with my now enlarged income from capital and the $5000, I can live as I have been (about $14,000 a year), travel, and so on, and save money

[1] Will D. Howe of Charles Scribner's Sons.

with no writing at all. Every cent from old and new books and magazines can go to capital, and before this five-year contract expires my income should be coming in from the other contract. I considered what seemed to me a very generous and thoughtful offer for several days, and have accepted, and signed the contract. Howe is returning to America with me on the *Berengaria.*

The gap is thus bridged. I have saved $16,000 in 1931, and believe I can save at least $30,000 in 1932, and $20,000 or more in 1933, besides the lesser amounts I saved before. For five years ahead I have no anxieties whatever, and then Main Street will be carrying me on with the canvassing edition. It seemed to me unfair to my wife, myself and to Scribner's not to accept, but I suppose Sedgwick and McIntyre will be much hurt.

From Ellery Sedgwick

Boston, February 23, 1932

I hope your attitude of fundamental optimism may be justified. I am free to say that I do not see light. The *Atlantic* has been a very tidy business, very conservatively managed, but we are treading water that has risen to our lips. *Harper's* is obviously losing money, and, between ourselves, I think *Scribner's* (the magazine of course) is on its last leg.

I have just come back from a visit to Washington and way-stations. Politically the only thing that can ruin Democratic chances is a fight in the Convention, of which they are really fearful at headquarters. My own prediction is that you can tell the winner six weeks in advance if you take the trouble to look at the price of wheat. If it is well above 80¢, the Republicans will keep their seats. If it is in the 60's, they will rise, bow, and pass from the stage. I had a few moments' talk with the President, who looked flabby and discouraged. The policy of his with which I most vigorously take issue is his attitude toward vacations. A holiday would have done wonders for him, but he is a man of no resources of mind or spirit beyond his administrative duties. He never reads except along lines that may prove "useful." Something he has learned from fate. He told me that every year there was a little stirring of optimism in January which was nipped in March. As for him, he would wait until March.

You will find this country a very different place. All the old buoyancy has gone, and Cynicism is King.

To Alfred McIntyre

February 29, 1932

You are in error in your letter when you state that you got me to take up again the idea of *The Epic of America* after I had apparently given it up. Letters to my wife, which we have recently been reading over, showed that I had this idea fully developed in 1926, and in the portfolio which I keep for ideas for books and magazine articles, there has always been a slip on which I have jotted down from time to time new suggestions for that work. I had never laid it aside, and it has only been a question of when, and for whom, I would write it. You did suggest to me the subject of *The Adams Family,* and I have always gladly acknowledged that fact. The book did very well, and because I have always wished to treat you, not simply on a business basis, but to fulfil every possible obligation to you which a gentleman could, I decided that you should be entitled to at least another book whatever arrangements I might make subsequently. It was for that reason that I did not hesitate to make the contract with you for the *Epic.* That, of course, has been the outstanding success of the year, and certainly, with a sale of 100,000 copies, my debt to you for the idea of the earlier book should certainly be paid. I had no thought whatever that when I decided that I ought to give you another book to make up for *The Adams Family* suggestion, my doing so could possibly be considered as laying the foundation for another claim to gratitude or obligation on my part toward you.

I may add, with regard to what seems to me the almost fantastic suggestion that I owe much to you for reviving in my mind the *Epic,* that if I had followed your suggestions as to that book it would never have been the success it has been. I never wavered from my original idea of its general conception, but during the last couple of months, when I was writing it in London, I received letters, and even long cables from Mr. Sedgwick, urging me to write it on different lines, and to make it what he called "vade mecum" or a sort of "Ploetz Manual."

To M. A. De Wolfe Howe

London, August 7, 1932

As you know, I was extremely tired when I finished the *Epic,* and then, after a very fatiguing trip home, had to settle down at once with a fagged mind to toil my way through a 275,000-word factual history of the U.S.A. By the time that was done and I had had another trip home, I was really so near the breaking point that I was a bit worried about myself. The last ten days at home almost ended the matter, as I found myself suddenly called upon to rescue the remains, less than one-third only in market value, of the fortune of a near relation, from the Trust Company which had displayed almost criminal incapacity and folly in investing. Tired as I was, I had to turn to in a hurry, frighten the Trust Company enough to make them cancel the Trust agreement and return all fees on its account, get the securities into the hands of my own bank, and then, with the conditions which prevailed in the market in May, with everyone in a blue funk, reorganize the structure of the whole estate with a view to safety, income, and eventual possibility of partial recovery of the portion lost. I finally dropped on the *Aquitania* more dead than alive. Over here I found all sorts of things awaiting me — continuance of advice and comfort to the above relation in long letters, a complicated re-drawing of my sister's will, the writing of four articles promised before I went to America, and a huge accumulated mail from strangers. Rest, badly needed, seemed impossible, day after day, of accomplishment, but I had a few days off in Sussex, and we are now back from a week in Paris. As I had not been to the continent for more than a year I felt that the complete change might do more good than just running down to the country somewhere here, and I do now feel better. The last five years have been a heavy strain, both in work and anxiety of all sorts, including seeing the property of my sister, myself and one or two others through the world crisis. I have done, however, all I set out to do and more, and as I think the world is rolling a bit less heavily now, I imagine that part of my extreme fatigue has been due to reaction after the strain. Without counting the additional income on what we have both saved, I have brought my sister's estate and my own through these past three years without the loss of a dollar in income and only a nominal shrinkage in market value; I have been able to add to my capital in three years what I had set out to add in hard work in nine; I have invested a good bit in bank stocks and so on at almost bottom (so far), which should bring a handsome profit in five years; the salary from Scribner's for the next five years relieves me from the old pressure of magazine articles; we are very comfortable in our two-floor flat here, and the drop in sterling has reduced my expenses here from a quarter to a third; finally with better prospects for the world at large I have emerged from a period of responsibility that was nearly crushing for a while, and I think it natural that I am tired. The doctor says I have done no harm to myself that is permanent or that will not be set right with rest.

From Allan Nevins

New York, August 24, 1932

. . . till July 4 I labored like a dog completing my life of Cleveland; and did complete it, in something like 275,000 words. Then till July 20 I labored like a nigger editing a book of selections from Lippmann's articles of this last year; that is, arranging them in some kind of topical order, deciding what should be deleted, annotating them to bind them together and explain the events they were built on, and writing a short introduction. Then the proofs began to arrive, and with it the usual worry of correction and minor revision. I had not felt like letting Mrs. Preston (Mrs. Cleveland that was) read the book till it was in proof sheets; that is, I had felt that sending her the manuscript was an imposition. The same way with Ogden of the *Times,* who wanted to read the book, and R. L. O'Brien, who was Cleveland's confidential secretary in the second Administration and is now chairman of the Tariff Commission. Moreover, some material came in late. It was only in July that I succeeded in wheedling out of Cleveland's one surviving and very aged sister a large bundle of his letters dealing with his marriage (she had given me others, including a set on his Buffalo life in the fifties, before) ; and it was only in July that I got at the bottom of the Cleveland-Woodrow Wilson row over the Graduate School at Princeton. It was quite a row, too. Altogether, the proofs have been quite a job. Last week I got the page proofs of the Cleveland, and the galley proofs of the Lippmann book, off my hands, and came up here to Vermont.

The life of Cleveland satisfies me. It is full of new material. I had many hundreds of new letters, some of them of the very first importance; I have had the manuscript diaries of William L. Wilson and Charles S. Hamlin; I have used the papers of Lamont, Bayard, Gresham, Olney, Fairchild, and many more, either unused before or else imperfectly explored; I have used all the newspapers of value; I have had the benefit of a secret history of the Wilson Tariff bill written by Jones, one of the Senate floor leaders, just after the Senate quarrel with Cleveland; I have had memoranda by all the survivors of that era; I have had Mrs. Preston's account of such episodes as the courtship and marriage; Dean West's account of the quarrel with President Wilson; and much, much more. It makes a book of almost 800 pages, but we are getting it out in one volume of moderate price — $5. I hope to heaven it sells. If it doesn't I shall be out a couple of thousand dollars which I spent in collecting all this material. The Book-of-the-

Month Club seriously considered taking it; got it down to their last group of two or three books; and then passed it over for a book on the *Mutiny on the Bounty*. It was too well documented, no doubt, for them — for it is as well documented as Pringle's *Roosevelt*, which they also passed over. Everyone who has read it likes it. One historical figure emerges from it, I think, a complete wreck — Olney.

Scribner's surprised me a week or two ago by writing to ask me to read the manuscript of your second volume. . . . I hope that the two volumes will be a great success, and indeed, I think that they ought to be. They fill a decided gap, and they are well calculated to meet the taste of the better part of the general reading public. Much will depend on the illustrations, and I have no doubt that Scribners, who can publish beautiful books when they put their minds to it, will serve you well there.

Nearly everyone in my circle of political and journalistic friends regards Roosevelt's election as highly probable. Betting ranges from 7 to 5 to 10 to 5 in his favor. O'Brien and Congressman Hamilton Fish tell me they think he is almost as good as elected. I know his friends think so. He is very strong in the Middle West, and of course the bitterness everywhere against the poverty of the past two or three years is tremendous. My own opinion of Roosevelt is low, but so is my opinion of Hoover, and I am so sick of the alliance of the Republican party and the most selfish and reactionary element in Big Business that I shall vote the Democratic ticket with pleasure if not enthusiasm. Roosevelt has been a lucky fellow; his name alone is worth a million votes, and the Jimmy Walker affair has unexpectedly worked out to his advantage. The recent rise in the stock market has as yet no industrial support that anyone can see. Employment and wages both fell heavily in July. As I write farm strikes are filling great parts of the Western country with bitterness, and there is a menacing demonstration of 10,000 Illinois miners against strike-breakers. Hoover's tactless handling of the bonus army made a very bad impression among all the veterans. A marked improvement in business and in farm prices might carry him to reëlection, but I shall be much surprised if he is not defeated.

The general opinion as I write is that Walker will land in the gutter within a week or ten days. His own lawyer obviously expects it. He has played his hand so badly, and has indulged in such obvious tergiversation and impudence at Albany, that he has lost many of his former friends. Curry, who is personally attached to him, will resent it, but I don't believe that many of the Tammany district leaders will mind seeing him ousted. His ejection will please the West and strengthen Roosevelt up-State. Meanwhile, Roosevelt will have a strong running-mate for governor here in Lehman.

To Wilbur Cross

London, August 30, 1932

I am fairly optimistic over the economic outlook in the U.S. but am much depressed by the political. Six months ago I would not have believed it possible that, had I had a vote at home this year, I could have hesitated to have cast it for the Democrats. Twelve years of Republicanism and the candidate seemed enough to determine the way the road led. But I find it hard to stomach Roosevelt; and with him, Garner, and the Democratic showing in the last Congress there seems to me to be little choice.

The trouble, however, goes deeper than the platforms and candidates of the present campaign. . . .

In the U.S. third parties are failures. The opposition party of progress must be the Democratic. Unfortunately its make-up as a "liberal" party has a narrower base than in most countries. In its fundamental attitude it has been right over and over again, as I contend it was right in 1896. But it has often been wrong in the specific remedies proposed, as in 1896. Our difficulty is that, unlike many of the older countries, the best brains at home for the most part go into business, and business men as a rule are not progressives. They want favors and as little risk of disturbance to established ways as possible. We have not the political career as open as in England, which provided the liberals with a Gladstone, a Campbell-Bannerman, etc. Nor have we the large classes of one sort and another who are intelligent and well-to-do without being active in business careers. Our "liberals" are to a great extent the farmers in bad times, the big bodies of voters moved by bosses where the democratic machine is dominant, as in New York, some professional reformers, likely to be cranks, the New Republic type of young intellectual, some older and better balanced intellectuals and so on. The party lacks a solid mass of intelligent citizens which it might have in opposition to the reactionary Republicans if the party had sound ideas and some chance of power. Except for a Congressman in a strongly local democratic district or a man in a democratic State, the outlook for national leaders is bad in a party which has come to power only three times since the Civil War if we count Wilson's two terms as one.

The nation needs the balanced functioning of a strong government and a strong opposition. Both parties need it for their own good. The Republican Party is strong. The point is how are we, in our peculiar circumstances, going to build up a strong Democratic Party, which will attract liberals and provide them with sound ideas and leadership? In other words, how are we going to add to the somewhat incoherent lot of followers in New York, the South and West, that leaven of sound men everywhere who can be made to reconcile liberalism with the stability of their business and jobs?

To Allan Nevins

London, September 4, 1932

I agree with you about politics, with which I am heartily disgusted. Hoover and the Republicans are beneath contempt and yet I cannot look with much equanimity on the chance of having Roosevelt, a weak panderer to the crowd, a paralytic facing the terrific physical strain of the presidency, as the only barrier between Garner and the White House. When Murray Butler was here in July I saw more or less of him and he thought the result might be very close. From what I can gather at this distance, Thomas is likely to poll a very heavy vote of the discontented independents as well as the socialists proper. I am at sea as to what the Walker situation means as it now stands.[1] As to business, I think we have seen the worst. In June at the very lows I bought about thirty different stocks, Nor. Pac. @ 6½, Great Northern @ same, Penn. @ 7, Nickel @ 4, Am. Lt. & Power @ 4, Louisville @ 9, etc. etc., with some banks and insurance companies, intending to hold them for three years. After I had done this, I had dinner early in July (did I tell you in my last letter?) with Murray Butler, just over from France, Lord Ryder, of the Cabinet, Sir Walter Layton (editor of *The Economist* and chief expert at Lausanne), and Francis Hirst (former editor of *The Economist*). There were just the five of us and the talk was intimate. They all agreed that the world had turned the corner in June. I also had tea the following week with Mellon, who having been privately if not officially bearish since Jan-

[1] James J. Walker, the dapper mayor of New York, had been exposed as vulnerable to charges of corruption in public hearings conducted by Samuel Seabury, and hastily resigned this month to avoid removal by Governor Franklin D. Roosevelt.

uary 1929, had turned very bullish. I think there are many signs of betterment, though I do not like much of what the government is doing, and I fear the veteran agitation again. But there is no use my giving you my opinion on American affairs with which you are in so much closer touch than I. I do not like at all a lot of the half-baked stuff, especially in economics, now being put out by such men as Harry Hazlitt, Stuart Chase, Elmer Davis, etc. Having been quite wrong on almost all that has happened economically, they now propose to reform the system! I have never known worse leadership than the country has been getting in every field. That, to me, is one of the dangerous elements in the situation.

I now have a clean slate as to work, all articles written for the moment and no book on the stocks. I have no idea what I shall try next, but shall start no book until after my next visit to America. We shall not go home until April as I weakly agreed to take another doctorate in June. Last June I declined three, because I was too tired to stay in hotels another six weeks and go trapesing over the country picking up sheepskins. One university offered to wait till this June, and I agreed. But I hate to think of losing May and June in England after spending the long dark winter here merely for another degree, which can do me no good at all.

From Allan Nevins

New York, September 25, 1932

This letter has a special purpose, and requires an early reply, so I shall place business before anything else. I shall also be blunt and direct. Lately I have been in communication, partly through Walter Lippmann, with the Dwight Morrow family. Mrs. Morrow is eager to have the biography of her late husband written by a distinguished hand. Her husband knew and admired your work, and on some suggestions of mine and Lippmann's she hopes she might interest you in the task. Her plan is to hire some competent man, at a good salary, to collect and arrange all the biographical data — to do the drudgery. You would then be asked to step in and execute the biographical masterpiece. She is quite ready herself, I understand, to make you a formal offer. But it is necessary for her to consult all the children, and perhaps other family connections, and secure their consent. So that now all that she wishes me to learn is whether you are, or could be, interested in her proposal.

Walter assures me she would make the most generous financial provision for the work. Since the Lindbergh tragedy she clings to this enterprise as one way of keeping her sanity, and it means more to her than anything else. Walter also tells me that the Morgan partners will throw open their archives. There would be a remarkable opportunity to lay bare the whole story of wartime and post-war financing as Morrow saw and assisted in it; to tell the story of his quite remarkable work in Mexico, with a good deal of the inside diplomacy of the Coolidge Administration; and of course to deal with an attractive and original personality. . . .

Your book is out here, as you know, and Scribner's have sent me a copy. What is more, I have agreed to write a review of it for the *Times.* They know I am a good friend of yours, and I have hence no compunctions in undertaking the job; for I tell you frankly, I am tired of writing reviews, and do this only because it gives me a chance to set your book in a fair light. I think Scribner's have done a capital job in illustrating it. It is one of the handsomest books I have ever seen for anything like the price. There are more typographical errors than there should be, but that is a characteristic of all Scribner books. . . .

Every sign here now points to the election of Roosevelt, and unless there is a sudden and striking change I expect to see him chosen by a staggering majority of the popular and electoral votes. Observers in the West tell me the bitterness there against Hoover is beyond belief — and I don't wonder. Here in New York he will do better, but the most seasoned politicians, including my friends Hamilton Fish and R. L. O'Brien, and such good observers as Lippmann, expect Roosevelt to win hands down.

To Allan Nevins

London, October 16, 1932

I am much obliged to you for acting as go-between in the Morrow matter, and scarcely know what to say. Certainly I could say nothing definite until I had taken the matter up with Scribners, which I am doing by this same post. In some ways the thing appeals to me, and in some it does not. I have, as you know, a soft spot in my heart for the house of Morgan, as the old man (father of the present J. P.) saved my father's financial life in a panic, and the doing of this would be a sort of return. I do not consider the house an unblemished lamb but it is unquestionably in my opinion the most broad minded and finest banking concern we have or ever have had in the U.S.A. I could therefore do the book with a considerable amount of sympathy and pleasure. I do not know much about Morrow beyond the somewhat bare facts that he was a partner of Morgan and resigned from making millions to give public service, which would also be a sympathetic subject. In addition, the possible financial terms which you somewhat vaguely hint at would be on the right side. I shall be 54 this week and as my family is short-lived, though I may live to be 90, my remaining working time is not of the endless vista sort that youth can look forward to. Five years ago I practically cut my modest fortune in two by marrying, and although I have never regretted it — quite the reverse — the problem of getting enough for two to be comfortable on in old age or illness has been a serious one. I have fortunately done well with my writing, but the taxes, both income and inheritance, seem to cut my independent income almost as fast as I can increase it. A $10,000 check I have coming to me in January, which a year ago I had hoped to save entire, now has to go entire to pay my income taxes next year; and the increase in inheritance tax means the having to save another $25,000 or so to leave my wife only where I would have left her last year before the new tax law. . . .

I realize that I cannot keep up the working pace of the last five any longer. I must do somewhat less work. I have therefore got to consider very carefully, at least for three or four years more, where best to expend my time and energy from the financial point of view. I am not a money-grubber. If I had been I should not have retired from my Stock Exchange firm to read and write, but I want to reach the point as soon as may be where we shall have $15,000 a year for old age, which, with the new taxes and death duties is not an extravagant figure. I have no idea what Mrs. Morrow would pay, or when or how.

From Henry S. Canby[1]

New York, October 21, 1932

I am answering your cable by letter since the important thing about the Lippmann essay is the essay and not the time, provided I can get it published sometime this autumn. By Lippmann as an American phenomenon I meant this. His articles are being syndicated to somewhere between four and five million people. Furthermore, they are being read to an extraordinary degree. When he came out for Roosevelt, last week, there were reverberations all over the country. He is discussed at every dinner party here in New York and I have found

[1] Editor, *Saturday Review of Literature;* Adams had offered to write on Lippmann.

university people who talked about him out in California last spring. I do not think any journalist with a message, so to speak, has gone so widely in recent years to so many classes. On the historical and social side you yourself, of course, would be a fair parallel. Lippmann, however, particularly in the last six months, has been a political influence also of very considerable importance. All of this makes an analysis of the man's mind and the nature of his influence viewed, so to speak, from the point of view of American history, extremely important.

To Allan Nevins

London, October 22, 1932

I rarely comment on reviews because I feel that they should usually be and remain wholly outside the sphere of personal relationships. In the case of your review in the *Times,* however, I cannot refrain from sending my most grateful thanks. You did not want to write it and you did, which is certainly reason for me to thank you. In the second place you have done me an extraordinary good turn. I did not expect high praise for the book in such reviews as might appear, and, as you say, had no idea of adding to my reputation. What I feared was a complete misunderstanding of the whole thing, perhaps flings at me for doing a mere pot-boiler to capitalize the success of the *Epic* when, in fact, I had signed the contract and planned this book before I had written a word of the *Epic*. What I badly needed someone to do for me was precisely what you have done in what seems to me one of the ablest, fairest and most discriminating reviews I have ever read in America. I do not see how you could have bettered a single word of it, and I wish every reviewer could read your article first, not because I want praise from them but understanding treatment. I am most deeply grateful to you.

I have, as I say, on principle rarely ever made a comment on a review, and until yesterday never an adverse one, and I am rather kicking myself that I did so in the case of Carl Becker whose review of the *Epic* in the April *American Historical Review* annoyed me very much. Did you see it? I would not have cared if he had pointed out legitimate faults in the book but he quarrels all through the review with the book because it is not in his opinion an epic (a title, of course, that I did not choose and fought not to have used). This over-emphasis on failure to fit a title would be rather unfair in any case I think but in this case is made much more so from the fact that Becker was evidently confusing all through an epic with a tragedy. Aristotle said that tragedy should purge the soul through the emotions of fear and pity, and when Becker complains that the book is not epical because it does not show "the tragic conflict between men's aspirations and the implacable decrees of fate," and does not cause his own soul to be "purged by fear and pity," it is quite evident he is thinking of tragedy. Aristotle said that the qualities of an epic were "a dignified theme, organic unity, and an orderly progress of the action." All this has nothing to do with fate, tragic conflicts, fear and pity, and when Becker belabors me in three paragraphs out of four in his review on the ground that the book is not an epic because it does not have to do with these things he is not only barking up the wrong tree but giving an unfair impression of the book to those who may know no more what epic and tragic is than he seems to himself. Being very tired yesterday and somewhat irritable perhaps, I wrote to him about this, rather shortly I fear, and wish now I had ignored it. It did make me rather angry, however, to be hammered in that way because of Becker's own slip — like the school boy who is whipped by the teacher when it is the latter who has made the mistake. A year or so ago I had occasion to point out to Alvin Johnson that Becker's article on Henry Adams in the Encyclopaedia of Social Sciences had more errors of fact in it than I had ever found made by any scholar in similar compass before. The article is really rather a scandal for what is supposed to be a scholarly work of reference. I think my letter was sent to Becker but he never commented on it. I imagine it annoyed him very much, for I am outside the academic pale of exact scholarship. I have never met Becker. What sort of chap is he? I never quite liked the fact that according to Fox he had agreed to allow his name to be used as one of the editors of our Macmillan series provided he would not have to do any work or even read the manuscripts. It does not seem a very scholarly way of earning money.

From Harry Hazlitt

New York, October 28, 1932

I am not a Socialist, and I don't think Norman Thomas a great man; nevertheless he seems to me personally superior in courage, sincerity, and economic understanding to either Hoover or Roosevelt. This sounds like the letter signed by the "writers" supporting Thomas; that is because I wrote that letter!

I think Hoover's reëlection would be a world disaster. If there were the difference between Tweedledee and Tweedledum in Hoover and Roosevelt I might vote for Roosevelt on the theory that the one chance in several million was worth taking. But Roosevelt grows worse day by day; he wobbles on the bonus where Hoover is definite; he denounces the Smoot-Hawley tariff in one breath and retracts this denunciation in another, either by promising just as much "protection" under him as under the Republicans, or by proposing some preposterous arrangement, like a separate treaty with each country for tariff reduction. I have not the slightest confidence in the man, and though I still think he will be elected in spite of Hoover's recent gains, I would not want it on my conscience that I voted for him.

From Carl Becker

Ithaca, November 1, 1932

I am sorry if you think that my review of your book did not do it justice. Perhaps it didn't. Still, it expresses, as well as I was able to do in short space my judgment of it. Whether that judgment is right or wrong I feel sure that a different title would not have changed it. The title merely gave me a convenient lead for indicating what seemed to me to be the qualities of the work. I was quite aware that it is tragedy that is supposed to purge the soul by fear and pity. You will note that what I say is "banishes all sense of epic grandeur and *tragic conflict* which the story of American history is so well suited to convey." At first the editor of the *Review* raised the query as to the use of the words 'purge the soul by fear and pity' in connection with 'epic.' When I pointed out to him that the words as I used them referred to the above words 'tragic conflict' he felt that the sentence as it stood was quite all right. I still think so. The closing paragraph might have been written even if the book had had some other title. It does not say, or mean to imply, that the book should have been an epic or a tragedy: it merely says that while the book is an interesting and valuable tract for the times (and surely tracts for the times are now much called for) it leaves one without a sense of the epic and tragic which might have been found in the story of American history.

From Worthington C. Ford

Paris, November 3, 1932

Why should you hesitate over the Morrow offer? Family biographies are apt to be dismal failures, ninety-nine in a hundred. But it would not be a family biography in your hands. Exactly the contrary. It would be history and of an unusual quality, for you would be dealing with the most important international questions, commercial, financial and treaty, that have so complicated today. You would be continuing your studies intensively on your generation and from papers closed to others, and the Civil War volume can wait. The Morrow would be passed on to others and — well, I will not predict, for I am much put out by what passes for biography. Take the opening, highly creditable to the Morrow family in making the offer to such a writer as yourself, and a good opening for making a notable contribution from you and also to your reputation. As history, it will be exactly in your vein and will give you an insight into the world's problems — from the bankers' point of view — that will be useful. I say bankers, because the credit system has been the guiding force, from colonial development to dollar diplomacy. I have read Bowers' Beveridge and was impressed by his skill in keeping Beveridge in the center and weaving around him a web of good history. His summary of the tariff fight of 1909 and of the Progressive Party and its disaster is excellent — not final, for who can write finality? but good, well documented and new. You will have treble the opportunity in the Morrow unless the popular estimation of the man is wholly wrong. Even if it has been wrong, there is a chance to tell a story of lasting importance.

From Walter Lippmann

New York, November 17, 1932

I had not seen your article in the *Outlook,* but I do remember reading another article of yours, I think in *Harper's,* which has always remained in my mind as prophetic. But this one is even more exact and impressive. My recollection is that I said in one of the articles that you refer to that the persons who foresaw the trouble were very few. At that time I had in mind Paul Warburg, Dwight Morrow, among Americans, and now I should add you. I myself realized all through the Twenties that the situation was thoroughly out of balance and that prosperity was on a false foundation, but I did not have any idea as to the violence of the crash nor its date. Luckily, I didn't have any money at the time to lose.

The state of mind here at the moment is not very hopeful from the point of view of the debt settlement and the other adjustments. Neither Congress nor the public at large appreciate how dangerous is the position of sterling, and those people who do appreciate it don't dare to expound it for fear of producing a panic. Roosevelt, I think, understands that aspect of the matter. Hoover, I believe, doesn't. Hoover has the authority and Roosevelt quite properly feels that he must not accept responsibility when he has no power.

From Carl Becker

Ithaca, November 21, 1932

I have just received your note. I see no reason why an author should not comment on a reviewer's treatment of his book. I am rather glad you did in this case, since I was glad to learn that the title was not yours. It is quite possible that I made too much use of the title. I myself have never found reviews of my own books very satisfactory as a rule; not because the reviewers haven't lauded them sufficiently — they have been cordial enough; but chiefly because it is not often that they have even been aware of the precise thing I tried to do. Maybe they are to blame for that; maybe the books are to blame. I realize that my reviews of other people's books may be unsatisfactory in the same way.

From Allan Nevins

New York, December 8, 1932

I should have written you long before; and the task has been deferred from day to day simply because I have had so much to say to you. I am glad you liked my review of your book in the *Times.* My idea in reluctantly writing it — as I told the book review editor, Donald Adams — was that I might put in its proper light a volume all too likely to be misjudged; the more likely, because your success has excited a good deal of jealousy among the more meanspirited of our craft. Many people told me they liked the review. Evidently it was liked at Scribners, for though I asked Howe not to use it in advertising, thinking that my name had been over-employed already by Little, Brown in your behalf, they have persistently done so. I have protested again, saying that I am sure you would like to have a change, and this time effectively. Your book is a great success. All the best-seller lists contain it. I must say that I feel a little mean-spirited envy sometimes myself! Fox and Muzzey like the text, and Fox thinks the publishers have done a superb job of illustrating it — as of course they have.

I have been reading proofs on the book, and am sending the first of them back to the publishers, with a few corrections which I forbear to mention. I ought to say that in my reports on your manuscript I did not list all the errors I found, but simply altered the text where I was sure I was right; as for example, where you named Palmer as the Democratic nominee in 1920 for Vice President. Since it was Franklin D. Roosevelt, that slip might have been noted by a good many people.

I am fearful that I may miss something still in the proofs, and shall try to get Muzzey to look at them; for I know you would not object.

On the question of the life of Dwight Morrow I have heard nothing of late from Lippmann, and believe nothing has been done. But I talked of the matter about three weeks ago with Will D. Howe. I told him that my own feeling was that you probably ought not to write such a book; and that certainly you ought not to engage to do it until you had scrutinized carefully the collection of papers to make sure there is something interesting to write about. Some men write interesting letters, make witty speeches, have wide and picturesque contacts; some who have equal opportunities are dull as ditchwater on all these counts. My supposition is that Morrow had a keen and alert mind, and wrote illuminating and important letters to friends. But it is just possible you might find a barren desert there, and would find your task flat and unprofitable. You have nothing to lose by waiting. I have surrendered all contact with the affair, for I don't know Mrs. Morrow, and Lippmann seems to be whirling frantically about from Washington to New York and Albany. I simply conveyed the general sense of your letter to them, and that is that.

As I also told Howe, I wish you would return to the field of pure history, and tossing the best sellers and book clubs overboard, write something like your New England trilogy again. I refuse to believe you are as hard up as you suppose. At any rate, the success of your latest book would, I think, put you in an entirely safe position. If I had one-fifth the savings you have, and one-third your income, I should consider myself a rich man; and I have young children, and am helping support three families besides my own. . . .[1]

The *Cleveland*, thank heaven, is doing well. It is in its fourth printing now (all small printings), and twice the blasted publishers have let the bookstores run out of copies. We shall probably sell five thousand copies in the first year, which is rated good for these depressed times, and for a $5 a book. Pringle hardly did as well with his *Roosevelt*. By the way, Pringle told me the other day that after his *Roosevelt* appeared, he got a letter from the executors of T. R.'s estate, enclosing a bill for $10,000! for use of the manuscripts. What is more, George Roosevelt (a nephew) threatened court action; and the publishers finally agreed to let the executors have all the earnings of the book between $10,000 and $15,000. Of course, it is not likely to earn $10,000. But the whole thing strikes me as one of the damdest outrages I ever

[1] A depression situation all too widespread.

heard of. Mrs. Roosevelt disapproved, and Herman Hagedorn and other friends, but George Roosevelt was adamant; said if he "dissipated the assets of the estate"—and the letters are assets—he would be liable to a penitentiary sentence. I begin to think my good friend Mrs. Preston (Mrs. Cleveland that was) an angel. She has certainly been a good sport about the book, which treats Grover roughly in spots—more roughly than Pringle treated Roosevelt; and she is coöperating vigorously in my issuance this coming year of a volume of Grover's letters, on an even division of royalties. . . .

Well, I must stop, though I would gladly write more. I wish I could see you and tell you of my troubles, for the financial burden I bear weighs on me heavily, and my hopes. We are all heartily ashamed of the attitude Congress takes on the debt question. You may assure your English friends that the prevailing feeling in this city is that if England pays another penny, until her debt is rigorously scaled down, she is more foolish than we suppose her; and that thinking sentiment here will support her in a thoroughly defiant position on the subject. We are glad to see Hoover go, and take the pestiferous gang of Smoots, Hawleys, Julius Kleins, and others along with him. O'Brien, chairman of Hoover's Tariff Commission, told me the Sunday before election (he dined with me) that he had lost all faith in Hoover's intellectual integrity, and that he believed that his reëlection would be the greatest calamity that could befall the country.

From Worthington C. Ford

Paris, December 18, 1932

Who ever intimated that your *March* was anything of a disappointment? Not I. On the contrary I thought it met all the requirements of such a book and in a way to extort my admiration. For I knew under what a pressure it had been written and to have obtained its purpose with so few omissions was a feat to excite wonder. I have given six copies to six persons, with the *Epic,* enjoining them to read them together—the *March* chapters first and then the chapter in the *Epic* that corresponds in time. It has worked remarkably well in the case under my immediate hand and the reader has become enthusiastic on American history. That is a pretty good test and would be my class method—if I had a class instead of a God-forsaken position in a foreign land where much of everything is offered, a bit damaged and under price. I am rereading Taine's French Revolution and am out for a set of Sorel on the same subject.

From Nicholas Murray Butler

New York, December 22, 1932

The late Mr. Charles Scribner took up with me the question of an autobiography, and as a matter of fact I began work on one in 1929. I chose as my title Across the Busy Years, and in order to preempt it the Scribners made formal notice of the fact that such a book was in preparation. During the summer of 1929 I made considerable headway, but have not been able to return to the job since then. There are two or three considerations which make it very difficult. One is the apparent vanity or egotism, no matter how much one suppresses his own personality, of describing in detail so many important happenings behind the scenes as I am able to describe covering a period of at least forty years. Another difficulty is the immense mass of material which I have in the way of memoranda, notes of conversations and important happenings, and correspondence of the most intimate character with all sorts and kinds of history-makers. My correspondence with Theodore Roosevelt alone fills six big volumes, each nearly the size of a "Webster's Dictionary.". . .

I quite understand your feeling about the debt situation, for I have been laboring at that problem since the Balfour Note was written in 1922. When the original settlements were made ten years ago it proved to be wholly impossible to get into the heads of our American official representatives any understanding whatever of the economic and financial calamity that they were so carelessly and so nonchalantly organizing. The paralysis of the world's trade, the forcing of nation after nation off the gold standard, and the complete disruption of foreign exchange relationships were all pointed to by me then as necessary results of the policy that was being entered upon. . . .

I have insisted again and again that the fundamental question is not whether the debtor nations can afford to pay, but whether the creditor nation can afford to receive. In my judgment it cannot for reasons which are clearly set out in the various speeches which I have pleasure in sending you.

A great change is going on in public opinion here, and by April 34 shall see a revolution similar to that which it took ten years to bring about in the matter of the repeal of the 18th Amendment. Labor organizations and farm organizations are demanding a re-study of this debt problem, and the influential papers and weekly periodicals published in small towns throughout the country are doing the same. Eventually all this will reach Washington and will have its effect.

It is my considered judgment that the default by France helps the situation greatly. I should not have wished England to default for obvious reasons, but France could default with impunity. The reason why I think so is that since the official mind at Washington has shown itself quite impervious to economic fact or to argument, it could only be reached by a knock-down blow. This is precisely what France has administered.

To M. A. De Wolfe Howe

London, January 26, 1933

My accident seven weeks ago was a close call. I was reading late at night with a celluloid eye shade of the usual sort on. With my mind wholly on what I was reading I struck a match to light my pipe and in an instant the world appeared to have burst into flames in my face. The shade was ablaze, as were also my moustache and hair, and I had sense enough to realize that at whatever cost I must keep my eyes shut tight. That left me rather helpless, however, and no one heard my call for help. Unluckily, at the moment Kay was in the bathroom on the floor below, with three doors shut between us, and the maids were down in the basement. I tried to rub and beat out my burning hair with my bare hands, forgetting the shade. I knew from the smell and sensation that my moustache and hair were on fire and must be put out. Somehow the fire as a whole did not go out and in despair of succeeding I clasped my hands in agony over my forehead. I *had* put out my hair, and when the shade burned up to my hands, it went out, but only after burning some of the flesh off the right one, and the skin from both. The skin was burned off my entire face except my chin, my eyelashes and brows were burned off and the lids deeply burned. Both doctors say I have only a miracle to thank that both my eyes did not go. I did not know until the lids were forced apart next day that they had not. Had the accident happened some years ago I might well have subsequently lost my eyes from infection and would almost certainly have been badly scarred, but thanks to the new treatment I hope to get off with practically no scarring. For four weeks, two nurses sprayed tannic acid on me day and night. I am still housed and shall have to be very careful as to the weather I go out in for at least two months yet, owing to the extreme tenderness and tendency to inflammation in all my new skin.

From Walter Mitchell[1]

Phoenix, February 14, 1933

I have had the pleasure of reading your *Epic of America,* and while I am no judge of such matters, and you have doubtless been deluged with complimentary letters about it, I venture to add mine to that long list. It is more thrilling than a novel. I got really excited over it, and that does not happen often.

Now comes the inevitable 'but.' You speak of the 'silver heresy.' It fell to my lot as a youngster to have to follow the debates in the Senate when the silver question was to the fore, and it has always seemed to me that the prejudice of people in the East 'who have' was so aroused as to what the 'have nots' might do, that the silver question was not able to get a hearing on its merits. This was exemplified by the continued nomination of Bryan, who was regarded as a radical on other grounds as well. For instance, after the 1896 election, I heard Senator Lindsay of Kentucky, who was one of the Democratic bolters on the gold platform, say to Senator Barry of Arkansas, that if at Chicago a man like Bland, whom they all knew and trusted, had been nominated instead of Bryan, there would have been no gold bolt. The question of silver coinage has never come up except when the dollar is worth more than it should be, and whenever gold has been discovered in sufficient quantities so that the per capita circulation has risen, the silver question has dropped out of sight. In other words, instead of its being a silver matter, the whole question at bottom seems to me to be that of a larger per capita circulation so that the value of the dollar might be more nearly what it ought to be in the light of what it can purchase.

Speaking of Bland, I was surprised that you gave him no credit for the whole silver movement. Bryan simply harvested Bland's crop. Indeed, had Bland permitted his managers at Chicago to make any deals at all, he would have been nominated, I am convinced, on the first ballot.

To Worthington C. Ford

London, March 1, 1933

Last night we made our first social plunge since my accident eleven weeks ago. It was at Lady Astor's and there was a huge crowd, a thorough old fashioned "rout," but of extraordinarily nice people, a far

[1] Protestant Episcopal Bishop of Arizona since 1926. He had been born and educated in Senator Richard P. Bland's Missouri.

better looking crowd than at the Embassy on our previous experience of that sort of thing here. Lady Astor gave a dinner first for Mellon,[1] the Prince being there, and the reception after began at half-past ten. When we had lunched there each time we had not been above the ground floor and I was amazed at the extent of the drawing rooms upstairs, all of which were open last night. Lady Astor and Mellon received, the Prince remaining in the dining room until about eleven. We began to think we were not going to see him at all although asked there to meet him! The scene was brilliant, the lights, flowers, stars and garters, decorations on everybody, and enough diamond coronets to pay the June instalment on the debt. I won't attempt a list of even a few of the titles there — *vide* the *Times* — the people more interesting to me being the political lights, Grandi, Baldwin, Macdonald, etc. etc. Some I already knew to speak to, as Lord Charnwood of the Lincoln *Life,* the Marquess of Lothian (formerly Philip Kerr, through whom I first met Lady Astor), and a few others. There were also a good many of the type of Sir Arthur Salter.

At eleven Lady Astor captured the Prince from the dining room and walked with him through the drawing rooms, introducing him. Luckily we were among those to whom she did so and we had quite a chat with him until she pulled him on to others. He is very boyish and it was amusingly like a mother taking a small child about to meet her guests. It was really almost funny! He is very shy and I think had been doing himself rather well at dinner. Kay had been worrying about her curtsey and had watched some of the other ladies making rather deep ones as he come in our direction. When introduced, however, he solved any difficulty by immediately holding out his hand to her and then to me, and saying "how d'you do" quite abruptly like a shy kid. Then he said "Where do you come from?" I said we were Americans, and he said in the same shy abrupt way, "What business are you in?" I said I was not in any, but wrote books, and that Dave Finley[2] (Chancellor of our Embassy) told me he had given him one of mine, *The Epic of America,* but I realized he would have no time to read it.

With that he stuffed his hands deep in his pockets and leaned back looking at me and said, "My God, did you write that?" I said yes, but had not supposed he had read it. He answered "My God, yes I

[1] Andrew F. Mellon had just concluded his service as Ambassador to Great Britain, 1931-32.

[2] David E. Finley, counselor in the London Embassy 1932-33, and later director of the National Gallery in Washington and chairman of the United States Fine Arts Commission.

did — every word of it. It is a marvelous book. It helped me a lot to understand America. You know I haven't been there now for ten years." He chatted a moment or two more about the book, showing he had read it, and then asked Kay if we were living here and how we liked it. She said she liked it so much that she would never go home if it were not for the income tax here. He laughed and said "My God, it *is* stiff, isn't it?" Finally Lady Astor took him by the arm and with a "Good Night" precisely like a small boy he was led up to someone else. In spite of his My Gods and perhaps an extra drink or two and his bashfulness, there was something very winning about him, and I can understand his popularity.

From Will D. Howe

New York, March 9, 1933

I think you would be astounded at the changes which have taken place since you left America. Of course, no one could sum up these changes in a few words, but I am going to try to give you one or two impressions, which I have received not only in New York, but in other places during the last two or three months, especially in the Middlewest and in Washington. It took us a long while to realize that we could not get back to 1929 and the rosy conditions of that era. I really believe that a large majority of the people in this country now realize that it will be impossible ever in our lifetime to return to these conditions. In other words, everybody realizes now that everybody must pay a price for what has been. Indeed, it is impossible to think of one's possessions in the old terms. The whole matter has to go through a readjustment. . . .

This last week has stunned the country. Of course, we read in the paper that there is a note of optimism and expressions of admiration as to leadership, but, if one can form an impression of things by going about and talking with various people, one certainly gets the impression that our country has simply been stunned. . . . Of course, everyone at this moment is awaiting almost breathlessly the next few hours in Congress.

From Worthington C. Ford

Paris, March 21, 1933

Yesterday I got from Morgan your gift[1] and can only repeat my high appreciation of the dedication and my admiration and affection

[1] His volume *Henry Adams,* dedicated to Worthington C. Ford.

— admiration for your great accomplishment and affection for your personal qualities. I sat up the night reading the *Life* and regard it as one of the best things you have done. You faced the *Education* — a competition apparently hopeless — and you have given the needed gloss to make that story understandable to the reader, whether ordinary or not. You have deftly touched its weaknesses without destroying the interest of the original, and you make Adams human — as he was — something other than his own depreciation of self that was in reality an appreciation remarkable for its detachment and justice. So, it is one more feather in your cap — or if you prefer, laurel crown.

From Worthington C. Ford

Paris, March 22, 1933

You will find an interesting situation in America, worthy your study and pen. The President has done well, but I question his ability to raise prices and fear he may stumble there. At present his energy is inspiring confidence and that is some gain. But the succession of revelations on banking methods may yet give more shakes and panics. He has two favorable years in which to make his mark — as Wilson did — and he has made a good beginning. On the other hand what is Germany aiming for? Her political drift towards monarchy is capable of explanation, but the agents and their actions are nearer Russia than Italy. To suppress Communism is one thing, but to suppress art is another, and the ostracism of scientists, scholars and musicians is a revival of a past which is of the darkest. I begin to wonder if I shall get to Bayreuth in July and if my nose, out of sympathy, is not taking on a Jewish shape.

To M. A. De Wolfe Howe

Washington, May 7, 1933

We landed in New York after an excellent passage, and spent ten most hectic days there, including three in which I had to take to my bed. The change in tempo not only between London and my birthplace but between a sick room of nearly four months and the whirl of engagements and publicity was too much, and I fell easy prey to a bug. Then we came here, where I have seen many interesting people and had the innumerable talks of the sort you know well in the Cosmos and elsewhere.

One of the outstanding ones was a whole evening with Hull, the Secretary of State. The night before MacDonald arrived he telephoned me about eight and asked Kay and myself if we could come at once, and we spent the evening with him and Mrs. Hull until 10:30. I like him very much, very simple, modest, unassuming, thoroughly upright, and in his own field very able. Fortunately that field, of economics, tariffs, and so on, is of more importance than the older problems of political diplomacy in the State Department at present. Without repeating the conversation I may say that I judged quite distinctly, even more from the questions he asked than from any direct statement, that the administration does not intend to use its vast powers of inflation if it is possible to avoid it.

I think they hope that the business improvement, now well under way, whether permanently or not, will continue sufficiently as to diminish very materially the demand for inflation, which always evaporates quickly when prices rise. It is a situation which has its dangers, but in my opinion there was nothing for Roosevelt to do but to pluck the nettle bravely and trust to his star and ours. He could not play the part of a Cleveland. The situation was more complex and dangerous. The present Congress contains many men of the stone age, and the more seasoned Congressmen realize it well. Roosevelt with admirable courage has skimmed all the scum off the boiling pot on the Hill and if all goes well the brew for the next meal may be clearer and less poisonous. So far he has surpassed my highest hopes, and has also made a profound impression on Europe.

What I gathered from Hull is confirmed by what I get elsewhere. One of the leading newspaper special correspondents at dinner the other night said that Roosevelt in his more intimate talks with them has several times emphasized the fact that his powers are permissive and not mandatory, giving the impression that he intends to inflate as little as may be if at all. I also dined with Gordon Auchincloss, Col. House's son-in-law, and he said the old man had said the night before that he thought he was himself something of a politician but that he was a child in the game compared with Roosevelt.

My own opinion is that business has really got off to a promising start. As Dun-Bradstreet point out, the improvement is no longer spotty but country-wide and on a broad front — rail earnings, car loadings, commodity prices, steel production, motor cars, wholesale and retail trade — and has now shown steady gains for several weeks well above seasonal — as well as that excellent index, electric power consumption.

To Lawrence Gipson

New York, June 3, 1933

I appreciate very greatly the suggestion as to the dinner, and Mrs. Adams and I would be glad to accept the invitation. There is only one point which embarrasses me somewhat, and that is the request that I give a talk at the dinner. To a professor used to facing a class, even if not larger audiences, I suppose it seems absurd, but in fact getting up and speaking before an assembly is such a nervous strain for me, and I do it so badly, that I no longer attempt it, other than a few words of thanks or something of that sort. When I was offered the degree at Lehigh I was also asked to make the address, and declined on the above grounds, and am not taking a doctorate at one of the most important western universities because they coupled it of necessity with the chief address of the day. I am at present utterly tired out with my three months hard work here at home following my four months' confinement to my room in London as a result of the bad accident to my face in December, and I not only have not the time in the next few days to prepare a "talk" but would dread the added strain of having to give one.

To Worthington C. Ford

London, August 21, 1933

I have been meaning to write, but the days are going by in a succession of from three to six books each on the Civil War, running through them and making my notes on slips. The present and its problems have receded and I am almost living in 1860-65, so absorbed is my mind in that period and its men. I am still tired but am better than when I landed from America and — knock wood — am sleeping better than for a year past, though none too deeply now. I have at least got away from the mild soporific I had to take for nearly a year and get a moderate and natural sleep on Bass Ale. . . .

Many thanks for the two misprints, which I have sent on to Scribners this morning. You spoke, I think, in a letter last winter, of my being weak in my treatment of the Civil War. Probably I was, and I would like to re-write certain passages in the light of all this reading I am doing, but, without troubling you with a long critique, I would be glad to know if some one point or more struck you, as I am now to write of it all at greater length. May I ask you also what you think of the conclusions reached by Owsley as to the ineffectiveness of the blockade and the unimportance of wheat? I have gone again carefully over his book *King Cotton Diplomacy* and think that, like most people who take new viewpoints, he rather overdoes his thesis, though it contains much truth. Do not bother to write at length on these topics, and not at all if there is a chance of our meeting at Emil's. . . . I agree with you in your scepticism as to Roosevelt, and am at sea as to what is in store for all of us.

To M. A. De Wolfe Howe

Florence, September 23, 1933

We have just had four heavenly days motoring through Tuscany and Umbria — Arezzo, Assisi, Perugia, Orvieto, Pisa, Volterra, San Gimingnano — the countryside at its best, the trees loaded with olives and the vines heavy with grapes. We may make another excursion to Ravenna, Rimini and San Marino, but in any case take the Rome Express to Paris Saturday, and go back to London a few days later to begin the Civil War! . . .

From this distance affairs in my native land seem to me extremely hazardous. I *hope* all will go well but I have no confidence in any one man, or group of men, being able to guide the complex economy of an industrial nation of 120,000,000 and trying to put economic laws "in reverse." This is not a slap at Roosevelt for whom I would have voted had I had a vote. He had to try the experiment, perhaps, as our new democracy is not of the sort to tighten belts or starve for five years. Nevertheless, I doubt very much if the experiment will work. *If* it cannot, or any similar one, and if the inevitable cycles are no longer to be "borne," then I see nothing but social disorganization. Perhaps we have stood the evils of capitalism as long as may be and are to fly to other systems which will have equal or greater evils. The eternal cycle of change.

In England things are really better, and more money is being spent than in some years. I feel that recovery in general can be glimpsed in many parts of the world. I am afraid we have set back our own recovery by loss of confidence, but may be wrong. I do not like Johnson's talk on the bally-hoo and prosperity processions. What use is it to ask me in the name of patriotism, to spend money on things I do not need when magazines cut their pay 25%, when as against my total expenses this year of $12,000 I am paying $13,000 in taxes with every prospect of increase, when the rise in inheritance taxes means that I must save nearly a year's income to leave my wife as well off as she would have been if I had died last year, when the threat is held over my head of a 50% reduction in purchasing power by a 50-cent dollar, when no one knows what will happen to bonds by inflation, when Public Service companies are being attacked in all directions, etc.? Perhaps all this is necessary but it does not build up capital or create confidence, the two things always hitherto essential to recovery from a deep depression.

To Governor Wilbur Cross

London, October 9, 1933

I am struck every time that I go to Italy with the extraordinary improvement in the life of the poorer people. I certainly have no use for dictatorships but Mussolini is the one genius among dictators whom the post-war period has thrown up. This time, for example, we motored among a great many of the hill towns in the Appennines and lower mountains. Fifteen years ago in the small villages and even larger towns the children would have been almost little savages, in rags with matted hair and vermin in their heads and with little or no morals whatever, begging for coppers and ready to render any sort of service, moral or immoral. Now they are well dressed, as neat as can be, going to school, walking along like self-respecting little citizens of a great nation. The change is really simply marvelous and both my wife and I rather dreaded coming back to London with its miserably dirty poor children, of whom we see a good many as there is a slum not far behind us from which the children come to the playground in the corner of the Gardens.

Conditions a few years ago going from England to Italy were all against Italy; now it is the other way. Six or seven years ago the swagger of the Black Shirts was extremely annoying; then even on the de luxe trains they would throw open the door of the railway carriage and look you over in an insolent way even if no remarks were made. That has passed now and the Black Shirts at railway stations are simply dignified and courteous. . . .

On the other hand of course there is still no freedom of speech or the press and I don't see how a great nation can continue without freedom of thought and expression. One has the feeling that Mussolini has cut the tree of national life off at the top and the little suckers are now growing up from the roots luxuriantly, but that does not mean that the tree itself will continue to thrive. . . . The area of freedom in Europe is narrowing. Sir John Simon was speaking of it in private conversation the other night. Torture is used in Italy, Germany and Russia and in that respect we seem to be going back to the Middle Ages. The Scandinavian Countries, Belgium, Switzerland, France and England now form all that is left of a genuinely free Europe. One feels a little as they must have felt in the days of the old Roman Empire when the Barbarian circle grew smaller round the threatened Empire.

To Governor Wilbur L. Cross[1]

London, December 11, 1933

The critical point here in Europe now is the German-Austrian situation. I have discussed this lately with [Lewis] Einstein who was for ten years our Minister for Czecho-Slovakia and who understands the Balkan situation fairly well; with Callender, who is the Representative of the New York *Times;* and with others. The point is whether the Hitler Government will try not only to swallow Austria but also to build up, either as a consolidated or federated State, a new Mittel-Europa. This is considered the real political problem over here. Confidentially, I know the British Cabinet is considering it. It has been suggested that one of the king's sons should go later on for the Winter Sports to the Tyrol and while there spend a night or two in Vienna — perhaps the Duke of Gloucester may go as a gesture to show Hitler that England is interested in Austria. I am afraid, however, that nothing will develop and that England will watch events until possibly it is too late as she did in 1914. At any rate, this is the storm centre of Europe, and it is possible that an article on the future of Middle Europe might be a good idea.

To Allan Nevins

London, December 26, 1933

I find it the way of this world that the person who can take care of his own affairs usually has to take care of others. I feel sorry for all those who went into debt, for example, in the late and unlamented boom, but as I did not, but kept my head and saved my money while my farming neighbors were mortgaging their farms to buy Hudson super sixes etc., and in two cases actually had the nerve to say I, as a "city man," ought to drive something better than a Chevrolet, I do not quite see the justice of cutting my savings to a fifty cent dollar to help them pay their debts. I realize the disastrous drop in farm prices and that they are out of line with some others, but have less sympathy

[1] Cross, still editor of the *Yale Review,* was well launched in his three terms as Governor of Connecticut, 1931-37.

than I might have with many individual farmers who were speculating as largely in lands and goods as were the Wall Street bulls in stocks. Between 1915 and 1929 most farmers had plenty of chance to lessen their mortgages and clear their homes, but not they. My next door neighbor put in parquet floors, a fine bathroom, sold his horse and bought a car, gave up his rowboat for fishing and bought a power boat, gave up his cow, pig and chickens, and so on. I, next door, denied myself and saved some money when I did not have much; and now the New Deal calls on me to pay his debts. This is exaggerated, but it has too much truth to be pleasant. I have been fortunate in having a best seller, but, not to speak of others, I have had to put up $1000 this year for one relation whom I considered far richer than I would ever be, and pay the funeral expenses of another. However, my lad, that is the way of the world, and I suppose it is good for us, though I do think you have a bit more than your share at present. At one time, my father, who was never rich, after his father lost his money in 1873, was carrying in good part thirteen relations besides his own family. If he had not always done such things, I suppose I would have easily $100,000 more, but I would not have had him different. On the tombstone of my 8th great grand-father is carved "Here lies an honest man," and as the generations go along such inheritances count more than money. . . .

As for book reviews. . . . I cannot see that they make the slightest difference, and I have ceased to have any intellectual respect for them. I say that without any sour grapes because in my short literary career of a dozen years I think I have had an extremely good press, both in American and foreign countries. But as to effect — the *Epic* had a less good press in America than almost any other book I have written, being sneered at in the *Nation, Sun,* and elsewhere, yet sold 140,000 copies, and made my reputation here in Europe, where it has been published and translated in four countries. The *Henry Adams* had a far better press at home, and an excellent one here in the English edition, though partly spoiled by Boni's padding it so, and has scarcely sold a copy. The public likes a book or it doesn't, the word goes round, and I can't see that the pundit reviewers count at all. . . .

I am delighted, and encouraged, that your *Cleveland* is in its 7th printing. It is a big and fairly expensive book, and that it should have sold so in these times speaks well for the public. I am looking forward to the *Letters,*[1] and hope they do as well. . . .

[1] *Grover Cleveland: A Study in Courage,* appeared in 1932; *The Letters of Grover Cleveland* followed in 1933.

I note that Harry Hansen,[1] quoting the *Socialist Review* the other day, said that I had "rehabilitated my fortune but lost my reputation in the last five years." As a statement not of opinion but of fact that comes fairly near being actionable for your old paper. To say I had to "rehabilitate" my fortune means that I had lost money, which I never did, though I never had any "fortune" in the American sense. "Reputation" offers difficulties, but leaving sales aside, as of course no indication whatever of reputation, it is within the past five years that I have been made a member of the American Academy, of the Royal Society, that my books have been widely noticed in Europe, highly spoken of by such papers as the London *Times* and Manchester *Guardian,* etc., and have brought me into contact with men of high standing who paid no attention to my earlier work. There is, however, an occasional note that makes me pause, sounded by people who think I ought to go back to research of some limited period. I have been having a long and interesting correspondence with Newton Baker, who clearly feels so. I am myself getting fed up with the idea that scholarship means only research and more research, and that wisdom, if one can acquire it, and the power to generalize and interpret, are somehow not "scholarly." Here in Europe the *Epic* is considered my best book because it is philosophical and interpretive and not mere fact-finding. . . .

P.S. I have read half of the Cleveland Letters and wish every American voter could read it. Without such intention on the part of the writer it is a terrible indictment of our modern democracy and the average man who runs and reads — the newspapers. Without any charm of style they give, taken together, a marvellously striking picture of what happens to an honest man when he tries to serve his country in public life. As a "case" the book is superb in showing the relations of the modern public to its public servants. You have done a most useful job in giving it to the public, and I hope it will be read and taken to heart. He indeed must be a brave man who, with any sensitiveness for himself or his family, would undertake a career of high elective office after reading it.

America's Tragedy: Return to Connecticut

Adams's first letter to M. A. De Wolfe Howe in 1934 referred to the troubles that forced him out of his Palace Court apartment and

[1] Harry Hansen, literary editor of the Chicago *Daily News,* 1920-26, was on the staff of the New York *World-Telegram,* 1931-48.

into a Holland Park residence in London. The transfer cost him time and mental turmoil, but at any rate he was still in his beloved London. He spoke also of the fact that some friends thought the new manuscript he had just completed, *America's Tragedy,* one of the best he had written. It was indeed a book of sweep and perception, and duly appearing that autumn, received good reviews, though later it disappointed him by its restricted sales. After *The Epic,* anything would have been disappointing, and the American public was as yet not greatly interested in the theme of sectional conflict. The Civil War boom would come later. It was under a feeling of some financial pressure that Adams, buying the Sheffield house at Southport in Connecticut, and facing the confusions of moving his household back to America, carried on the tasks required by his new contract with Scribner's.

His disenchantment with the New Deal grew steadily from 1934 to 1936. It was not the massive governmental interventions on behalf of the farmers, laborers, and underprivileged generally that he condemned — he approved them; it was the heavy expenditures, drastic taxation, and unbalanced budgets accompanying the Social Security program, with an appearance of financial carelessness, that disturbed him. Some aspects of the reforms in banking and public utilities control also alarmed him. Although the increase in industrial production and national income in these years was remarkable, Roosevelt himself was anxious over the mounting national debt, and showed this anxiety in vetoing the veterans' bonus bill and cutting back W.P.A. expenditures. Adams feared that in climbing out of the slough of depression the government was stumbling into new disasters. At the same time, he warmly approved of practically all the foreign policy measures of the President and Cordell Hull.

To M. A. De Wolfe Howe

London, February 14, 1934

The move, the law suit, the getting settled in and all took up a whole month, and put me so far behind with my book that I have had to work very steadily and hard since then until I sent it to Scribner's on January 31st as promised. I then immediately had to turn to writing a history of the last year in America, as the first supplementary chapter for the subscription edition of the *March,* and next do a long-delayed article for the *Times.* Meanwhile I have dictated an average of fifty letters a week, but the letters to my friends have mostly remained unwritten. The few readers the book has yet had in manuscript appear to like it. Allen Boyd says it is the best I have done, and my wife and sister say it is fully up to the *Epic* if not better, but of course I have no idea how it may strike others or the public.

Speaking of the *March,* Schlesinger[1] is here in London lecturing, and in sending regrets to a tea for him the other day I at last told him I thought he had been quite unfair in his review of the *March* in international or American affairs. On the whole, I agree with you as to Roosevelt, though I feel rather that we are walking a tight-rope across Niagara. With you, I prefer the professors to the bankers but would prefer a rather more "right-wing" lot. A right-wing professor is likely to be far off from a left-wing banker! I am betting personally on our coming out of this all right eventually, but the bill in taxes is going to be colossally, and I think unnecessarily, big.

From Worthington C. Ford

Paris, May 17, 1934

For your amusement I enclose a letter from my successor in the M.H.S.[2] He had sent to me a copy of the *New England Quarterly* (Morison's magazine) in which is a notice of your Henry Adams volume, signed B de V. Who B de V. was, I had not the least idea; but happening to pick up the newly issued volume of American Historical Writings I noted Bernard De Voto and wrote Mitchell a remonstrance against admitting such a note in the magazine and said it was "nasty." I had in view letting Morison know that his magazine ought not to allow personal prejudices to control, as he himself is subject to prejudice which he does not conceal. I have given Mitchell permission to print what he wishes of my letter. If it results only in "pistols and coffee," I can handle it. If it results in a libel suit, you will be held responsible. I am sending to you the *Quarterly,* which need not be returned. If you are curious about De Voto look in *Who's Who.* His excuse is rank, for he is nothing but a potboiler.[3]

[1] Arthur M. Schlesinger of Harvard University.

[2] His successor in directing the Massachusetts Historical Society was Stewart Mitchell, best remembered for his biography *Horatio Seymour of New York.* The Morison here named is of course Samuel Eliot Morison.

[3] Bernard De Voto, whose books included *Year of Decision, Across the Wide Missouri, Course of Empire,* and *Mark Twain's America,* was an author of distinction. He had a vein of pugnacity and malice that justified Miss Amy Loveman's remark, "He is his own worst enemy."

To Miss McAfee

London, July 1, 1934

Through the New York *Times* European representative late last evening I got through to Berlin by phone and got the last news. The papers this morning do not carry one particular bit, which was that Hitler stated that Von Hindenburg was very ill and a specialist had been sent to him.[1] Perhaps "shot while resisting arrest" will be changed to "died from a pill"! Francis Hirst is writing a little book on liberty and he said a day or so ago to me "who would ever have dreamed thirty years ago that in writing on liberty in Europe I would have to have a chapter on the re-introduction of torture!?" . . .

It is true in the last war men did submit to the draft. On the other hand, ever since the Civil War the pension grabs have indicated what I said, viz. that when men do go to war, or after, they consider themselves as entitled to be a separate class in the community thereafter, to be pampered and paid for the rest of their lives. So the Civil War soldiers, the Spanish War and the Great War. They did submit to the draft as you say, but the hully-balloo of public sentiment, the impossibility of resisting the government in most cases, etc., perhaps had as much to do [with] it as a stern sense of duty.

Also we do pay our taxes, some of us. It is that or perjury and perhaps jail. But it is not altogether from a sense of duty to the nation. Up to a point we realize from town meeting days that someone must pay. If a village wants to build a school it does not go to New York and hold up a bank with a pistol. It has to tax its citizens. On the other hand, a considerable part of my taxes I do not pay from a sense of duty. I pay because there is nothing else to do. We all use every loophole legally to escape. Even the Governor suggested a Connecticut loophole to me! I paid last year in Federal Income tax about $8000. Mr. Morgan and many others paid none.

To Miss McAfee

London, August 10, 1934

Affairs at home appear to me to be more and more discouraging. I agree with much of what you say as to utilities but I think a very distinct difference ought to be acknowledged between operating com-

[1] President Paul Von Hindenburg had appointed Hitler Chancellor in January, 1933, and Hitler had gained dictatorial powers by special enactment of the Reichstag. Hindenburg remained a figurehead in the presidency until his death in 1934.

panies and holding companies. Many of the latter have been outrageous in capitalization and management. But this applies much less to operating companies, or even holding companies where the holdings have merely united companies operating in a single limited district, like the Consolidated Gas. . . . On Long Island, when I lived there my family budget for all expenses was about $8000 a year. Of that my electric light bill accounted for from $1.50 a month in summer to about $4.50 in winter, yet people talk as though the Long Island Lighting Company were an octopus sucking the blood of the people! As to government-owned plants working as a yardstick I think that all bunk. We have had Commissions for years working on fair rates. If they cannot determine them have a Federal Commission for the purpose.

I am also getting fed up with experiments with the currency. A "dollar" ought also to be a yardstick, but how can any business man or investor go ahead and plan for the future if he does not know what a dollar is going to be in another year or even month? How could anyone agree to deliver so many "yards" of goods or "tons" of coal if he did not know what Roosevelt would rule would make a yard or a ton when the contract matured? A gold dollar was bad enough as a measure of value, but at least you then had two things to balance against each other — a dollar of certain gold content and the supply of products to be bought and sold in terms of it. Now you have the increased uncertainty of not knowing whether one man may declare the dollar to be this to-day and that tomorrow.

Take also the railroads. Roosevelt had pointed out their importance and we have been taxed hundreds of millions to help keep them going. They began to do better. Suddenly they are taxed some three hundred million a year for pensions. Why the rails any more than the chewing gum industry or any other? Why not suddenly say that chemical industry must pension all its employes and their widows as an experiment regardless of what happens to their stockholders?

If I am no longer a Roosevelt man I am not a "Tory," whatever he may choose to say when he calls names instead of arguing. I realize the need for immense social changes and am willing to bear my share of the burden, but I am no longer willing as an investor and citizen to stand for putting money into industry when any one branch may be ruined without notice by the fiat of one man. There has been enormous dishonesty among business leaders and politicians, but the only "culprit" the government seems to be able to punish is the honest stockholder and investor. So far I personally have not suffered.

To Robert Underwood Johnson[1]

London, August 24, 1934

I had not realized that the Academy did not admit actors as actors. It is rather an interesting point, about which I am not prepared to argue, whether acting is, *per se,* an art. I can see that a line has to be drawn somewhere, and that the finest dancer in the world would not be eligible for the Academy. On the other hand I have always thought of acting as exemplified in, say, a Modjeska or a Bernhardt, as art of a high order. As actress a Bernhardt would not be eligible in an Academy of Letters but I should vote for her, I think, in an Academy of *Arts* & Letters. From the standpoint of art it seems to me that she was far more important than many of the now forgotten authors who at one time and another have been elected among the French "immortals". . . . The medium, of course, is a transient one but such an artist leaves his or her impress upon the living tradition of the high art of dramatic presentation, and after all a drama is written to be acted and not merely read. In creating a great stage character the actor does create and not merely interpret, as a performer may interpret a musical composition. I do not recall who wrote the stage version of Rip Van Winkle but for forty years I have carried the impression of old Joe Jefferson in the part. Jefferson, not the author, created Rip for the American people.

In these days when the actor is struggling to maintain the tradition of the legitimate stage as against the movies, often at great sacrifice and for the love of art, might it not possibly be a wise move and a beneficial one for the Academy to accord him status as artist rather than entertainer. Without the actor we cannot continue to have the great drama as we have known it from Greek days down. The dramatist would have to turn scenario writer, or a mere closet dramatist, writing only to be read. I think there is always loss of life when the dramatist loses contact with the stage and writes without thought of it. . . .

I have read with interest the list of candidates. Lippmann of course I want to see in. Woodbridge is good. The two artists I do not feel competent to pass on but shall probably vote for. I know Rollo Ogden[2]

[1] Poet; associate editor of the *Century Magazine* under Richard Watson Gilder, 1881-1909, and the editor until 1913; co-editor with C. C. Buel of the four-volume *Battles and Leaders of the Civil War* (1887); and secretary of the American Academy of Arts and Letters, 1904-17.

[2] Rollo Ogden (1856-1937) was successively editor of the New York *Evening Post,* where he succeded E. L. Godkin and Horace White, and (beginning in 1922) the New York *Times.* His work was almost entirely journalistic, although

and rather question his name. The best you yourself say is that "he is a man of high character and literary traditions." That is true but those are scarcely sufficient qualifications merely in themselves for election to the Academy. The chief objection to the *Times,* and it is an important one for the paper and in connection with Ogden, is that its editorial page is extremely weak. It has the best news of any paper in the world, but no one ever looks to the *Times* for guidance in a crisis. I am fairly intimately connected with the *Times,* and I think my criticism is generally concurred in. It does not dare "take a line." One has only to think of Dana and Greeley and others. One turns to the Hartford *Courant,* Lippmann in the *Herald,* or the Baltimore *Sun* rather than to the *Times* for interpretation and comment. Ogden's literary work outside of his journalism is sound but small in volume and not so outstanding as to make him an Academician. This is the way I feel on first reading your letter and I write quite frankly. Moreover, I think we already have one of the *Times* editors, Finley, as an Academy member and it might look badly to take two members out of fifty from the staff of a paper which is notoriously rather weak in its editorial writing.

To Allan Nevins

London, August 31, 1934

What you say about my new book was most encouraging. I have no hopes of more than a moderate sale and more or less bludgeoning by the academics, who, like Schlesinger, will accuse me of potboiling. I appreciate what you say as to research and one of these days may go in for some such subject again and such a treatment. Living over here it has been impossible, for I simply have not had the strength to carry on research on a grand scale on my American visits while doing all the other things, socially and in business, which such visits have entailed. . . . The kind of writing I shall undertake after we live in Southport will depend on several things, the ease of getting away from home, the resources of the Yale Library, my own degree of energy, etc. As to Columbia, I know nothing of teaching whatever. I question whether I have the accurate, extensive and detailed knowledge requisite. I am unfitted in every way for ordinary teaching or lecturing. Such a seminar plan as you suggest sounds less formidable, but I doubt if it would

---

he published a brief critical biography of William Hickling Prescott, and a longer life of Godkin that has generally been regarded as badly organized and inadequate.

pay me. It would take much time and energy from writing, the more as the work would be new to me. It would mean living in New York or a constant running back and forth from Southport. . . .

All you had to say was of great interest and I am looking forward to a good talk with you. I see Dennett[1] goes to Williams. I have not read his *Hay* but glanced at it in the Century Club, and am glad it has been a success. Your series must be doing well, and your *Cleveland* was certainly a fine book. I am obliged to you for saying all you could of the little *Henry Adams.* I think I explained to you why Mrs. Adams has yet to remain behind the scene. The real influence on Henry was not merely the suicide, and to base his psychology even in part on that would be more misleading than to say nothing. It is impossible to say all in print at present, so I have taken the knocks on that score in silence at present.

To Miss McAfee

London, September 6, 1934

I have just got off an article, called for in a hurry by the New York *Times,* in which I come out for the first time in a distinctly critical view of F.D.R.'s policies. I suppose it will appear in the next few weeks. I am immensely disappointed by the muddle in which the party seems to me to be getting us, genuinely disappointed as an independent who wanted to tie up to the Democratic party and believed two years ago that it had a magnificent opportunity. For the first four months or so I thought Roosevelt would use it as it ought to be used, but I feel now he is leading us into quagmires and quicksands instead of on to firm ground. I would have liked a very progressive program, would have stood for one even which might have gone much farther than I would, though I am willing to go far, but all I can see now is a jumble and mess in which we are not so much building a new house to live in as a nation as washing away the foundations on which any house can be built in which Americans want to live.

To Miss McAfee

London, September 15, 1934

News from America, both in public print and private letters, is very disquieting. Personally, perhaps because I am still very tired in spite of

[1] Tyler Dennett, who had been chosen president of Williams College, had written an admirable biography, *John Hay: From Poetry to Politics* (1933), in the American Political Leaders Series which I established and edited.

the Chaplaincy rest, I feel more uneasy and discouraged than at any previous period in the depression. It is particularly disheartening to read of our going from bad to worse while at the same time reading of improvement in many parts of the world. Conditions in England have been steadily improving for considerably more than a year now, though there has been a slight set-back in the past month or two. Canada is in better shape, and Australia surprisingly improved. Even South America is on the up-grade as we continue downward. . . . The government . . . is destroying the confidence I might otherwise feel. In fact, I no longer have any at all, and am now passively waiting to have my financial throat cut.

I have been pretty consistently right as to economic conditions for the past eight years; I did not go into debt or speculate in the boom; I have worked hard and saved a considerable amount of money even in the five depression years; but it has all been taken away by the devaluation of the dollar, taxation, etc., which have been due to the foolishness and mismanagement and dishonesty of others. I am getting tired of the policy of robbing Peter to pay Paul when in many cases Peter has been a conservative, saving, hardworking person and Paul has been a fool, borrowing money to speculate with in stocks, land, crops, etc., or to buy cars, radios and everything he has wanted. At Bridgehampton there was not a farmer in the whole community who did not have from one to two or three cars all far more expensive than my Chevrolet, and who was not riding high, wide, and handsome. Now I am taxed to help them carry the "crushing burden" of debt. Of course I do not mean that this is the whole story for the whole country but there is a lot of truth in it which does apply to the whole country. . . .

Our great prosperity during and after the war would have permitted the clearing off of a tremendous amount of private and public debt and the putting of almost every one in a position to stand not a rainy day but many rainy months. Instead of that most people went in for whoopee, and now those who did not but kept their heads are paying the bills for those who did. I am wondering what road we Americans are going to have to travel before we get through. For the first time I am beginning to get worried about the stability of our most fundamental institutions. The way we are going now events, not intentions, may push the administration where they may have had no intention of ever going. That is the way, more often than not, that the biggest changes come. . . .

In 1791 when the United States had the opportunity of buying

French assignats at a low figure and so paying off its debt to France, Jefferson assured the French Minister that "the Government of the United States have no idea of paying their debt in a depreciated medium" and that in all payments allowance would be made for the depreciation in French money. We have gone down grade a long way since then when we insist on paying Panama the annual rent agreed on in gold dollars in our new 60 cent ones! I can recall no time when the morality of our government has been so low, as I point out in the article when mentioning the constant talk about our not having more depreciation until we have induced people to buy government bonds. It seems generally to be assumed that it will be all right after that to pay them back in dollars of less value than we borrowed from them. During the war I subscribed in all to over $50,000 of Liberty bonds. . . . Now I would not buy ten cents' worth of our government obligations, and I have no less an example to follow than George Washington himself.

To Miss McAfee

London, October 24, 1934

Last night I was writing to Henry Canby about cabbages and kings and I rather took him to task for having such a lot of instructors, assistant professors, professors, etc. — anything connected with a college except the janitor — write reviews, whereas here in England men of culture such as Harold Nicolson, Lord Eustace Percy and others did much, with the result that instead of getting a meticulous factual study with the usual points that on such a topic the author knows nothing or that he has not footnotes, or that he did not write this sort of book instead of the one he wanted to write, and without getting at the philosophy of the thing, one does often get at the heart of what the author was trying to do. The press has always treated me well, better than I have deserved, and this comment is not sour grapes at all, but the difference between the review in the Sat. Review at home by Coles (whom Owsley did up most neatly in the October *Virginia Quarterly* and who does not know even his subject) and the one in a recent Sunday *Times* here in London by Lord Eustace Percy who realized that the book was not a report of research but a study in a topic — the development of sectional or international hatred — which, as he says, has had little treatment in political economy, shows what I mean. In general, the specialized American professor is not a man of broad humane culture. What with the Ph.D. grind, the early years of low salary, early marriage, education of the children and so on, the poor man, unless he or his wife have money, has no chance. He has got to write, has to show that he can pick flaws in anyone, etc. . . .

Congressman George H. Tinkham of Boston spent Sunday afternoon with me — self-introduced. Although a Republican, he has represented the Democratic Back Bay district of Boston for twenty-eight years, and this year is the candidate of both parties. From what I learn he has been very right in his financial predictions. He now, like the president of the Union Carbide Company, predicts a ten-cent dollar (purchasing power) by 1937. I have myself been becoming more and more anxious. I am not a timorous person, and bought stocks at the very bottom in May, 1932, when America was scared white. Nor do I go with the crowd, for I predicted and sold out for the crash in 1929. But I *am* scared now for the first time. In enormous outlays for relief and public works, in piling up short-time obligations of government, etc., we are going the classic way of Europe in the early 1920s.

From Worthington C. Ford

Paris, October 29, 1934

I have read your *America's Tragedy* with delight and much to my advantage. For again you tell a familiar story but in a new light and with a broader and deeper understanding. As a study of social conditions, North and South, it deserves all praise, and it is quite a feat to so bring them into relations with the social differences of today. The first five chapters I found easy and enjoyable reading and could not but notice the ease with which you marshal your facts in the most telling way. When you come to the war the effort involved is a bit felt by this reader. (You note that I confine it to myself.) The great complexity caused by the many currents, as disrupting in their effect as war itself, gave me at times an impression of confusion and repetition. For example, in each chapter some incidents of fraternizing on the part of the combatants. Was your purpose to show that more bitter the feeling between the North and South the better the feeling between the armies? The last chapter is at your best, philosophic and to the point, a lesson in politics and in government delivered with the mastery of full experience. I do not go so far as to say that this is your best book, but I do say that it maintains your high standard and in parts rises to a high degree of eloquence.

To Members of the Academy of Arts and Letters and The National Institute of Arts and Letters

[1935]

At a meeting of the Directors of the Academy on March 23rd, it was suggested that I write to all of our fellow members of the Academy and Institute to tell them of an enterprise in South Dakota of which I then spoke and in which I have become greatly interested.

To be as brief as I can, the story is this. About three years ago I was told by my friend Leland D. Case, the editor of *The Rotarian* magazine (I am not a Rotarian), about a movement which had started in his Alma Mater, Dakota Wesleyan University at Mitchell, S.D. He asked me if I would lend a hand. The little organization was called "Friends of the Middle Border," and as it happened three of its ten incorporators were members of the American Academy — Stewart Edward White, the late Hamlin Garland, and myself.

The movement came straight out of the grass roots in good old American fashion. It has also been old fashioned in that those trying to do something with and for it, have not asked for help. What these people on the spot are doing has been done without running to Washington for government aid, or to anyone else, but the growth has been vigorous and indicates that both the movement and need are vital. The thing is living and growing. Not only has a museum of arts and letters been started but the collections have so grown that the group is now planning for a museum building, the architect of which is Lawrence C. Licht, well known, and whose brother is in the office of our fellow member William A. Delano. I mention this only as one of the many accidents which has brought this little institution into so many different sorts of contacts with the Academy and Institute. For example, among the members of its Advisory Board are William Lyon Phelps, John Sloan, John Erskine, Carl Sandburg, William Allen White, as well as Stewart White and myself. In addition to these Academy and Institute members the list is a distinguished one.

Many people have become interested and contributed in one way and another. "Billy" Phelps gave a most helpful collection of books; John Taylor Arms gave one of his most beautiful etchings; the family of Hamlin Garland has given portraits of Garland and a notable collection of memorabilia of all sorts; Stewart White has given manuscripts; Mrs. Gutzon Borglum donated important items from the studio of her late husband; Nancy C. Hahn, the sculptress, gave the original plaster cast of her noted statue, "Pioneer Woman," the bronze of which is in

St. Louis; Harvey Dunn gave his finest painting, "Dakota Woman"; I have given various things, including books, etchings, and what they say out there is probably the only original Albrecht Dürer in that whole section of the United States; others have given generously, and the gallery now contains examples of the work of Audubon, Catlin, Hargens, Levon West, Deming, Grant Wood, and other painters, as well as rare books and much else.

It should be noted that this is the only museum in the whole vast area covered by the states of the two Dakotas, and perhaps we might include Montana and Idaho. It is the only place where young and old Americans of that section can see original works of art. You never know when from such new contact a spark of inspiration may fire some youngster, but it is an experience also for the old. Recently a retired farmer became so rapt in contemplation of Dunn's Dakota Woman that he had almost to be pulled away by the relatives he had come to visit!

What I have noted represents only a small part of what has been given — illuminated missals, historical objects of importance in teaching the history of the section and the nation, and many other things, but I must not make this letter too long.[1]

From Worthington C. Ford

Paris, January 31, 1935

Many thanks for your letter, the greater because taken out of time and occupations making heavy demands on you. My congratulation on the Athenaeum Club. If there is a chance of your being in England in the future, have your name up for full privilege. You will never be a political refugee, for whom England has had such kindness, but you may decide that the U.S. is not a restful haven and come back to London. A membership is a recognition — well merited in this case. Were I a younger man, by thirty or forty years, I would be tempted to commit suicide having the disability I now have. Your picture of sectional division is well supported, but it offers nothing to a man like myself. Also, your speculation on the political trend is fruitful in suggestion. At present the Republicans are ultra conservative and unable to frame a policy. The Supreme Court may help them, but such a

[1] At a meeting of the directors of the Academy, Charles Dana Gibson said at once he would contribute some of his work, John Taylor Arms that he would provide another etching, and Van Wyck Brooks and William Lyon Phelps that they would send books.

technical decision as the hot-oil one will not carry them far. The defeat of the entrance into the world court hamstrings the President's foreign policy, but think of running a campaign on that vote, when many democrats and the real Progressives — LaFollette and Shipsted — voted with Borah-Johnson. The President can correct the hot-oil decision by new legislation, but our policy of isolation is now indefinitely fixed. And that means, too, that Hull's liberal commercial policy stands little chance of acceptance. However, we can wait and I want in 1936 to vote for F.D.R. unless some frightful blunder comes to his discredit. Inflation I believe to be unlikely. I enclose the program of a Chambertin dinner at Rouzier's. There is none of the vintage of 1911, but you may be sure those named on the slip are good, above the average and far above what other restaurants serve. Were you here I would take you, just for the experience. You ought in your next visit go to the *caves* of Thomas-Bassot, as it would enable you to lay the foundation of your Connecticut *cave*. Well, you are off at the end of the month. May the journey be good and profitable to both and a safe return. If you return to Holland Park, I shall hit you in the summer. . . . Of course K would have gone to the Chambertin dinner.

To Miss McAfee

London, May 10, 1935

Many an individual Englishman makes me angry at times but they are certainly a wonderful nation, and I take off my hat to them. They are simple, honest, conscientious, flexible, with a strong social sense, courageous, not soft. I asked Mrs. McConaughy of Wesleyan what she felt was her strongest impression here, and she said at once, "the *decency* of everybody." I was interested in all you had to say but what worries me most about my own country is the character of our people, and the Secretary of State told me that was what also worried him most. The Bonus grab, for example, is indecent to an extent that no one home seems to realize.[1] There is first the demand, never satisfied, of a large part of the able-bodied men of the country to be given colossal sums of money for no real reason at all, as in the case of Spanish and Civil War "veterans." Then there is the accepted belief everywhere that everyone in politics can be bought. Every newspaper takes

[1] The Patman Bonus bill, for immediate payment of adjusted-service certificates that were not to mature until 1945, passed both houses of Congress by heavy majorities, but failed in May, 1935, by a narrow margin in the Senate, to override a Presidential veto.

it for granted, as does everyone, that because the President has given billions to spend, of course he can crack the whip and get more from Congress than otherwise. Again, that while Congress may not believe in the Bonus, of course Congressmen have to vote for it to some extent, etc. etc. Then there is the constant voting by Congressmen to please their constituents or some special group with the open understanding that the President will use his veto. How can one have respect for a legislature made up of venal and weak hypocrites? I spoke in the "Letter," in the part cut out, of the levity of our public life. Well, I read in the paper that the Senate passed the $2,000,000,000 Bonus Bill amid scenes of great hilarity largely caused by Huey Long.[1] It seems to me that the voting away of two billions of the people's money is not an occasion for hilarity even if there *is* a mountebank in the room.

To Wilbur L. Cross

London, May 17, 1935

I am sorry I could not have written my letter after the Jubilee.[2] No one who was not in London to feel the spirit of it can conceive what it meant. It has been extraordinary from every standpoint. As someone said the other day, if England established a Socialist Republic the King would be elected first president.

The story goes round, which if not true is *ben trovato* and true in interpretation of the people, of a Communist in Whitechapel who asked his neighbor if he were going to decorate his house for Jubilee. When told he was, the enquirer said "Fine! I wish I could but you see I am a Communist!" Many stories are true, as given in the sensational press but also reported to me by eyewitnesses. At Sunderland House, where a ball was being given, the crowd outside began dancing to the music coming from the open windows. They then called "louder," and the guests came down to the street and danced with the crowd on the pavement. This was not what we would call a drunken party but this is really becoming, for a while at least, "Merrie England" again. There has been any amount of community singing with all classes in the crowds. In Piccadilly, a crowd last Saturday night called for the band

[1] Senator Huey P. Long of Louisiana was shot in Baton Rouge and died September 16, 1935.

[2] Adams was writing a periodic letter on English affairs to the *Yale Review*. King George V celebrated the twenty-fifth anniversary of his accession on May 6, 1935. A great procession rolled through London, and the King reviewed the fleets at Spithead — just before they were ordered to the uneasy Mediterranean. An economic revival coincided with the Silver Jubilee.

to come out and play. The mounted police — all the police have been marvellous in their tact and good nature with unprecedented masses of people — edged in with their horses, but were rather nonplused when instead of moving on they stopped to pat the horses! Never have I seen such crowds or such happy and good-natured ones. One of my maids sat on the curbstone all night from ten in the evening until twelve next day to see the procession. She said the street was filled by four A.M., all laughing and joking, and dancing to while the time away. England has not been so confident or happy in twenty years and more. The contrast is not pleasant when I look at my own country. Except for a European War, England is I believe the safest, sanest, most contented land in the world today, unless we add Sweden and Norway, and I go home in the spring from a sense of duty as an American only. . . .

It *is* a great country, and I think it will win out. The dark shadow comes from the continent, especially that old home of the barbarians, Germany. In the present increase of uneasiness caused by the death of Pilsudski, Mussolini's adventure in Africa, the imminent downfall of the gold currencies, capital is flowing in here, which I think largely the cause of the fall of ten cents in the dollar in a week or so, rather than our own fantastic finance. If America were not my country, nothing would induce me to emigrate to it today from here, either for security or comfort.

To Miss McAfee

May 26, 1935

Hull, the Secretary of State, in Washington told me he was getting discouraged — between ourselves — about the willingness, or rather unwillingness — of even well educated Americans to take the trouble to think. It reminded me of a dinner I was at in Washington on a preceding visit. Over here not long ago I gave a dinner, and among the men were Hirst, former editor of the *Economist,* Gooch of the *Contemporary Review,* and so on.[1] The talk was utterly delightful, witty, informed, wide-ranging. This week I am giving another for Herr Von Devall, London correspondent of the *Frankfurter Zeitung,* and others, and expect again good talk. Well, in Washington at the dinner I speak of there was also a select group. There was Charles Warren, Davis (who ran for president), J. M. Beck, an ambassador, and about four

[1] Francis W. Hirst, economist and journalist; George P. Gooch, one of the editors of the *Cambridge History of British Foreign Policy,* and author of important books of European history.

others of equal note. In the smoking room after dinner all of us were placed in a circle, like a Farmers Grange meeting in Bohunk, a pitcher of ice water on the table, and talked for about forty-five minutes before rejoining the ladies. The entire conversation was made up of personal anecdotes, of a very mild interest, and funny stories. That is no exaggeration. Not an idea was started or anything important touched on.

To Mrs. William Vanamee[1]

June 3, 1935

I have just been writing a short review for the *Saturday Review* of Henry Osborn Taylor's little book just out. This has brought to my attention the fact that he is not a member of the Academy. He is now, both by age and achievement, the dean of American historians.[2] In 1927 he was president of the American Historical Association, and is a member of the Institute. His long life, beginning in poverty, has been devoted to the highest ideals of both life and scholarship, and his dozen or so volumes represent a high level of scholarly thought and devotion. Especially in his six volumes on the classical, mediaeval and 16th century periods he has made a wider sweep through the past of men's thoughts and ideals than any other American historian. He is now, I believe through his marriage into and inheritances from the Isham family, a wealthy man, but for his first fifty years he clung to his ideals of comparative poverty and constant study. The combination of both life and work would warrant his consideration, I think, and as he is nearly eighty, any action, if it is to be taken at all, should not be long delayed.

To Miss McAfee

Oxfordshire, July 20, 1935

We go home about April 1, but it will take two months at least probably to make changes in the house, even though minor, build book cases etc. and there is no chance of my being settled for writing until into the summer.

It will be an interesting year to be home. Personally, I have begun to consider Roosevelt a tremendous incubus on the Democratic Party, though I may be wrong, I am not through with the party but I am with

[1] Assistant secretary of the American Academy of Arts and Letters.

[2] Henry Osborn Taylor, author of *Ancient Ideals, Thought and Expression in the Sixteenth Century,* and *The Medieval Mind,* and out this year, *A Layman's View of History.*

him. In all American history I cannot recall a single other President who has gone back so completely on his campaign pledges. When you read his speeches and think what he has done it is staggering, almost unbelievable. Yet he made the pledges not when times were good, but after two years of depression. The platform has also been completely scrapped, and yet never in history has one stated so definitely that it was "a covenant," as it said, with the people. Nor do I like his attitude toward the Supreme Court and the unconstitutionality of the laws he urges.

To Miss McAfee

August 11, 1935

America is not divided into the city-folk, the rich and wicked, and the country-folk, the poor and the honest, not by a jugfull. This is not defending the business men who were either crooked, as many were, or mistaken in judgment as many were, but merely to make others in American life — the political leaders, the people themselves — take their share also of the blame.

But this topic, as also Roosevelt, are too big for a letter to-day. Incidentally, I think his latest attack, on those who avoid taxation by buying tax-exempt securities, is a very mean and demagogic one. When the law and the governments, state and national, say "here is an investment which will yield so much and on which you will be taxed; here is another which yields less but on which you will not be taxed," what possible case has Roosevelt got against those who choose the tax exempt one? Does he really believe that during the war, when the Federal government put out tax-exempt bonds, that the purchaser should have paid, first, the higher price, and then been morally bound to pay a tax also though the government did not levy it? It is absurd. The government itself is deeply dishonest in its income tax laws and yet he apparently thinks the citizen ought to make presents to the government.

For example, since 1932 I have had to handle an estate which was brought to me almost wiped out. About $125,000 had been placed in bad investments and shrunk to $32,000. Many of these I had to sell. As the income was only about $3,000, the tax allowance for loss was of no use, as there was nothing to set it off against in taxes. But the securities I bought have not appreciated to a value of over $60,000. If I sell them to get into safer things, though the estate still shows a loss of $40,000 and no real profit, the widow will be taxed on the "profit" of $28,000 as though it were a year's income, merely because I shifted from one set of securities to another. Had I kept the old ones and had they risen, and did I now sell them, I could claim a loss of $40,000, but because I changed horses the government will claim a profit of $28,000. What would we say of a banking house that played that sort of game with its depositors.

To Miss McAfee

London, August 30, 1935

I was interested in the report of Governor Cross, and I myself believe that Roosevelt is honest as to his intentions *in his own mind.* I do not question his moral fervor or honesty but I do now question his intellectual integrity, which is quite a different matter but perhaps even more important. As for myself, and there must I think be large numbers who feel the same way, I consider that Roosevelt has almost completely broken his pledged word on what I consider fundamental matters. In 1932 he received about 22,500,000 votes; Hoover 16,000,000; Thomas 730,000. That summer had seen almost the lowest ebb in American morale, lower in some ways than in the later banking crisis. But look at the election. The Socialist vote was only 730,000, the Communist and other radical groups practically negligible. The 16,000,000 votes for Hoover can be considered only as conservative. How about the 22,500,000 for Roosevelt? Aside from mere desire for a "new face" and a turning over on the bed of pain, it is fair to examine the platform and the candidate's speeches to try to discover what the people who voted for him wanted.

Both platform and speeches were almost wholly conservative. Roosevelt insisted that the great need was for economy in government expense, that as president he would be an example to all in this respect, people and state governments as well as national, that he pledged himself to this and that "nothing in the campaign transcends in importance this *covenant* with the tax payers of this country." Again he said that the budget *must* be balanced, borrowing stopped, etc. or else the government was on the road to bankruptcy. He promised to reduce expenditure "drastically." Again he said, speaking of how the Hoover administration had financed deficits by loading up the banks with government paper, that "it is my pledge and promise that this dangerous kind of financing shall be stopped." . . .

Such fundamental pledges, covenants, and, as the platform said, "contracts" with the people have been broken as I have never known any other party to break pledges before in our history. Nor, to a great extent, has there been any need of doing so. Much of the money spent and powers demanded have been for social experimenting for which neither he nor the party had received any mandate at all from the voters. In fact, the contrary was the case. The 16,000,000 Hoover votes were conservative. The 22,500,000 for Roosevelt himself must be considered, if speeches, platforms and pledges are of any account at all, as being given in large part because of what was promised, and what was promised was conservatism in finance with certain specified reforms which those of us who were for Roosevelt — and I was — desired. I hoped at last we were to have a liberal and advanced party which at the same time would be sound.

That is why I feel so bitterly about being betrayed. Had Roosevelt done the magnificent work he did in the banking crisis, and then tried to put his pledges into effect, and later suggested his farther-reaching reforms — or at least plans — in a way that would have allowed of discussion and education, he might have carried us along perhaps. But, as Lippmann has pointed out, he has lost his head, and wants to rule as though we were to carry on government forever on a crisis basis. Did you see the article I mean? I am going to have a couple of fairly hard attacks on him, and so am glad to have you act as his advocate to keep me from going too far. Personally I think this last session of Congress disgraceful. What place in self-government by the people is there for "must" legislation, backed by the power of a pork barrel of astronomical dimensions, required to be passed without having given either the legislature or the people any time to consider it all carefully? And if pledges of such gravity and solemnity as those of 1932 are to be broken so lightly as never to be recalled even, what becomes of our method of elections? Why go through the farce?

To Miss McAfee

London, September 20, 1935

As you say, we may wait now to see whom the Republicans put up, and what Republicans put him up! Nothing in my opinion was more detestable than the Republican administrations from Harding to and through Hoover. I have no use for the general ideals of the Republican Party, and that is why my present disappointment is keen.

It will not, probably, be many months now before we shall be settled in Southport, and then we can talk things over better than writing them. Also we shall know much more about them. At present I have no idea when we shall move, except that it will be not later than

March. Whether it may be sooner, even in a few weeks, depends on Mussolini.[1] People are not jumpy here but there is deep anxiety, and I have no wish to get caught in a general war. Were we travelling with a few suitcases, I would not bother, but with an empty house at Southport waiting for us, with my lease here soon up, and with all my entire household goods here, it would be no joke suddenly to find that I could not get them out, as my aunt and uncle were caught in Paris in their house there without warning in 1914.

England does not want war and will go as far to avoid it as possible, but her back is quite definitely up. Whether she would allow the Abyssinian adventure to go on while she stood by after all that has been said, no one knows. There is a good deal of talk of sanctions, and the one I have heard most of — in circles which count — is that of closing British ports to the belligerents. As the Italian army is getting a large part of its essential water supply from the British works at Adana, that would mean turning off the water faucet for the Italians. But Mussolini says sanctions mean war. I think the British policy, as before 1914, has been blundering, and has led to Mussolini's getting his bear by the tail so he cannot let go. He counts on one campaign definitely but high officers in the British army, whose opinions are worth something, say he could do little toward real conquest, if then, in less than four campaigns. Meanwhile Italian bonds are unsaleable here in London though offered at 10%.

To M. A. De Wolfe Howe

London, October 22, 1935

As you know, I bought a house at Southport a year and more ago which is now vacant. My lease here is up in March, and we had all our plans made for going home with the Lares and Penates in January so as to have a couple of months to alter and decorate the house and move in by April before the heats begin. The international situation, however, is hastening us.

I do not look for war in Europe at present, but the tension is very great. I agree with Chamberlain who said last week that we are here at the beginning and not the end of a crisis, and that for a long time

[1] Rejecting a peace formula of the League of Nations, Mussolini began the Italian invasion of Ethiopia on October 2, 1935. The League Council at once condemned Italy, and nearly all the League states imposed sanctions upon her. An Anglo-Italian crisis followed, which threatened to end in war until Sir Samuel Hoare of Britain and Premier Pierre Laval of France took steps to lessen the tension.

ahead Europe will be very uncertain and will probably face a succession of crises. A letter from Ford to-day, approving of my flight, says that this is also his opinion. My situation is peculiar. If we were tourists with only hand luggage I would not change plans and run. If we had intended to remain several years, I would remain. But we have *got* to go soon, and had planned for January. It is, therefore, only a question of how many weeks to remain, how much worry is worth, and what chances we care to take. Tension may or may not later end in war. My belief is that there will be none for six months if at all. But every war comes suddenly when it comes; a spark is thrown into the powder box — Lexington in the Revolution, Sumter in the Civil War, the *Maine* in the Spanish war, the murder of the Archduke in the World War. . . .

On the whole, I decided not to bother myself over a few extra weeks at the end of eight years, and so we are off, D. V., before the end of November. I shall rest more easy when we and the things are in New York. I have two women to get across, two large steel cans with everything I own including all silver, family portraits, and so on, which are not replaceable, fifty-five cases of books, a large packing case with my sister's things, four trunks and a fleet of bags.

From Alfred M. Landon

Topeka, December 3, 1935

I note that you are quoted by the Associated Press as saying "the trend toward definite dictatorship has been apparent for half a century, the result of natural forces unleashed by the tremendous increase in population," which "necessitated governmental attention to the people's welfare."

I would like to have the full text of your remarks if you will be good enough to send them to me.

From Wolf Von Dewall[1]

London, February 1, 1936

Everybody is frightened of Germany. The Rhineland Question is very much to the foreground. When Neurath was here he gave the assurance that we would in this regard not take any unilateral action but he certainly did not promise that we shall remain satisfied with the conditions as they are. I have the feeling that the whole situation will

[1] London correspondent of the *Frankfurter Zeitung*.

soon compel the English to take a bold move. If they allow the situation to remain in its unhealthy and dangerous stagnancy they must fear that it cannot be controlled any longer. Therefore, they as the leading power will have to make another attempt of bringing France and Germany together. There are, of course, advisers who suggest encirclement and Litvinov, when he was here, did not make a bad impression, but I trust that good British common sense will tell the leading men of this country that that would be the most direct way to hell. In spite of what most English papers say I still feel convinced that Hitler would follow an energetic British lead — if he feels that it is meant sincerely. After all, he has shown many times that he wishes to keep on good terms with Britain. Thus, even if the German Foreign Office declares now that as long as the present war goes on it would not be practical to discuss the projected Western Air Pact, I think this must not be taken too seriously. Let us hope that young Mr. Eden will be the right man.

From William Allen White

Emporia, Kansas, March 28, 1936

I greatly enjoyed reading your "The Living Jefferson." It seems to me you have done a gorgeous job. I was interested in what apparently is a quotation from the *Federalist* in which you use the quotation, "The rich and wise and good." Can you tell me where I can find it? I should like to look it up if you can give me anything like the chapter and page where I can find the phrase, and I can learn in what connection it occurs.

You certainly have done a service to your country. The book is particularly timely.

From Ezra Pound

Rapallo, Italy, April 28, 1936

Re/ yr/ article (Scribner) on F.D.R. or rather the quotation of it in Readers Digest April, which is all that has yet been washed up on this coast.

If Frankie had a god damn fool program in 1932. Parts of which were in flat contradiction with FACTS, and no better than wall st. or hoover, what's wrong with his having learned at least as much as he has learned?

You birds in the N.Y. magazine ring give me the ear ache. Does Scribner or any of the other old bleederies, or in fact do YOU dare answer the enclosed 8 questions?[1] . . . Constitution O.K. but the massed filth of N.Y. publishing has been against clear discussion of money and credit.

Note date of publication of Van Buren's autobiography//. Also note the N.Y. objection to ANY thought not already masticated and proved to be bunk by London.

Have long wondered to what extent yr/ generation of writers accepted in the U.S.A. ever dared read anything unaccepted by the ring.

To Allan Nevins

Southport, July 31, 1936

I do not drive the car any more than I can help, as I dislike the new American cars with their low tops and mouse trap windows, and also the traffic on main roads. Of course, from here we have to take one of the worst, I am told, the Boston Post. Kay enjoys driving but gets tired after 80 miles or so, and we have not the American complex of long and fast tours. I also miss having a decent road map. There seems to be no such thing as a decent road map in America, which is odd considering that Americans have more cars than any other nation. After trying to find something anything like 50% as good as the Bartholomew maps in England or those of France or Italy, I wrote to the map division of the Library of Congress, and they agreed with me that there were no good maps. The elaborate 320-page "Connecticut Guide" done by the CWA and completed with funds, as it says, from the FERA, is a lovely example of wasted money and how not to do it. The map is made evidently by some one who does not know the first principles of map making and is extremely confused and unreliable. The only good map I have seen of this part of one of the oldest and most densely settled parts of the U.S.A. belongs to Professor Roe, and he had to make it himself by taking a Geological Survey map (always good) and bringing it up to date (it has not been revised for twenty years!), and marking the good and bad roads on it himself. The Library of Congress told me the best map for the small roads was the rural delivery map of the Post Office for my county, and I got that, but it also is inaccurate. I don't want a map of the highway from here to Atlanta or Tucson but of the roads in my neighborhood, and apparently there "ain't any such animal." So, we are exploring slowly and gently, sticking our noses into fine looking wood roads which may peter out in a ravine without room to turn, and so on. We could stick

[1] Enclosure lost.

to the main highways and traffic but that is just what we do not want to do, and we have not yet had time to drive enough to do much exploring.

Southport itself is delightful, and we are well content with it and our house. Social life is naturally not as entertaining as that of London, but we did not expect it to be, and are wholly satisfied. As old Jonathan Trumbull told his son when he wanted to be an artist, "Connecticut is not Athens." I am glad, however, in the present state of Europe, to have all my belongings safely home. It is not as cool here as the East End of Long Island, but not bad, and in the hot spell the thermometer never got to 90 when it was over 100 in town. The water is only about 800 feet from my house and we can see bits of it through the trees. There is nothing whatever of the suburban about the place, although some men do go to New York daily. One never hears it even mentioned, however, and we might be in New Hampshire or Vermont. A couple of years ago when here on a flying visit I was at the house of one of the leading lawyers, and he said, "Well, what do you think of things?" In the previous three weeks I had lunched with the British Foreign Minister in London, and been to see the Secretary of State in Washington, so I said "Things in the United States or Europe?" His answer was "Oh, I mean things in Southport"! That is Southport — a sort of Cranford with motor cars. But I like it.

You say you would like to talk politics with me. Perhaps it is just as well we can't. We are good friends who think differently. You can't convince me, and I know I can't change you. Emotion is running high in this campaign, and will run higher. I knew of three luncheon parties already among ordinarily nice and sensible people which have been broken up by guests walking out of the room when the political talk got too hot. What I do not like is the impugning of motives on both sides. There is much Roosevelt-phobia among the antis but there is also a lot of maligning among the Rooseveltities. I do not want a Harding-Coolidge regime and want liberalism but because I believe that in the long run Roosevelt is leading away from true liberalism I was called a reactionary and Tory by one of my best friends the other day. . . . You say Roosevelt has "kept the country moving." I think he has given it diarrhoea.

Factual History: Europe at War

As 1938 came, with the United States recovering from the "recession" of the previous year, with France gaining the upper hand in

Spain, and with Japan achieving control over a great part of China, Adams busied himself in Connecticut with less ambitious labors than before. He still wrote steadily for the best magazines. After plowing through the first volume of his history of the British Empire, which he published in 1938, he pressed doggedly into the second, which appeared in 1940. The subject had looked inspiring, but the necessity of squeezing too many facts into too narrow space clipped the wings of his muse, and gave him a pedestrian pace. He found more real sense of creation in the six-volume *Dictionary of American History* which he had conceived and planned, and for which as early as 1938 he was writing many of the best articles. His Pegasus, however, had become too much of a workhorse to delight him, or his best friends.

In American affairs the happy fact of the time was the decay and ultimate collapse of isolationism. He felt a deep sympathy with friends in Britain who told him in 1940-41 how badly they felt over the apparent failure of Americans to perceive the perils that confronted civilization after the fall of France. His dislike of Roosevelt's third-term candidacy was mitigated by a sense that the Democratic Party might be more dependably alert to the world crisis than the Republican Party. He well remembered who had slain the League cause, upheld the stupid neutrality legislation, and given so much trouble to his friend Cordell Hull.

From Isaiah Bowman

February 14, 1938

Dear Adams and Beard:

Reading your three letters to the New York TIMES, I am amazed that neither of you makes reference to the real Bible of this pioneer business, namely Bowman's *Pioneer Fringe,* a work published in 1931 by the American Geographical Society and containing the LAST WORD. Chapter two has something specific to say on women in pioneering.

All of which goes to show that some good men have their lapses and that both of you have read nothing new on the subject for the past eight years. This reminds me of the fellow who said that it is not what we know that makes trouble in the world, it is what we do not know and are so sure about.

Now I was brought up in a log hut, learned to clear the land at a tender age, drove a plow at ten, and in general did the work of the land as it was done in 1888, in a still heavily wooded part of eastern Michigan. Moreover, I was born in Canada, and did not reach the

Hudson until I was 23½ years old. So take a back seat, both of you, and the next time you write anything on the pioneer send it to me to be edited! I expect this advice to be strictly followed since I have long counted both of you, and still count both of you, as among my best friends.

More power to both of you and more knowledge of the pioneer fringe as developed by

Yours sincerely,
Isaiah Bowman

To Allan Nevins

Southport, April 5, 1938

I am making a hurried trip to town tomorrow to deliver Vol. I of the *British Empire* to Scribners, and have a heap of articles to do immediately for magazines as well as for the Dictionary. If I can clean up in a month or so I would like to have a change before starting reading and note-taking for Vol. II, but do not know where to go. I hate motoring, visiting tires and does not rest me, and I don't go in for golf or other sports. In London I could always easily get a complete change, either by going a short distance in England itself or by running over to the continent, but here, except for some changes in the landscape, there is no mental rest. The people I might meet out of London did not talk about Roosevelt, the stock market, and every other topic that I have to think of a good deal, and talking meant a change even when I did not go to France or Holland, or, in less time than it takes to go to Chicago — to Italy. Over there there were endless cities to go to with their interest of history, art, or architecture and life, but here I do not care a rap to go again to Boston, Washington, Hartford, Pittsburgh, Philadelphia or what-not. I am not decrying America. I am merely speaking of one aspect of it for me when I am tired.

To Allan Nevins

Southport, September 27, 1938

I have agreed to lunch with Theodore Roosevelt, Jr., if he can make it that day — at his request and I do not know what about. I would much rather talk to you about your new enterprise of the magazine, of which I should like to know more. I have not yet seen your book on history and indeed have read almost nothing outside the immediate need of the moment.[1] I am really dead tired, and discouraged about all

[1] The "new enterprise" concerned the magazine that eventually emerged as *American Heritage;* the book was *The Gateway to History.*

the world problems. The storm about put the finishing touch to me although the house came through safely as well as ourselves. It was a terrifying experience, and trees were coming down all around us, the house next door being crushed under two.

What do you know about the Assoc. Prof. Strayer who wrote such a fiendishly nasty review about me in the Saturday Review? I think Canby treated me badly, not only in the review but in printing a big picture which was not in the book to emphasize one of the reviewer's sneers. Incidentally, he seems to write carelessly for he spoke of Wat Tyler as being assassinated. If you know the way he was killed, as given, e.g. by Oman in his *Great Revolt of 1381* you know how absurd it is to talk about an assassination. I had two men, including Davies, read the book for slips, and while there are some, I know and are bound to be when you are sweeping through 2000 years, I cannot believe that there are, as he says, so many as to make the book unsafe to use. Of course it is hurting my library sale, I suppose.

From Harold Callender

London, October 9, 1938

I feel that the old Empire is growing weak and shaky at the heart. Britain slowly prepared, without exerting herself much, for a war in 1941, while the Germans prepared for one in 1938; hence Chamberlain's diplomacy of last month. Without any historical insight whatever, I suspect that you cannot long run an Empire, or even maintain one, by these methods. London was almost defenceless against aircraft, the R.A.F. was not much more than half as strong as the German air force, the army had only a few modern guns, when it looked like war ten days ago. Yet four years ago Churchill had warned of German armament — Baldwin at first denying that Germany was ahead in the air, then admitting he had been wrong. Here there was, and is, complete confusion, even in the government, which vaguely feels that this country must arm some more but pretends to be hopeful because Hitler and Chamberlain signed a bit of paper saying the two countries would never go to war. The Conservatives are so frightened of Bolshevism that many still defend Hitler, whose regime they think is a slightly exotic kind of conservatism. The Empire which was acquired in a fit of absentmindedness may be lost in a similar fit. "The people are all right but the governing class lacks guts," said a friend of mine in the Foreign Office. . . .

The British now think the crisis is past and that they can settle down to tranquility while Hitler absorbs most of Europe, though they expect to have to throw him a colony or so (the snag is to decide which and whose). They then think he will suddenly become reasonable and peaceful; basing their expectations, I suppose, upon his record and utterances. I sometimes think the British are too stupid to survive. If you read Chamberlain's speeches in the House, especially the last one, you will at least see why. In your second volume you doubtless will consider the lethargy of the Empire today, the economic weaknesses of Britain, the diminished security of naval power, and the viability of the Empire — which, I suppose, depends upon the survival of this country as a naval power and an economic power. . . .

To Worthington C. Ford

Southport, January 1, 1939

As to the USA I can only say that the prospect for 1939 is fairly good, better than for 1938, though the outlook is very mixed yet, chiefly on account of the apparent insistence of the administration on continued spending and heedlessness of any call to ever balance the budget. There can be but one end to that. We are certainly in for ten years of deficits and a debt of how much over $40,000,000,000 nobody knows, or, in Washington, seems to care. Resistance to one-man government, however, with not a kitchen but a slop-room cabinet of young Cohens and Corcorans, *et al.*, seems really to be growing.[1]

Bad appointments continue as usual, such as the new Secretary of Commerce who has been engaged in social welfare work all his life and knows nothing of business, and of Murphy, who ignored court orders and fostered the sit-down strikes, as the new Attorney General. They will both be confirmed, I think. Mrs. Roosevelt has gone on the Board of Directors of son Jimmy's insurance company because it is considered that in his new Hollywood job he should not continue on the Board.[2] She admits she will attend only a meeting or two a year and

[1] Benjamin V. Cohen, who became associate general counsel of the Public Works Administration, helped draft the Securities Exchange Act of 1934, the Public Utility Holding Act of 1935, and other important New Deal legislation. Thomas G. Corcoran, a special assistant to the Attorney General, 1932-35, and counsel to the Reconstruction Finance Corporation from 1934, also helped congressional committees write various measures. The pair were much berated by opponents of Roosevelt and the New Deal.

[2] James Roosevelt, son of the President, had begun his business career as an insurance broker in 1930, being associated successively with the Gerard Company and the John Paulding Meade Company of Boston until 1932, and then with a New York firm. Later he became one of the principal officers of the Samuel Goldwyn interests in motion picture production.

will only represent him. Why, if it is improper for him to be a member, the President's wife should be chosen to be his stool pigeon is rather inexplicable. However, she says that this year she will, like other citizens, pay the income tax on what money she gives to charity, which is a glimmer of returning decency. I think FDR had one of the greatest chances any president ever had, and he took hold well at the start but he certainly muffed the ball later, and has taken many steps it will be hard for anyone to retrace. I agree with his social outlook and humanitarianism, but to distribute a national income fairly there must be a large and sound income to distribute, and the piling up of deficits, destruction of all investment confidence, and ultimate inflation can bring no good to anybody. That leads to cruelty to *all* and not amelioration for some.

However, I live from month to month, and by April may have my taxes paid for this year and begin to make some money for my own expenses and savings. The taxes, some $6000 this year, have driven me into the radio field, and I am acting as historical consultant for the Du Ponts' "Cavalcade of America" on the air. It is considered the most useful program educationally and has taken a number of prizes. It runs for 26 weeks, and I have only about 3 weeks solid work examining the scripts, for which I get $4500. Whenever I get into a contract with big business or mass production such as radio, I say "ain't Nature wonderful?" Meanwhile I continue my work on the five-volume *Dictionary,* which I think is really going to be good, owing to the cooperation of some 500 scholars, my second volume of the *British Empire* articles, and so on.

From Worthington C. Ford

Paris, April 2, 1939

I was in London for two weeks last month. . . . The city was cold, wet and dreary. The trenching in the parks, distribution of gas masks and steel shelters and the incessant discussion of A.R.P. and like reassuring things, were disturbing. At the Museum one could always find a desk, something quite unusual, and I found my great comfort there. I had looked for an invasion of refugees, but there was no evidence of it. Even my club may close its doors, as it has suffered so heavily in membership. The world is changing rapidly and a contest must come, soon or late, to prove if it is worth living in. Thank heaven concessions to the dictators appear to be checked and their normally keen appetites will not be made the keener by throwing human sacrifices to them.

To Mrs. James Truslow Adams in Southampton

Southport, Friday, August 25, 1939

Dearest Monk xxxx

It is hard to write for there is at once so much and so little to say. Your own notes seem to come from a different world with their news of swims and picnics and so on while the world is waiting from moment to moment for the possible knell of our civilization and all our personal hopes and lives. Night before last I made up my mind at last that war was inevitable barring a backdown by Hitler and telegraphed to add about $10,000 to Amy's and my cash balances. In New York yesterday nobody was talking of anything but the European situation. I think Sunday will be the dead line. All Americans have been warned to leave Europe at once unless they have to stay. London and Paris are blacked out at night, and the French have asked all Parisians who can leave to evacuate the city at once. . . .

I shall certainly be glad when I have you again but you might as well stay as planned and have a good time — I have just been down to listen in to Paris. They expect war except for the miracle of Hitler's giving in. The population of the eastern front of France is being evacuated as fast as possible and taken to the west. People are leaving Paris by thousands as fast as they can get away. The French general at the head of the army has been placed in command of all French and British forces. The British navy is holding the Baltic and North Seas. Paris believes the zero hour will be tonight at 12. . . .

This afternoon I am supposed to be writing an article for the *Times* but writing is hard under this strain. I shall never forget this August. The August of 1914 was bad enough, but I was 25 years younger then, and we did not then know how terrible modern war could be.

From Worthington C. Ford

Le Vesinet, France, October 15, 1939

I have little fear that anything will happen in this place, some twelve miles from Paris, with no military features. Living is changed. Our houses are darkened, windows painted and heavily curtained, curfew at nine o'clock, street lights out or obscured, reams of A.R.P., and trenches in squares and churchyards.

At the beginning every possible precaution was imposed. We carried gas masks to market, sealed our cellar windows (against gas), were told to lay in a stock of sand, and to watch the step of others as well as our own. We had one "alerte," a false one, two or three days after the declaration of a state of war, none since. I am unique and fortunate. I cannot hear the siren and remain unmoved. It may give me a reputation for cool courage or bring a reproof from the police. Paris is the City of the Dreadful Night. By day the streets are deserted, few bus lines in operation, a restricted Metro service and few taxis. All windows are striped with paper to prevent splintering of glass, shops are open three hours in the morning and three in the afternoon. No opera, a limited comedie, few theaters. Museums are closed — the Louvre emptied of its principal features, and the same for the Biblio-Nationale. The hours of the theater end at 9 (to be extended this week to 10). After dark Paris is really dark, lights extinguished or subdued, houses sealed and few persons or vehicles in the streets. Restaurants close at 9 — such as have not shut down completely. The railway stations are dark, windows of cars curtained and lights painted out — as are the lights and shiny parts of autos. As an exercise in thorough preparation it is superb, and there is no complaint. It is impossible to praise too highly the morale of the people and their confidence in their cause and defense. The Communists alone have suffered — not unjustly.

From Mayor F. H. LaGuardia

New York, February 14, 1940

You are quite right that the stock mass production of spaghetti in the usual run of restaurants is anything but what it should be. I would recommend the Vesuvio, at 163 West 48th Street. I used to go there and the kitchen was excellent. I had to quit because the politicians became too numerous. I just can't stand being in the same block with them. Then there is the Grotta Azzurra, 387 Broome Street, I have never been there but I am told that their kitchen is real Italian.

If you will call Gorini at Henri's, 15 East 52nd Street, and tell him exactly what you want, I am sure you will have it properly prepared there. Their kitchen is French but the chef is Italian and prepares dishes specially. At Little Venice, 126 West 13th Street, ask for Leo and tell him to prepare exactly what you want. Be sure to caution him not to put in too much oil and salt. When they want to show off they over-season.

I shall be happy to have a chat with you if you will drop in sometime when you are in the city.

From Allan Nevins

Columbia University, February 19, 1940

I have nothing but praise for the first volume of the *Dictionary of American History.* It seems to me to do you, Mr. Coleman, and Scribner's great credit. Your foreword is very well done indeed. So far as I have read in the work it contains no errors — though in the article Bimetallism I think the author somehow inadvertently gives the impression that the coinage of silver dollars in this country stopped in 1873. No doubt as I keep on consulting the book I shall find some slips, and when I do I shall let you know.

Let me say also that both Commager and I find the book extremely convenient. It is going to be enormously useful. Your principle of having a great number of short articles, instead of a moderate number of inclusive articles, is exactly right. And anyone looking into the volume will be delighted to find unexpected treasure there. Think of having an article on the Century Dictionary, and another on Building and Loan Associations, and another on Camp-Followers — all interesting! It is a real public service, this Dictionary.

By the way (see Bathtubs) is it really true that Boston made use of the bathtub in 1845 unlawful except on advice of a physician, or is that a "fact" drawn from the ingenious hoax-article that H. L. Mencken wrote on the subject?

From Alfred R. McIntyre

Boston, April 2, 1940

I have looked over the proposed revision of *The Epic of America* as shown in the marked pages and the new typed pages. I would wish that you had given more space to the Roosevelt New Deal period of almost eight years. In the first revised edition, published November, 1933, the inauguration of Roosevelt is mentioned on page 405 and the next few months are dealt with in not quite six pages. In the contemplated 1940 edition Roosevelt and the New Deal get four of these six pages plus three and a-half new typewritten pages, so I would think that you covered seven and one-half years in, at the most, two pages more than you used to cover six months in the previous edition. I realize your feeling that it is difficult for you to write about the New Deal without taking a position that would be disliked by a great many people, but, even so, can't you write considerably more about it and still, to quote your letter of December 18, 1939, "treat the last few years rather generally?"

To Dr. Walter Damrosch

May [?], 1940

I have your letter of the 1st and am in entire sympathy with your point of view as to the present difficulties between the National Institute of Arts and Letters and the American Academy. As a member of both, I greatly deplore what seems to me an entirely unnecessary stirring of the waters. I have the story not only from your letter but also from one or two other confidential sources and there seems to be no question whatever about how the situation has arisen. While the matter was pending, I expressed my disapproval of the amendment to the constitution of the Academy and wrote to Mrs. Vanamme, insisting that the members of the Academy should be informed of the reasons for the suggested change. I never got any satisfaction but my objections to the change should be on file in the Academy office. So far as I know, and I have been a member of the Academy for some twelve years, we have never been consulted as to anything that was going on. It is true that we have a luxurious building in what is still a very inaccessible location. Had I been consulted I would, for example, have opposed the building of the concert hall with its magnificent organ which so far as I know has never been used. I am utterly opposed to the emphasis which is placed in America on "plant." For example, at Oxford and Cambridge in England, the common rooms, although they may have portraits on their walls of distinguished men who have made the Empire for the past three or four hundred years, have simple wooden Windsor chairs for the boys to sit on while they talk. I was almost nauseated when I was taken through the new Graduate School at Yale which I attended and found the way that the Harkness money was used. The common room there is like the lounge of a golf club for multi-millionaires and the effect on the boys is that they cannot talk intelligently unless they sit in upholstered easy chairs costing perhaps two or three hundred dollars apiece. I thoroughly agree with you that the Academy should live in comparative poverty or at least in decent simplicity instead of bowing to the will of one man who happened to inherit many millions as the adopted son of a railroad magnate of a not very savory period of American finance.[1] If he who has never done anything himself of note in the Arts is to tell the fifty mem-

[1] Archer M. Huntington (1870-1955), benefactor of the Academy, was the adopted son of Collis P. Huntington (1821-1900), one of the builders of the Central Pacific Railroad and later president of the Southern Pacific.

bers, who are supposed at least to have done something, exactly what they shall do, or he will stop his contributions, I would personally be inclined to sell the confounded building and thumb my nose at it. We have enough of an endowment to have some permanent rooms somewhere and there is no more comfortable chair in the world than the old fashioned wooden Windsor. I would rather sit in one of those than in the magnificent thrones which are provided for us.

To say that no protests were made against this change is not only absurd but is a lie. My own protest is either on record or has been destroyed. I am wholly with you in this matter and am enclosing as requested my signed disapproval of the amendment.

From Francis W. Hirst

London, June 2, 1940

Things look much better than they did a week ago, when the Germans declared they were exterminating our expeditionary force. They have had a lesson which will not quickly be forgotten, and if the French, who let them through at that fatal gap, can now hold them up and drive the barbarians back, we may see before long a revolution in Germany. The perfidy of Leopold is equal to that of the traitor Arnold or any other traitor in history. I wonder how it is that these perfidious brutes with their vile Gestapo, can inspire a Fifth Column in so many democratic countries. Mussolini seems still to be hesitating and trembling between the German devil and the deep sea of the British Navy. I hope he will refrain, even though I think we should probably be able to deliver such smashing blows that Fascism would crumple up.

It staggers me that the Republican leaders of New England stock have so little sympathy for the Allied cause. I suppose they are counting votes and think that isolationist sentiment plus hostility to the New Deal will win them the Presidential election. If you had sent us a few thousand good aircraft in the last two or three months, it would have made a vast difference, as our pilots are far superior to the Germans and we have a good reserve of them.

I hope you are both well. In spite of all this sorrow and anxiety we keep composed and I find it possible to go on working as usual, (though I can't earn one fifth of what I could a year ago by journalism!). This flight of our American friends via Ireland at the instance of the United States Government is not very intelligible to me.

From William Allen White

Emporia, July 30, 1940

I have your letter about the petitions that are being circulated by the Committee to Defend America by Aiding the Allies. Here is the answer: These petitions were not composed in the office of national headquarters in New York. We allow the various local committees a certain amount of autonomy. They are more or less free agents going in the general direction that we are going.

The clause you object to was circulated in New York and circulated on a petition in Chicago several weeks ago but later was taken out — probably at the suggestion of the national committee. I agree with you entirely that we cannot afford to send help that might endanger our work, into continental Europe. That is a problem that will have to be worked out carefully.

Personally, I realize that famine and typhus are already stalking continental Europe. Typhus is a louse disease; and I shouldn't wonder if this war that was started by a louse may end by a louse. Any way, when the famine begins to gnaw at the entrails of Germany, the Germans will not be able to put down the famine-revolting peoples of Holland, Denmark, Belgium and France. And I verily believe that, by that time, we will be perfectly safe in feeding revolting nations. But not until they have lined up in revolt.

I haven't the slightest doubt that it is now unsafe to feed anyone in continental Europe because I realize that what happened to your young friend in France will happen all over the continent if we try to feed those whom the Germans have conquered.

To return to the petition — If I were you in this case I should scratch out the objectionable point and go ahead and circulate it.

It is purely a local matter and most of our local chapters do not include that questionable clause.

From Charles Scribner

New York, August 1, 1940

I had not heard before of your idea of writing a book on *The American* and I could not be more enthusiastic about it. This enthusiasm is shared by everyone in the office who I have spoken to. I think you are just the person to write such a book and for a good many years to come this will be a most timely subject. It would also give a wide scope for your powers without involving any great amount of research.

I would be glad to send you a contract for it at once if you are in accord. Maxwell Perkins wonders if you have read Madison Grant's *The Conquest of a Continent* or Dixon Wecter's *The Saga of American Society*. The latter is now at work on a book on the American Hero which we plan to publish in the early winter. He is not suggesting these as source books in any sense but thinks that they might furnish you with some ideas in building your theme.

From Van Wyck Brooks

Westport, Conn., August 6, 1940

May I suggest to you that MacLeish's *The Irresponsibles* is a very moving statement that may turn the tide in American literature.[1] It seems to me important for a number of reasons. It affirms the autonomous function of the man of letters, who has aped the artist, cringed before the scientist, or served as a mere instrument of agitation. It asserts the free will of the winter, too long forgotten in a world that has been dragged by fatalism.

This is the voice that has always spoken for poets and writers who have stood for truth, courage and freedom. I know of no document of our time that is more likely to rouse our thinkers and set our intellectual world in action.

To Charles Scribner

August 12, 1940

I was delighted with your letter of the 9th and to know how well pleased you were with the project of a book on "The American." I think it is something which I could do fairly well and would be very much interested in doing. . . . Suppose we say in the contract from 100,000 to 150,000 words. As yet I have not had time to think over the structure. . . .

With regard to the permanent arrangement which we have had for ten years of which over eight years have elapsed, I may say that it has also been very happy for me and I would be glad to renew it in some form which would be mutually satisfactory to both of us. I like to know that, in addition to my independent income, there is a certain amount which I can count upon and I think it has a certain soothing influence on my mind for the work which I do.

[1] Archibald MacLeish published his essay *The Irresponsibles* this year.

I have not as yet talked much with Coleman[1] about the idea of a one-volume historical atlas to go with the *Dictionary of American History,* although we have discussed it to some extent. I note what you say about the supplementary illustrated volume for the *Dictionary of American Biography.* Of course I would like to have a hand in that if in the course of a year or two you decide to bring it out. I am still rather yearning after a purely pictorial history of the United States, and the more I think of it, the more I think that it might be practically without any text at all. Such a volume as a supplementary volume to the *D.A.B.* would naturally be all portraits, but a similar supplementary illustrated volume to the *D.A.H.* would have very great variety which I think would be of much interest to libraries and homes. . . .

Saturday, Malcolm Johnson, whom young Theodore Roosevelt calls his partner, was up to luncheon and spent four hours. What Doubleday, Doran want me to do is to bring Beck's book on the Constitution up to date.[2] There has been no revision since 1924, although the book is still selling, and they are anxious to keep it on their list, but if they do so they want to have it revised. Of course the consent of the Beck heirs would be necessary. What they suggest, if they can get the consent, is for me to write a short introduction of about three pages and a couple of additional chapters covering the course of the Constitution from 1923 to the present, with a slight revision here and there of the existing text, such as where it refers, for example, to Coolidge as the President at the time. They suggest a division of royalties between the Beck heirs and myself and an advance of $500 to $1000 depending on the amount of work which might be involved.

From Harold Callender[3]

Washington, October 19, 1940

Most of my New York friends, like all of your guests, are for Willkie (largely on domestic grounds) and I find myself in hot water whenever I suggest that domestic issues are secondary or less than secondary. On this point, I hope you noticed two letters in last Sunday's New York

[1] R. V. Coleman, the able managing editor of the *Dictionary of American History,* to whose wide knowledge of the American past and editorial skill Adams frequently paid tribute.

[2] James M. Beck, whom President Harding had appointed Solicitor General in 1921, and who held that office until 1925, then going into Congress from Philadelphia for four terms, had published *The Constitution of the United States* in 1922. As a conservative defense of individualism against federalism, it attained considerable influence. Beck died in 1936.

[3] Of the New York *Times* staff.

Times (Oct. 13th, opposite editorial page), one on the third term, the other on the isolationist allies of Willkie, including McNary. I shudder to think of McNary as President; and having had a long talk with him, I do not shudder to think of Wallace in that office. Again I am thinking chiefly of foreign relations, which events seem to me to compel one to do. I am not fond of Roosevelt, who appears to me a bit shifty on some points; but I am shocked by the bitter division in this country (of the same kind that broke France); and whatever the long-run result, I feel sure that a change-over now would inevitably slow up the whole machinery of government and armament at just the moment when stability of policy and continuity of authority are absolutely vital. In Europe a change of government means merely that a different set of ministers sit at the cabinet table while the rest of the machinery goes on unaltered, but here the shift of personnel is vast and (because of the two-month interval) the confusion is prolonged. We have a government and foreign policy which are known to the world; if we change the first the world will wonder whether it means changing the second too, and in the circumstances any change would be welcomed by Berlin and Tokyo, because nothing else could be worse from their points of view. Some of Willkie's most eminent supporters have told me his election would mean a more moderate foreign policy — and that is just what I think is most to be feared. I am sure the strengthening of the fleet at Pearl Harbor and the advice to Americans to leave the Orient greatly impressed Japan, and I fear that any moderation here at this time would be very risky and would increase the chance of war.

In comparison with these considerations, the T.V.A. seems to me trivial (though Willkie in Oregon seemed to have changed his mind about the T.V.A., or at least about government sale of power); and the rest of the New Deal (which, so far as I can make out, is mostly accepted by Willkie) seems unimportant. These are things to be dealt with after the infinitely greater question of the survival of Britain and this country is decided. Nothing else matters now.

From Jan Smuts[1]

Union of South Africa, November 8, 1940

Please also accept my thanks for your book *The Epic of America* which I have been reading since its arrival last week with much interest. It is a good story told wonderfully well, and I am glad you have given me the pleasure to read it.

[1] Prime Minister of the Union of South Africa.

We are passing through a most significant period of history, in which a most determined attack is once more launched on the great human values which have resulted from our phenomenal advance in the West and these values are being tested as never before. To an historian like you this era must therefore present outstanding interest. Perhaps your *Epic of America* may only be the forerunner of that *Epic of the West,* which will tell the story of our Western Civilization since the foundations were laid by Athens and Rome and Jerusalem.

From Allan Nevins

New York, November 12, 1940

We have moved from 147th Street out to Bronxville, at 122 Park Avenue; a delightful house, where we and the children are very happy. I work at home two days a week, and on the others can drive in to Columbia in about twenty-five minutes, so that the arrangement is quite convenient. . . .

Now that the *Rockefeller* is out, I am working tooth and nail on Volumes I and II of my history of the United States from 1846, and I must say that it engrosses me more than anything I have ever undertaken. The *Rockefeller* sold, as Bill Howe probably told you, about 6,000 sets before publication, and seems to be going reasonably strong. But as I labored like a dog on it for four years, and spent about $3,000 of my own money in research, stenographic costs, verification, index-making, and so on, I am not likely to make more than poor days' wages on it.

And what are you working on? I note that you stood with Willkie in the recent contest. If the election had concerned only domestic issues, I would have been strongly with you. But defeating Hitler is the first item on the road back to sanity and prosperity; and I could not stand the possibility that Hiram Johnson, Taft, Ham. Fish, and the other isolationists would take control in 1941 as the Lodge-Borah isolationists took control in 1921.

From Harold Callender

Washington, January 12, 1941

Thanks very much for the excellent booklet on Britain; it ought to do some good; there is plenty of room for enlightenment on the subject. I'm glad your friend Willkie showed more sense than Hoover or Landon; it was wise from the partisan point of view as well as helpful; for we're in this thing and can't crawl out. We're going to rescue an Empire that came near committing suicide; and then I suppose we shall say the time has come to be nice to the poor Germans after Hitler has cut his throat and the Germans put in another Prince Max and cry "Kamerad." I greatly fear an outburst of human kindness, as before; though what will happen in the next three months may serve to defer it — for they will be devilish months, and while I feel moderately hopeful, I admit I have misgivings about night bombing, against which there is as yet virtually no defence, and about shipping and about appeasers here like Kemper, president of the Chamber of Commerce of the U.S., who seems to have learnt nothing about Hitler. I'm told that Wall Street is full of appeasement, and if that is so then here is another would-be suicide who must be saved from himself. These innocent business men imagine Hitler is a crusader for capitalism. It's odd to find here the same arguments I heard in Holland, Belgium, Norway, Sweden and England a year ago.

From Charles Moore[1]

Moorelands, Gig Harbor, Washington, March 2, 1941

Here is a suggestion which possibly you can do something with. The pessimism which the acting Librarian of Congress and his ilk are boasting to have brought about was induced by *The Education of Henry Adams* and its vogue; by his history of the Jefferson and Madison administration, and by his letters. Their effect on historians came first; then the public took up the critical, deprecatory attitude. None with less ability could have exerted such influence. About 1907 I became acquainted with a Coolidge of Quincy, who told me he was attentive to Henry Adams's sister. One afternoon he went to the Adams house to ask her to go for a buggy-ride. She was not at home and he asked Henry, lately returned from London. Coolidge, by way of making conversation, said: "You must have met many interesting people in London. Gladstone, what did you think of him?" "Oh, he's no good." "How about Disraeli?" "Oh, he's no good." I heard President Eliot tell of his last visit to Henry Adams. As he was going down the stairs H. A. called to him: "Charles, Brooks is the only one of us who has got things right." "In which," Dr. Eliot dryly remarked, "undoubtedly

[1] Chairman of the National Commission on Fine Arts 1915-37, acting chief of the Division of Manuscripts in the Library of Congress 1918-27; an eminent student of city planning; and author of biographies of Charles H. Burnham and Charles Follen McKim.

Brooks would agree." "Brooks," H. A. continued, "says that this democracy of ours is all a damned fraud." "Such a statement coming from the great-grandson of one President, the grandson of another, and the son of our most valuable statesman, were the saddest words I ever heard spoken." The same Mr. Coolidge told me he met Charles Francis Adams coming from the polls in Quincy. The old man was puzzled. He had voted and yet had his ballot in his hand. The two returned and on investigation found that he had voted his laundry-list!

I hope you are enjoying Connecticut life. One feels foolish trying to say anything of the European situation, it changes so fast. Moderately recent letters from Lord Charnwood[1] tell of his son's bringing his wounded men out of France in the great escape, of Lady Charnwood, alone in her upper chamber and bedridden, being nearly thrown from her bed by a bomb. They are now in Sussex in "safety," and he is recovering from an attack that for a time paralyzed and blinded him. He could dictate and sign letters.

From John A. Danaher[2]

U.S. Senate, March 4, 1941

I am sorry to be so delayed in acknowledging your letter of the 24th with your pamphlet "An American Looks at the British Empire." The principle upon which this H.R. 1776[3] is based is so startlingly new to American foreign policy that I simply cannot believe it should pass. The Committee Report, and more particularly the background, clearly shows that it is intended to accept interpretations of obligations upon us by virtue of the Kellogg-Briand Pact, and thus to implement the Pact. I believe the reasoning to be devious and unsound and definitely contrary to our understanding when we ratified the Pact in 1929. In addition, interminable commitments may flow from our recognizing by action under this bill (if it becomes law) in that, by our conduct, we will have represented to a beneficiary nation that we deem its defense "vital" to our defense. The bill does not adopt the word "material" nor refer to a nation with whom we have "sympathy," it proceeds solely on the basis that defense of any such nation is deemed "*vital*." Thereafter, the whole action of our country will depend solely and simply on

[1] Godfrey Rathbone Benson, first Baron Charnwood, best remembered for his admirable life of Abraham Lincoln (1916).

[2] A graduate of Yale who was Republican Senator from Connecticut 1939-45, then being appointed by President Eisenhower to the Court of Appeals.

[3] The Lend-Lease Bill.

what the President chooses to do in furtherance of the representation to any such beneficiary nation that we have found its defense vital to us.

From Burton K. Wheeler[1]

Washington, March 6, 1941

You apparently have been listening to some propaganda to the effect that those of us who are opposing the bill are filibustering, and if so you have been misinformed. No speech has been made on the floor of the Senate that has not been directly to the point on this bill. The American people were led to believe that this was a defense bill. I challenge you to read the bill and then say there is anything in it that is for the defense of the United States, unless you consider that England, China, Greece and any other country that the President may name, is our first line of defence.

Secondly, the bill has been heralded as an "Aid to Britain" Bill. This is true, but it is much more than that. It is a bill to give to the President dictatorial powers far beyond that ever given to any President of the United States.

During my eighteen years in the Senate of the United States I know of no important legislation being defeated by filibuster. A filibuster is never effective except as a temporary purpose toward the close of the session. We could not defeat this bill by filibustering, and as far as I am concerned we are not going to try. We are going to insist it be thoroughly debated even though we may be in the minority.

The propaganda and misrepresentations that were carried on at the outset of this debate, together with the general propaganda for war for months past, makes me feel that the bill should be thoroughly discussed. There are vital questions of national and international policies involved as well as grave questions of constitutionality.

To Winifred H. Bonnell[2]

March 10, 1941

I have been thinking over a great deal the question of the windows in the Washington Cathedral and have really devoted more time to it in one way and another than I should have. . . .

I believe in the great plan which might be worked out for making the windows representative of the development of the best in America

[1] Senator from Montana 1922-48, and a leading isolationist.
[2] Of the National Cathedral Association.

together with the Biblical story that the fundamental fact of our diversity of races or nationalities should find a place but I think the plan as outlined to me is too mechanical and individual. Because you have outlined three personalities to each nation, I think you have already got into trouble. For example, you have given three Scandinavians, Leif Ericson, Gustavus Adolphus, and Swedenborg. I am speaking here only of the mechanical division of those who have influenced America by nationality and not by their importance. In my opinion although we have had many races in this country, the English race or British has been far more important in its influence than any other. They founded the United States and from them we inherit our law, political institutions, language, and literature, and the whole mold into which immigrants of other races have had to fit themselves. Yet because of your division by nationalities you honor only three English as contrasted with three Scandinavians who were far less important or as contrasted with six French, counting the Huguenots as mainly French. As to the individuals chosen I will speak of them later but I am thinking here only in terms of the general plan for the twenty-six windows. Your division is four-fold, first as to races or nationalities; second, listing great pathfinders; third, great rulers, and fourth, great leaders.

I think that this hampers you in the choice of individuals, if you can have only so many from each race and will tend to distort the picture of America as a whole as giving every race equal influence in the development of the America of today. Also as I wrote before I think it will make trouble for you as you go on if you are not going to continue this racial division. I say racial for convenience so as not to repeat national each time. I do not see why we should start with it. You will have to consider many other races as they come into the American picture such as Irish, Scotch-Irish, Scotch, Germans, Italians, Poles, Jews, and nearly a score more. As a minor difficulty will come the question of the Negro. What are you going to do with him if you show three Indians and no Negro? The Negroes number about thirteen million and by their labor, their contribution to our folk lore, our music, and in other ways have contributed much to American culture. . . .

Coming to the English, I think as I have said above that we ought to have a great many more than three, and even of the three you have chosen, I do not quite see the reason for William Penn. It is true that he founded Pennsylvania and on a liberal religious basis but I do not think that he was the most important founder of any colony either from the standpoint of founding the colony or of his religious views.

You know how much language and literature have to do with the building up of the ideology of any people and I would say that such Englishmen as Wycliffe who first translated the Bible into English, Shakespeare, or the translators of the King James Version of the Bible were all more important to us than Penn. The constant reading of Shakespeare and the Bible has been of enormous influence for generations in America.

To Van Wyck Brooks

Southport, March 21, 1941

I have just finished reading your *New England Indian Summer* and I want to congratulate you most heartily on it. It is a magnificent piece of work, and this is the first time in a long life and some twenty odd years of writing that I have written so to an author. I would like to have a talk with you about it some time and it has been a matter of regret to me that I have not seen you more frequently at the meetings of the Academy. . . .

Naturally I was intensely interested in all you had to say about Henry Adams and I am not sure whether or not you know the central tragedy of his life. I know that you say that his wife committed suicide, which of course is absolutely true, although the present head of the family, Charles Francis Adams, formerly Secretary of the Navy, denies it. Although this fact is true, it does not explain all of Henry Adams in relation to his wife and in my little account of him, I did not mention even the suicide for reasons which I could give you in conversation, and because I did not do so, Alexander Woollcott in the *New Yorker* said that I might have refrained from doing so because of old fashioned gentility, but he thought it was "spinach." The fact is that Woollcott did not know the whole story whereas I did, and it was a story which could not be told in print but which I will tell you when we have a chance to have a chat again. I got it from my dear old friend, Worthington Ford, who was a friend of Henry Adams, and who died two weeks ago on the steamer returning to America, and also from Mrs. Don Cameron who, as you know, was Henry Adams' best woman friend, and also from Lady Milnes Gaskell. I visited her in Wenlock Abbey and she insisted that I sit in the chair that Henry Adams used to occupy across the fireplace from her and her husband in the old days, and she also told me the story. When we get together some day, I will tell it to you if you do not already know it.

I would question whether Senator Lodge was wholly a "victim of a day of small things." In my opinion he was rather the small thing himself at the end of a great era in New England. He was like an apple which had gone bad because it had a worm in its core. Several scholars have been asked to write his life and have declined and like that of John Hancock, I doubt if it well be written. Nobody can write it without using the papers which the family possesses and if they use those papers, they are more or less bound not to paint the real man. . . .

I agree with you about Channing and his lack of interest in personality. I recall one winter when I was doing research work in the Library of Congress, as I did for about fifteen years, I lunched with him every day and although he was doing research work for his history, he amazed me by saying that in all the years that he had spent in Washington, he had never gone out to Mt. Vernon to see how Washington had lived, although he had written much about Washington.

I note again that you say that Charles Francis Adams had undertaken a diplomatic history of the Civil War but it had never been completed. In fact Adams wrote a three-volume life of his father who was the American Minister to England during the Civil War. He had as aid in one volume, my friend, Worthington Ford, and in the second volume, Professor E. D. Adams. The three volumes which cover the diplomatic history during the Civil War are finished and I believe are in manuscript form in the Massachusetts Historical Society Library, but E. D. Adams (who was no connection of the family any more than I am) wrote and published two volumes called "Great Britain and the American Civil War," using a lot of the C. F. Adams' material. C. F. Adams, the younger, felt that the heart had been taken out of his own book and it has never been published. There was a considerable amount of bad feeling about all this which I need not go into but the C. F. Adams' work is complete, although not published.

From Senator Josiah W. Bailey[1]

Washington, March 28, 1941

Let me say to you that on the evening in which the first Reconstruction Finance Bill was passed in 1932, there were some of us who realized what it meant. The Government was throwing itself in between the people and the disasters of the depression. We knew that there would be no end to the process and that the Government itself would in all probability be consumed. It is a singular reflection that I was

[1] A graduate of Wake Forest College in North Carolina and a resident of Raleigh, Bailey served in the United States Senate 1931-46.

rebuked by Senator Hugo Black for voting for the bill. I told him that I was voting for the bill understanding what it predicated. We had been informed by the White House that, unless the bill should pass, there would be an immediate collapse of enormous proportions. I was hoping to head off the collapse. We did postpone it, but that is all. Meantime, we had set a precedent which has plagued us ever since. Senator Black voted against the measure. It may be worth your while to know that Senator Robinson told me, with authority from the White House, that unless the bill should pass by midnight, the banks throughout the New York District would be closed the following morning at nine o'clock, and this, of course, would mean the closing of banks throughout our country. He told me that he had authority from the White House to say this and that he needed a few Democratic votes. Whoever writes the history of this era should get all the facts in connection with that particular situation. Senator Reed of Pennsylvania knows the facts as he was actively in charge of the legislation and I think was acting on behalf of the White House. His speech is in the Record. You may recall that at that time the Republicans were in power and that the number of Republican Senators and Democratic Senators were about equal. I had hoped that we might avert the disaster and then frame a policy, but the truth is we were framing the policy. Within a few weeks, I was receiving a flood of letters from North Carolina saying, "you have relieved the banks and the railroads and the insurance companies, now you must relieve the little people."

From Van Wyck Brooks

Westport, March 31, 1941

I have just come home after a winter in Washington and I find here your delightful letter. I regret so much not having seen you at the meetings and hope I can make up for this lost time soon. Naturally all you tell me is of the greatest interest to me. What a store of knowledge you have about all these writers, whom I have known only through the printed page; and you may imagine how eager I am to hear the story of Henry Adams. I supposed there were depths upon depths below all that had ever been published about him. Of course I had read your *Adams Family* and your life of Adams and I can well imagine that much could not be printed. The suicide was so bold a fact that I should not have mentioned it if the *New England Quarterly* had not printed a long article on it. What lay behind the fact was the important matter, and one can imagine that this would not be for print while

H. A. remains a semi-private person. This is only one of the most interesting points you raise, which I should be so happy to discuss with you. What an extraordinary tale about Edward Channing! — and about the incidents of dictation at H. G. Leach's! I was also most interested to hear about the C. F. Adams history and to read your notes about Senator Lodge. When I suggested that he represented a "day of small things," I meant specifically *in New England*. It was a day of big things indeed for the nation at large, as you say; and one of my problems in my later chapters was to retain the *regional* note at a time when New England was merging in the nation. But I must not inflict upon you any more of my handwriting, which is not too clear! I only hope that I may soon have a chance to talk with you. Perhaps you are going to the Academy meeting on Monday, April 7th, and perhaps in any case you will let me drop in again some afternoon at Southport. In Washington I met Justice Roberts at dinner and he spoke of a delightful visit he had had with you.

To the Saturday Review

April 19, 1941

Recently the world of American scholarship was shocked to learn of the sudden death at sea of one of its greatest figures, Mr. Worthington Ford, on the ship on which he was escaping to America from France. "Escape" is not quite the word to use, for Mr. Ford, with his indomitable courage, never attempted to escape from anything, but at last the government had ordered all Americans out of that beleagured country. He had written to me from his home near Paris that by lack of proper coincidence of age and wars he had never seen one, and was determined to do so before it was too late. He was then eighty-two. Well, he saw one, and after the Germans had forced him with a suit-case from his "farm," as he called it, to the Pyrenees, and thence to Marseilles, he obeyed government orders, and sailed. We were all looking forward to greeting him, but he did not reach America. For him it was not tragic. It was peace after a long and full life, a release from a world which was daily becoming increasingly the negation of all he cared for. It is fitting, however, that the journal of American Letters should take space for an "Ave atque Vale" for a man who did so much for American intellectual life as did Worthington Ford.

Those who loved him (as I did for twenty years), and they were almost all those who had known him, of all ages, retain a singularly strong impression of him. He was a remarkable combination of a very great scholar, of a man of the world, of a Humanist to whom nothing human was alien, and above all of a great gentleman. A century and more ago, Emerson in his essay on "The American Scholar," sensing the growing disintegration of *Man,* in the Greek myth, into various-functioned *men,* had written of them as being "minutely subdivided and peddled out, that is spilled into drops" by over-specialization.[1] A half century later, Gamaliel Bradford in his essay on the same topic wrote that the scholar "soon becomes aware that other men regard him rather with respect than affection, and he schools himself to it."

Neither of these remarks, wise though their authors were, applied to Ford. He never broke into drops "which cannot be gathered." He remained in the Greek sense "the Man," and did not suffer amputations from his learning. He faced and welcomed life from all its angles. He was not merely one of the greatest historical scholars America has produced, who knew probably more about the manuscript sources than any other living when he died, and who in addition was a noted statistician and economist, but he also knew his wines and their vintages, his food and where in the capitals of many countries to get it, his music and his theater. A younger man, like myself, could turn trustingly to him for advice on all these subjects, and delicate points of gentlemanly ethics as well, receiving ever the soundest advice, given with the affectionate interest of a father.

Last Labors to Make History Accessible

Adams had the satisfaction, in his last years, of seeing the three useful reference works that he had planned brought to completion. The six-volume *Dictionary of American History* appeared in 1940, the *Atlas of American History* in 1943, and the four-volume *Album of American History,* a pictorial record, in 1948. No good reference library could do without the first, and few large libraries failed to acquire the others. While these were appearing his last interpretive study of the American past was completed: *The American* (1943). Serenely busy, happy in his wife and home, and with many friends in easy reach, he devoted his leisure to the American Academy of Arts and Letters, the Bridgeport Savings Bank, the frontier museum he befriended in South Dakota, and above all to reading.

[1] Mistakenly published in the *Saturday Review* with word "over-speculation."

From Allan Nevins

Columbia University
September 15, 1942

This time I went to England to help the Board of Education install more American studies; and in two months I was all over the island, from Fifeshire to Brighton and from Hull to Bristol. I spoke to thousands of teachers, and conferred with hundreds of education officers. Britain is stripped down to essentials, but they have organized their services so well that they have ample food and clothing. As one of the greatest armies in the world now lies in the island and grows greater every day, they are crowded; train travel is a nightmare, and I have had to sit in a bleak station till dawn because no hotel could take me in. Fuel is going to be short for domestic use this winter. But the British have not lost any of their confidence in victory. . . .

From Lawrence Henry Gipson

Lehigh University
October 10, 1942

First of all I want to tell you how happy I am that you are to review the new volume of my series. It has certainly been most heartening the way you have upheld my hands, in moving forward, in my rather ambitious undertaking. My books need every bit of favorable publicity that can honestly be given; the sale has been most disappointing and I do not want my publisher to become discouraged. If I could get away from my work I should so much appreciate having the chance to discuss with you this vexing problem. Of course, I realize that only the more scholarly portion of the American public is interested in a rather detailed account of the last twenty-five years of our colonial history; but it seems as though we should be sufficiently matured as a nation to guarantee that the libraries of the country, by and large, would add the series. For I feel that it is a contribution of some importance which serious students should be anxious to consult.

To Miss Felicia Geffen[1]

Southport, November 9, 1942

I am just writing so that you will have it on authority that it seems to me we could invest at least $15,000 of our funds in the general ac-

[1] Assistant secretary-treasurer of the American Academy of Arts and Letters.

count especially with this last little thousand that has come in from the mortgage of the land under water. I would be willing to invest in either the insurance stock suggested by Oliphant or any other which they suggest as first class and trust that this time the Guaranty will not be hesitant. I think with the little increase, as I figure it, of $50 a year from the trust account in charge of the Bank of New York and the income received from our own savings, we ought to increase our income at least $600. Of course we cannot figure with common stocks on an absolutely certain income year in and year out but certainly all that we add helps to offset any declines and perhaps may have the good fortune to be a permanent increase. I may say that the Academy is the only institution that I know of living on endowments which is in the position of living way within its means, saving capital, and adding to income. The Massachusetts Historical Society wrote me there must be some magic in it.

To Captain B. H. Liddell Hart[1]

Southport, December 18, 1942

I have your letter of November 23rd and it was very pleasant to hear from you again. As perhaps you know, we came home from London about six years ago and even then had to pay war risk insurance on my furniture only because of the mouthings of d'Annunzio when he was talking about sinking Malta below the seas. I am glad to have got all my belongings over here, especially as my library in which you visited me in London was blown to bits, but we do miss England. . . .

As perhaps you know, although my family have been in America for 300 years, owing to intermarriages in the last generation I have about as many first cousins among the English as I have among the Americans and on both sides they are very busy in this war. So far, the only casualty has been a very nice young English cousin who died at Mombasa after three years' hard fighting in Abyssinia without a scratch and another who is in a prison camp in Germany. Another went through the evacuation of Dunkerque; another was on the Burma Road and is now in a hospital on the Tibet frontier waiting for an operation to try to bring together the severed ulnar nerve of his arm and has just been awarded the Military Cross by Britain; another is with the R.A.F. in North Africa. These are my English cousins.

[1] Military Correspondent of the London *Daily Telegraph,* 1925-35, of the London *Times,* and author of *Scipio Africanus* (1926), *The Remaking of Modern Armies* (1927), and *Sherman* (1930).

From Allan Nevins

Columbia University
March 5, 1943

I have delayed replying to your much-appreciated letter until I knew where I would be on the day you say you come to town, March 9th. Alas, it appears that I shall have to go to Washington again. As you probably don't know, I have for quite a long time now been spending two days a week working for the OWI. It is almost incredible to me, and would be quite incredible to anyone else, how much this messes up my working time. Partly, of course, my work suffers from the fact that I usually come home exhausted, for travel is difficult these days. But just try giving two-sevenths of your week away, and you will be astonished how you are crowded in the remainder.

Will Howe had told me that your new book is done, and I congratulate you on it. I am sure that it will be one of the books of the year. But I had not heard about the *Atlas*. That is well worth getting out. I cannot tell you how many historical workers have expressed to me their appreciation of the *Cyclopaedia*. In England last summer I found a few people with sets — Dennis Brogan, for example; and they said it is indispensable. I use my own set constantly. It is too expensive; I wish that Scribner's could have sold it for half the price; but you did a most useful piece of work on that opus.

I hammer away at my long history, and will in time have two volumes finished. Meanwhile, I am like you in having to do a lot of odd jobs. But I have ceased to let myself be dragged out for public speaking. After both my trips to England I was beset by invitations that I could not well refuse, and I no doubt reached a good many people in a useful way by my voice. Apart from the O.W.I., I give some time to the Writers' War Board, and to the newly projected magazine *Transatlantic*. . . .

My brother is in North Africa, and is a brigadier-general. For a time he was civil administrator of Oran — till they handed over to the French there. Now he is with the staff in Algiers — that is, with Eisenhower's staff.

From James A. Van Kirk[1]

Mitchell, So. Dakota,
March 17, 1943

May I express our very great appreciation of your gift of the George

[1] Supervising Director, Friends of the Middle Border.

H. Wright etching, *Back to Earth,* and the other four pictures which have arrived this week?

Your letter of March 8 interests us very much indeed. Among the more important acquisitions of Friends of the Middle Border are a salon-sized oil, *Dakota Woman,* by Harvey Dunn, the gift of the artist — this painting is insured for $3000 —; the plaster cast of *Pioneer Mother* by Nancy Coonsman Hahn, a 'permanent loan' by the artist — this is the original of a piece in Forest Park, St. Louis, and is a gift in all but name —; the Coursey Collection of Dakota Literature, a gift from Major O. W. Coursey of Mitchell of some 300 books on Dakota and by Dakota authors — this gift forms the nucleus of our regional literature collection —; the manuscripts of Stewart Edward White's *The Westerners* and *The Claim Jumpers,* of Horace Cramer's *Marginal Land,* and of *McGillycuddy, Agent* by Julia B. McGillycuddy; a group of long-hand manuscript pages by Hamlin Garland, a number of his photographs, an Indian beaded letter-holder from his study, and two portraits of Hamlin Garland by his daughter, Constance Garland Harper, all the gifts of Mrs. Harper — Hamlin Garland was one of the incorporators of Friends of the Middle Border.

To Miss Felicia Geffen

Southport, May 21, 1945

I wonder whether anything has been done about the membership of Ezra Pound[1] as a member of the Institute. Perhaps improperly, although I am a member of the Institute, I think constantly in terms of the Academy but still it does grate a little on me when a man who has been indicted as a traitor by the United States government can still be a member of the Institute. He has now been captured and in due course will be tried and perhaps killed. He is one of those Americans who have lived their lives in Paris and gone rotten at the core. As a matter of fact, if you will think it over, Paris is a tremendously stimulating place for awhile but sooner or later you have to get away or you too go rotten. Think of a few of the men who have been members of

[1] Pound, whose eminence as a poet was unquestioned, and who had been a leader of international distinction in the movements called imagism and vorticism, had resided in Italy from 1924 onward. He had used the radio to broadcast Fascist doctrine to America during the Second World War, had been indicted for treason, and was brought to the United States after the defeat of Mussolini. He was pronounced insane by a federal tribunal, and committed to a federal hospital. The Institute dropped him from its rolls.

the Institute or the Academy such as my cousin, Edwin Abbey, Whistler, Henry James, and others in Arts and Letters, who have got all they could from Paris and then have gone either to London or returned. I only know one who has stayed in France and she came to America frequently, Edith Wharton, who maintained what I think is complete sanity. Pound went crazy as to America and so did a good many others. Possibly it is better that we should not attempt to prejudge the case which will undoubtedly be decided by the courts now that Pound is in custody under a charge of treason, but it does annoy me to have a fellow like that a member of the Institute.

To Allan Nevins

Southport, September 25, 1945

I still have three downs — your friend, Franklin, Hirohito, and the C.I.O. I think before the disappearance of Franklin, you had changed your views a bit but I also think you came back and changed them again, so I do not know how you feel about him, and as a young and very progressive thinking man, you may like the C.I.O. I am a thorough good Tory. I would like to drink six bottles of port after supper and damn the Liberal Party and so to bed! I used to think I was a Liberal but as I see some of these youngsters now getting hold of the magazines which used to be Liberal and satisfying to me, I don't know where I stand. I was speaking to a Catholic here, the other day, and said I did not know just what I had done because one of his church papers had given me an awful lambasting whereas the Catholics had always treated me with great courtesy including the Archbishop who always put me on his list of recommended books for last year. The paper was the *Commonweal* and when I told the Catholic professor what the paper was, his answer was, "Don't mind that, it has changed hands and has gone over to the control of a lot of young men who believe they are very advanced thinkers." I don't know whether I am advanced or completely in reverse but there is something that does not jibe between myself and a lot of the so-called Liberals of today.

To Leland Case, Rotarian[1]

May 13, 1946

I think something could be made of your idea as to the American Dream being translated into international affairs. Without trying to

[1] Dean at Dakota Wesleyan.

outline it now, I just suggest one or two ideas that come to mind. One is that America has always been a land of dreams in spite of the fact that Ellery Sedgwick said that I could not call my "Epic of America," "The American Dream" as I wanted to. His objection was that no red-blooded American would pay $3.50 for a dream. Red-blooded Americans have always been willing to gamble their last peso on a dream and the one phrase from my whole book which has become journalese is "the American dream." I could say something about that quite briefly in rehearsing what I mean by it. I could also emphasize the part which the empty land and the frontier played in building up that dream which would fit in with your San Francisco meeting. I could even say something about the starting of San Francisco and the prices which the ordinary person got there for all sorts of things including $50 for a cat to kill rats, and $1.00 a newspaper, and so on. In other words, there has been the empty land which made opportunity and the various factors making for tremendous rise in prices which also made opportunity.

Now the land both in the United States and more or less throughout the world is fairly well taken up. There is not much empty land left but there is the new frontier of science. This, however, is a different frontier and includes an industrial civilization with a large population in proportion to the land and so on. But there is another point — one thing which has made America so different from Europe although we are made up of perhaps eighty different races, has been the way in which we have had to get along together. In other words, the European nations from little ones like Belgium and others are still living on a thousand centuries or more of history and hatred with their neighbors. We have been able to get along in America with all of our neighbors of all colors and all races because in part, we were not a nation based upon long historical past with the hatred and all that came with it, but a nation that was based on people who lived together, with the same dream and the same way of life.

Now that has a little to do with the peace of the modern world possibly. I personally like differentiation. If I had lived 100 years ago, I would have liked to have been able to go to Cairo and see one kind of architecture and civilization, or to Tokyo and seen another, or to one of the Chinese cities and seen another. Just because I am so strongly individualist, it rather annoys me to see pictures of modern Japanese, Chinese, and other cities which look very much like Times Square, with skyscrapers and all the rest. It is no more of what one dreams of in

Tokyo or Hongkong or Calcutta than Canal Street in New Orleans is like the old Canal Street of 100 years ago. Canal Street in New Orleans today might just as well be 6th Avenue in New York. Nevertheless, all these things do in a way bring people together. They make them have the same ideas, the same desires. A Japanese woman of high caste and high rank in society who fifty years ago had her beautiful Japanese silks, might have nothing in common with her Parisian sister who had a gown of satin, but now they are all dressing alike, they may begin to think a little more alike. In a way this is a pity but it also may make somewhat toward peace eventually.

To Bob Heinl

Dec. 5, 1946

I have done a good deal of historical writing and editing and would be glad to help you in any way that I could but most of my work has been quite different from yours. I may say that in many cases, the approach and technique have had to be different. I have never had a research assistant for all the 40 or 50 volumes I have written or edited and so cannot be too helpful to you from that angle but I would like to say one or two things so that you can turn them over in your mind and we would be more prepared to talk in the comparatively short time which unfortunately we shall have together.

I think every historian and writer develops his own technique. For many of my books, I worked as follows. I had a fairly large library of American history at my place on the east end of Long Island. When I decided to write on a certain subject as, for example, my 3-volume history of New England, what I did was to go through all the books which I had which in any way related to what I had to do. Speaking purely technically, what I did was to take an ordinary sheet of typing paper 8 x 11, fold it four times and split it into four slips. I would then go through such books as I had on my shelves and putting at the head of each slip the name of the book and as I went through it, put on my slip line by line, the page and the topic which I [thought] would interest me perhaps when I came to it in my writing and then put that into the volume. I also kept track of the bibliographies at the bottom of the pages or at the back of the volume, and also the bibliographies as published by the American Historical Association. I would buy special sets of expensive volumes I thought I might have to use constantly from my friend, Everitt in New York, with the understanding that I could return them to him when I got through for 80% of what they cost — in other words, I rented them for 20% of their market value. This saved me a lot of trouble and gave me material always on my shelves until I got through with that particular volume. There were also a great many rare volumes which I could not afford to buy even if they were in the market, and old newspapers and so on, which I would consult at the Library of Congress in the three or four months which at that time I regularly spent in Washington. I would go to Washington with perhaps a list of 900 books to look at. I had the run of the Library and going through the shelves could tell at a glance that some book which I had on my list was of no use, and put it back, and others I found might take me two or three days to make notes on. There were also the newspapers and the maps. These notes I made on separate slips for each topic which is important, and I sometimes came back from my stay in Washington with 2,000 slips of notes. Then back at my home I would take those slips from Washington and the New York slips which I had in the volumes in my own library and put them all together. It was obvious that a good many referred to matters which would only come in the later chapters of the book and others in the earlier. I would separate these more or less and then as I started a chapter, I would go to all my slips that belonged to that period and look up my references and notes. That is the way I built up a good deal.

Those were the three narrative volumes of the History of New England. I had about 100 volumes of early Colonial records such as Plymouth, Massachusetts. Rhode Island, Vermont, and so on in my library.

On the other hand, I had to interrupt this work on account of contracts to do the volume which I did for the 12 volume *History of the United States* published by Macmillan which was all social and economic, with no military or political history interwoven. This meant a lot of newspaper work. Speaking of not having had a research assistant, I may say that wanting to go through twenty years of the Maryland *Gazette,* I went to Annapolis and stayed two weeks, and read 2,000 issues of the *Gazette.* Of course, I could have told some girl or young man to do it for me and to give me what they thought the most important items on slavery, political relations of the colony to England and so on. However, it certainly paid me to do all the work myself. Reading those twenty years of the *Gazette* week by week as it came out, I lived in Maryland from 1730 to 1750 and I got a great many items that probably a research assistant would not have got and also a great many things that I would not have asked a research assistant to look for. Finally, I also lived myself into that period in a way in which I could not have done if someone had simply sent me a bunch of notes on certain topics.

To Alfred C. Howell[1]

Southport, December 17, 1946

It was very pleasant to hear from you again and I wish that I might see you and also your new office. Unfortunately, I rarely go to New York and have been there only four times this year, the last time not below 155th Street. Possibly I shall do better in the coming year. You say that you have *almost* retired. I have completely retired and refuse to do practically any writing whatever, no magazine articles, no more books, and only a little editorial work. Between my age and I am now in my 69th year and the fact that with a 60-65% income tax, and a 35-40% inheritance tax, I really cannot make any money either for myself or my wife, there is no sense in keeping on longer. I have said what I could about American life and America and I have seen so many writers and historians keep on writing too long because perhaps they had to pay the butcher and grocer or because they could not live without seeing their names in the paper, ruin their reputations that I think I am rather sensible to know when to stop, and I have. I wanted to choose the right date so I quit on Labor Day in September. You had better quit also because you have lived a long and full life, and what is the use. I do not know what your work or hours may be but for the last two years, the summer neighbor across the street who sublets the house of friends of ours for the summer months, and is vice-president of the Central Hanover Bank and Trust Company, leaves here at 7:15 in the morning and does not get home to dinner until after 7 in the evening. I asked him one day last summer what the heck was the use of being vice-president of the Central Hanover at his age and living that kind of life. He told me he was beginning to think very seriously about it himself and he didn't see any particular use.

Sincerely yours,
JTA

You may, or may not, know that I increased the "Open Fund" of the Academy in the Guaranty by $182,000 this year. Not bad for cashed in profits and savings! The other funds are in legals and do not allow much brain work.

[1] Of the Guaranty Trust Co., New York City.

To Allan Nevins

Southport, December 17, 1946

You have evidently been doing things but I have not the faintest idea of what you were doing all summer in the American Embassy in London. I know the government sent you to Australia and that you would have gone on to New Zealand and South Africa if you had not jumped off the stone wall or whatever it was. I probably should know what you were doing in London but I do not, but congratulate you on your having had a very interesting experience there, as you say, with Harriman. I knew, of course, of your winning the $10,000 prize and that you had these two volumes coming out with Scribner's which I shall be very glad to look at when they appear,[1] although I am not doing very much reading now. I am quite a bit older than you and cannot any longer keep up the pace which you set as to work. In fact, I quit completely in September and except for cleaning up a certain amount of editorial jobs, I am not going to write any more. . . .

I think I am making a record for a New Yorker and a suburbanite. I have not been on the New Haven railroad now for more than two years nor in the subway in New York for fifteen years. The record is getting to be really almost too precious to break and I am very comfortable out here although I do miss seeing people in New York. I was at the meeting of the Academy and Institute and missed you there although fortunately not for the same reason that I missed a number of others like Charles Dana Gibson, Clayton Hamilton, Billy [William Lyon] Phelps, Arthur Train, and Steve [Stephen Vincent] Benét, who have passed on. In addition there were a number who always used to come like Herbert Putnam and old Mather,[2] who was something of a bore, but an accustomed fixture, so that the meetings are becoming quite different from what they used to be.

To Allan Nevins

Southport, January 14, 1947

What you say about England is just what I get, except that those who write to me from there are not so keen about the Labor government as you report them to be. I get in my mail a great deal of criticism.

You ask why I have stopped writing. It is partly because I am get-

[1] *Ordeal of the Union,* which was awarded the Scribner Centenary Prize.

[2] Frank Jewett Mather (1865-1953), the Marquand Professor of Art in Princeton University, sometime art critic of the New York *Evening Post,* and author of important books on art.

ting old and will be 69 this year and am tired and have watched other men like Charles A. Beard and others write too long and I think it well to stop while I still have some reputation. I have to write an additional chapter every year for the so-called "subscription edition" of my *March of Democracy* for the loose-leaf volumes. I get only $500 for the chapter but I have to clip papers all during the year and it gives me something to do, and the sales are about $1500 a year more, so I shall keep that up, but I cannot see myself facing the beginning of writing a whole new book. I am willing to build a chicken coop but not plan a large building.

I would like very much to see you and in regard to the last point that you bring up, I am going to talk to my lawyer. I think you are right, that I should begin to think about a literary executor, although I have never thought of myself particularly as a literary man. In spite of the innumerable letters which I have torn up and thrown into the scrap basket, there are, however, some 25 filing cases or so of letters which I have felt were important enough to keep. . . .[1]

As to writing my life, I do not think it will be worth writing, but I am at present dictating a 150-page account of my family for several hundred years.

To Rabbi Aaronsohn[2]

Southport, May 5, 1947

Although I had expected to only skim your book, which was one of many which are sent to me by authors or publishers, I read every word of it. It is an extremely moving book — in fact, so moving, that it is hard to speak of it adequately. The style is good and carries the reader along on an easy flow of a most interesting narrative, which incidentally, is one of the best accounts of one of the racial and cultural factors which have helped to make the America I love. In a previous letter, I said I judged the book was autobiographical, and if it is so throughout, I was pained to come to the account of your wounding and the loss of your eyesight. If that be true, what a glorious career you have run! I will not intrude myself upon you with the praise of an outsider but shall merely say that your whole career has been remarkable, and one in which not only you, but your fellow religionists and all good Americans can share in the pride.

[1] This was an overstatement; but these letters were brought by the editor of this volume to Columbia University, where many more were added to them.

[2] Rabbi Michael Aaronsohn of Cincinnati, Ohio.

Our background has been different, but as I read along, I was struck by some coincidences. You speak of having started on $3.50 a week. That is exactly what I got when I started, after I had a degree of Bachelor of Arts from the Brooklyn Polytechnic and a Master of Arts from Yale, but I learned a lot in the job I had, as you did. Also, it was for me luncheon money, because my father although not rich, was comfortably off, and I did not have to help the family. Another coincidence was that we were both in World War I, and while you had trouble in passing the physical examinations, I did also. I was then forty and of course many years over draft age with a somewhat bad heart. I wanted to get into the chemical warfare division but ended up in the Intelligence, working on my specialty of maps and at the Peace Conference, had charge of all the confidential maps on which the new boundaries were being drawn. Another coincidence, although it turned out more happily for me than unfortunately for you, was that when living in London for a few years, I had an accident which the doctors thought had blinded me. I had not then written the *Epic of America* or some other of my more important and most profitable books, and if my eyesight had not been restored, it would have been quite a different life for my young wife, who is twenty years younger than I, and myself ever since. Whether I would have had your courage or not, I do not know.

I had not meant to ask you to re-write your views as to Zionism but merely wished that I might perhaps use your letter which is a most interesting one if you did not object. I have never been a literary agent and have never employed one myself, and this year have stopped all writing completely. It is possible that I might get one magazine or another to publish an article of perhaps 2,000 words or more from you but do not want to bother you to do it and do not wish to involve you in what has become an extremely emotional situation. As your view is rather different from that of Rabbi Wise and some others and of course from the revolutionary movement in Palestine which I fear is hurting the cause of the Jews everywhere, it is possible that the *Atlantic Monthly* or *Harper's Monthly* might be glad of an article unless it is now too late, owing to the fact that the matter is up with the United Nations.

I would be glad to have your permission to show a copy of your letter to some people including possibly President Truman. The whole matter makes me exceedingly depressed because many people who were not anti-Semitic before, do feel that the Zionists in the Holy Land are doing things which they simply cannot approve of and that if they are going that way there, they might elsewhere. The whole situation is bad and requires the most careful handling and the most wise writing on both sides.

Bibliography of Works by James Truslow Adams

BOOKS

Some Notes on Currency Problems. New York, Lindley & Co., 1908.

Speculation and the Reform of the New York Stock Exchange. Summit, N.J., 1913. Privately printed by James Truslow Adams.

Memorials of Old Bridgehampton. Bridgehampton, L.I., 1916. Privately printed by James Truslow Adams. Reprinted by Empire State Hist. Pub., and by Friedman, I. J., 1962 (Kennikat).

An Address Delivered upon Founder's Day before the Colonial Society of Southampton, L.I., June 12, 1917. Privately printed by James Truslow Adams.

History of the Town of Southampton, East of Canoe Place. Bridgehampton, L.I., Hampton Press, 1918. Reprinted, ltd. ed., by Friedman, I. J., 1962, and by Empire State Hist. Pub., 1962 (Kennikat).

Notes on the Families of Truslow, Horler, and Horley from English Records. Bridgehampton, L.I., 1920. Privately printed by James Truslow Adams.

The Founding of New England. Boston, Atlantic Monthly Press, 1921. Reprinted by Little, Brown (paperback pub. in Toronto), 1963; reprint by Peter Smith, 1963.

Revolutionary New England, 1691-1776. Boston, Atlantic Monthly Press, 1923.

Rhode Island's Part in Making America; an Address Delivered at Rhode Island College of Education. R.I. Educ. Circ., R.I. Dept. of Pub. Instruction, Providence, 1923.

New England in the Republic, 1776-1850. Boston, Little, Brown, 1926. Reprinted by Peter Smith (Penguin paperback), 1960.

Provincial Society, 1690-1763. New York, Macmillan Co., 1927. New edition, Macmillan, 1938.

Hamiltonian Principles. Boston, Little, Brown, 1928. (Extracts from the writings of Alexander Hamilton, selected and edited by James Truslow Adams.)

Jeffersonian Principles. Boston, Little, Brown, 1928. (Extracts from the writings of Thomas Jefferson, selected and edited by James Truslow Adams.)

Our Business Civilization: Some Aspects of American Culture. New York, A. & C. Boni, 1929. (Collected essays.) Published as paperback by Boni (Bonibooks), 1930. Republished in England under title *A Searchlight on America,* with introduction by Douglas Woodruff, Routledge, 1930.

The Adams Family. An Atlantic Monthly Press book, Boston, Little, Brown, 1930; London, Oxford Univ. Press, 1932 (with different title page); Blue Ribbon Books, 1933; New edition, Hillary House, 1957.

The Epic of America. Boston, Little, Brown, 1931. Translated into French, German, Danish, Hungarian, Italian, Portuguese, Rumanian, Spanish, and Swedish. Numerous subsequent American and foreign editions.

The Tempo of Modern Life. New York, Boni, 1931. (Collected essays.)

The March of Democracy (2 vols.). New York, Charles Scribner's Sons, 1932-1933. Vol. 1, *The Rise of the Union;* Vol. 2, *From Civil War to World Power.* English edition under title *History of the American People,* Routledge, 1933. *The March of Democracy, a History of the United States,* continued by Jacob E. Cooke and others (7 vols.), Scribner's, 1965. Published by Hillary, 1966. Rev. ed., 7 vols. by Scribner's, 1966 (by direct subscription only).

Henry Adams. New York, A. & C. Boni, Inc., 1933. Published by Routledge, England, 1933.

New England's Prospect. With Henry S. Graves, Edward A. Filene, and others. New York, American Geographic Society, 1933.

America's Tragedy. New York, Charles Scribner's Sons, 1934.

The Record of America. With Charles Garrett Vannest, with maps, workbook, and guide. New York, Charles Scribner's Sons, 1935; new editions, Scribner's, 1938, 1949.

The Living Jefferson. With G. Freeland. New York, Charles Scribner's Sons, 1936. (Also published in London.)

Building the British Empire, to the End of the First Empire. New York, Charles Scribner's Sons, 1938. (Also published in London.)

Contributing editor of *New Frontier Social Science Series,* 3 vols.: *America's Progress in Civilization,* by George Earl Freeland and James Truslow Adams. New York, Charles Scribner's Sons, 1936.

Empire on the Seven Seas; The British Empire, 1784-1949. New York, Charles Scribner's Sons, 1940; also published by McClelland (cheaper edition).

America Looks at the British Empire (America in a World at War, No. 1). Farrar, paperback, 1940. Same book under title *America Faces the War,* paperback, London, Oxford University Press, 1941; also *An American Looks at the British Empire (America Faces the War, No. 2),* London, Oxford University Press, 1941.

Dictionary of American History, 6 vols. New York, Charles Scribner's Sons, 1940-1960. Editor-in-chief, James Truslow Adams; Managing Editor, R. V. Coleman. 2nd ed. (revised), 6 vols., Scribner's, 1942; Vol. 6 (Supplement), 1940-1960, Editors, J. G. E. Hopkins and Wayne Adams, Scribner's, 1961; 7 vols. by subscription only, Scribner's, 1966; another edition, London, Oxford University Press, 1940.

Concise Dictionary of American History. New York, Charles Scribner's Sons, 1962. Abridged from *Dictionary of American History* by James

Truslow Adams, edited by Wayne Andrews; Advisory Editor, Thomas C. Cochran.

Constitution of the United States, by James Montgomery Beck, revised and enlarged by James Truslow Adams, New York (Toronto), Doubleday, 1941.

The American: The Making of a New Man. New York, Charles Scribner's Sons, 1943.

The Atlas of American History. New York, Charles Scribner's Sons, 1943. Editor-in-chief, James Truslow Adams; Managing Editor, R. V. Coleman; edition by Saunders, S. J. R., 1943; edition by Scribner's, 1966.

Frontiers of American Culture. New York, Charles Scribner's Sons, 1944; Saunders, S. J. R., 1944.

Album of American History, 5 vols. New York, Charles Scribner's Sons, 1944-1949. Vol. 1, *Colonial Period;* Vol. 2, *1783-1853;* Vol. 3, *1853-1893;* Vol. 4, *End of an Era;* Vol. 5, *Index, 1917-1953;* Managing Editor, R. V. Coleman; Assoc. Ed., W. J. Burke; Art Director, Atkinson Dymock; Vol. 5, Ed. J. G. E. Hopkins; Art Director, LeRoy H. Appleton; another edition by Scribner's, 1960; revised edition, Vols. 1-5, Scribner's, 1961; 6 vols. by subscription, Scribner's, 1966.

Big Business in a Democracy. New York, Charles Scribner's Sons, 1945; Saunders, S. J. R., 1945.

SELECTED ARTICLES

"On the Term British Empire," *Amer. Hist. Rev.,* April, 1922.
"Unexplored Region in New England History," *Amer. Hist. Rev.,* July, 1923.
"Historic Determinism and the Individual," *Atlantic,* Oct., 1924.
"Our Dissolving Ethics," *Atlantic,* Nov., 1926.
"Home Thoughts from Abroad," *Atlantic,* Oct., 1927.
"Our Racial Amnesia," *Harper's,* Jan., 1928.
"Jefferson and Hamilton Today," *Atlantic,* April, 1928.
"The Mucker Pose," *Harper's,* Nov., 1928.
"Cost of Prosperity," *Harper's,* Dec., 1928.
"Our Lawless Heritage," *Atlantic,* Dec., 1928.
"Business Man's Civilization," *Harper's,* July, 1929.
"Hoover and Law Observance," *Forum,* July, 1929.
"Sweetness and Light, Sixty Years After," *Atlantic,* Nov., 1929.
"Diminishing Returns in Modern Life," *Harper's,* April, 1930.
"Presidential Prosperity," *Harper's,* Aug., 1930.
"Portrait of an Empty Barrel," *Harper's,* Sept., 1930.
"Emerson Re-read," *Atlantic,* Oct., 1930.
"Pollyanna, Our Patron Goddess," *Forum,* Nov., 1930.
"War Debts," *Forum,* April, 1931.
"Responsibility of Bankers," *Forum,* Aug., 1931.
"Tempo of Modern Life," *Harper's,* Sept., 1931.
"Future of American Government," *Forum,* May, 1932.
"Our Whispering Campaigns," *Harper's,* Sept., 1932.
"Rights Without Duties," *Yale Rev.,* Sept., 1932.

"America's Lost Opportunity," *Scribner's,* Oct., 1932.
"Walter Lippmann," *Sat. Rev. Lit.,* Jan. 7, 1933.
"America Revisited," *Yale Rev.,* June, 1934.
"My Methods as a Historian," *Sat. Rev. Lit.,* June 30, 1934.
"Liberty, Is It Worth Fighting For?" *Scribner's,* May, 1935.
"Letter from England," *Yale Rev.,* June, 1935.
"Test for American Business," *Yale Rev.,* Sept., 1935.
"Responsibility Under Relief," *Woman's Home Comp.,* Oct., 1935.
"Remaking the Nation: How Fast?" *Read. Dig.,* Sept., 1936.
"What Happens to a Party When It Makes a Sweep," *Yale Rev.,* March, 1937.
"What the Supreme Court Does for Us," *Vital Speeches,* March, 1937.
"The American Constitutional Crisis," *Contemp.,* April, 1937.
"How Can Our Democracy Be Preserved?" *Read. Dig.,* April, 1937.
"Man Must Organize," *Rotarian,* April, 1937.
"Bryce's America: 1888-1938," *Sat. Rev. Lit.,* June, 1938.
"Is Decline of the Profit Motive Desirable?" *Rotarian,* July, 1938.
"What Shall Washington Control?" *Read. Dig.,* Sept., 1938.
"Is Capitalism Doomed?" *Read. Dig.,* Nov., 1938.
"Is Thinking Going out of Style?" *Rotarian,* Jan., 1939.
"Shield of Our Liberty: The Bill of Rights," *Read. Dig.,* Jan., 1939.
"From Flatboat to Ship of State," *Rotarian,* Feb., 1939.
"Why Historians Get Headaches," *Rotarian,* Jan., 1940.
"Balance of Powers," *Scholastic,* April, 1940.
"Civilization Cannot Die," *Cur. Hist.,* July, 1940.
"Our Stake in the British Empire," *Am. Merc.,* Aug., 1940.
"Worry Was Ever with Us," *Rotarian,* Aug., 1940.
"What Does Col. Lindbergh Believe?" *Cur. Hist.,* Sept., 1940.
"Six Most Important American Women," *Good H.,* Feb., 1941.
"Worthington Chauncey Ford: 1858-1941," *Sat. Rev. Lit.,* April, 1941.
"Forces That Make Us the United States," N.Y. *Times,* July, 1941.
"Democratic Fashion," *Sat. Rev. Lit.,* Sept., 1941.
"Shall We Writers Fail Again?" *Sat. Rev. Lit.,* April, 1943.
"Connecticut Yankee and Other Characters," *Yale Rev.,* Dec., 1943.
"Needed: Post-War Capital," *Rotarian,* Jan., 1944.
"Why Are We Americans Different?" *Read. Dig.,* April, 1944.
"I Was at Versailles," *Rotarian,* July, 1944.
"Unity of the United States," *Va. Q. Rev.,* April, 1945.
"Yes, Mr. Shaw, but; Synthetic Colloquy over Six Questions Between George Bernard Shaw and James Truslow Adams," *Rotarian,* April, 1945.

OBITUARIES OF ADAMS

Amer. Hist. Rev., July, 1949.
Newsweek, May 30, 1949.
Pub. W., June 11, 1949.
Time, May 30, 1949.
Wilson Lib. Bul., Sept., 1949.

Index

Aaronsohn, Rabbi Michael, 301-303
Abbey, Edwin Austin, 10
Adams, Abednego, Virginia ancestor of JTA, 4
Adams, Amy, sister of JTA, 16, 43, 83, 141, 146, 161, 197
Adams, Brooks, author, brother of Charles Francis and Henry, 35, 163, 175
Adams, Charles Francis, treasurer of Harvard, former Secretary of the Navy, 58, 60, 162, 163, 175, 283, 286, 287, 289
Adams, Charles Frederick, great-uncle of JTA, 9, 175
Adams, Francis, first English ancestor of JTA, 3
Adams, Francis Peake, great-grandfather of JTA, 4, 7, 8, 159
Adams, Henry Augustus (or Austin), 9, 10, 58, 94, 145, 168, 174, 175, 181, 182, 184, 185, 187, 196, 197, 244, 286
Adams, Herbert, sculptor, 131
Adams, James Truslow, publications:
The Adams Family, 48, 79, 89, 200, 207, 212, 214, 288
Album of American History, 99, 100, 290
The American: The Making of a New Man, 97
America's Tragedy, 48, 72, 73, 74, 76, 77, 101, 252
The Atlas of American History, 99, 100, 290
Building the British Empire, 88, 89, 268
Dictionary of American History, 77, 96, 99, 100, 153, 267, 274, 279, 290
Empire on the Seven Seas, 88
The Epic of America ("The American Dream"), 48, 58, 68, 70, 71, 72, 79, 89, 90, 91, 101, 200, 206, 207, 209, 210, 212, 214, 223, 229, 232, 233, 243, 274, 280, 281, 302
The Founding of New England, 33, 34, 37, 38, 89, 101, 113, 190
Frontiers of American Culture, 100, 101
Henry Adams, 48, 234, 241, 249
History of the Town of Southampton, East of Canoe Place, 23
The Living Jefferson, 72, 74, 75
The March of Democracy, 48, 77, 79, 80, 87, 90, 96, 208, 301
Memorials of Old Bridgehampton, 22
New England in the Republic, 39, 145, 184
Our Business Civilization, 49, 63, 94
Provincial Society, 1690-1763, 40, 41, 79, 101, 197
Revolutionary New England, 37, 101, 113
Some Notes on Currency Problems, 22
Speculation and the Reform of the New York Stock Exchange, 22
The Tempo of Modern Life, 49, 63, 94
Adams, Mrs. James Truslow. *See* Seely, Kathryn
Adams, John Quincy, 58, 59, 60, 91, 159, 160, 162, 163, 175, 186
Adams, Josephine Truslow, professor at Swarthmore, 9
Adams, Leonie, 7, 9
Adams, William Newton, 5-7, 8, 10, 11, 12, 18, 106

Adams house, 158
Aiken, Conrad, 93
Albert, King of Belgium, 28, 29
American Academy of Arts and Letters, 65, 85, 253, 254
American Council of Learned Societies, 77
American Historical Association, 37
Anderson, Sherwood, 93, 170
Andrews, Charles M., historian, 10, 86, 123, 126
Archbishop of Canterbury, 178
Armstrong Cork Company, 10, 12
Arnold, Matthew, 94, 168, 173-177, 184, 186
Ashley, Sir William, professor at Harvard and Birmingham, 127, 128
Astor, Lady, 54, 178, 232, 233, 234
Atlantic Monthly, 36, 97, 160, 161, 186, 192, 203, 213, 302

Bacon, Leonard, 98
Bailey, Josiah W., senator, 287-288
Baldwin, Stanley, Prime Minister of England, 54, 58
Barnes, Harry Elmer, author, 137
Barrie, James M., 77
Bartlett, Robert, 24
Beard, Charles A., 98, 301
Beck, James M., 96, 257, 279
Becker, Carl, 62, 79, 174, 223, 224, 225, 227
Beebe, William, 24
Begahot, Walter, 90
Bell, D. W., Undersecretary of the Treasury, 95
Benét, Stephen Vincent, 300
Benson, Godfrey Rathbone (first Baron Charnwood), Lincoln biographer, 95, 233, 283
Bentley, William, 120
Berwind, E. J., 33
Beveridge, Albert J., Lincoln biographer, 146, 169, 226
Binkley, William C., 74
Black, Hugo, senator, 288
Blizzard of 1888, 11-12
Bolton, Charles K., author and editor, 180
Boni, Albert, 58, 59, 61, 62, 63, 64, 65, 76, 145, 160, 166, 168, 181, 183, 184
Bonnell, Winifred H., of the National Cathedral Association, 284-286
Bonsal, Stephen, 55
Bowers, Claude G., 192-194, 204
Bowman, Isaiah, president of the American Geographical Society, later president of Johns Hopkins, 24, 25, 26, 41, 103, 104, 105, 267
Bradford, Gamaliel, 290
Brady, James H., governor of Idaho, 19
Brett, George P., head of Macmillan, 43, 171, 173, 197
Bridgehampton, Long Island, 17, 21, 22, 23, 32
Bridges, Robert, 51
Brigham, Clarence, 156
Brooklyn Polytechnic Institute, 3, 14
Brooks & Company, English banking firm, 5
Brooks, Richard, counsin of JTA, 8
Brooks, Theodore, uncle of JTA, 8; cousin of JTA, 9
Brooks, Van Wyck, 278, 286-289
Brownell, William Crary, 77
Bruce, P. A., author and economist, 41
Brusilov, Alexei, Russian general, 36
Bruun, Geoffrey, 89
Buchan, John, 54
Butler, Nicholas Murray, president of Columbia, 65, 188, 189, 191, 204, 205, 219, 230
Byrd, William, 41

Callender, Harold, of the New York *Times,* 76, 269, 279-282
Cameron, Mrs. Don, 286
Campbell, Charles Stewart, 158
Canby, Henry Seidel, editor of the *Saturday Review,* 125, 126, 129, 171, 172, 200, 205, 222, 251, 269

Case, Leland D., editor of the *Rotarian,* dean at Dakota Wesleyan, 253, 295-297
Century Club, 46
Chamberlain, Austen, 54, 262, 269, 270
Channing, Edward, 289
Charnwood, Lord. *See* Benson, Godfrey Rathbone
Charwelton, Manor of, 159
Chase, Stuart, 185, 220
Churchill, Winston, 269
Clarendon, Lord, 34
Cleveland, Grover, 228, 229, 241, 242
Cohen, Benjamin V., 270
Colby, Bainbridge, 26, 27, 109
Coleman, R. V., of Scribner's, 99, 100, 279
Columbia University, 81. *See also* Butler, Nicholas Murray
Commager, Henry Steele, 75, 78
Communists, 256
Conrad, Joseph, 46
Cook, Albert S., professor at Yale, 22, 24, 113
Coolidge, Calvin, 2, 91, 129, 155, 170, 266
Corcoran, Thomas G., 270
Cornell University, 154
Coursey, Major O. W., 294
Craven, Avery, 74
Creel, George, 111
Croly, Herbert, 90
Cromwell, Oliver, 35
Cross, Wilbur L., Governor of Connecticut, editor, 57, 65, 75, 76, 82-85, 175, 180, 185, 218, 239, 240, 256, 260

Damrosch, Walter, 85, 275-276
Danaher, John A., senator, 283-284
Darrow, Whitney, of Scribner's, 76
Dashiell, Alfred, editor of *Scribner's Magazine,* 56
Davis, Elmer, 220
Day, Clive, professor at Yale, 33
Delano, William A., 253
Dennett, Tyler, president of Williams, 249
Depression, the Great, 72, 78, 200
Dodd, Mead & Company, 17
Dos Passos, John, 93
Dougherty, Paul, JTA's schoolmate, 14
Dreiser, Theodore, 93
Dunn, Harvey, artist, 254, 294
Dürer, Albrecht, 254
Duveen, Lady, 178
Dyer, Mary, Quaker martyr, 34

Edwards, Jonathan, 38
Einstein, Lewis, Minister to Czechoslovakia, 76, 175
Eisensohn, Sister M. Alfreda, 19
Eliot, Charles William, president of Harvard, 282
Endicott, John, 34
Erskine, John, 253

Farnell bookstore, Brooklyn, 13, 14
Fascists, 153, 154
Feuchtwanger, Lion, 95
Finley, David E., counselor in the London Embassy, 233
Fish, Hamilton, 60, 217
Fiske, John, historian, 152
Fitzgerald, Scott, 76
Flexner, Abraham, 186, 205
Flint, Charles R., capitalist, 18
Ford, Henry, 45
Ford, Worthington C., 36, 45, 54, 58, 61, 62, 66, 68, 87, 95, 156, 167-169, 174, 187, 197, 198, 203, 209, 225, 229, 232-235, 237, 244, 252, 254, 270-273, 287, 289, 290
Foster, Elizabeth, 74
Fox, Dixon Ryan, 36, 40, 43, 122, 174, 182
Freeman, Douglas, 77
Friends of the Middle Border, 101, 253, 293
Frost, Robert, 169, 195
Fuess, Claude M., 61
Furlong, Major Charles Wellington, 107-109

Galsworthy, John, 77
Garland, Hamlin, 253, 294
Gaskell, Lady Milnes, 196, 197, 286
Geffen, Felicia, of the American Academy of Arts and Letters, 96, 291-292, 294-295
George V, King of England, 82, 256
Gibbs, Sir Philip, 54
Gibson, Charles Dana, 300
Gipson, Lawrence, historian, 151, 237, 291
Glasgow, Ellen, author, 170
Godkin, E. L., 90
Gooch, George P., historian, 49, 55, 257
Grant, Robert, 65
Grayson, Dr. Cary, 31
Greene, Evarts B., 39
Greenslet, Ferris, of Houghton, Mifflin, 61, 62, 166-169, 179

Hagedorn, Herman, 229
Hahn, Nancy Coonsman, sculptress, 253, 294
Hamilton, Clayton, JTA's schoolmate, 14, 300
Hamlin, Charles S., 216
Hampden, Walter, JTA's schoolmate, 14
Hansen, Harry, literary editor, 242
Harding, Warren G., 2, 129, 266, 279
Harper, Constance Garland, daughter of Hamlin Garland, 253, 294
Harper Brothers, 36, 43, 56, 64, 162, 177, 188, 203, 210, 213, 302
Hart, Captain B. H. Liddell, correspondent, 292
Haskins, Charles H., dean of Harvard, 103, 113
Hazen, Charles Downer, 65
Hazlitt, Henry, literary editor, 52, 65, 79, 97, 177, 208, 210, 220, 224
Heinl, Bob, 297-299
Hirst, Francis W., editor of the *Economist,* 49, 55, 76, 97, 219, 245, 257, 276
Hitler, Adolph, 58, 76, 245, 269, 282
Hoare, Sir Samuel, 262
Hoover, Herbert, 67, 91, 93, 111, 156, 170, 177, 189, 193, 194, 198, 201, 208, 211, 217, 224, 225, 229, 260, 261
Houghton, Mifflin Co., 61, 166-169
House, Colonel E. M., 28, 103, 104
Howe, A. W., 18
Howe, Mark A. De Wolfe, 36, 45, 46, 60, 64, 65, 97, 121, 134, 147-154, 156, 158-163, 165, 169, 176, 178, 182-186, 187-190, 194, 199, 201, 205-207, 212, 214-215, 228, 231, 235-236, 238, 242, 243, 262
Howe, Wallace, 158
Howe, Will D., of Scribner's, 77, 228, 234, 281, 293
Howell, Alfred C., 299
Howland & Aspinwall, merchants, 5
Hudson, Manley O., 113
Hull, Cordell, 55, 86, 96, 235, 236, 243, 267
Huntington, Archer M., 275

Ickes, Harold, Secretary of the Interior, 55, 56
Indians, 35

James, Henry, 51, 295
James, William, 15, 90
Jameson, J. Franklin, 59
Jamestown & Chautauqua Railroad, 15
Janney, J. A., 18
Johnson, Allen, editor, 152, 175
Johnson, Alvin, 57
Johnson, Charles, writer, professor at Rutgers, 36
Johnson, Douglas, geologist, 29
Johnson, Gerald W., historian, 97
Johnson, Malcolm, 279
Johnson, Robert Underwood, poet, 19, 247-248
Johnston, Charles, of the *Atlantic Bookshelf,* 182
Judd, Orrin, Solicitor General of New York, 97

Kerr, Philip, 178

Knightley, Sir Charles and Lady, 159
Kohlsaat, Herman Henry, 119
Korff, Baron, Menshevik Russian leader, governor-general of Finland, 31

Ladd, George Trumbull, 15
LaGuardia, Fiorello H., 273
Landon, Alfred M., 75, 263
Lansing, Robert, 24
Lardner, Ring, 76
Laski, Harold, 54
Laval, Pierre, Premier of France, 208, 262
Leach, Henry Goddard, editor of the *Forum,* 56, 289
Lewis, Sinclair, 93, 170
Licht, Lawrence C., 253
Lindbergh, Charles A., 221
Lindley, Allen L., 18
Lindley, D. A., 18
Lippmann, Walter, 24, 25, 57, 75, 93, 103, 146, 176, 210, 216, 220, 222, 223, 226, 228, 248
Little, Brown & Co., 59, 61, 64, 66, 76, 157, 184, 202, 206, 207, 212, 227
Lloyd, Lord, governor-general of Egypt, 53
Locke, John, 38
Lockwood, L. V., author, 40
Lodge, Henry Cabot, 62, 289
Long, Huey P., 256
Low, Seth, family, of Brooklyn, 6
Lvoff, Prince, 31

Mabie, Hamilton Wright, 13, 16, 17
MacLeish, Archibald, 278
Matanzas, Cuba, Adams estate, 4
Mather, Cotton, 34
Mather, Frank Jewitt, professor at Princeton, 300
Maury, Brooklyn school head, 13
Maverick, Maury, Texas congressman, 75
McAfee, Helen, of the *Yale Review,* 57, 75, 76, 211, 245-246, 249-252, 255, 257-262
McClellan, Elizabeth, author, 40
McConaughy, James C., president of Wesleyan, 80, 171
McIntyre, Alfred R., of Little, Brown, 59, 160, 202-203, 214, 274
McNitt, V. V., editor of *McNaught's Monthly,* 57, 67, 138, 139
Meadows, Idaho: promoted by JTA, 18-19
Mellon, Andrew F., Secretary of the Treasury, Ambassador to Great Britain, 49, 91, 92, 118-119, 156, 219, 233
Mencken, Henry L., 37, 75, 79, 170
Meredith, George, 77
Merritt, Carroll B., of Scribner's, 76
Mezes, Sidney Edward, 24, 103, 104
Michelena family of Venezuela, 5
Mill, John Stuart, 90
Mitchell, Walter, Episcopal Bishop of Arizona, 232
Moley, Raymond, 55
Moore, Charles, 95, 282-283
More, Paul Elmer, 94
Morgan, J. P., 245
Morison, Samuel Eliot, 36, 37, 65, 179, 180, 186, 190, 244
Morrow, Dwight, 78, 208, 220, 221, 222, 225, 226, 228
Mucker pose, 63, 95
Muirhead, Findlay, editor of the Blue Guides, 134
Muirhead, James Fullerton, Baedeker editor, 49, 66, 134
Munsey, Frank A., newspaper editor, 1
Mussolini, 54, 58, 154, 205, 239, 257, 262, 276, 294
Muzzey, David S., historian, 201, 227

National Institute of Arts and Letters, 253
Nazimova, Alla, actress, 10
Nevins, Allan, 59, 129, 130, 133, 145, 149, 154, 163-164, 167, 176, 195-198, 199-200, 203-205, 210-211, 216-218, 219-222, 223-224, 227-229, 240-242, 248-249, 265-266, 268-269, 274, 281, 291, 293, 295, 300-301

New Deal America, 82
Newton, Mary R., great-grandmother of JTA, 4
New York *Evening Sun,* 1
New York *Herald,* 1
Nicolson, Harold, 78, 251
Northumberland, Duke of, 158

Ogden, Rollo, 16, 247, 248
Osgood, Herbert Levi, professor at Columbia, 122

Pacific & Idaho Northern Railroad, 18, 19
Page, Thomas Nelson, 77
Palace Court: JTA's London home on, 47, 48, 66
Palfrey, John Gorham, historian, 33, 152
Parkman, Francis, 152
Peake, Mary, wife of Abednego Adams, 4
Pearl Harbor, 280
Percy, Lord Eustace, 251
Perkins, Maxwell E., of Scribner's, 76
Persian: studied by JTA, 21
Phelps, William Lyon, 85, 142, 159, 253, 300
Pollock, Sir Frederick, 50
Pound, Ezra, 264, 294, 295
Pulitzer Prize, 36, 57, 128
Puritans, 33-38
Putnam, Herbert, Librarian of Congress, 188, 209, 300

Quakers, 34
Quincy, Josiah, mayor of Boston, president of Harvard, 149, 162

Ramsdell, Charles W., 74
Read, Conyers, 88
Rhode Island State College, 36
Rockefeller, John D., 281
Roosevelt, Mrs. Eleanor, 229, 270
Roosevelt, Franklin Delano, 40, 55, 57, 74-76, 84, 86, 90, 91, 208, 217, 218, 219, 224, 225, 226, 236, 238, 240, 241, 243, 246, 249, 259, 260, 261, 266, 267, 268, 274
Roosevelt, George, 229
Roosevelt, James, 270
Roosevelt, Theodore, 90, 129, 217, 228, 230
Roosevelt, Theodore, Jr., 268, 279
Royal Society of Literature, 65
Royce, Josiah, 15
Russell, Bertrand, 93

Sandburg, Carl, 253
Santayana, George, 15
Saturday Review of Literature, 204, 222, 242, 251, 258, 289-290
Schermerhorn, Edward, 20, 21, 44, 45, 47, 154
Schlesinger, Arthur M., 36, 40, 43, 46, 79, 174, 182, 244, 248
Scribner, Arthur H., 56, 76
Scribner, Charles, 56, 72, 76, 77, 88, 89, 210, 212, 213, 215, 227, 230, 237, 268, 277, 278-279
Sedgwick, Ellery, editor of the *Atlantic Monthly,* 36, 48, 56, 66, 67, 122, 155, 157, 158, 159, 160, 162, 168, 173, 177, 182, 184, 186, 191, 203, 213, 214, 296
Seely, Kathryn (Mrs. JTA), 29, 43, 44, 45, 46, 113-127, 131, 132, 135-144, 155, 272
Sergeant, Elizabeth Shepley, of the *Atlantic Bookshelf,* 182
Sewall, Samuel, 40
Sheffield, Joseph E., philanthropist, 81; house, 81, 102
Sherman, Stuart P., 125, 129, 149, 194, 195
Shirley, William, royal governor of Massachusetts, 38
Shotwell, J. T., professor, 103, 205
Simon, Sir John, 54
Sinclair, Upton, 93
Singleton, Esther, author, 40
Sloan, John, 253
Smith, Adam, 91
Smith, Alfred E., 75

Smuts, Jan, Prime Minister, Union of South Africa, 280-281
Snowden, Philip, 54
Southampton, Long Island: history of, 23
Spencer, Herbert, 90
Spreckels, John, sugar magnate, 10
Stefansson, Vilhjalmur, Arctic explorer, 24
Stevenson, Robert Louis, 77
Stokes, Frederick A., & Company, 17
Strachey, Lytton, 94, 166
Strayer, J. R., 88, 269
Summit, New Jersey, 21
Sumner, William Graham, 90

Taft, Charles P., 57
Taft, William Howard, 57, 193
Taylor, Henry Osborn, 168, 171, 191, 194, 255, 258
Taylor, Moses, merchant-banker, 6
Thorndike, Ashley, professor at Columbia, 174
Thwing, Charles F., president of Western Reserve, 175
Tinkham, George H., congressman, 252
Train, Arthur, 300
Trotter, Reginald G., 89
Truman, Harry, 302
Truslow, Francis Adams, 4
Truslow, James, uncle of JTA, 13, 16
Truslow, James Linklater, grandfather of JTA, 10, 11, 12, 16
Truslow family: history of, 10-12
Tunney, Gene, 159

Vanamee, Mrs. William, of the American Academy of Arts and Letters, 258, 275
Van Doren, Carl, 79, 149
Van Doren, Irita, 149
Van Dyke, Henry, 65
Van Kirk, James A., 293-294
Von Dewall, Wolf, correspondent, 263
Von Hindenburg, Paul, 245

Wales, Prince of, 54, 233, 234
Walker, James J., 217, 219
War of 1812, 39
Warren, Charles, 257
Washburn, Mr., of American Antiquarian Society, 161
Washington, George, 4
Watson, Sir George, 81
Webster, Daniel, 157, 159, 160, 173
Weeden, W. B., author and economist, 40
Weeks, Edward, editor of the *Atlantic Bookshelf,* 64, 66, 179, 181, 203
Wells, H. G., 93, 98
Wells, Thomas, editor of *Harper's Monthly,* 56
Wertenbaker, Thomas J., historian, 40
Wesleyan College (University), 80, 81, 145, 163, 169, 195
Wharton, Edith, 77, 295
Wheeler, Burton K., 284
Wheelock, John Hall, poet, 77
White, Henry, diplomat, 176
White, Stewart Edward, 253
White, William Allen, 95, 253, 264, 277
Willkie, Wendell, 95, 279, 280, 281
Wilson, William L., 216
Wilson, Woodrow, 24, 30, 31, 90, 95, 103, 129, 216
Wise, Rabbi, 302
Wister, Owen, 65
Wolfe, Thomas, 76
Wood, General Leonard, 8
Woodruff, Douglas, 64

Yale Club, 1, 2, 46
Yale Review, 51, 57, 66, 206, 240
Yale University, 8, 9, 14, 15, 24, 75, 81, 123, 159, 172, 185, 248, 275, 302